The Polo Gr

The Polo Grounds

Essays and Memories of New York City's Historic Ballpark, 1880–1963

Edited by STEW THORNLEY

MCFARLAND HISTORIC BALLPARKS, 5
Series Editors David Cicotello *and* Angelo Louisa

McFarland & Company, Inc., Publishers
Jefferson, North Carolina

LIBRARY OF CONGRESS CATALOGUING-IN-PUBLICATION DATA

Names: Thornley, Stew, author.
Title: The Polo Grounds : essays and memories of New York City's historic
ballpark, 1880–1963 / edited by Stew Thornley.
Description: Jefferson, North Carolina : McFarland & Company, Inc., 2019 |
Series: McFarland historic ballparks ; 5 |
Includes bibliographical references and index.
Identifiers: LCCN 2018059695 | ISBN 9780786478972
(softcover : acid free paper) ∞
Subjects: LCSH: Polo Grounds (New York, N.Y.)—History. | New York Giants
(Baseball team)—History. | New York Mets (Baseball team)—History. |
Baseball fields—New York (State)—New York—History. | Baseball—
New York (State)—New York—History.
Classification: LCC GV417.P65 P65 2019 | DDC 796.3576/87471—dc23
LC record available at https://lccn.loc.gov/2018059695

BRITISH LIBRARY CATALOGUING DATA ARE AVAILABLE

ISBN (print) 978-0-7864-7897-2
ISBN (ebook) 978-1-4766-3358-9

Front cover photograph: Yankees rookie Gil McDougald hitting
a grand slam in Game 6 of the 1951 World Series against
the Giants at the Polo Grounds (collection of Stew Thornley)

Printed in the United States of America

McFarland & Company, Inc., Publishers
Box 611, Jefferson, North Carolina 28640
www.mcfarlandpub.com

To my wife, Brenda Himrich—
the best wife in the world
(and a great baseball fan)

Table of Contents

Preface and Acknowledgments

Stew Thornley

The classic period of ballparks began in 1909 and extended through the construction of Yankee Stadium in 1923 or, if one wants to carry it further, to the stadium constructed in Cleveland in the early 1930s.

By the time baseball expanded its number of teams in the 1960s, most of the classic ballparks were still being used, mixed in with an array of other stadiums in cities that had gotten major league teams over the past decade.

After World War II, the trend was toward stadiums away from the central city. Where once the location of a ballpark was valued because of the availability of public transportation, by the 1950s, a car-oriented society was more interested in spacious areas with plenty of parking.

Another shift—this one in the 1960s—was toward multipurpose stadiums. For many years, football gridirons could be fit into baseball fields, though the configuration of seating and layout was not the best for those tenants. As professional football grew in prominence, the National Football League was important enough to get equal treatment in new stadiums.

Efficiency—a means of satisfying two sports in one stadium—led to functional facilities, but for baseball, it also led to a loss of charm and character. The "cookie-cutter stadium" model popped up in many cities, circular ballparks with symmetric distances in the outfield as opposed to quirky configurations of many of those from the classic period. The stadiums looked alike and, combined with artificial turf in many, created a 30-year period of sterility for baseball venues.

By the 1990s, football and baseball had reached the point that each had enough clout to get a stadium of its own in many markets. This led to a retro look for ballparks, which had distinct features and appearances. Baltimore, with Oriole Park at Camden Yards, took the lead in this wave, and its new ballpark returned to the core of the city, helping to revitalize Baltimore's harbor region. Other cities followed with the return closer to downtown areas, places that were able to combine parking ramps with public transportation. The ballparks added amenities and comforts and could be characterized as entertainment centers with baseball as the focal point. Above all, the new parks became greater revenue producers for teams, who sought to maximize income.

Although most baseball fans would agree that the retro period beats the cookie-cutter era, the newer ballparks still cannot provide the genuine character and charm as those from the classic period. A century ago, ballparks often had their dimensions determined by the space available, sometimes within the confines of a city block and hemmed in by other features of the surrounding area.

Many young fans enjoyed merely looking at the stadium diagrams printed in a variety of publications. Each of the classic ballparks had a distinct look, and one could imagine the view from the seats, looking out to the outfield walls.

For me, one ballpark that was hard to imagine by just looking at a diagram was the Polo Grounds; its bathtub configuration, short distances down the lines, outfield fences emanating from the foul lines at 135-degree angles, and notched center-field fence left me clueless as to what it looked like to those in the stands.

Fortunately, the Polo Grounds was a much-photographed ballpark, and it was not hard to find pictures from all angles that showed its shape and size. I collected images of the Polo Grounds, fascinated by each one. In 1997, I finally took the time to roam through the former site of the ballpark, now occupied by high-rises. The ballpark was long gone, but the bluffs on one side, the river on the other, and a walk down the stairs from the 155th Street viaduct where I had parked gave a sense of the place and some feeling for what the area was like during the years baseball was played in it.

My first book on this park, *Land of the Giants: New York's Polo Grounds*, was published by Temple University Press in 2000. The research and writing of it led me to envy those who had the chance to know the Polo Grounds firsthand, and I was grateful to many people in the late 1990s who shared their experiences with me. One of them was Larry Ritter, author of the incomparable *Glory of Their Times*. He and I became friends, and Larry provided a great deal of information that I used then and now use again in this book.

For this project, I appreciate the work of all the contributors, whose names will appear within the text. Approximately 70 players who played at the Polo Grounds sent me their memories, and a number of fans did the same.

Ron Selter provided the dimensions and configurations for the Polo Grounds, as he has done in other books in the McFarland Historic Ballparks series, and John Pastier added his architectural analysis, which he has likewise done elsewhere in the series. Others contributed heavily researched essays, and people such as Arnold Hano and Jerry Schwab were among those who shared their memories of the park.

Bill Lamb was a great contributor with his profiles of Giants owners and landowners of the property where the various Polo Grounds were erected. Dan VanDeMortel wrote a fantastic summary of the shooting of Bernard Doyle prior to a Giant game in 1950.

James Forr organized a group of writers for the Memorable Games section. Gary Mintz publicized this project with the New York Giants Preservation Society. As with many other books on baseball history, the Society for American Baseball Research (SABR) was prominent in this project, and most of the contributors are members of SABR.

Thanks to series editors David Cicotello and Angelo Louisa (as well as Angelo's wife, Pam) for their guidance and support.

A collection is a team effort. And the team that I have assembled for this tribute to the Polo Grounds is a top-notch group.

The Polo Grounds, though gone for more than 50 years, lives on through the many photographs taken inside and outside the stadium (collection of Stew Thornley).

Editor's Note: A number of stadiums bearing the name Polo Grounds occupied several sites in Manhattan. The original Polo Grounds, north of Central Park, had two diamonds in 1884, and some researchers count these separately. Others count this site as one ballpark. As a result, when the different stadiums are identified in the essays of this book, the numbers may go up to either four or five. However, because of the content of each essay, readers should have no problem understanding which numbering system is being used for that essay.

The Polo Grounds
Owners and Overlords

BILL LAMB

For more than 75 years, the Polo Grounds of New York stood at the epicenter of major league baseball. In 1881, the construction of the original ballpark, an edifice located just north of Manhattan's Central Park, gained fledgling professional leagues a foothold in New York City (NYC) proper, the commercial and sporting center of the nation, and did much to establish the game on the national scene. Within a decade of its erection, the ballpark would have a world baseball champions banner hoisted over its diamond. Three subsequent iterations of the Polo Grounds, all located some distance away in far north Manhattan, would also host championship teams.

Presented below are biographies of the club owners who guided the fortunes of the New York Giants, the principal tenant of the Polo Grounds throughout its history. It was these men—and women, too—who financed, built, and maintained the various ballparks that housed the franchise. Giant club owners, however, did not exercise exclusive control over the Polo Grounds, for while they had paid for and owned the actual ballparks, they were only leaseholders of the real property upon which the four Polo Grounds sat. Also profiled herein are the Polo Grounds' landlords: James Gordon Bennett, Jr., and James J. Coogan, additional parties of significance in the Polo Grounds saga.

John B. Day

A prosperous cigar manufacturer originally from Connecticut, John B. Day may fairly lay claim to being the founder of major league baseball in New York City. Prior to Day's arrival on the scene, the National League (NL) New York Mutuals and earlier professional clubs bearing the name New York had played their games mostly in Brooklyn, then the nation's third-largest city and a municipal entity separate and distinct from New York.[1] In 1880, Day financed the operation of an independent professional baseball club that began playing its games in Brooklyn, but he relocated to grounds originally laid out for polo in Manhattan before the season was completed. Subsequently outfitted with substantial grandstands erected by Day, this playing field, dubbed the Polo Grounds, would soon host a pennant-winning team in the major league American Association (AA). A still grander ballpark built by Day in far north Manhattan and a National League champion team would follow before the decade was out. Sadly, Day's success as a baseball magnate was short-lived. His wealth diminished by the bruising Players League (PL) War of 1890 and then lost by reversals in his business fortunes, Day spent the second half of his life in greatly reduced circumstances, eking out a living on the margins of baseball and commerce.

The ill-starred John Bailey Day was born in Colchester, Connecticut, on September 23, 1847, the third of five children born to Yankee farmer Isaac Henry Day and his wife, Sarah (née Williams).[2] Following graduation from the Golden Hill Institute in Bridgeport, Day went into the cigar manufacturing business with brother-in-law Charles P. Abbey.[3] The firm, Abbey & Day, flourished, with production and wholesale outlets placed in Hartford and Middletown, and a warehouse in Gildersleeve, Connecticut. In time, the business expanded to New York, opening a large tobacco processing plant on the lower eastside of Manhattan. Resident proprietor Day took up offices near the financial district, while relocating himself and his wife, the former Ella Davis of Portland, Connecticut, to a brownstone mansion on posh Fifth Avenue. As befitted his station in life, Day soon adopted the mien and trappings (frock coat, top hat, cane, carriage) of Gilded Age gentry. He also became a member in good standing of Tammany Hall, the corrupt political organization that controlled the Democratic Party in New York City.

From an early age, Day had been a baseball enthusiast, fancying himself a pitcher. Once in New York, he organized and played on various amateur nines in and around the city. This led to a fateful encounter with Jim Mutrie, an unaccomplished player in assorted New England leagues then at loose ends in Manhattan. Mutrie, who had energy, a keen eye for baseball talent, and considerable organizational ability, was in attendance when pitcher Day was battered from the mound in a meaningless mid-summer 1880 game. According to popular lore, Mutrie then approached the deflated hurler with a proposition: Mutrie would scout, sign, and manage a top flight baseball team for Day if the well-heeled capitalist would bear the costs.[4] Day was willing, and in short order, Mutrie had stocked the roster of the new team—formally named the Metropolitan Club of New York—with first-rate talent, much of it coming from the Unions of Brooklyn and the recently disbanded Rochester Hop-Bitters.

On September 16, 1880, the Mets made a successful debut, defeating the Unions, 15–3, on the grounds of the Brooklyn club. The victors, however, were destined for Manhattan, once an expanse of open field was discovered

John B. Day owned the Metropolitan and was the first owner of the team that became known as the New York Giants.

in an affluent neighborhood just north of Central Park. Owned by James Gordon Bennett, Jr., the socialite-sportsman publisher of the *New York Herald,* the grounds had been laid out for polo matches among the athletic rich but was otherwise available for sporting use. On September 29, 1880, professional baseball was inaugurated at the "Polo Grounds," with a Mets victory over the Nationals of Washington before a throng of some 1,000 spectators.[5] Playing an assortment of local semipro, college, and amateur nines thereafter, the Mutrie-managed Mets completed an abbreviated first campaign with a commendable 16–7–1 log, which included a 15–6 victory over Manhattan College in which club owner Day hurled a complete game. With this modest taste of success, Day was smitten with club ownership.

To underwrite his ambitions for the club, Day incorporated the Metropolitan Exhibition Company (MEC), with himself as president and principal stockholder. Tammany Hall cohorts Joseph Gordon,[6] Charles T. Dillingham, and Walter Appleton were enlisted as minority MEC shareowners and served with Day as the corporation's board of directors. But in actuality, John B. was in full and unilateral control of club affairs. Once he secured a long-term lease to the playing field from Bennett, Day began construction of a spacious grandstand and other seating accommodations at the Polo Grounds. Again piloted by Mutrie, the 1881 Mets played a mixed Eastern Championship League-freelance schedule of 151 games, including 60 contests against National League competition. At season's end, the team's respectable 18–42 performance against the NL prompted the organizers of the rival American Association to offer Day a place in their new major league. But for the time being, Day declined. The 1882 Mets schedule would again consist of a mix of games between major league opposition and local nines. And again, the Mets would play the big leaguers tough, winning 29 of 74 contests against NL foes while taking all but one game against AA teams.

In 1883, John B. Day entered the ranks of major league club owners—and in a big way. To some surprise, Day declined an invitation to place the Mets in the National League, the longer established and more prestigious of the two major circuits. Rather, the Mets joined the American Association, with Mutrie remaining as field manager and MEC stockholder/director Gordon appointed club president. Thereafter, Day boldly announced that an entirely new MEC-owned club would be placed in the National League. The nucleus of this team, originally called the Gothams, or simply the New-Yorks, would consist of budding stars like Buck Ewing, Roger Connor, and Mickey Welch, plucked from the roster of the defunct NL Troy Trojans. Standout Providence pitcher-infielder John Montgomery Ward would also be wearing a Gotham uniform, while the remainder of the squad would be formed from free agents, castoffs, and other nonentities. Veteran backstop-manager John Clapp would do the field managing while Day himself would serve as the Gothams' club president.

To accommodate the two major league clubs that would be using the Polo Grounds, a second diamond with a separate grandstand was laid on the property.[7] As accorded with its preferred status as Day's club, the Gothams were given the established field on the southeast corner of the Polo Grounds, while the Mets were consigned to a new, landfill-based playing surface placed on the southwest quadrant. When the Gothams and Mets played home games simultaneously, the two diamonds were separated by only a canvas fence, an awkward arrangement that occasionally required outfielders from one league to chase long hit balls onto the field of a rival circuit.[8] Differences in standing between the two MEC clubs were reflected at the gate, as well. The carriage trade sought by Day for the Gothams was charged 50 cents general admission while the working classes cultivated for the Mets would get in for a quarter. Potent liquid refreshment, however, was available at each venue, thus defying the league-wide ban on alcohol sales at NL games.

The aspirations of the MEC brain trust were confounded in 1883. Behind the stellar pitching of Tim Keefe, a Troy refugee deemed unworthy of the Gothams by management, and the astute generalship of Mutrie, the Mets finished a commendable fourth (54–42) in the AA race, while the Gothams fared no better than sixth (46–50) in the NL standings. This disconcerting situation continued in 1884 when an improved Gotham nine could rise no higher than fourth place and had to suffer the embarrassment that accompanied the late-season dismissal of new manager James Price, caught for a second time embezzling club funds. Meanwhile, the Mets, banished for most of the season to an ill-conceived new ballpark erected along the East River,[9] rode the hitting of infielders Dave Orr (.354) and Dude Esterbrook (.314), superb pitching by Keefe (37–17) and Jack Lynch (37–15), and the leadership of skipper Mutrie to capture the American Association flag. The Mets balloon, however, was quickly punctured in the postseason. In the precursor of the modern World Series, the Mets were swept by the NL Providence Grays in three noncompetitive and poorly attended games played at the Polo Grounds.

Events during the off-season manifested John B. Day's intention to make a champion of the Gothams. And to that end, the Mets would be sacrificed. First, manager Mutrie was transferred to the NL club. Then, he and Day engaged in some rule-bending chicanery to bring Met stars Keefe and Esterbrook over. Shortly before the start of the 1885 campaign, Mutrie chaperoned the two on a vacation voyage to Day's onion farm in Bermuda, the trip ostensibly a reward for sterling work during the previous season. Once Keefe and Esterbrook were safely out to sea, the MEC released them from the Mets roster. While Keefe and Esterbrook were incommunicado somewhere on the Atlantic, the ten-day period that other clubs had to sign them as free agents elapsed. Once that happened, Mutrie inked the two to Gothams pacts. Upon discovery that star players had been slipped out of the league, the American Association executive board howled in protest. But all it could do was ban Mutrie from the league, an empty gesture as Mutrie had already left for the NL. The AA directors also voted to expel the Met franchise, but quickly reconsidered. Instead, the Mets were fined $500 for the manner in which Keefe and Esterbrook had been released. The Mets were also required to post a bond, a sort of guarantee that the team would complete its 1885 AA schedule.[10] When the time came, a gutted Met team played out the season as obliged but plummeted to seventh place in the standings. But this was of little concern to Day and his MEC associates. In December 1885, the Mets were sold for $25,000 to Staten Island amusement impresario and local railroad magnate Erastus Wiman, who promptly removed the franchise to his St. George Grounds, a ferry ride away from Manhattan.[11]

Fortified by its new acquisitions (which also included future Hall of Fame outfielder Jim O'Rourke, late of Buffalo), the Gothams posted a dazzling 85–27 (.759) record in 1885. But this was good for only second place in the NL, as the Cap Anson–led Chicago White Stockings had been two games better. In addition to a change in fortunes, the New York club also underwent a name change as well. During the early part of the 1885 season, the New York Gothams acquired the handle Giants, the moniker by which the club would soon become famous.[12]

As the standing of his franchise increased in the NL, the stature of John B. Day among his fellow magnates rose with it. Along with dominant club owners A.G. Spalding (Chicago) and John I. Rogers (Philadelphia), Day was chosen to represent the league on the important Joint Rules Committee of Organized Baseball. He was also appointed to the NL Board of Arbitration and became a heeded voice in league executive conclaves. Top salaries, first-rate road accommodations, and bonhomie—John B. was on familiar terms with many of his charges—also garnered the New York magnate esteem and good will in the player ranks.[13]

In 1888, the Giant players rewarded Day's amity by bringing home the 1888 NL pennant. Home-game attendance of 305,455 also paced the circuit. New York then made its triumph complete by downing the AA St. Louis Browns in a postseason match of league champions. Unfortunately for Day, he did not fare as well against a different adversary: city planners determined to complete the local traffic grid by running a street through the Polo Grounds outfield. Rearguard maneuvers, both legal and political, had forestalled the project during the 1888 season, but by early the following year it had become evident that the Giants would have to find a new playing field, the Tammany connections of the club's owners notwithstanding.[14] At first unable to locate suitable grounds in Manhattan, the Giants opened the 1889 season in Jersey City and then switched to the St. George Grounds in Staten Island, erstwhile home of the now-disbanded Mets. But by June, negotiations between Day and James J. Coogan, the wily estate agent for the vastly propertied Gardiner-Lynch family, afforded the Giants a lease to a vacant tract of property in far north Manhattan. Within three weeks thereafter, the small army of workmen engaged by Day had erected a usable, if unfinished, ballpark on the grounds. When completed that winter, this handsome facility on 155th Street and Eighth Avenue would seat more than 14,000 and be dubbed the New Polo Grounds.[15] On July 8, 1889, the Giants inaugurated their new home field with a 7–5 victory over Pittsburgh, a harbinger of the second-half success that would see New York nip the Boston Beaneaters at the wire for the NL pennant. The Giants then successfully defended their world champions title, defeating the AA Brooklyn Bridegrooms behind the hurling of unlikely mound heroes Cannonball Crane and Hank O'Day.[16]

Day's enjoyment of the triumph was tempered by a sense of foreboding. The 1889 season had been conducted amidst simmering player discontent, longstanding player resentment of the reserve clause having been exacerbated by the imposition of a tight-fisted salary classification scheme, adopted by the NL over Day's objection. Even as the Giants rallied for the pennant, plans for a new major league, one controlled by the players themselves, were taking shape. And the chief promoters of this nascent rival, from visionary organizer John Montgomery Ward to chief recruiters Tim Keefe and Jim O'Rourke, all wore a New York Giant uniform. Still, Day remained confident in his franchise's future. Despite rumblings of player secession, Day turned down a $200,000 offer for the club tendered late in the 1889 season by Polo Grounds landlord Coogan.[17]

On November 4, 1889, the players' intention to form a new major league was publicly announced.[18] As New York was the very font of the rebellion, Day's Giants would be particularly hard hit by player defection. The Giants quickly lost the team's entire regular lineup to the Players League, save for aging pitcher Mickey Welch and outfielder Mike Tiernan. To counteract the attrition, the National League formed a War Committee chaired by the hard-nosed Spalding, with Day and Rogers as the other members. The two leagues then began maneuvering. Ward and his comrades, genuinely fond of Day and eager for a defection in NL ownership ranks, attempted to entice Day to their side by offering him a lucrative position in PL executive offices. Ever the NL loyalist, Day refused and was soon busy trying to lure PL enlistees—notably Giant star Buck Ewing and second baseman Danny Richardson—back to the NL fold. But to no avail.[19] Thereafter, Day adopted a litigation strategy, instituting reserve clause-based suits against Ward, Keefe, Ewing, and O'Rourke. The courts entertaining such actions, however, were uniformly unpersuaded, declining to grant Day any form of relief.

With his roster depleted and the start of the 1890 season on the horizon, Day took the first of the steps that would hasten his financial ruin: he tendered Indianapolis club owner John T. Brush a $25,000 note in exchange for Jack Glasscock, Jerry Denny, Amos Rusie, and others under contract to the just-liquidated Hoosier franchise.[20] Long-term implications aside, the move yielded an immediate benefit. Day would now be able to put a presentable team on the field. And he would need to, for the interleague competition in New York would be cutthroat. In a display of hubris and disdain, War Committee chairman Spalding had arranged the NL schedule to place his league's teams in direct head-to-head competition with the upstart PL whenever possible. This made the atmosphere in New York particularly fraught, as the PL had erected its playing site (Brotherhood Park) on grounds immediately adjacent to the New Polo Grounds. Only the stadium walls and a ten-foot-wide alley separated the two ballparks.[21]

The fan allegiance question was settled on Opening Day when 12,013 attended the debut of the star-laden Ewing "Big" Giants, while only 4,644 chose to watch Day's "Real" Giants play next door. As the 1890 season progressed, both teams drew poorly, but Day's nine suffered more. By season's end, only 60,667 fans had paid their way into the New Polo Grounds, less than one-fifth the attendance of only two seasons before. With receipts unable to cover club expenses, Day began to allocate funds from his tobacco business to keep the Giants running. But this failed to stanch the tide of red ink, and at midseason the New York Giants were on the verge of bankruptcy. NL club owners summoned to a private conclave in Brooklyn were stunned by the degree of Day's distress. To avert the collapse of the National League's flagship franchise, Spalding orchestrated a financial bailout on the spot, pledging $25,000 to Day in return for stock in the Giants' club. Boston co-owner Arthur Soden did the same, while Philadelphia co-owner Al Reach and Brooklyn's Ferdinand Abell made smaller investments in club shares. John T. Brush, meanwhile, agreed to convert Day's outstanding $25,000 players payment note into a Spalding/Soden-sized stake in the Giants' operation.[22] When word of the arrangement leaked, the press took to referring to the strapped club owner as John *Busted* Day. But with the aid, the New York team managed to stagger to the 1890 season finish line, its 68–63 record good for sixth place.

While the PL Giants had posted a more respectable (74–57) third-place finish, franchise backers had received no return on their investment. To the contrary, they, like Day, had lost a good deal of money during the 1890 season. Unlike Day, Wall Street financier Edward B. Talcott and his PL partners were not unabashed lovers of the game. To them, baseball was mostly another business venture. That made them receptive to settlement overtures. Preempting consolidation of the two leagues as a whole, Day and Talcott swiftly reached an agreement to merge the New York clubs, cutting out John Montgomery Ward and his players' board in the process. Day, onetime friend of the renegade players, had been adamant that player representatives be excluded from NL-PL consolidation discussions. Said Day, "The players have nothing to say at all. They have not lost the money during the last season and, consequently, they have no interest at stake. The capitalists on both sides will do the negotiating. The players will have to do what they are told to do."[23] Talcott concurred, brushing off objections by Ward. "I don't propose to have Mr. Ward or anybody else criticize my business methods," Talcott declared, testily. "Nor shall I allow Mr. Ward to tell me how my financial interests must be arranged. The fight cannot go on another year, for baseball will become a dead sport. Ward can say what he likes but it cannot alter matters with us a particle."[24] With its New York operation co-opted, the Players League passed from the baseball scene, its remaining backers scrambling to reach consolidation or buy-out agreements with NL counterparts. By late-November 1890, a triumphant A.G. Spalding could accurately proclaim, "The Players League is as dead as the proverbial doornail."[25]

Though it may have been dead, the brief existence of the Players League had exacted a grim toll on the fortunes of John B. Day. Competitive pressures had drained MEC coffers and prompted Day to tap his tobacco business to keep the Giants afloat. And when this proved inadequate to the task, Day had been forced to seek financial aid from fellow NL owners, whose combined investment in the New York franchise now exceeded Day's own.[26] Worse yet was Day's new arrangement with his former PL rivals. Unlike Spalding, Soden, Brush, and the other silent club partners, the Talcott faction would be active in management affairs and quickly wrest operational control of the Giants franchise away from Day. An early sign of Talcott ascendency was conveyed by the selection of the team's playing site for the 1891 season. Day had built and paid for the New Polo Grounds less than two years earlier and the stadium was a fine baseball venue. But Brotherhood Park was the home base of the Talcott forces, and Talcott himself was responsible for the ten-year lease that the PL Giants had signed with landlord Coogan. With no intention of having an idle ballpark on his hands, Talcott had Brotherhood Park renamed the Polo Grounds and designated as the permanent playing field of the New York Giants. Day's adjoining stadium, retitled Manhattan Field, was relegated to hosting college football, track meets, horse racing, and other secondary sports. Day's diminished stature in the new Giant operation was also reflected in the treatment of his old friend and collaborator Jim Mutrie. Although he continued as the Giants' manager at Day's insistence, Mutrie was shorn of effective command, supplanted in authority by Buck Ewing, the former PL Giants' leader. At the conclusion of the 1891 season, Mutrie was unceremoniously severed from franchise employ, with Day powerless to stop it. John B. continued to hold the title of club president for another season but was now little more than a figurehead. Control in the Giants' front office was exercised entirely by the Talcott forces.

In February 1893, Day resigned. At a farewell meeting of franchise stockholders, John Montgomery Ward, a small-stake Giants shareholder, offered a motion of thanks to the departing club chief. Although he and Day had had their differences, Ward pronounced himself "deeply grieved to see Mr. Day retire from the presidency."[27] The motion was thereupon seconded by John T. Brush, who added "a glowing tribute to Mr. Day as a baseball president, a companion and a gentleman."[28] Upon unanimous adoption of the testimonial, Day, "overcome with emotion," could do no more than reply, "I thank you, gentlemen."[29] And with that, the founding era of the New York Giants passed into history.

The remainder of Day's life was spent in ever-tightening straits. He was now only a marginal shareholder in the baseball franchise that he had started and his tobacco business was in serious decline. Soon, Day was obliged to close his Manhattan tobacco processing plant. From then on, he would eke out his existence on the periphery of baseball.

In March 1896, NL president Nick Young appointed Day the league's National Agreement liaison to the minor leagues.[30] The following spring, Day relinquished the post to make probably the strangest decision of his baseball career: acceptance of the offer to manage the Giants, tendered by new franchise commander Andrew Freedman, a Tammany Hall friend of Day who had acquired control of the club from the Talcott faction. Without managerial experience and saddled with a mediocre lineup, Day lasted until early July, posting a 29–35 log before being fired by the impatient Freedman. Several years thereafter, Day returned to baseball as supervisor of NL umpires, issuing widely ignored directives against rowdy behavior on the field.[31] In January 1902, Day made a peculiar reappearance on the game's executive stage. With NL magnates locked in bitter stalemate over the league presidency—the factions being evenly divided between supporters of A.G. Spalding and incumbent Nick Young, the candidate of Freedman and John T. Brush—Day offered himself as the perfect compromise choice. John B. would even serve his first year in office free of charge. To no great surprise, Day's offer was politely ignored by the warring sides.[32]

In March 1903, Day resurfaced at the side of former MEC partner Joseph Gordon when the long anticipated entry of the American League into New York was announced. News accounts identified Gordon as president of the new franchise, with Day being described as "associated" with the operation.[33] As for the club's prospects, Day stated, "I feel sure that the New York public will appreciate our efforts, and that the new club will be a success. We have a splendid team under contract and our grounds will be the finest in the country."[34] While Gordon would serve as ceremonial New York Highlanders president for several years thereafter—the club's actual bosses being the less presentable Frank Farrell and Bill Devery, characters from the Manhattan demimonde—Day quickly settled back into obscurity, with no further connection to the Highlanders being known.

In 1906, Ella Day died. Sometime later, Day remarried, taking a middle-aged Connecticut woman named Agnes Wallis as his second wife. By 1910, the couple was living in rented premises in Brooklyn, Day having spent the previous year as president of the Metropolitan Baseball Club, "a fast semi-pro nine in Carlstadt, NJ."[35] He also spent time peddling his personal Day brand cigars to friendly saloon owners and shopkeepers. From there, Day's fortunes continued to wane. Although his name was periodically listed among attendees at major league baseball functions,[36] Day's only remunerative connection to baseball was the five dollars a game that he made as a ticket-taker at the Polo Grounds. John B. also began to experience health problems, suffering a series of small strokes that hampered his mobility. By 1920, the Days were back in Manhattan, their meager income supplemented by rent paid by lodgers sharing their apartment and by Agnes Day's sewing.

Finally, in the fall 1923, Day's plight became public knowledge via press reports. Agnes, now terminally ill with cancer, extolled her husband's past glory to visiting newsmen. "He doesn't look a great man now," she said, "but he was. A tobacco man when he came here in the Eighties. He was worth nearly a million…. When he used to visit [his cigar factory] in Middletown, Connecticut … whistles blew and work was suspended to greet him."[37] Mildly embarrassed by the situation, Giant executives hastily arranged a Polo Grounds benefit game for Day and Mutrie, discovered living in near destitution on Staten Island. The game, between the defending World Series champion Giants and a minor-league Baltimore team featuring alumnus Babe Ruth, drew a disappointing crowd of only 5,000 but the modest gate was supplemented by contributions from Charles Comiskey, Garry Herrmann, and other major league baseball dignitaries. Day was also granted a small pension by the National League.[38]

After Agnes died, Day spent his final years living with friends in nearby Cliffside, New Jersey. On January 25, 1925, he died from the effects of a fifth stroke. John B. Day was 77 years old. Following an Episcopal funeral service in Manhattan, Day was interred in the family vault at Center Cemetery in Portland, Connecticut.[39] Childless, he was survived by unmarried sister Fanny Day and three nephews. Respected and well liked in his heyday and thereafter largely forgotten, Day was a good man and a lifelong lover of baseball. But deeply ingrained traits of personal honor and institutional loyalty left him ill-equipped to deal with the fast-changing diamond scene of 1890 and the profit-minded entrepreneurs who entered the game with it. Perhaps the most prominent casualty of the Players League war, John B. Day is best remembered as the earnest founder of the New York Giants, the first great franchise in the storied history of baseball in the big city.

The Talcott Group

During the years between the founding and ownership of the New York Giants by John B. Day and the tumultuous club stewardship of Andrew Freedman, the franchise was controlled by a group of men who viewed baseball mostly as a business opportunity. Although he never held the title of club president, the unquestioned leader of this group was Wall Street financier Edward B. Talcott. Perhaps a more avid baseball enthusiast than his associates, Talcott was originally enticed into the game's ownership ranks by his friend Albert L. Johnson, the Cleveland trolley car magnate and initial bankroller of the Players League. In late 1889, Talcott assembled the financial backers of the New York entry in the new circuit. When the Players League failed after the 1890 season, the Talcott group (Talcott, Edwin A. McAlpin, Cornelius C. Van Cott, and Frank B. Robinson) merged their franchise with that of John B. Day. In short order, the PL men largely displaced the financially strapped Day in management of the Giants' affairs. An able man, Talcott took the lead in restoring the franchise to fiscal health. He also approved the player acquisitions that made the Giants competitive on the diamond once again, as evidenced by a New York capture of the 1894 Temple Cup. But despite this success, baseball had not provided the return on investment anticipated by Talcott and company. So in January 1895, they sold their controlling interest in the New York Giants to Freedman and left the game.

With the exception of stockbroker Frank B. Robinson (about whom little is known), the Talcott group was composed of prominent New Yorkers of wealth and

Edward B. Talcott was the head of a group that financed the New York entry in the Players' League and then took over the Giants.

political influence. Leader Edward Baker Talcott was of particularly distinguished lineage, descended of English gentry that reached American shores in the 1630s. His more immediate forbearers included a colonial governor, military commanders, and business leaders.[40] Born in New York City on January 21, 1858, Talcott was the fifth of seven children born to Frederick Lyman Talcott and his wife, the former Harriet Newell Burnham. The elder Talcott was a successful banker and commodities broker known as the "Cotton King." His son Eddie (as the baseball press called him) was educated at Fort Washington Institute. At age 16, he entered Talcott & Sons, the family banking house. Several years later, Talcott joined the brokerage firm of Charles F. Hardy & Company, where his youthful energies were seasoned by trips to Europe on company business. In 1879, the 21-year-old Talcott married Sara Roberson, a relation of future U.S. president Grover Cleveland. Sadly, none of the couple's three children lived beyond age six.

In 1880, Talcott returned to the family firm as a partner. Three years later, he went out on his own. Purchasing a seat on the New York Stock Exchange, "the boy broker of Wall Street" proved an adept trader and was soon a wealthy man. He also became a force in New York City Democratic Party politics but steadfastly declined to stand for elective office or accept appointment to a local government post. Rather, Talcott preferred to exercise his considerable influence behind the scenes.[41] In his leisure time, Talcott was an active clubman, holding membership in the Manhattan and New York Athletic Clubs, as well as the Atlantic Yacht Club. A baseball fan since childhood and "himself a pitcher of no mean ability,"[42] Talcott was also frequently in attendance at Giant games in the Polo Grounds.

Ten years older than Talcott, Edwin Augustus McAlpin was also a scion of privilege. Heir to a tobacco-producing fortune, McAlpin was born in upstate Ossining, New York, on June 9, 1848, the favored son of David Hunter McAlpin and his wife, Adelaide.[43] Following graduation from Phillips Academy in Andover, Massachusetts, McAlpin entered the New York City office of D. H. McAlpin & Company in early 1861. When the Civil War broke out, McAlpin enlisted in the Union Army as a drummer boy, but his father quickly had the youngster discharged from duty because of his tender age. The call to military service, however, ran deep in young Ed McAlpin. As soon as he reached the age of majority in 1869, McAlpin enlisted in the state militia as a private. Able and energetic, he soon ascended to officer rank. In 1885, he was promoted to colonel and placed in charge of the 71st Infantry Regiment of the New York State Guard. Upon taking command of this flagging unit, Colonel McAlpin "aggressively cut dead wood from the ranks and reorganized the leadership cadre to such an extent that it became virtually a new regiment."[44] All the while, McAlpin remained in the employ of the family tobacco business, eventually assuming partnership. The firm prospered during McAlpin's tenure, ultimately becoming an industry giant, the American Tobacco Company. On the domestic front, McAlpin married Anne Brandreth, the daughter of a wealthy patent medicine manufacturer, in October 1870, combining her fortune with his own, while fathering five sons. Like the wealthy Talcott, McAlpin's leisure activities included following the New York Giants, but his politics were different. McAlpin was a staunch Republican, active in party affairs in his native Westchester County and serving as mayor of his birthplace.[45]

Unlike Talcott and McAlpin, Cornelius C. Van Cott rose from humble origins. Born in Greenwich Village on February 15, 1838, Van Cott received only a few years schooling before he entered the workforce as a printer's apprentice.[46] Later, he became a carriage maker, working for an employer who was also the foreman of a local fire company. At age 20, an intrigued Van Cott joined Hose Company No. 7 and began his rise through the service. Connection to a fire company also abetted Van Cott's entry into politics. Affable and ambitious, he quickly rose in Manhattan Republican Party ranks. In time, Van Cott's labors on behalf of the party were rewarded by his appointment as Inspector of Customs. Meanwhile, his 1860 marriage to Fanny Thompson produced a son named Richard, with whom Cornelius would maintain a close, lifelong bond.

In 1872, Republican Mayor William Havemeyer appointed Van Cott to the NYC Board of Fire Commissioners. Reappointed by both Republican and Democrat mayors thereafter, Van Cott would hold the positions of Fire Commission Board president and secretary, sinecures that facilitated Van Cott's entry into banking and insurance, the fields where he made his fortune. An acolyte of U.S. senator and New York Republican Party powerbroker Thomas S. Platt, Van Cott was elected a New York state senator from Manhattan in 1887. Two years later, Platt arranged his appointment as postmaster of New York City by President Benjamin Harrison. All the while, Van Cott retained his position as chief executive of the West Side Bank and the newly formed Great Eastern Casualty and Indemnity Insurance Company.[47] Although spawned by a baseball playing family— various Van Cotts had played for the amateur New York Gothams in the 1850s[48]—Cornelius preferred fishing, hunting, and other field pursuits.[49] Still, his wealth and political position made Van Cott an attractive prospect for those organizing a new baseball club in New York.

Decades after the event, *New York Times* sportswriter John Kieran penned a nostalgic column about a tape-measure home run hit by Giant slugger Roger Connor during the 1889 season. After the ball had soared over a distant Polo Grounds wall, "Eddie Talcott, broker and baseball fan, jumped up and started a collection.... [Spectators who] chipped in [included] Col. McAlpin and [Albert] Johnson. They gave Roger a big gold watch."[50] But Talcott, McAlpin, and Johnson were up to more than just taking in games together at the ballpark that summer. Each was preparing to assume a pivotal role in the rival baseball league that Giant shortstop John Montgomery Ward would unveil at season's end: the Players League. Johnson would contribute heavily to the early financing that got the PL off the drawing board. McAlpin would assume the position of league president, while Talcott was the driving force behind the new league's cornerstone franchise in New York. Ward masterminded the player defections that stocked Players League rosters, including the virtual en masse movement of NL Giant personnel to the PL Giants. Talcott did most of the rest. He leased vacant ground adjacent to the New Polo Grounds from the Gardiner-Lynch family via estate agent James J. Coogan and footed the bill for the erection of a brand new ballpark (Brotherhood Park) directly beside it. Talcott also secured well-heeled acquaintances to share the financial burden of the new franchise.

On November 15, 1889, the New York Base Ball Club Limited filed incorporation papers in Albany. Listed as franchise principals were financial backers Talcott, McAlpin, and Cornelius Van Cott, and Giant stars Tim Keefe and Buck Ewing.[51] A month later, the club was formally organized, with Van Cott and Talcott becoming franchise president and vice-president, respectively. Stockbroker and McAlpin brother-in-law Frank B. Robinson, another sizable club investor, was elected secretary-treasurer, while McAlpin, Keefe, and Ewing joined the club officers on the franchise board of directors.[52] A good-sized crowd for the home opener at Brotherhood Park augured financial success, but it was not to be. With five major league teams (NL New York Giants, PL New York Giants, NL Brooklyn Bridegrooms, PL Brooklyn Ward's Wonders, and AA Brooklyn Gladiators) all playing their home games within a few-mile radius, there simply was not enough fan patronage for the turning of a profit. The situation elsewhere was no better, as the fan base was inadequate to the task of sustaining so much professional baseball. By 1890 season's end, each of the three majors was in extremis.

Although the Players League had the cream of the playing talent, PL club backers were a different breed from National League magnates like A.G. Spalding, John T. Brush, and Arthur Soden, hard-nosed capitalists but also true lovers of the game, in for the long haul. Conversely, most of the PL club owners were baseball fans, but they all were businessmen first and wanted a foreseeable return on their investments. And nowhere was this more the case than in New York. As the season drew to a close, Players League president McAlpin issued brave statements about the circuit's intention to carry on, despite financial hardship. Followers of the game were, therefore, stunned by the announcement that McAlpin's franchise partner Ed Talcott and John B. Day had decided to cut their losses via consolidation of New York's PL and NL clubs. With its indispensable New York franchise co-opted, the Players League quickly collapsed, much to the dismay of John Montgomery Ward and his cohorts. Even more disturbed by events was Players League secretary Frank Brunnell, who rained abuse on McAlpin and Talcott, branding them "traitors" who had "thrown down" the league to preserve their own wellbeing—all to no effect.[53] The Players League was dead, and the melded New York Giant club would play in the National League.

On January 24, 1891, the concerned parties met to reorganize the franchise under the laws of New Jersey. Club ownership ranks were dominated by the Talcott group, which now held slightly over half of the Giants' stock. Other NL club owners (Spalding, Soden, Brush, et al.) controlled just over one-quarter combined, while the stake of John B. Day and his MEC associates had been reduced to about 15 per cent of the club stock. Former PL organizers Ward, Keefe, and O'Rourke, plus a few others held the remaining odd stock lots.[54] The new organization was christened the National Exhibition Company, the corporate handle used for all the ensuing years that the New York Giants would be in existence. Greatly respected in baseball circles, Day was bestowed the title of club president. But executive power would actually be wielded by VP Talcott and his allies. The next two seasons were trying ones for the Giants, both on the field and at the gate, where Polo Grounds attendance remained far off the norm of the late 1880s. The Talcott group strengthened its hold on franchise operations by purchasing the bonds had to be issued to cover club indebtedness. By the close of the 1892 season, club president Day was little more than a ceremonial Giant executive. Shortly thereafter, his resignation from office rendered Talcott control of the franchise complete.

Talcott and McAlpin declined the post of new club president, citing the pressure of their other obligations. However, with Democrat Grover Cleveland returned to the White House, Van Cott would have free time, having resigned his patronage post as New York City postmaster. But as before, the franchise course would be steered by Talcott, the *New York Herald* reporting that it was "an open secret that [Van Cott] has but little knowledge of the national game, and that Mr. Talcott will be 'the power behind the throne.'"[55] Having reconciled with now NL Brooklyn player-manager John Montgomery Ward, Talcott then decided to improve the Giants' balance sheet by upgrading the product on the field through securing Ward for New York. Ward cooperated in the move via an unsubtle threat to retire unless given his release by Brooklyn. For $10,000 or a share in Giant gate receipts—accounts differ—Ward was secured as New York player-manager for the 1893 season.[56] Shortly after his installation at the helm, Ward dispatched aging icon Buck Ewing to Cleveland in exchange for young infielder George Davis, whose Hall of Fame career blossomed once in a Giant uniform. With fireballer Amos Rusie performing yeoman work on the mound and Ward and Davis anchoring the infield, the Manhattanites began to climb in NL standings. Attendance surged as well, with the 387,000 patrons drawn to the Polo Grounds for the 1894 season setting a new major league attendance record. Capping New York's season was a four-game sweep of the NL pennant-winning Baltimore Orioles in the 1894 postseason Temple Cup match.

Notwithstanding the improvement in the team's fortunes, it appears that baseball club ownership had not produced the financial return anticipated by the business-minded Talcott group. By late-1894, they were ready to leave the game and were thus receptive to discreet sale inquiries made by Andrew Freedman, a Tammany Hall insider and real estate millionaire. Indeed, so anxious were Talcott and the others to get out, they sold their controlling interest in the Giants' franchise to Freedman at a bargain-basement price variously estimated at $48,000 to $54,000.[57] On January 25, 1895, Freedman officially took control of the New York Giants, bringing the Talcott regime to its end.

Life after baseball was not particularly kind to erstwhile club president Cornelius Van Cott. Restored to the position of NYC postmaster following the election of Republican president William McKinley in 1896, Van Cott soon overextended his business interests and eventually had to assume liability for considerable commercial debt. Worse yet, scandal erupted at the post office. In 1904, government inquiry into suspected financial wrongdoing led to the dismissal of his brother, Whitfield Van Cott, from postal service employ, and the arrest of his beloved son Richard, a post office cashier, on embezzlement-type charges. Cornelius himself was under investigation when he took ill in his office on October 25, 1904. Within minutes of arriving home, Van Cott suffered a fatal heart attack. He was 66 years old. Following funeral services at St. Paul's Methodist Episcopal Church, Van Cott was laid to rest in Cypress Hill Cemetery in Brooklyn. Despite Van Cott's late-life embarrassments, the *New York Times* remembered him kindly, as both "enemies and friends were agreed as to his genial personality, his somewhat old-fashioned good manners, and his unfailing affability."[58]

Fate smiled more favorably on McAlpin and Talcott. In 1895, New York governor Levi P. Morton appointed McAlpin to the post of state adjutant general, with the military rank of major general. But a quest for the vice presidential spot on the Republican Party ticket for 1896 sputtered when McAlpin delivered a poorly received speech at the national convention in St. Louis.[59] All the while, McAlpin remained involved in the family's lucrative tobacco business and active in civic affairs and boy scouting. He died of a cerebral hemorrhage at his mansion in Ossining on April 12, 1917, aged 68. Following a funeral at the local Presbyterian Church that he had long served as a trustee, Edwin Augustus McAlpin was interred at Vale Cemetery in Schenectady, New York.[60]

Only in his mid–30s when he left the game, Eddie Talcott spent the remaining years of his long life mostly out of the public spotlight. He continued his frequent attendance at the Polo Grounds and could be relied upon to predict a Giant pennant at the start of each season. In 1897, Talcott joined the brokerage firm of Bell & Company and the following year reportedly earned over one million dollars during the five month run-up to the Spanish-American War. In 1901, Talcott sold his seat on the New York Stock Exchange for a handsome sum and only dabbled in the market thereafter.[61] Later that year, A.G. Spalding floated Talcott's name as a potential buyer of Andrew Freedman's Giant franchise holdings during Spalding's fight with Freedman and John T. Brush over the NL presidency.[62] But Freedman had no intention of selling out to Talcott or any other buyer proposed by Spalding, and the dispute over the league president election was ultimately resolved in Freedman's favor by the courts.[63]

By 1910, Talcott and his wife had relocated to the New Jersey shore, where Talcott kept a low profile, giving his occupation as a stockbroker for Hudson, Ivey & Company to census takers. Following the death of Sara Talcott, Ed remarried, taking widow Mary Howell Grover as his second wife in 1925. Talcott's name last appeared in the press under peculiar circumstances. A spinster heiress named Louise Williston attempted to enlist Talcott's aid in her effort to gain release from a New York mental asylum.[64] By now, however, Talcott was old and ailing and could provide no assistance. He died after "a long illness" at his home in Point Pleasant Beach, New Jersey, on April 6, 1941.[65] Edward Baker Talcott was 83. Following a wake in nearby Mansquan, Talcott was buried at Woodlawn Cemetery in the Bronx.[66] With that, the Talcott group passed into history.

Andrew Freedman

Chroniclers of the game have rarely been kind to Andrew Freedman, principal owner of the New York Giants from January 1895 to September 1902. According to one club historian, Freedman was "naturally arrogant [with] a bad temper at the end of a very short fuse."[67] In much the same vein, Bill James memorably described him as "George Steinbrenner on Quaaludes with a touch of Al Capone" and "just this side of a madman,"[68] while another commentator has awarded Freedman the distinction of being "the most loathsome team owner in baseball history."[69] But Andrew Freedman's stormy tenure as the Giants' owner was, in fact, only a chapter in the life of one of New York City's most prominent turn-of-the-century figures. To Freedman, ownership of the Giants was little more than a pastime, a diversion from the weighty business and political affairs that dominated his life. As a consequence, his stewardship of the club was mercurial, with frequent managerial changes, angry ultimatums to fellow magnates, and battles with the sporting press being alternated with periods of complete indifference by Freedman to his baseball interests. In short, club ownership did not show Andrew Freedman at his best.

The future Giant boss was born into a Manhattan family of middle-class German-Jewish immigrants on September 1, 1860. His father, Joseph Freedman, was a prosperous grocer while his mother, Elizabeth Davies Freedman, tended to the children, of whom Andrew was the second of four.[70] A precocious grammar-school graduate, Andrew was enrolled in preadmission courses at the College of the City of New York (CCNY) at age 14 but proved

Andrew Freedman had a tumultuous tenure with the Giants in the 1890s.

an indifferent scholar, dropping out of CCNY at the end of his freshman year.[71] Freedman began his working life in the employ of a dry goods house but soon gravitated to real estate, the field where he would make his first fortune.

To enhance his prospects, 21-year-old Andrew Freedman joined Tammany Hall, the corrupt political machine that controlled the Democratic Party in New York City. There, he attached himself to Richard Croker, a rising Tammany star. In time, Freedman would become a financial advisor, business associate, and close personal friend of Croker. In 1886, Croker assumed control of the Wigwam (as Tammany Hall was informally known) and installed his protégé Freedman on the finance committee, Tammany's all-powerful policy-making board. Freedman's association with Croker, combined with his native intelligence and a fierce energy, all but guaranteed success in the real estate world. Dealing extensively in tony Fifth Avenue properties and acquiring vast tracts of land in the then sparsely populated Bronx, Freedman quickly amassed a fortune via sale of property at inflated prices to local businessmen, city contractors, and others requiring the favor of his patron, Boss Croker. By the time that he reached age 30, he had become a very wealthy man.

Freedman's interest in baseball is usually traced to his appointment as receiver of the bankrupt Manhattan Athletic Club in 1893. His administration of club affairs included management of Manhattan Field (née New Polo Grounds), only recently the home of the Giants and still an important New York sporting venue. Freedman began taking in Giant games (Manhattan Field and Polo Grounds III sat on adjoining sites) and soon developed a liking for the sport.[72] With time on his hands following Tammany's defeat in the municipal elections of 1894 and awash in money, he quietly began acquiring blocks of Giant stock, at times using circus impresario James A. Bailey as a front.[73] Then in January 1895, Freedman made his move, capturing majority control of the franchise by buying out Edward B. Talcott and his allies.[74]

Wealthy, politically connected, and a native son, the youthful (age 34) Freedman's acquisition of the club was initially well received. The *New York Herald* predicted that Freedman "will wear well.... He is young, with excellent business ideas, liberal in his dealings, pronounced in his ideas of right and wrong, and quick to recognize an advantage."[75] Baseball luminaries joined in well wishes for the new owner. A.G. Spalding, having only recently divested himself of his own ownership share of the Giants, stated, "That from what I hear, Mr. Freedman is a clever businessman and will prove successful. I hope he makes a lot of money."[76] Just retired star John Montgomery Ward, whose sale of his small share of Giant stock had helped to make Freedman's control of the club possible, also applauded the new magnate, particularly after Freedman ratified Talcott's appointment of Ward favorite George Davis as the team's playing manager for the upcoming season.[77] Overlooked in the glow of good feeling was a dubious opening move by the novice owner: elimination of the post of managing director of the club. Despite limited prior contact with and understanding of the game, Freedman would exercise the duties of franchise commander personally as the Giant president.

With the nucleus of the 1894 Temple Cup champions returning, great things were expected of the Manhattanites, but the team started the new season sluggishly. Impatient New York scribes were quick to assign blame, as did Giant fans, and the new club owner was not exempted from their censure. Although in many ways an able man, Freedman's background had not conditioned him to public criticism. Combative and surprisingly thin-skinned, Freedman reacted badly. He began by firing his managers. Davis, Jack Doyle, and Harvey Watkins would all be relieved of duty during the 1895 season.

Freedman also had trouble with his players, particularly star hurler Amos Rusie, who chafed under the owner's disciplinary measures.[78] Nor did Freedman enjoy cordial relations with his fellow magnates, most of whom found him abrasive and impossible to get along with.[79] Worse still, Freedman got into fights—at times, literally[80]—with the writers on the Giant beat, occasionally denying them admittance to the Polo Grounds or refusing to communicate about club matters. *New York American* sportswriter Charles Dryden retaliated by publishing imaginary interviews with Freedman, complete with maladroit quotations designed to make the polished owner appear an ignoramus.[81] A public relations nightmare, Freedman quickly managed to alienate most of the baseball world.[82] In the meantime, his team staggered home a disappointing ninth-place finisher (out of the 12-team NL).

Unhappily for Freedman, his fortunes fared little better with the Giants the following campaign. Crippled by the absence of Rusie, who sat out the entire year rather than capitulate to tight-fisted salary terms, the Giants finished the 1896 season a distant seventh, 27 games behind pennant-winning Baltimore. In the offseason, the Freedman-Rusie impasse was finally resolved via the unsolicited intervention of fellow NL club owners who—without Freedman's knowledge or approval—quietly induced Rusie to return to the Giants for the 1897 season by settling $5,000 on him. Indignant when he found out, Freedman refused to contribute to the settlement and fumed at the magnates' intrusion into his running of the Giants.

Buoyed by Rusie's return, the Giants surged to third place in 1897. The team also benefited from the inattention of its owner, now largely preoccupied with political matters. With Richard Croker returned from Europe and reinstalled as Tammany chief, Freedman threw himself into the successful mayoral campaign of Tammany candidate Robert Van Wyck. Following Van Wyck's inauguration, Freedman declined appointment to office, choosing instead to remain a backroom powerbroker in the new administration. At Croker's urging, however, he did accept the position of treasurer of the National Democratic Party. In 1898, Freedman expanded his business empire by becoming a principal of the Maryland Fidelity and Guarantee Company, a municipal insurance and bonding operation that proved a lucrative new source of income for him.[83] But as Freedman's commercial interests flourished, his reign as a major league-team owner was about to enter a malevolent period that would beget serious repercussions for the game.

In late July 1898, Freedman paid a now infrequent visit to the Polo Grounds to take in a game against Baltimore. In the fourth inning, Ducky Holmes, a former Giant, struck out. On his way back to the bench, Holmes responded to the gibes of New York fans by referring to Freedman as a *Sheeny,* an anti–Semitic putdown. When umpire Tom Lynch refused an enraged Freedman's demand that Holmes be ejected, Freedman ordered the Giants off the field. Lynch thereupon forfeited the game to the Orioles. In the aftermath, Freedman insisted upon league action against Holmes, branding his remark not only personally offensive but "an insult to the Jewish people and the Hebrew patrons of the game."[84] The season-long suspension of Holmes thereafter imposed by the league provoked an ugly reaction. Boston players circulated a petition denouncing Freedman's "spirit of intolerance, of arrogance and prejudice toward players, a spirit inimical to the best interests of the game,"[85] while *Sporting Life* decried punishment of Holmes for the "trifling offense" of "insulting the Hebrew race."[86] Holmes' lawyer, meanwhile, obtained injunctive relief from a friendly local judge and Holmes ended up spending only a few days on the sidelines.[87]

Needless to say, Freedman bristled over the outcome, playing every Giant game versus Baltimore under protest for the remainder of the season. But what truly incensed him was not so much the resolution of the Ducky Holmes affair but the position taken by his fellow owners. Branding the suspension illegal (because it had been imposed without a hearing), the other NL magnates had sided with Holmes and urged the league board of directors to lift the suspension. To Freedman, a proud man sensitive to slights, this stance and Holmes' reinstatement represented nothing less than league countenance of a gross personal insult. And Andrew Freedman would not abide it.

Freedman's revenge would take the form of a punishing financial lesson for the other NL owners. Although Freedman adversaries like Cincinnati owner John T. Brush and Baltimore boss Harry von der Horst were well-heeled businessmen, they lacked the financial wherewithal to conduct their baseball operations at a loss indefinitely. Andrew Freedman was different. While not in the plutocrat class of a Vanderbilt, Rockefeller, or Carnegie, Freedman was truly wealthy with a personal fortune that was likely the equal of his fellow magnates put together.[88] In his eyes, owning a baseball club, like opera patronage and collecting French landscape paintings, was a pastime, not a livelihood. Thus, he could well absorb the injury that would accompany his singular plan for retribution—ruination of the NL's most important financial asset, namely, Freedman's own New York franchise. By whatever methods required, Freedman would ensure that the Giants began fielding noncompetitive teams. Immediately thereafter, Giant fortunes nosedived. The 1899 season would see the team plummet to 60–90, a full 42 games behind pennant-winning Brooklyn. Repelled by the situation and with no end in sight, fans avoided Giant games in droves.[89] As intended, the attendance falloff delivered a crippling blow to the finances of the NL, particularly hurting the smaller market clubs that had come to rely on healthy receipts from Giant contests. The league's distress gave Freedman no end of satisfaction. As the Giants' dismal season drew to a close, Freedman declared, "Base ball [*sic*] affairs in New York have been going just as I wished and expected them to go. I have given the club little attention and I would not give five cents for the best base ball [*sic*] player in the world to strengthen it."[90] And as even his detractors knew, Freedman meant it.

With their horizons bleak and certain of Freedman's ruthlessness, the NL owners soon entreated for peace. But reconciliation with Freedman would come at a high price. First and foremost was submission to Freedman's demand for reduction of the NL to an eight-club circuit and the elimination of syndicate club ownership—the twin policy prescriptions that fig-leafed the deeply personal nature of Freedman's bitterness toward the league. The owners also acceded to Freedman's demand that the Giants receive the pick of the players available from the liquidated franchises. In addition, the league agreed to reimburse Freedman the $10,000 that the annual rent of Manhattan Field cost him, lest the grounds be available for use by some future competitor. Last, but an important matter of principle to Freedman, the NL refunded the $1,000 fine imposed on the Giants for forfeiting the Ducky Holmes game—with 6 percent interest.[91]

Another ramification of the mollification process was the emergence of a wholly unexpected alliance between Freedman and principal antagonist John T. Brush, the league's most influential magnate and heretofore leader of the Freedman opposition in NL owners ranks.[92] Little immediate benefit from the Freedman-Brush collaboration accrued to their respective franchises, as the Giants and Reds alternated as the league's cellar dwellers for the 1900 and 1901 seasons. But both men had larger endeavors on their mind than the immediate pennant races. Freedman, in fact, had taken to almost entirely ignoring the Giants, his energies consumed by the task that would yield his most enduring legacy: construction of the Interborough Rapid Transit line, New York City's first true underground railway system.[93] Brush, meanwhile, was busy at work on a longtime pet project, a scheme to convert the independent franchises of the National League into a jointly held trust.[94] As Brush envisioned it, NL assets would be pooled into a holding company managed by a board of regents. Players and managers would be licensed by the board and assigned to various clubs consistent with establishing competitive parity. Costs would be controlled by means of stringent salary caps and by the manufacture of baseball equipment by a trust subsidiary. Apportioned profits to trust shareholders would be meted out at season's end.[95]

When Brush broached the trust proposal to him, Freedman, anticipating adverse press and public reaction, was skeptical but, in time, agreed to bankroll the scheme. The fine details of the trust were later hammered out by Brush, Freedman, and fellow owners Arthur Soden (Boston) and Frank de Haas Robison (St. Louis) during private meetings held at Tower Hill, Freedman's secluded estate in Red Bank, New Jersey. Failure to secure a fifth magnate's vote, however, would prove fatal to the scheme as the trust forces would be stalemated during contentious NL owners meetings held in December 1901. Legal proceedings pitting Freedman against anti-trust champion A.G. Spalding ensued, with Freedman taking a battering on the public relations front even as his lawyers prevailed in court.[96]

Rejection of the trust was not the only setback being suffered by Freedman. Of far graver consequence was the ouster of the scandal-plagued Van Wyck regime in the New York City elections of November 1901. Shortly thereafter, Richard Croker resigned his post as Tammany chief and took up residence in the British Isles, far beyond the subpoena power of the incoming reform administration. As noted by the observant, Croker's departure drastically reduced the political power of Andrew Freedman, an insider sans electoral constituency whose influence was derived solely from his close personal ties to the fallen Tammany chief. Taking particular heart from this situation were those in the baseball world eager to see a club from the new American League installed in New York. The most likely candidate for transplant to Gotham was the reincarnated Baltimore Orioles, then under the direction of player-manager and part-owner John McGraw. At least temporarily, however, AL moving plans were frustrated by an audacious counterstroke masterminded by Brush, now effectively in charge of the NL as chairman of a three-owner governing committee. Taking advantage of McGraw's restiveness under the disciplinary yoke of AL president Ban Johnson and with the connivance of Freedman, Brush induced McGraw to force his release by the Orioles. Immediately thereafter, McGraw inked a four-year contract to manage the Giants. With major assistance from Maryland politico John "Sonny" Mahon, Brush then covertly maneuvered majority control of the stock in the cash-strapped Baltimore franchise into Freedman's hands. Under its new ownership, the Orioles immediately set about releasing the team's best players, all of whom then signed with the Giants (Joe McGinnity, Dan McGann, Roger Bresnahan, Jack Cronin) or the Reds (Joe Kelley, Cy Seymour). Only quick action by Johnson saved the franchise for the AL. Taking advantage of league charter provisions activated by an ensuing Baltimore game forfeiture (for lack of players), Johnson promptly stripped Freedman of the title to the franchise and placed the club under direct presidential control for the remainder of the season.[97]

The following spring, the AL, with new club ownership procured by Johnson, would endeavor to transfer the Orioles to New York. But Andrew Freedman would be there to provide opposition to the move, even though he was no longer officially connected to the game. On August 12, 1902, Freedman, his interest in baseball near extinguished and besieged by the myriad demands of the subway project, had announced that he had appointed John T. Brush managing director of the Giants and transferred day-to-day control of club operations to him (while Freedman retained the title of club president). A month later, Freedman severed his connection with the club, selling his controlling interest in the New York franchise to Brush for approximately $200,000, a purchase that Brush financed largely through the sale of his own Cincinnati club to local interests. But Freedman was still an actor to be dealt with by major league baseball. His oversight of the rapid transit project gave Freedman considerable sway over New York real estate, which he used to stymie AL entry into Manhattan for months, condemning for putative subway purposes any site that AL president Johnson took interest in. With the start of the 1903 season approaching, only the acquisition of a desolate north Manhattan mesa overlooked by Freedman afforded the AL a foothold in New York.[98]

Looking back, the eight years of Freedman stewardship can fairly be adjudged the darkest in New York Giant history. The club had been a contender only once (1897) during that span and had reached bottom (a 44–88 last-place finish) by the time that Freedman had abandoned the game. However, perhaps more enervating than the Giants prolonged poor play was the atmosphere created by Freedman. Essentially a dilettante when it came to baseball, Freedman periodically left the Giants directionless. But team fortunes sank even further when Freedman's attention returned to the club. Chronically impatient with his club's standings, Freedman inflicted 13 managerial changes on the Giants during his tenure as franchise owner. Worse yet, Freedman's peevish battles— with players, umpires, fellow owners, league officials, the sporting press—and his ferocious vindictive streak drained vitality from the NL's flagship enterprise and hurt the game itself in the process.

Fortunately for baseball, Giant fortunes quickly rebounded under the new Brush-McGraw regime and a pennant winner was produced within two years. But Andrew Freedman also prospered. No longer distracted by baseball club ownership and largely relieved from duty in the political world as well,[99] Freedman concentrated his energies on the complex financing and construction schemes that made the subway system operational by 1904 and Freedman an even richer man. Losses subsequently suffered in the Panic of 1907 were more than recouped by the sale of another Freedman insurance venture, the Casualty Company of America, for a handsome price in 1909. In addition, Freedman served as a director of various construction, rapid transit, waterfront, theater, and railroad companies while holding stock in numerous other going concerns, including the Wright Brothers flying machine company. He also continued to reel in hefty fees from conservatorships and other court-appointed positions.[100]

Although scorned by baseball, Freedman was held in high esteem by the business and social elites of New York. His circle included 1904 Democratic presidential candidate Alton Parker, banker August Belmont, Jr., theater owner Lee Shubert, Tammany powerhouse T. P. Sullivan, helmsman Cornelius Vanderbilt III, prominent political lawyer DeLancey Nicholl, financier Jacob Schiff, and retailing giant Nathan Strauss, most of whom also served on the board of a charitable foundation established by Freedman.[101] Diversions included the opera, art collection, yachting, and the ownership of racehorses.

Freedman even took to raising purebred Holsteins at Freedmanor Farms, a livestock operation situated on his Red Bank estate.[102] In addition, he spent considerable time on golf courses near his properties in rural New Hampshire.[103]

In late 1914, Freedman served as best man when Richard Croker, his long-estranged first wife having finally died, married his mistress. The following year, Freedman's tautly strung constitution began to unravel. He suffered from bouts of exhaustion before experiencing a complete nervous breakdown in November 1915. Confined to his Manhattan apartment suite and attended by 24-hour medical care, Freedman had a stroke and died on the morning of December 4, 1915. He was only 55. A glowing *New York Times* obituary extolled his business and civic accomplishments, describing Freedman as the person "who did more than perhaps any other man to make possible the subway system in this city."[104] Freedman's tenure as owner of the New York Giants was noted in passing.

A bachelor,[105] Freedman bequeathed lifetime incomes to his aged mother and spinster sister, both of whom were comfortable in their own rights, while personal mementos were left to Croker, Belmont, and other friends.[106] The bulk of the $7 million Freedman estate, however, was designated for the erection and maintenance of a nonsectarian residence for the affluent fallen on hard times. First opened in 1925 and expanded six years thereafter, the Andrew Freeman Home, an exquisite four-story limestone palazzo sited on the Bronx's Grand Concourse, was declared a New York City landmark in 1992 and currently hosts civic and cultural events.[107] Sadly, few entering the premises today are familiar with the mansion's namesake.

As shown above, Andrew Freedman was not the one-dimensional ogre portrayed by the game's writers. He was an astute businessman and political operative but lacked the temperament and baseball expertise required for success as a club owner. In the final analysis, both baseball and Andrew Freedman would have been better off if they had never met.

John T. Brush

Beset by a chronic illness and often in pain, John T. Brush was not an obvious candidate for a leadership role in turn-of-the-century baseball. But Brush's afflictions camouflaged a fiercely competitive spirit and a will of iron. For 25 years, Brush was the most influential club owner in the National League, a champion of causes that affected, for both good and ill, the fortunes of the national pastime in its turbulent early years. A self-made man, Brush had risen from rural poverty in upstate New York to become a prosperous mercantile and civic leader in his adopted hometown of Indianapolis. Not an athlete himself, John T. first seized upon baseball as a vehicle for advertising his retail clothing business. But he soon developed an abiding passion for the game, eventually relinquishing oversight of the business to others in order to focus his energies almost entirely upon the operation of major league clubs, first in Indianapolis, then Cincinnati, and ultimately New York.

John Tomlinson Brush was born on June 15, 1845, in Clintonville, New York, a remote upstate hamlet situated near the Canadian border.[108] He was of Scots-Irish stock and born into a family that had just lost its breadwinner. His father, also named John Tomlinson Brush, had died a month earlier at age 35. Soon thereafter, widow Sarah Farrar Brush and her four young children relocated to the village of Lawrence, New York, where

Sarah succumbed shortly after the 1850 U.S. Census was taken.[109] The Brush orphans were then taken in by grandfather Eliphalet Brush and his second wife, Melinda Pier Brush.[110] Work on the Brush farm in Hopkinton was hard and the accommodations spartan. Cramped living quarters required young John and older brother George to sleep in a barn. Escaping agricultural drudgery at age 17, John took a short course of study at Eastman's Business College in Poughkeepsie, winning a $25 prize for a pen sketch of an eagle.[111] Thereafter, Brush journeyed to Boston, where he got his first taste of the retail clothing trade.

On September 2, 1864, 19-year-old John T. Brush enlisted as a private in the 1st New York Artillery Regiment and likely saw action at the Civil War front. Mustered out unscathed in June 1865, he proceeded to Troy where, in time, he was befriended by George Pixley, a principal in the newly formed retail clothing business of Owen, Pixley & Company. Within a few years, Brush advanced from clothing salesman to store manager to partner in the company. Somewhere along the way, he met Margaret Agnes Ewart, a woman about whom little is known except that she was born in upstate New York and married John T. Brush on October 18, 1869. Daughter Eleanor Gordon Brush was born in Albany in March 1871.

More than 100 years after the fact, Natalie Brush de Gendron, a late-life Brush daughter by his second wife, asserted that the Margaret-John Brush marriage was not a happy one and that the couple divorced shortly after Eleanor's birth.[112] But census and other records appear to tell a different story. First of all, Margaret bore Brush a second child, a daughter named Adalaide who did not survive infancy.[113] Moreover, New York census records place John T. Brush, wife Margaret, and daughter Nella (Eleanor) under one roof in Lockport, New York, the place where Brush managed an Owen, Pixley store in 1873–1874. Later in 1874, Brush was dispatched to Indianapolis as Owen, Pixley expanded operations westward. After frustrating delays, a company outpost, whimsically named the When (as in *When* will it open?) Store, opened its doors on March 20, 1875. With consumer interest whetted by Brush's improbable flair for advertisement and promotion, the operation became a resounding success, eventually becoming the largest department store between New York and Chicago.[114] The store's boss quickly immersed himself in the civic affairs of his new hometown and soon became a leading figure in various community and fraternal organizations. All the while, U.S. and local

John T. Brush was involved with several major league teams and is best remembered as owner of the Giants.

census data have John, Margaret, and Eleanor Brush living in Indianapolis. But all may not have been well in the Brush marriage. Beginning in the early 1880s, Indianapolis city directories list John and Margaret Brush as residing at different addresses, with Margaret identified as the widow of (the very much alive) John T. Brush.[115] On June 9, 1888, Margaret Ewart Brush died quietly in Indianapolis. Despite the prominence of her husband, no obituary was published in the local newspapers.[116] All that is known is that Margaret was laid to rest in the Brush family plot in Crown Hill Cemetery in Indianapolis.[117]

Local legend has it that John T. Brush first became enthused about baseball upon reading a Spalding guide confiscated from an idle store clerk. Or that Brush's interest in the game stemmed from accepting stock in an Indianapolis ball club as payment for a debt. The facts are more prosaic. In his youth, Brush had been a catcher for neighborhood teams in upstate New York, a hotbed of the early game. Later, he seized upon baseball as a vehicle for advertising the When Store. In 1882, Brush organized a municipal baseball league, building a diamond with a grandstand in northwest Indianapolis for league games and engaging Jack Kerins as player-manager for the When Store team. After the professional game mushroomed to three major leagues in 1884, Indianapolis was granted an American Association franchise. Historical accounts differ on whether or not Brush owned the one-year AA Hoosiers, but it seems more likely that Joseph Schwabacher, "a local liquor dealer beat Brush to the franchise."[118]

Determined to remain involved in the game that he was now thoroughly smitten with, Brush backed an Indianapolis team in the newly formed Western League the following year. Outclassing the competition, the club record stood at 27–4 when the Western League collapsed in mid–July. Brush then made overtures toward acquiring the National League's Detroit Wolverines but was rebuffed. He and other Indianapolis investors had better luck purchasing the financially ailing NL St. Louis Maroons. Taking the title in early 1887, the investment group promptly moved the franchise to Indianapolis, with Brush becoming the club vice president. By July, Brush was in the top spot, club president Louis Newberger having resigned in disgust after a number of Hoosier players were arrested in an Indianapolis brothel.[119]

In addition to guiding the lackluster fortunes of the Indianapolis club, Brush threw himself into the administration of the National League, serving on various policy-making committees. The adoption of one Brush initiative by the league, a tight-fisted salary classification plan, was a major cause of the player revolt that led to the debilitating Players League War of 1890. Ironically, Brush himself was among the first casualties of that conflict, with the NL liquidating his Indianapolis franchise as a preemptive wartime measure. But Brush had no intention of being forced to the sidelines. He exacted stiff reparations from the league, remained a member of the NL ownership council, and obtained the promise of the next available franchise from fellow magnates. Then in July 1890, he took a stake in the New York Giants, accepting club stock in lieu of payment for Indianapolis players sold to the personnel-depleted Giants. By April 1891, Brush was back in National League ownership ranks, having outmuscled rival claimant Albert Johnson for the rights to the Cincinnati venue. With the backing of his friend and minority club stockholder N. Ashley Lloyd (co-owner of his family's prosperous Cincinnati pharmacy chain), Brush assumed the position of club president of a reorganized Cincinnati Red franchise. There for the ensuing decade, Brush served as a convenient target for the brickbats of *Cincinnati Gazette* sportswriter Ban Johnson and other local scribes aggrieved by the noncontending nines that Reds management put on the field. A dour man of somewhat sinister appearance (think mustachioed cartoon villain Snidely Whiplash)[120] with a penchant for backroom intrigue, Brush was often the recipient of bad press, particularly during his years in Cincinnati. If that bothered him, he rarely showed it. And hostile press commentary had no effect whatsoever on Brush management strategies.

The highlight of the decade for John T. Brush occurred away from the diamond. On June 6, 1894, the 49-year-old widower married Elsie Lombard, a stage actress barely older than his daughter Eleanor. The birth of Natalie Lombard Brush a year later only increased his joy. Brush reveled in his new domestic life. Elsie excelled as a hostess and soon the Brush mansion, renamed Lombardy in her honor, became a standard destination for theatrical stars (Sarah Bernhardt, Henry Irving, Ellen Terry) and literary lions (Arthur Conan Doyle, James Whitcomb Riley, Booth Tarkington) sojourning in Indianapolis. Meanwhile, Eleanor Brush had married Harry N. Hempstead, a capable young Philadelphian whom John T. would come to rely on. But as good as things were going on the family and business fronts, Brush achieved little success as leader of the Cincinnati Reds during the 1890s. The club was a reliable nonfactor in NL pennant races.

A nonresident owner unloved in Cincinnati, Brush had long had his eyes on another franchise: the New York Giants. Brush had retained his minority interest in the Giants through the various changes in franchise command, but his ambition to assume control of the club himself had been frustrated by the stealthy accumulation of a majority stakehold by Andrew Freedman. Brush and Freedman did not get along and were regularly at odds in gatherings of NL club owners. They even came to blows in the taproom of a Manhattan hotel. But at an October 1899 meeting brokered by Boston boss Arthur Soden, the two reached an understanding, and soon thereafter began to work in concert—often to the dismay of fellow magnates and a hostile sporting press. Among other things, Brush and Freedman collaborated on the contraction of the National League from 12 clubs to eight, the contentious baseball trust scheme, the gutting of the American League franchise in Baltimore, and efforts to keep the AL out of New York.[121] By 1902, however, baseball club ownership had lost its charm for Freedman, now preoccupied with the myriad tasks attending completion of the NYC subway project. As soon as Brush could raise the necessary purchase price, an estimated $200,000, Freedman would transfer his majority interest in the Giants to him. Most of the capital required was obtained by Brush through sale of the Reds to a consortium of Cincinnati politicos. Faithful sidekick Ashley Lloyd would supply the remainder, becoming a junior partner of Brush in New York, just as he had been in Cincinnati. On September 30, 1902, Brush achieved a longstanding baseball goal. He assumed the position of majority owner and president of the New York Giants.[122]

Brush and incumbent Giant manager John McGraw quickly set about reversing the club's recently dismal fortunes. The two men, both products of impoverished childhoods in upstate New York and intensively competitive, meshed perfectly. Brush left roster decisions and diamond strategy entirely to his manager and reaped almost immediate dividends. The Giants captured the NL pennant in 1904. But much of the luster of that accomplishment was lost when the club declined to meet the American League winners in a postseason championship match. The following year, the Giants repeated as NL pennant winners and then captured the 1905 World Series crown, defeating the Philadelphia A's in a celebrated all-shutout Series played under rules devised by Brush that remain largely in effect to this day.

Although his baseball fortunes were ascendant, Brush's health was precarious. Since

1890, he had exhibited symptoms of locomotor ataxia, a painful wasting disorder almost invariably a manifestation of syphilis.[123] During the previous decade, he had frequently been ill, often critically so, and was now largely confined to a wheelchair.[124] In a bow to his lack of mobility, Brush took to observing home games seated in his massive Deauville limousine, usually parked along the right field foul line. Elsie Brush was often at John T.'s side, while daughter Natalie was permitted to sit in a field box but sheltered from Giant players. The chivalrous Christy Mathewson was the only Giant whom Brush would permit to be introduced to the young and impressionable Natalie, much to her disappointment.

One final baseball challenge awaited John T. Brush. In April 1911, an early morning fire almost totally destroyed Polo Grounds III (née Brotherhood Park), the wooden ballpark that had served as the Giants' home base for the past 20 seasons. Brush wanted to rebuild but, faced with his own fast-approaching mortality, had to weigh the high cost of stadium reconstruction against the future financial needs of his family. Thus, he would not go forward with rebuilding plans unless Elsie approved. Happily for New York baseball, she did. And within less than two months, the Giants were playing home games in a new concrete-and-steel ballpark, the iconic bathtub-shaped Polo Grounds IV. At season's end, the NL pennant-winning Giants opened the World Series at their new ballpark, losing to the Philadelphia Athletics in six games.

A National League pennant in 1912 was John T. Brush's last hurrah. Following another World Series failure, this time defeat in a heartbreaking eight games (the series had one tie game) to the Boston Red Sox, a rapidly failing Brush convened a meeting of the board of the National Exhibition Company, the Giants corporate alter ego. There, son-in-law Harry Hempstead, long a board member, was designated board president-in-waiting and Brush successor. John T. then embarked upon a health-restorative railway trip to the West Coast. But he never made it, dying outside Seeburger, Missouri, on November 25, 1912. John T. Brush was 67. Days later, dignitaries from throughout the baseball world attended Brush funeral services at St. Paul's Episcopal Church in Indianapolis. Grief-stricken pallbearer John McGraw spoke for the assemblage when he remarked, "A gamer, braver man never lived."[125] Brush was then interred in the family plot at Crown Hill Cemetery.

To perpetuate his memory, the Polo Grounds was retitled Brush Stadium, but the name never took public hold. In 1946, John T. Brush was among those named to the Honor Rolls of Baseball, a second-tier Cooperstown accolade that immediately faded into oblivion.[126] Now, a century after his death, Brush is all but forgotten by baseball, an undeserved fate for a man who spent the better part of his working life in service to the national pastime.

Harry Hempstead

Getting his affairs in order, an ailing John T. Brush chose to entrust the care of his family and his ball club to son-in-law Harry Hempstead and longtime friend and baseball junior partner Ashley Lloyd, naming them executors of his estate. It would prove a sound decision. Men of principle and sober judgment, the two would view their paramount responsibility as safeguarding the financial security of the Brush heirs: widow Elsie Brush, her teenage daughter Natalie, and Eleanor Brush Hempstead, John T.'s daughter by his first marriage (and Harry's wife). Following Brush's death, executive command of the Giants was assumed by new club president Hempstead, who would follow Brush's example in handling club affairs, leaving roster and game strategy decisions to John McGraw, while overseeing fiscal operations of the franchise himself. But unlike John T. Brush, Hempstead had no burning desire to stay connected to the game. And threats to the Giants' bottom line presented by the upheavals attending the 1914–1915 skirmish with the upstart Federal League (FL), and thereafter by World War I-related curtailment of the 1918 playing season, disturbed Hempstead, undermining his confidence in the suitability of baseball as a long-term family investment. Thus, when the opportunity presented itself in early 1919, Hempstead largely divested the Brush women of Giant ownership, forfeiting in the process the financial windfall that would accompany the game's oncoming explosion in popularity.

Although no stranger to the game—he had been a decent player himself in his youth[127]—Hempstead's expertise lay in retail business, not baseball. Born Harry Newton Hempstead in Philadelphia on June 25, 1868, he was the youngest of six children of Orlando Gordon Hempstead and his wife, Eliza (née Tyler).[128] O. G. Hempstead, originally from Connecticut, made a handsome living as head of a customs brokerage firm and his offspring were raised in comfortable circumstance. Following graduation from a Philadelphia prep school, Harry matriculated to Lafayette College, a top-flight liberal arts-engineering institution located in Easton, Pennsylvania. There, he leavened a rigorous course of study with extracurricular activities, including intramural baseball. But for the most part, Harry focused on academics, first as an engineering major, thereafter concentrating on chemistry. He graduated with a bachelor of science degree in 1891, but not before reputedly blowing a hole in a chemistry lab wall by misadventure with a volatile formula.[129]

Although educated to be a chemist, Hempstead began his working life in the freight transportation business, serving as vice president of the Morris European and American Express Company in New York City. During that time, he met Eleanor Gordon Brush, daughter of Indianapolis department store magnate John T. Brush by his late first wife, Margaret. Courtship ensued, and on October 10, 1894, Harry and Eleanor were married. The subsequent birth of sons Gordon Brush Hempstead (1899) and John Brush Hempstead (1904) would make their family complete.

John T. Brush's son-in-law, Harry Hempstead, took over the Giants after Brush's death.

In 1898, the Hempsteads relocated to Meadville, Pennsylvania, where Harry became president of the Garfield Chewing Gum Company. Four years later, his father-in-law ful-filled a long-held ambition, acquiring majority ownership of the New York Giants. And the Brush acquisition was not without consequence for the Hempsteads. Wishing to con-centrate his attentions on operation of his new baseball franchise, Brush prevailed upon Harry to move his family to Indianapolis and assume oversight of the Brush clothing business, including the flagship When Store. With Hempstead serving as When Store manager and doubling as When Clothing Corporation treasurer, Brush was free to plot the course needed to return the long downtrodden Giants to pennant contention.

In November 1902, Hempstead took a position on the board of the National Exhi-bition Company, the Giants' corporate shell.[130] He was reappointed to the board five years later.[131] But no actual power rested in that body, as Brush ran the business side of the franchise unilaterally, while manager McGraw took care of matters on the playing field. The arrangement was a success both on the diamond (where NL pennants were won in 1904 and 1905, with a World Series victory in the latter season) and at the gate, where the Giants annually led the game in attendance. Indeed, a major league-record 910,000 fans passed through Polo Grounds turnstiles in 1908, when the pennant was lost to the Chicago Cubs in the replay of a tie game necessitated by the infamous "Merkle boner" late in the season. The Giants captured NL pennants in 1911 and 1912, as well. But with the health of club boss Brush now in rapid decline, regime change was in the offing.

At a hastily convened meeting of the NEC board in early November 1912, Harry Hempstead was designated club president-in-waiting. Later that month, John T. Brush died. Uncertainty followed in the wake of Brush's passing, with rumors rampant that the Giants would be sold by the Brush heirs.[132] Hempstead moved quickly to meet the situ-ation. Days after the Brush funeral, he released a public statement declaring that the family would retain its interest in the New York franchise and that on-field operations would remain in the hands of manager McGraw.[133] Shortly thereafter, Hempstead jour-neyed to New York and was formally installed as president of the Giants.

Although well known in Indianapolis business circles, the 44-year-old Hemp-stead was a mystery to baseball fans. The *Cincinnati Enquirer* informed readers that the incoming Giant boss was "a young man of engaging personality and quiet business tem-perament … [who has been] a careful and quiet student of the game for many years."[134] His stewardship of the franchise would be aided by the counsel of Ashley Lloyd, who retained his minority ownership interest in the Giants.[135] The majority owners of the New York Giants, however, were the Brush family women, each of whom was apportioned a one-third share of John T. Brush's stock in the club under the terms of his will. As Natalie (then age 16) was still a minor, this put Mrs. Brush in effective control of the franchise. Fortunately, Elsie Brush shared her late husband's esteem of Harry Hempstead and was content to leave disposition of club affairs to his judgment.[136]

Continuing the recent thaw in one-time frosty relations between the Giants and their American League rival, Hempstead made the Polo Grounds available to the ballpark-dispossessed Highlanders for the 1913 season and beyond, adding a $50,000 annual rental fee to the Giants' balance sheet.[137] Otherwise, Hempstead resolved to maintain the status quo, an intention reflected in the prompt signing of McGraw to a new $30,000 per year contract. The Giant skipper responded by bringing home a third consecutive National League pennant. But for a third straight time, the New Yorkers fell in the World Series, losing the 1913 fall classic to the Philadelphia A's in five games. Soon thereafter, McGraw began to chafe under the Hempstead administration, particularly resenting his diminished influence on franchise direction. During the previous decade, he and John T. Brush had worked in tandem on all aspects of club operation. New club president Hempstead, however, kept McGraw at arm's length, ceding complete authority on player contracts and game strategy to the fiery manager, but not seeking McGraw's input on business and other matters related to franchise welfare—a blow to long-held McGraw aspirations to ascend to a front-office post. On matters pertaining to franchise operation, Hempstead relied upon the advice of Ashley Lloyd and club secretary John B. Foster.[138]

Although customarily a listener rather than a talker when in the company of other baseball leaders, Hempstead was quick to sound the alarm about the danger posed to the 1914 season by the Federal League, a one-year minor league circuit now asserting major league status. To reduce player receptivity to FL inducements, Hempstead persuaded fellow NL club presidents to concede certain contract-related demands being made by the players, a strategy subsequently rewarded by the loyalty of Christy Mathewson and other New York stalwarts when the Federals came calling. The following January, the steely businessman beneath the genial Hempstead exterior was put on rare public display. With the financially strapped International League franchise in Jersey City likely to be overwhelmed by the relocation of the Federal League champion Indianapolis club to Newark, baseball powers proposed to save the Jersey City Skeeters by moving the franchise to the Bronx. Such a placement, however, required the permission of the New York Giants, which held territorial rights to the venue. But Harry Hempstead would not grant it. In his view, the stationing of another professional baseball club in New York might impinge upon the financial interests of the Brush family women. Notwithstanding considerable pressure from American League president Ban Johnson, International League president Ed Barrow, and *The Sporting News,* Hempstead would not yield. Hence, the Jersey City franchise remained in New Jersey. Months later, the Federal League received similar treatment from the Giant boss. The plan to relocate a Federal League club to Manhattan was promptly thwarted by Hempstead, quietly dispatching his agents to scoop up the East Side building lots that had been designated as the site for the Federal League club's ballpark.[139]

The Federal League expired following the 1915 season, but not before exacting, in the opinion of Harry Hempstead, a fearsome toll on the game's well-being, particularly its minor leagues. Citing calculations by NL officials, Hempstead observed that the minors had contracted from 49 leagues in 1913 to 26 presently, while more than 5,000 former players had lost their place in the professional ranks, all of which Hempstead attributed to the havoc caused by the conflict with the Federals. "The man who thinks wars are good for base ball [*sic*] has never had anything to do with a club in time of war," he declared.[140] Still, the "likeable and affable" Hempstead was "at the center of one group of good souls" who advocated reconciliation with Federal League backers during an interleague peace conference.[141] One such FL backer was Harry F. Sinclair, a swashbuckling oil tycoon who had owned the Newark Peppers and wanted to stay in the game. In the winter of 1915–1916, Sinclair set his sights on acquisition of the New York Giants and rumor of a sale soon abounded. When queried on the subject, Hempstead—ever the businessman—revealed that "while he had received no definite offer for the club, he would sell [the Giants] if the offer was alluring [and] that he was open to proposals."[142] But the prospective sale foundered when Sinclair declined to meet the Hempstead asking price of $2 million, an amount that Sinclair deemed "beyond all reason."[143] That outcome was agreeable to many Gotham baseball followers, including influential *New York Sun* sportswriter Joe Vila, who wrote that "if Hempstead remains in control there will be no regret as he is a clean sportsman and thorough gentleman."[144] Thereafter, Hempstead penned a first-person editorial on the rosy prospects presented by the 1916 season, provided there was improved on-field behavior by players and the game was conducted "according to the theories and ideas of the managers."[145]

Unlike his late father-in-law, Hempstead was not fixated on baseball. During his tenure as Giant president, he continued oversight of Brush family business operations in Indianapolis, served as a trustee of his alma mater, Lafayette College,[146] and enjoyed winter sporting activities in Lake Placid. The 1917 season brought a second National League pennant to the Hempstead headquarters, but things had not gone smoothly. Hempstead's relations with manager McGraw remained distant, and the Giants' roster now contained types not to the club president's liking, particularly defiant second baseman Buck Herzog whom Hempstead suspended late in the season for refusing to accompany the team on a road trip to Boston. And the season finale again proved a disappointment, the Giants losing the 1917 World Series in six games to the Chicago White Sox. Of far more long-term concern to Hempstead was the effect American entry into World War I might have on major league baseball. Although the 1917 season was not seriously affected by the war effort, 1918 would prove a different story. Player ranks were thinned by the call to military service and defense-plant work, the regular season was abbreviated, and the fall classic hurriedly completed by September 11. All the while, attendance at Giants games plummeted. The gate for 1918 home games was only 256,618, barely half that of the previous season and not one-third the Polo Grounds' attendance of a decade earlier. The major leagues as a whole had fared no better, each circuit losing more than one million patrons from the preceding season. Drastic measures were needed to restore the game to good health. To that end, Hempstead and Boston Red Sox owner Harry Frazee proposed the installation of former U.S. president William Howard Taft as an all-powerful one-man executive-in-charge of major league baseball.[147] But while the Taft proposition and competing remedies were mulled on the sports pages, major changes in the operation of the New York Giant franchise were in motion behind the scenes.

Major league baseball was on the verge of a golden era. The game would enjoy immense popularity in the 1920s, with ballpark attendance skyrocketing and club investors reaping the rewards. But Harry Hempstead did not see this. In January 1919, Hempstead saw only hard times ahead, with baseball being no place for the Brush women and their money. His inclination to sell the ball club, however, produced a split in family ranks. Elsie Brush trusted Hempstead's judgment and would do as he advised, while Natalie, although now a young adult, would do what her mother told her. But Eleanor Hempstead was another matter. A private woman but fiercely protective of her father's legacy (and with a good head for both business and baseball), Eleanor refused to part with her share of the Giants' stock.[148] Still, the holdings of Elsie and Natalie Brush were sufficient to convey majority control of the franchise to potential buyers. On January 14, 1919, Hempstead announced "with great regret" the sale of the New York Giants. The new club owners were a syndicate headed by Manhattan stock speculator Charles A. Stoneham. Giant manager McGraw and New York City magistrate Francis X. McQuade were small-stake syndicate members and invested as club officers, McGraw becoming vice president and McQuade treasurer, with Stoneham assuming the club presidency. The sale price was generally reported as $1 million.[149]

Relieved of the responsibility of running the Giants, Harry Hempstead carried on as president of the Brush family clothing business until he retired from the post in 1922. A New York resident for most of the past decade, Hempstead spent his remaining years in affluent leisure, alternating his time between a Park Avenue apartment in Manhattan and a Westchester County mansion, while not traveling abroad. He continued to be active in the affairs of Lafayette College, was elected NYC Alumni Association president in 1920, and he served on the college board of trustees until 1936. During these years, Hempstead remained mostly out of public view, except for a brief flirtation with the Giants. During one of the frequent Stoneham-McGraw-McQuade spats, it was reported that Stoneham was entertaining an offer for his Giant stock tendered by Hempstead emissaries.[150] Nothing came of it, and Stoneham would remain in control of the club until his death in January 1936.

In March 1938, Harry Hempstead suffered a stroke at his Park Avenue apartment. He lingered for ten days thereafter, dying on March 26 at age 69. Following funeral services, he was buried in the Brush family plot at Crown Hill Cemetery in Indianapolis.[151] An able but cautious man, Hempstead served the interests of family and baseball diligently but was risk averse and lacked the vision required to usher his club into baseball's approaching golden age. Compared to others who had held the franchise reins, Harry Hempstead left no more than a modest imprint on New York Giant history.

Charles A. Stoneham

No essay-length profile can fully encompass a life as eventful as that of Charles A. Stoneham's. Although remembered today only as majority owner of the New York Giants during the Roaring Twenties, Stoneham's contemporaries were just as likely to associate his name with the New York Curb Exchange, horse racing, legal troubles, the Manhattan night club scene, Tammany Hall, gambling casinos, and highly publicized scandals in both his business and private lives. Stoneham did little to court attention, but his activities proved irresistible to the press, as Stoneham seemed to personify a popular Prohibition Era stereotype: cutthroat business operative by day, boozy bon vivant by night. As Giant chief executive, Stoneham avoided the clubhouse and tried to stay out of the limelight, leaving, as did his predecessors, field control of the club to manager-vice-president John McGraw, and thereafter to manager-first baseman Bill Terry. Meanwhile, Stoneham busied himself with other concerns. The formula proved a successful one. During the 17-season Stoneham regime, the Giants won five NL pennants and were World Series champs three times.

Charles Abraham Stoneham was born in Jersey City on July 5, 1876, the older of two sons born into a working-class Irish Catholic family.[152] His father, Bartholomew F. Stoneham, a Civil War veteran born in New York City, worked as a bookkeeper while his Irish immigrant wife, the former Mary Holwell, tended to Charles and younger brother Horace (born 1879).[153] The death of their father in 1894 roughly coincided with the entry of the Stoneham brothers into the workforce. Charles began as a board boy with a mining stock brokerage firm. Adept with numbers and innately shrewd, he quickly advanced to the position of stock salesman, a profession at which he excelled. On the domestic front, Charles was first married around 1896. Although the surviving evidence is fragmentary, it appears that his wife, Alice Rafter Stoneham, died five days after giving birth to daughter

Mary in January 1898.[154] The 1900 U.S. census lists Charles as a widower, living with his toddler daughter Mary and other relations at his mother's home in Jersey City. Shortly thereafter, he married Johanna (Hannah) McGoldrick of New York City, who quickly bore him two sons: Charles A., Jr. (born 1901) and Horace (1903).

By 1903, Stoneham's success as a stock salesman provided him the financial wherewithal to form his own mining stock brokerage, a partnership named O. F. Jonasson & Company, complete with an office on Broadway in Manhattan. Younger brother Horace joined him as the firm's cashier. Business fortune smiled on Charles A. Stoneham and life was good until spring 1905, when family tragedy was followed by the first public scandal in Stoneham's life. On April 25, 1905, four-year-old Charles Jr. drowned while playing in a local extension of the Morris Canal. Shortly after the child was buried, Stoneham family mourning was interrupted by the suicide of wealthy widow Olivia Gray at the upscale Imperial Hotel in Manhattan. Found in the dead woman's room were letters addressed to Stoneham bearing the salutation "Dear Sweetheart" and reproaching Stoneham for his ill treatment of her, the particulars of which were fully republished in the press.[155] Stoneham denied consorting with Mrs. Gray, protesting, "I cannot understand how my name came to be used by the woman, and all I can suppose is that someone used my name."[156] But Stoneham denials were not taken seriously, particularly after business partner C. C. Bamberger informed the press that the deceased was a client of the Jonasson firm and had recently been in Stoneham's company at an uptown hotel.[157] Three years later, another unsavory precedent was set in the life of Charles A. Stoneham. He was sued by an investor named Webster who alleged that he had been defrauded by Stoneham's brokerage firm.[158]

Around 1909, stock quotations provided by Charles A. Stoneham & Company began appearing in newspapers. Stoneham was now an operative in the New York Curb Exchange, a frenetic, unregulated open-air marketplace for the purchase and sale of stocks that did not qualify for registration on respectable exchanges. Many curb exchange brokerages were actually bucket shops, establishments wherein the customer was sold what purported to be a derivative interest in a stock or commodity future, but no transfer or delivery actually accompanied the transaction. Rather, the order went in the bucket, with the customer, in effect, betting against the broker on the stock's rise or fall.[159] The potential for fraud here was enormous and many jurisdictions, including New York, made operation of a bucket shop (as opposed to maintenance of a facially licit, if risky, curb exchange brokerage) a criminal offense. Still, bucket shops flourished. For a compulsive gambler like Stoneham—he was a regular at race tracks,

Charles A. Stoneham had dealings in a number of New York activities, including ownership of the Giants.

casinos, and other gambling haunts—stock speculation/bucketing converted his pleasure in endeavors of chance into his livelihood, and he prospered. In time, Charles A. Stoneham & Company would have operations in Boston, Providence, Chicago, Detroit, and elsewhere, in addition to its home base in Manhattan. By the advent of World War I, Stoneham was rich, so well-heeled that he could afford to lose $70,000 to Arnold Rothstein's Partridge Club playing roulette one evening—over the telephone![160] But gambling was hardly Stoneham's only vice. He was also a heavy drinker with a fondness for the opposite sex. With wife Hannah safely stashed in their Jersey City home, good-time Charlie nightly prowled the Manhattan demimonde, usually with drink in hand and often with a chorus girl mistress on his arm.

In January 1919, rumor of a sale of the New York Giants was rife, with NYC candy manufacturer George Loft and Broadway showman George M. Cohan considered the most likely franchise purchasers. Surprise therefore greeted club president Harry Hempstead's announcement that a majority interest in the Giants had been sold to a syndicate headed by Charles A. Stoneham, a figure unknown to most New York baseball fans. The faithful were comforted, however, by the fact that the revered Giant manager John McGraw was part of the new club ownership group.[161] New York City magistrate Francis X. McQuade, a well-known Tammany regular, was another minority stockholder. By most accounts, the Giant purchase price was $1 million.[162] In introducing himself to local baseball followers, Stoneham asserted a lifelong allegiance to the Giants; he had been a rooter for the club since the 1890s' heyday of star outfielder (and fellow New Jersey Irishman) Mike Tiernan.[163] Stoneham then created a stir—while causing some discomfort in the club-owner fraternity that he had just joined—by declaring that Giant players would all receive salary increases for the 1920 season.[164]

Like John T. Brush before him, Stoneham had total faith in John McGraw, leaving roster decisions and game strategy entirely to the Little Napoleon. Stoneham was also liberal with his checkbook, bankrolling the improvements sought by McGraw. Otherwise, Stoneham withdrew, avoiding locker room contact with Giant personnel and watching game action from a window in his distant Polo Grounds office. The formula produced prompt and positive results. Paced by the play of future Hall of Famers Frankie Frisch, George "Highpockets" Kelly, Dave Bancroft, and Ross Youngs, the Giants captured four consecutive National League pennants (1921–1924), and bested the Babe Ruth–like New York Yankees in two of three intercity World Series. All the while, club coffers swelled with revenues generated by NL record-breaking fan attendance, with the Giants drawing between 820,000 and 980,000 patrons every season through 1924.[165] Other Stoneham sporting ventures, including his racing stable and a Havana racetrack (the Cuba-American Jockey Club that he had purchased with McGraw in October 1919), were also thriving. But trouble was brewing on the stockbrokerage front.

In late 1921, Stoneham dissolved his own stockbrokerage firm, recommending that clients transfer their investments to the firm of Hughes, Dier, & Company. Many did, and were wiped out when the firm, now called E. D. Dier & Company, collapsed in January 1922. Investor losses were estimated at $4 million.[166] Subsequent bankruptcy court proceedings uncovered evidence that Stoneham had been a silent principal in the Dier firm, and a slew of civil lawsuits were subsequently instituted by Dier investors seeking to have Stoneham held liable for their losses.[167] A far graver problem soon confronted Stoneham: the implosion of E. M. Fuller & Company, a notorious Manhattan bucket shop. Summoned to testify before bankruptcy commissioners, Stoneham was unable to provide a plausible explanation for the $147,000 that he had passed to Manhattan sheriff (and Tammany powerbroker) Thomas F. Foley through Fuller accounts. The Giant owner's claim that the money was a personal loan to Foley subsequently formed the gravamen of a perjury indictment obtained by federal prosecutors.[168]

Stoneham's denial of the charge and his resolution to go to trial placed baseball leaders in an awkward position. Although fellow owners were clamoring for Stoneham's ouster as the Giants' president, NL president John Heydler felt powerless to act. Notwithstanding the discomfort caused the league by widespread fan attention to the charges, Heydler declared, "I have neither the inclination nor the right to discuss Mr. Stoneham's affairs outside of baseball." He continued, "As [NL] President, I have only to do with Mr. Stoneham as a club owner and league member," adding, on that account, that he had found Stoneham to be "a good sportsman, fair and straight in all his league dealings … and reasonable in his official dealings with my office."[169] The silence of Commissioner Landis bespoke a similar disinclination to pursue action against Stoneham, at least for the time being.[170]

The troubles facing Stoneham expanded exponentially when a new federal indictment was unsealed in January 1924. Stoneham's involvement in the Fuller operation now yielded fraud, theft, and other charges exposing him (and brother Horace A. Stoneham) to lengthy prison terms upon conviction. Worse yet for baseball, Stoneham's co-defendants included brokerage business associates also connected to the New York Giants: Ross F. Robertson, a director on the Giants' corporate board,[171] and Stoneham attorney Leo J. Bondy, legal counsel for the Giants. After a trial punctuated by bitter wrangling between the trial judge and prosecutors and postverdict allegations of jury coercion, Stoneham and the other accused were acquitted.[172] Stoneham's legal problems, however, were far from over. Civil judgments obtained against him by defrauded investors plagued him, while ceaseless attorney's fees taxed his bank account.[173] Although the Giants continued to draw well,[174] Stoneham needed money and sought to enhance the revenue derived from his leasehold on the Polo Grounds by renting the ballpark to boxing promoter Tex Rickard, a summer opera company, professional soccer teams, and college football, with mixed financial returns.[175] Whatever his money troubles, Stoneham gave no thought to selling the Giants, intended as a legacy for son Horace, then getting his feet wet in club management. But reduction of the owner's financial resources meant that manager McGraw would no longer have unfettered access to the Stoneham checkbook.

No sooner had Stoneham put his brokerage-related headaches behind him than he was confronted with an ugly internal fracas in the Giants' front office. The Stoneham-McGraw-McQuade triumvirate had long been a troubled one, and replacement of McQuade as club treasurer during a May 1928 meeting of the National Exhibition Company board precipitated a very public falling-out. In time, McQuade filed suit to regain his corporate office, alleging, among other things, that Stoneham had used NEC funds to finance personal ventures. Stoneham admitted making use of the money but maintained that he had long ago repaid the corporate treasury, with interest. Going on the attack, Stoneham accused McQuade of padding the Polo Grounds free-pass list with a multitude of McQuade cronies and of threatening Stoneham with physical harm when Stoneham complained. The McQuade suit dragged on for several years before a $42,827 judgment obtained at trial by plaintiff McQuade was vacated on appeal and his lawsuit dismissed.[176]

While the McQuade-Stoneham lawsuit was playing out, the 30-year tenure of manager John McGraw came to an end. Frustrated by his recent inability to win a pennant and probably suffering the early effects of the prostate cancer that, with uremia, would ultimately claim his life, McGraw resigned midway through the 1932 season. His successor, star first baseman Bill Terry, quickly succeeded where McGraw had not, leading the Giants to the 1933 NL crown. The Giants then assumed the mantle of baseball champions for the first time in more than a decade, defeating the Washington Senators in a five-game World Series.

The reign of club owner Charles A. Stoneham was also approaching its end, hastened by the onset of Bright's disease (kidney failure). As Stoneham's health continued to decline, son Horace took on a more visible role in the Giants' front office. In late December 1935, Charles journeyed to Hot Springs, Arkansas, but its medicinal waters did not restore his health. Lapsing into a three-day coma, Stoneham died there on January 6, 1936. He was 59. The Stoneham funeral was a curious affair. Unlike the requiem of most club owners, the Stoneham funeral mass at All Saints Church in Jersey City and subsequent interment at nearby Holy Name Cemetery was a private affair, closed to all but wife Hannah, son Horace, a few other family members, and a handful of New York Giant officials. Three days later, the Stoneham will was filed for probate by executor Leo Bondy. The estate would be divided equally among Hannah and the two Stoneham children, Mary and Horace.[177]

Some three months later, the shroud placed over the Stoneham funeral became understandable: Charles A. Stoneham had had another "wife" and family ensconced in Westchester County. In April 1936, a former showgirl named Margaret Leonard filed a court petition as Mrs. Charles Stoneham seeking support and maintenance for herself and children Russell Stoneham, age 16, and Jane Stoneham, age 12. While the petition was pending, Margaret Stoneham was permitted to mortgage the Greenburgh, New York, residence where she, Charles, and the children had resided.[178] Whether the long-suffering Hannah Stoneham or her son Horace were previously aware of Charles' second family is unknown, but neither ever publicly acknowledged it. The existence of the second family, however, was no mystery to will executor Bondy and Charles' brother Horace. Both men served as trustees of a fund that Charles had set up for the benefit of children Russell and Jane.[179]

In terms of moral character, Charles A. Stoneham—serial philanderer, shady stock speculator, ethically-challenged businessman, and quasi-bigamist—was easily the worst person ever associated with Giant ownership. But in purely baseball terms—with five NL pennants and three World Series titles in a 17-season span—the Stoneham years were arguably the best in Giant history.

Horace Stoneham

In January 1936, boyish Horace Stoneham inherited stewardship of the New York Giants from his late father. Over the ensuing two decades, Horace would devote himself single-mindedly to the club's success. Then, confronted with poor financial prospects, a declining fan base, and a decaying ballpark, he decided upon a course once unimaginable—relocation of New York's most venerable sports club to the West Coast. Gotham sportswriters and legions of Giant fans never forgave him and thereafter took delight in Stoneham's many travails as owner of the San Francisco Giants. Guided by a traditionalist unable or unwilling to adapt to changing times, the club was in serious financial trouble by the time that Stoneham took his leave of the game in January 1976. Although many in baseball liked the genial Horace Stoneham, few expressed regret at his departure.

Born in Jersey City on April 27, 1903, Horace Charles Stoneham was the younger son of enterprising stock speculator Charles A. Stoneham and his second wife, the former Johanna (Hannah) McGoldrick. Horace never knew older brother Charles A., Jr., who died as a four-year-old in a drowning accident, but had the childhood company of his half-sister Mary and the domestic help engaged by the Stonehams.[180] Following attendance at local parochial schools, Horace was enrolled at Loyola Academy in Manhattan, where he compensated for underperformance in the classroom by excelling on the school's ice hockey and baseball teams. After further academic grooming in prep schools—and eventually graduating from the Pawling School in upstate New York—Horace matriculated to Fordham University in the Bronx. He lasted four days.[181] His father then dispatched Horace to California for a sobering encounter with a pick and a shovel in the copper mines. The experience, surprisingly, agreed with Stoneham, fostering the ambition to enter engineering school. Sadly, Horace later recalled, "I wasn't smart enough," and the following year he headed to the Giants' spring training camp in Florida, where a long apprenticeship in the club front office commenced.[182] While learning the ropes, Horace met and began courting a young dancer named Valleda Pyke. The couple was married in 1924, and soon had two children, Mary Valleda (born in 1925) and Charles Horace, called "Pete" (1927).

Charles Stoneham always maintained that he had purchased the Giants in order to pass the club on to his son and steadfastly resisted offers for the Giants from prospective buyers. But before Horace inherited the club, he would be thoroughly schooled in all aspects of franchise operations. He worked in the ticket office, assisted the grounds crew, learned the intricacies of handling travel accommodations, and was given responsibility for scheduling non-baseball events at the Polo Grounds. When Charles' health began to fail in the mid–1930s, Horace steadily assumed more front-office responsibilities. Thus, when Charles died in early January 1936, Horace's succession as franchise boss was a smooth one, his youth notwithstanding. When he formally took office as New York Giants president, the 32-year-old was reported to be the youngest chief executive in major league baseball history.[183] The ball club whose fortunes the youthful Stoneham would now oversee was a veteran one, studded with future Hall of Famers like Bill Terry, Carl Hubbell, Mel Ott, and Travis Jackson. Emulating his father's relationship with John

Horace Stoneham took over the Giants from Charles and continued to own the team for many years after it moved to San Francisco.

McGraw, Horace gave Manager Terry a wide berth, avoiding the club locker room and watching game action from the same distant clubhouse office window that Charles Stoneham had used. The immediate results were gratifying—at least until World Series time. The Giants captured the NL pennant in both 1936 and 1937, only to lose the fall classic each year to the Yankees.

Although Terry had hung up his first baseman's glove after the 1936 season, he continued as manager through the 1941 season. When Ott succeeded him, Stoneham assumed a higher profile, becoming, in effect, general manager as well as club president. During the 1940s, the Giants were also-rans in National League standings as the St. Louis Cardinals and local rival Brooklyn Dodgers vied for the league pennant most seasons. Like many other franchises, however, the Giants benefited from the post–World War II surge in fan attendance. From 1946 through 1951, more than one million patrons passed through the Polo Grounds turnstiles each season. The revenues generated by a robust gate were important to Stoneham for, unlike a coming generation of club owners, he was not some multimillionaire businessman dabbling in baseball. The New York Giants represented Horace Stoneham's almost exclusive source of income.

A frequent criticism of the Stoneham regime was that it was suffused with nepotism, a tradition started by Horace's father. Although he left the baseball side of the Giants' operation entirely to vice president-manager John McGraw and his managerial successor Bill Terry, Charles Stoneham found club employment for family members. He hired footloose son Horace, first assigning him to menial tasks and then to the Giants' front office. Charles also bestowed incomes via the franchise corporate board upon his brother Horace A. Stoneham and reputed brother-in-law Ross F. Robertson. As club president, Horace followed this example. His cousin, another Charles A. Stoneham, was long a Giant scout and later farm system director. Nephew Charles Stoneham "Chub" Feeney was recruited to the Giants' front office right after his law school graduation, while son Pete Stoneham was made a junior club executive while still in his 20s, just as Horace had been. Worse yet to some observers, Horace often formed emotional attachments to veteran Giant players, treating them like family members as well, and, as a result, was reluctant to part with their services—even when their usefulness to the club had waned.[184] In midseason 1948, however, the Stoneham sentimentality was little in evidence. With the G-Men stuck midpack in NL standings (37–38), Stoneham abruptly fired 23-year club member Mel Ott as manager, replacing him with the stormy Leo Durocher, a move that so upset Horace's daughter Mary Valleda that she "didn't speak to [Stoneham] for a month."[185] But the team rallied under Durocher's direction, and the Giants would be a pennant contender for most of Lippy Leo's eight-season managerial tenure.

Belying his reputation as a hidebound traditionalist, Stoneham also pursued innovation, at least for a time. Beginning in the late 1930s, he invested heavily in developing a minor league farm system for the franchise. With Cleveland boss Bill Veeck, Stoneham was in the vanguard of the movement of spring training to Arizona, relocating the Giants' long-time Florida training camp to Scottsdale in 1947. That same year, Stoneham was one of the first baseball club owners to embrace television, signing a contract for the telecast of Giant home games with the local NBC station (then called WRCA-TV). Far more important, Stoneham quickly embraced integration once Brooklyn and Jackie Robinson had breached the color line. By 1949, the Giants' lineup featured former Negro League standouts Monte Irvin and Hank Thompson, with the incomparable Willie Mays soon to join them.[186] Stoneham was also quick to explore the foreign player market, and soon modest talents like Ray Noble (Cuba), Ruben Gomez (Puerto Rico), Ramon Monzant (Venezuela), Ozzie Virgil (Dominican Republic), Valmy Thomas (Virgin Islands), and Andre Rodgers (Bahamas) were accorded spots on the roster, with Latin greats like Orlando Cepeda and Juan Marichal, plus the Alou brothers and Jose Pagan, to follow after the club arrived in San Francisco. But the venture that cemented Horace Stoneham's place in baseball annals was the relocation of the storied New York franchise.

Although the Giants had experienced some recent success—winning NL pennants in 1951 and 1954, and the World Series in the latter year—the club was now playing a decided third fiddle to the Yankees and Dodgers with New York-area baseball fans. In 1956, no more than 629,179 fans attended Giant games at the Polo Grounds, little more than half the number of just two seasons earlier and only a fraction of the Yankees' (1,491,138) and Dodgers' (1,213,562) gate. The Giants' ballpark was falling into disrepair and the north Manhattan neighborhood where the Polo Grounds sat had changed for the worse, much to the discomfort of fans coming in from the Westchester and New Jersey suburbs. Meanwhile, after 50 years of stability, major league franchises were on the move—the Boston Braves to Milwaukee in 1953, the St. Louis Browns to Baltimore in 1954, and the Philadelphia A's to Kansas City in 1955. And soon rumors of relocation were attached to the New York Giants.

In years past, Stoneham had publicly denied any intention of moving his franchise.[187] But that changed, particularly after proposals for the construction of a new sports stadium on Manhattan's west side were abandoned by city officials. Horace had now come to the conclusion that New York "could not support three baseball teams."[188] Testifying in July 1957 before a Congressional subcommittee probing the relocation of baseball franchises, Stoneham declared that "if our club doesn't make an immediate move, it is faced with the problem of diminishing income and may lose the opportunity to move later."[189] Stoneham set his immediate sites on Minneapolis, where the Giants maintained an American Association franchise. But soon another prospective transfer location emerged: San Francisco. Aggressively, albeit quietly, promoted by Bay Area officials and with a Giant-friendly fan base derived from a decade of Arizona spring-training baseball, San Francisco was soon designated the new hometown for the New York club.[190] Years later, Stoneham dismissed the widely held notion that he had served as a cat's-paw for Brooklyn boss Walter O'Malley, intent on moving the Dodgers to Los Angeles and needing a relocation partner to saddle with San Francisco, a less-desirable West Coast venue. Said Horace, "If Brooklyn had picked San Francisco first, I would not have gone to Los Angeles. San Francisco was the place I preferred. Believe me when I say, San Francisco first, Los Angeles never."[191]

Abandonment of New York was hard for Horace Stoneham, personally. A fun-loving man and a prodigious drinker like his father (but without Charlie Stoneham's more disreputable vices), Horace had been a regular at Toots Shor's famous Manhattan watering hole, at times drinking until daylight with the owner, comedian Jackie Gleason, New York sportswriters, and other pals. Long separated from his wife and with an often-distant relationship with his two adult children, Stoneham was frequently lonely in San Francisco and at his winter home in Scottsdale. His remedy was to corral friends, club officials, sports scribes, and/or anyone else handy inside a convenient hotel room and drink, talk, or argue the night away. In February 1958, however, the fondness for alcohol that ran deep in the Stoneham men produced dire consequences: 30-year-old Pete Stoneham was arrested on vehicular homicide charges arising from a fatal drunk-driving accident outside Phoenix.[192]

Whatever the Stoneham family hardships accompanying the move to California, the San Francisco Giants were a success in their inaugural season, with the third-place (80–74) club drawing 1,272,625 fans to bandbox Seals Stadium, their temporary home while a new ballpark was under construction. In their second West Coast season, the Giants, with fresh muscle in the form of Orlando Cepeda, Willie McCovey, Jimmy Davenport, Felipe Alou, and Willie Kirkland lending ample support to Mays, closed to within four games of the pennant-winning Dodgers in the NL standings, while home attendance (1,422,130) continued on the upswing, as well. The pitching of 24-game winner Jack Sanford and the addition of Dominican right-hander Juan Marichal, on his way to becoming the finest Giant hurler since Carl Hubbell was in his prime 40 years earlier, pushed the club to the NL top in 1962, providing Horace Stoneham his fifth and final pennant as the franchise's president. Only a heart-breaking 1–0 loss to the Yankees in Game 7 of the World Series marred the Bay Bombers' campaign.

The Giants continued to draw well in the larger confines of Candlestick Park, attracting a then-club record 1,657,912 fans in 1966. But soon troubles overtook the club. The windy, often cold, new ballpark was inhospitable to both players and fans. Willie Mays was beginning to slow down. And starting in 1968, competition in the form of the newly-arrived Oakland A's had arrived in the Bay Area.[193] Athletics owner Charles Finley was the very antithesis of Horace Stoneham: flamboyant, promotion-minded, attention-getting, innovative. His teams dressed in gaudy colored uniforms, including white shoes, and sported mod moustaches. A mechanical rabbit supplied new baseballs to the home plate umpire. A mule named Charley O. grazed before games in the outfield. More important than Finley's gimmicks and promotions, the A's had talent: Reggie Jackson, Catfish Hunter, Sal Bando, Vida Blue, Joe Rudi, and others. Meanwhile, the Giants, with Marichal, McCovey, and flashy Bobby Bonds supplanting the aged Mays, remained competitive for a time, winning a NL Western Division crown in 1971. But after that, it was no contest, either at the gate or on the field between the three-time (1973–1975) World Series champion A's and their also-ran neighbors. By 1975, Giant attendance was down to 522,919 and calls for a change in club ownership were regularly sounded in the baseball press.[194]

Stoneham was far from blameless for this unhappy state of affairs. He had stayed at the helm too long, refusing to adapt to changing times or to relinquish responsibility to subordinates, as other club presidents had long ago done. Although Chub Feeney and other Giant front office executives may have been in nominal charge, Stoneham retained final say on trades, managerial changes, club policy, and other matters of substance. To the end, he held a stodgy disdain of ballpark promotions. For Horace, the game by itself was more than sufficient attraction for baseball fans. And the complexities of modern sports finance were beyond him. The Stoneham family had acquired the Giants late in the Deadball Era, and Horace ran the franchise much as if the calendar had not changed. In sum, he had become an executive dinosaur.

In January 1976, after dalliances with prospective purchasers who intended to relocate the Giants to Denver or Toronto, a financially-pressed Stoneham relinquished control of the franchise to San Francisco real-estate magnate Bob Lurie. The sale price was reportedly $8 million, or about eight times what it had cost his father to acquire the club 57 years earlier. In retirement in Scottsdale, Stoneham became a rather sad figure. He remained dear to his older sister Mary, but she lived in faraway New Jersey. Horace had little contact with his estranged wife or his children, and none at all with the half-siblings that his father's liaison with Margaret Leonard had produced.[195] Stoneham also severed most contact with baseball, occasionally attending Giant spring training games in Arizona, but declining invitations to club functions in San Francisco, including affairs intended to honor him. On Christmas Day 1989, he fell at home and fractured a hip. Old and alone, Horace Charles Stoneham died in a Scottsdale nursing home on January 7, 1990. He was 86. Following funeral services at Our Lady of Perpetual Help Roman Catholic Church in Scottsdale, cremated Stoneham remains were interred at St. Francis Cemetery in Tucson.

During the 40 years that Horace Stoneham served as club president, the Giants won five National League pennants and the 1954 World Series. Although that record was not quite the equal of his father's, Horace was a far better man: honest and fair-minded in his business dealings and, apart from a lifelong drinking problem, without serious vices. He had been devoted to baseball and the Giants. Horace's legacy, however, was marred by the length of his tenure at the top. He stayed at the club helm too long and refused to change as changing times required. And whether for good or ill, Horace Stoneham will forever be remembered as the man who removed the Giants from New York.

James Gordon Bennett, Jr.

Rare is the baseball reference work that contains an entry on James Gordon Bennett, Jr., the socialite-sportsman who published the *New York Herald*. As far as is known, Bennett never played in a baseball game. Spending most of his adult life living in France, he may never have even seen one. Bennett's connection to the game was based entirely on real estate. In the 1880s, he owned a sizable grass field located in an affluent Manhattan neighborhood just north of Central Park, the site upon which the original Polo Grounds would be erected. Although Bennett was probably a complete stranger to the game, many New York baseball fans had doubtless heard of him, as Bennett was one of the late 19th century's most famous New Yorkers—notwithstanding the fact that he was present in the city only occasionally. The prominence of his newspaper and tales of his high profile, often eccentric, lifestyle, made Bennett a household name in much of Gotham.

James Gordon Bennett, Jr., owned the land occupied by the original Polo Grounds.

Born in Manhattan on May 10, 1841, James Gordon Bennett, Jr., was the oldest of three children of James Gordon Bennett, the immigrant son of a well-to-do Scottish family, and his wife, Henrietta (née Crean).[196] Bennett Sr. founded the *New York Herald* in 1835. The following year, he captured public attention and readership for the newspaper through lurid front-page coverage of the murder of a prostitute named Helen Jewett. Over time, the *Herald* became more respectable. By 1845, it was the most popular, and profitable, newspaper published in the United States.[197] From the beginning, the publisher groomed his son to succeed him. Gordon (as he was called to distinguish him from his father) was educated by private tutors, both in New York and Paris. As a young man, he was commissioned in the U.S. Navy and saw Civil War service. Upon discharge, he underwent training at the *Herald*, assuming the post of managing editor in 1866.[198] Gordon then took command of the paper upon his father's death in 1872.

Bennett was a dashing figure, heavily involved in both New York high society and the sporting world. He was also given to outlandish behavior. His engagement to the daughter of a socially prominent physician was abruptly terminated, reportedly after a drunken Bennett urinated into a fireplace during the engagement party. Thereafter, he spent most of his time in Paris and elsewhere abroad, dictating orders to *Herald* editors via trans-Atlantic cablegram. A European base also afforded Bennett the opportunity to exercise his passion for sports, particularly those of the "novel and hazardous" variety.[199] Among the unfamiliar sports that captured Bennett's fancy was a British favorite, polo. During one of his periodic sojourns back in New York, Bennett established the Westchester Polo Club. To provide the new organization a place to play, Bennett had a polo field laid out on vacant grassland that he owned in Manhattan on 110th Street, just north of Central Park. But soon the club began playing matches closer to home on the grounds of Jerome Park Racetrack in the Bronx, leaving the Manhattan polo field little used.

The exact circumstances that brought the Bennett-owned polo field to the attention of baseball entrepreneur John B. Day and his manager, Jim Mutrie, are unknown. But Day and Mutrie were looking to relocate their new professional club, the Metropolitan of New York, from Brooklyn, where teams from New York invariably played, to New York City proper.[200] With Bennett back in Paris, it is doubtful that he took an active part in arranging for his north of Central Park field to be made available for baseball. But in any case, professional baseball made its debut in New York on September 29, 1880, with the Mets defeating the Nationals of Washington on Bennett's polo grounds. Thereafter, Day obtained a leasehold on the property, and set about building permanent grandstands around the playing field, which formally assumed the name *Polo Grounds*. By the end of the 1888 season, after which the ballpark was surrendered to city planners intent on extending the local traffic grid through the outfield, the Polo Grounds had been enlarged into an impressive edifice capable of accommodating some 12,000 fans.[201] All the while, Bennett remained ensconced in his Paris apartments, dispatching daily directives to harried *Herald* editors in New York and otherwise busying himself with romantic affairs, yachting, balloon racing, exotic foreign travel, and the like.

On May 14, 1918, James Gordon Bennett, Jr., died from a recurrence of pneumonia at his villa in Beaulieu-sur-Mer on the French Riviera, aged 77. He had lived an eventful life, the details of which were recounted in a respectful full-page obituary published in the rival *New York Times*. Bennett's lifelong passion for sport was duly noted—but neither the Polo Grounds nor baseball was mentioned.

James J. Coogan

His name forever attached to the palisades that towered over the Polo Grounds, James J. Coogan lingers in public consciousness a century after his death. Baseball has enshrined New York Giant Bobby Thomson's 1951 pennant-winning homer as "The Miracle of Coogan's Bluff," while the oeuvre of Hollywood icon Clint Eastwood includes the popular 1968 detective-western *Coogan's Bluff*. But while cultural artifacts may preserve his name in memory, they shed little light on the life of the actual Coogan. Originally a Bowery furniture dealer and later a gadfly New York City politician, Coogan is sometimes identified as the owner of the Polo Grounds. Or as the landlord of the property on which the ballpark was situated. But Coogan was neither. Rather, his connection to the Polo Grounds stemmed from his service as estate agent for the Gardiner-Lynch family, the wealthy New York clan that

James J. Coogan is the name behind Coogan's Bluff, a term still associated with the Polo Grounds.

Coogan married into. Later installed in high political office as a Tammany Hall factotum and living at ease on his wife's fortune, life turned out well for James J. Coogan.

Although the genealogical evidence is somewhat contradictory, it is likely that James Jay Coogan was born in County Carlow, Ireland, on December 16, 1845.[202] He joined family members who had preceded him to New York City at about age seven.[203] Although he later obtained a legal education, graduating from New York University Law School, young James Coogan was trained to be an upholsterer for the furniture business that his father Patrick (sometimes given as Peter) Coogan had established with other family members. In time, James, along with his brothers Edward and Thomas, assumed control of the operation. By the late 1870s, the Coogan brothers were proprietors of a thriving business, dealing new and used furniture from a large outpost located on the Bowery in lower Manhattan. Coogan Brothers Furniture had several stores in midtown as well.[204]

With his furniture business prospering, Coogan lived comfortably. But his standard of living skyrocketed in 1883 when Coogan married into money, taking as his bride 22-year-old Harriet Gardiner Lynch, youngest daughter of the tea merchant William L. Lynch and heir to a vast Gardiner family inheritance. By her mother, Harriet was descended from Lion Gardiner, the 17th-century merchant-soldier for whom the eastern Long Island landmark Gardiner's Island is named.[205] By the 1880s, the Gardiners ranked among New York's oldest and wealthiest families, with large holdings in Manhattan and Long Island real estate. The year after James' betrothal, the Coogan alliance with the Gardiner-Lynch clan was cemented when brother Edward Coogan married Evelynn Lynch, Harriet's older sister.[206] With her own husband deceased, family matriarch Sarah Gardiner Lynch entrusted oversight of the Gardiner estates to new son-in-law James. The family properties included a meadowland in far north Manhattan recently reclaimed from the Harlem River. The most arresting feature of the property was its boundary, a 115-foot-high escarpment that would, in time, provide a dramatic backdrop for major league baseball. But the encounter with baseball was several years into the future for James J. Coogan. Presently, he was preparing the launch of a political career.

Coogan's first attempt at office was stillborn. In 1886, he sought the endorsement of the Central Labor Union, a federation of city trade unions, as candidate for New York City mayor. Despite pledging to spend $200,000 on his election campaign if nominated, Coogan received scant support and eventually sat out the mayoral contest. Two years later and bolstered by Gardiner family funds, he tried again. Rebuffed by the major political parties, Coogan managed to capture the mayoral nomination of the fringe United Labor Party. Notwithstanding the $100,000[207] of family money poured into the campaign, Coogan finished a distant fourth to 30-year-old Tammany Democrat Hugh J. Grant, still the youngest person ever elected mayor of New York. While unsuccessful in his bid for office, the vicissitudes of New York City politics were now about to bring Coogan into contact with baseball.

Although the 1888 season had been a successful one for the New York Giants at the gate—a then-record 305,455 fans attended home games—and on the field—a National League pennant had been capped by the team's defeat of the American Association champion St. Louis Browns in the postseason precursor of the modern World Series—a sense of foreboding had pervaded the Giants' headquarters throughout the campaign. The continued existence of the club's ballpark was in peril. The Polo Grounds had long been objectionable to the moneyed class who resided in the surrounding north Central Park neighborhood, and the alderman who represented them had finally pushed through the City Council a traffic improvement plan to extend the local street grid—right through the Polo Grounds outfield. Rearguard legal and political action had staved off condemnation of the ballpark for a time, but there was little chance that the Polo Grounds would survive to see the 1889 season. In recognition of the inevitable, Joseph Gordon, a member of the Giants' corporate board of directors and well-versed in city real estate,[208] pressed a new ballpark location on club president John B. Day: an expanse of vacant meadowland in far north Manhattan owned by the Gardiner-Lynch family.

Although miles removed from midtown, the area was fortuitously serviced by a station on the New York and Northern elevated railway. And the ground itself, already used for picnics and pickup baseball games tolerated by the property owners, was ideal for the construction of a ballpark. Unhappily for Day, the property was not for sale, as the Gardiners rarely, if ever, sold family-owned real estate. And while the family was amenable to renting the property, Day could not reach agreement with their wily estate agent, James J. Coogan. With the 1889 baseball season on the horizon and negotiations with Coogan stalemated, Day published an extraordinary notice in the *New York Times*. It advertised for "a party to purchase from the present owners ... that plot of land bounded by 8th and 9th Avenues and 155th and 157th Streets" which Day would then lease from this property angel for "5 to 10 years at a rental of $6,000 per year."[209] To no great surprise, the notice went unanswered, and Day's Giants were forced to begin the 1889 season playing at a derelict ballpark in Jersey City. Swift transfer to grounds inconveniently located on Staten Island did little to improve the club's situation. By June, Day and Coogan had resumed negotiations and an agreement was soon reached on a multiyear lease of the meadowland property, oftentimes called the "hollow."[210] But in an economy that he would come to regret, Day declined a Coogan offer to rent the hollow in its entirety and would lease only as much of it as was needed for the site of a new ballpark.

As soon as the lease was signed, work on the construction of the new Giants ballpark commenced at a breakneck pace. With material salvaged from the original Polo Grounds, the small army of workmen enlisted by Day produced a usable, if unfinished, ballpark within a remarkable three weeks. When completed over the following winter, the ballpark, called the New Polo Grounds, would be a handsome, if oddly pear-shaped enclosure, capable of seating about 14,000 baseball fans (and far more for college football, track meets, horse racing, and other sporting events later hosted there). But unfortunately for Day and ensuing ballpark owners, the topography of the surrounding area afforded a view of field action for nonpaying spectators, as well. Freeloaders standing high above on the 8th Avenue Viaduct, the Harlem Speedway, and the stairway of the elevated train station had an excellent vantage point, while more distant views of the playing field were available to those standing atop a stretch of the palisades soon dubbed Dead Head Hill.

Once playing inside their new ballpark, the Giants surged in the NL standings, coming from the middle of the pack to nip the Boston Beaneaters at the wire for the pennant. New York then successfully defended its World Series crown, defeating the American Association Brooklyn Bridegrooms in a nine-game postseason match of league pennant winners. As the 1889 season was drawing to a close, Coogan, intrigued by the money-making possibilities of baseball club ownership, made a $200,000 offer for the Giants.[211] Day turned him down, another decision that he would shortly have cause to second-guess. For no sooner was the 1889 season over than a rival baseball circuit emerged: the Players League. The brainchild of visionary Giant shortstop John Montgomery Ward, the PL would soon have most of the National League's best players under contract, including virtually the entire roster of Ward's former team. Worse yet for Day, the new rival would station its flagship franchise in New York, erecting a ballpark (Brotherhood Park) literally feet from the New Polo Grounds on available hollow property leased from the Gardiner-Lynch estate, courtesy of James J. Coogan. Coogan then tried to pressure Day into vacating the New Polo Grounds, threatening to terminate the Giants' lease on the underlying property.[212] But Day was not cowed, and his club would play out the season at their ballpark, albeit before drastically reduced crowds.

At the conclusion of the financially ruinous 1890 season, the Players League folded. In New York, the rival ball clubs merged. Under the new regime, John B. Day remained nominal president of the Giants, but the club front office was dominated by Edward B. Talcott and his PL allies. As Talcott was personally responsible for the ten-year lease on Brotherhood Park signed in 1890, that ballpark assumed the name *Polo Grounds* and became the Giants' home field. The New Polo Grounds, in turn, was renamed Manhattan Field and leased to the Manhattan Athletic Club. Prohibited from hosting major league baseball games, Manhattan Field became a site for college football, with the annual Yale-Princeton game drawing throngs to the venue. A *New York Times* account of the 1893 Thanksgiving Day clash made note of the 29,000 fans seated inside Manhattan Field and the "good many thousands" standing above the stadium confines observing the game from "Coogan's Bluff," the first published usage of the appellation.[213]

By then, James J. Coogan's interest in baseball had pretty much abated. Not so his desire to attain political office. In July 1892, it was reported that Coogan was now a member in good standing at Tammany Hall. And given his access to the Gardiner-Lynch family fortune, he was a plausible Tammany Congressional candidate for the fall elections.[214] But financial embarrassment would soon put a damper on Coogan's political prospects, at least temporarily. While his wife and in-laws were rich, Coogan himself was not. Indeed, disastrous fires at several Coogan Brothers furniture outlets and generally adverse business conditions attending the Panic of 1893 placed the fortunes of James J. Coogan in precipitous decline. By late 1893, he was broke and obliged to declare personal bankruptcy. In his petition to the court, Coogan professed to being "entirely penniless and dependent for shelter upon his mother-in-law" Sarah Gardiner Lynch, with whom he, wife Harriet, and their children lived on Manhattan's posh Fifth Avenue.[215] Coogan further averred that he had conveyed his share of the furniture business to his brothers and that the real property that he oversaw was all owned by Mrs. Lynch.[216] Meanwhile, civil judgments obtained by unpaid Coogan Brothers creditors continued to be entered against Coogan and his brother Edward.[217]

In time, press attention to Coogan's financial distress waned. By mid–1897, Coogan was again active on the political front, paying court to Tammany chieftain Richard Croker. According to one published report, Coogan was likely to be Tammany's candidate in the upcoming New York City mayoral election.[218] In the end, the Democratic Party nomination would go to another Croker vassal, City Court Judge Robert Van Wyck. Meanwhile, Coogan was back in court, sued by his brother Edward for conspiring with his mother-in-law, Sarah Lynch, to deprive Edward of assets derived from the liquidation of Coogan Brothers.[219] To avoid entangling daughter Harriet's inheritance in the litigation, Mrs. Lynch conveyed title to the property undergirding the Polo Grounds to Harriet.[220] The final outcome of the case is unknown, but presumably it was settled out of court.

In January 1899, Coogan's political aspirations where finally fulfilled when Boss Croker designated him to fill the post of Manhattan Borough president, the office made available by the death of incumbent Augustus W. Peters.[221] The borough president's office was largely ceremonial, leaving Coogan little to do. But he got himself in trouble anyway, voting in Southampton, Long Island, rather than Manhattan, in the 1899 elections. Political rivals promptly demanded his ouster from office as a non–Manhattan resident. The purchase of a new Fifth Avenue mansion cured the Coogan residency problem, while a $100,000 contribution from the Gardiner family funds to the 1900 presidential campaign of Democrat hopeful William Jennings Bryan squared Coogan with party elders. However, Coogan, like the other Tammany retainers, was turned out of office in November 1901 by a Gotham electorate angered by the shenanigans of the scandal-plagued administration of Mayor Van Wyck.

From then on, Coogan largely withdrew from public life. He still tended to Gardiner estate duties, collecting rentals, including those paid by owners of the New York Giants. In addition to the $15,000/year lease of the property on which Polo Grounds III (née Brotherhood Field) sat, club owners also rented the adjoining property, where Manhattan Field slowly fell into disuse and was ultimately reduced to the open field that it had once been. Still, the site remained on the rent rolls, bringing another $10,000 annually into family coffers.[222] But for much of the time, Coogan relaxed at Whitehall, a resort mansion in Newport, Rhode Island, purchased in 1903. Seven years later, Whitehall became the scene of a legendary feud between Newport gentry and the formidable Harriet Lynch Coogan. Harriet took offense when none of her neighbors would attend a coming-out party for her daughter Jessie. When fire seriously damaged the mansion in 1911, Harriet refused to have it repaired, leaving Whitehall to decay into a rotting eyesore that would dismay the neighbors for the next 30 years.[223] In May 1911, meanwhile, her husband announced a grandiose plan to convert the now vacant Manhattan Park site into a $6 million amusement park/amphitheater/exhibition hall.[224] But nothing ever came of it.

Slowed by heart disease, Coogan was largely retired when he succumbed on October

24, 1915, passing away in the family suite at the Hotel Nederland in Manhattan. He was 67. Following a funeral mass at St. Patrick's Cathedral, he was interred at Calvary Cemetery in Queens. The passing of James J. Coogan, however, did not sever the family connection to baseball. For the next 32 years, his widow would oversee Gardiner family properties, including the Polo Grounds site. Legend has it that Harriet Coogan did not trust the mail and would collect the rent personally at the Giants' offices each month. Under the terms of a 30-year lease entered between the club and Mrs. Coogan in 1932, the Polo Grounds rent came to $50,000 a year through 1947, $55,000 a year for the 15 years after that. Once the lease expired, ownership of the Polo Grounds was vested in the Coogan family, but the Giants would retain the right to sublet the ballpark for the indefinite future.[225]

Harriet Gardiner Lynch Coogan died on December 18, 1947, aged 86. Incredibly, she left no will. But son Jay Coogan generally represented family interests after Harriet's death. The Giants fled New York after the 1957 season. But pursuant to the terms of the 1932 lease, the club continued to pay rent on the Polo Grounds until 1962. The aged ballpark was now obsolete and in poor condition, but necessity dictated its use by the expansion New York Mets for the 1962 and 1963 seasons. By then, however, the Polo Grounds had long been targeted for condemnation by city officials, a move furiously resisted by Jay Coogan on behalf of his family. Litigation dragged on, until the city ultimately prevailed before the New York Court of Appeals, the state's highest tribunal, in 1967. As compensation for their extinguished right to the underlying real estate, the Coogan heirs were awarded $2,872,882. The San Francisco Giants got $1,466,006.90 in compensation for the ballpark itself. However, by the time of final judgment, the Polo Grounds was only a memory. In April 1964, the ballpark had been demolished, bringing to a close a memorable chapter in the history of both New York City and major league baseball.

NOTES

1. Brooklyn and the other outer boroughs of present-day New York did not become incorporated into the city until 1898.

2. The biographical data presented herein is mostly derived from Bill Lamb, "John Day," http://sabr.org/bioproj/person/c281a493. Sources for that profile include the John B. Day file maintained at the National Baseball Hall of Fame Library, Cooperstown, New York; U.S. Census data accessed via http://www.ancestry.com; David Pietrusza's biographical article of Day in *Baseball's First Stars*, Fred Ivor-Campbell, *et al.*, eds. (Cleveland: Society for American Baseball Research, 1996), and certain of the newspaper articles cited below, particularly the Day obituary published in the *Hartford Courant*, January 26, 1925.

3. Abbey, the husband of the elder Day sister Anna Eliza, was an expert in the cultivation and processing of tobacco, according to his obituary in the *Hartford Courant*, August 18, 1917.

4. Peter Mancuso's informative Society for American Baseball Research (SABR) BioProject profile of Jim Mutrie relates that the popular first-meeting story was disputed by the venerable Henry Chadwick. According to Chadwick, Mutrie was introduced to Day at a meeting prearranged by members of the New York baseball press. Peter Mancuso, "Jim Mutrie," http://sabr.org/bioproj/person/430838fd.

5. In a first-person newspaper article published years later, Day recalled his anxiety when the Nationals were late arriving to the grounds and spectators took umbrage at the prospect of seeing the Mets play a pickup team instead. See "John B. Day Tells of Bitter Hour," *New York Times*, February 6, 1916.

6. Reminiscing in the early 1950s, Blanche McGraw described Gordon as Day's brother-in-law. See Mrs. John J. McGraw, with Arthur Mann, *The Real McGraw* (New York: David McKay Company, 1953), 170. A diligently researched history of the early Giants does the same. See James D. Hardy, Jr., *The New York Giants Base Ball Club: The Growth of a Team and a Sport, 1870 to 1900* (Jefferson, NC: McFarland, 1995), 32. But genealogical inquiry controverts the notion that Day and Gordon were in anyway related. The two were simply friends whose wives shared a common maiden name: Davis.

7. As per Philip J. Lowry, *Green Cathedrals: The Ultimate Celebration of Major League and Negro League Ballparks* (New York: Walker, 3rd ed., 2006), 148.

8. Authorities disagree on just how often such competing Gotham-Met games were played at the Polo

Grounds. For more, see Stew Thornley, *Land of the Giants: New York's Polo Grounds* (Philadelphia: Temple University Press, 2000), 16–20.

9. Constructed amid factory smokestacks on a former landfill site, Metropolitan Park was soon adjudged both unplayable and a health hazard. By midseason, Met games were played there only when the Polo Grounds were being used by the Gothams. Lowry, 148–149.

10. For a more detailed account of the affair, see David Nemec, *The Beer and Whisky League: The Illustrated History of the American Association—Baseball's Renegade Major League* (New York: Lyons & Burford, 1994), 91–92.

11. As reported in the *New York Times*, December 5, 1885. After two desultory seasons on Staten Island, the Met roster was purchased for parts by Brooklyn club owner Charles Byrne. The AA then transferred the franchise hulk to Kansas City.

12. Although widely attributed to Mutrie, the nickname *Giants* may actually have been coined by a *New York Evening World* sportswriter. See Mancuso, 7–8.

13. Years after he left the game, former Giant outfielder John Henry recalled that Day "travelled with his men on many [road] trips and nothing was too good for the players." And when he felt "that his players were tired and needed relaxation, [Day] would order champagne and wine for them and do other things for their comfort," as per an unidentified circa 1923 newspaper article contained in the John B. Day File, National Baseball Hall of Fame Library, Cooperstown, New York.

14. Although Day himself was little more than a Tammany member, the other Metropolitan Exhibition Company stockholders were heavily involved in local politics—particularly Joseph Gordon, elected to the New York state assembly from a Manhattan district in 1888. But even a Sachem heavyweight like Gordon proved unable to save the Polo Grounds from demolition.

15. For a more detailed account of Day's ballpark woes, see Bill Lamb, "Manhattan Field (New York)," http://sabr.org/bioproj/park/8a2a9a1f.

16. Crane and O'Day posted all six Giant victories in best-of-ten game series. Hall of Famers Tim Keefe and Mickey Welch were winless for New York.

17. As reported in the *New York Times*, September 6, 1889. In the article, it was estimated that since it was formed in the fall of 1880, the Metropolitan Exhibition Company operation of the Giant and Met franchises had yielded corporate shareholders Day, Gordon, Dillingham, and Appleton a $750,000 profit.

18. See the *New York Times*, November 4, 1889. A verbatim reprint of the players' declaration of war and an apt summary of the situation is provided in Mike Roer, *Orator O'Rourke: The Life and Times of a Baseball Radical* (Jefferson, NC: McFarland, 2005), 169–172. For a more expansive treatment of Players League hostilities in New York, see Hardy, 92–133.

19. The unrequited wooing of Ewing and Richardson received ample press coverage, much to Day's chagrin. See, e.g., *Chicago Tribune*, February 18, 1890; *Boston Globe*, February 19 and 23, 1890; *Sporting Life*, February 26, 1890. The reported vacillation of Ewing, however, would earn him the lasting mistrust of many in the Players League ranks.

20. Over the strenuous protest of Brush, the Indianapolis (and Washington) franchises had been dissolved by the National League as an early wartime measure. As Brush was the author of the salary classification plan that precipitated the Players League strife, irony abounded. But Brush, a resilient and resourceful department store magnate, converted the situation to his advantage, capitalizing on Day's distress to advance a long-term Brush objective: control of the New York Giants.

21. In a short-sighted move, Day had declined to lease the entire meadowland on which the New Polo Grounds was constructed. This left ample room for the construction of a second ballpark on the remainder of the tract, which landlord James J. Coogan had no compunction about renting to the Players League backers.

22. As later recounted in *Sporting Life*, January 9, 1892. See also, Harold Seymour (with Dorothy Mills Seymour), *Baseball: The Early Years* (New York: Oxford University Press, 1960), 238.

23. As quoted in the *Chicago Tribune*, October 15, 1890.

24. As per the *Chicago Tribune*, November 7, 1890, and *Sporting Life*, November 8, 1890.

25. As quoted in the *Chicago Tribune*, November 22, 1890.

26. The subsequent issuance of bonds purchased by others to cover franchise indebtedness reduced Day's ownership share even further. By fall 1891, New York sportswriter George H. Dickinson calculated that Day's stake in the New York Giants constituted less than 10 percent of the club's stock. Fellow MEC members Joseph Gordon and Charles Dillingham retained even smaller holdings, while Walter Appleton no longer was listed among franchise's stockholders, as per *Sporting Life*, October 17, 1891.

27. As quoted in the *New York Times*, February 10, 1893.

28. *Ibid.*

29. *Ibid.* Day was succeeded as Giant president by Cornelius C. Van Cott, a Talcott faction member.

30. As reported in the *New York Times*, March 4, 1896.

31. See, e.g., *New York Times*, April 13, 1900.

32. As reported in the *New York Times*, January 21–22, 1902.

33. See, e.g., *Boston Globe* and *Chicago Tribune*, March 13, 1903.

34. As quoted in the *Chicago Tribune*, March 13, 1903.

35. According to the Day obituary published in the *Hartford Courant,* January 26, 1925.

36. See, e.g., *New York Times,* March 4, 1914, placing Day in attendance when the Giants and Chicago White Sox were greeted dockside upon their return from a world tour, and *New York Times,* February 16, 1916, listing Day as in the audience for former president Taft's keynote address at a major league banquet.

37. As per an unidentified 1923 newspaper article in the John B. Day File, National Baseball Hall of Fame Library, Cooperstown, New York.

38. As reported in the *New York Times,* October 5, 1923.

39. As per obituaries published in the *Hartford Courant* and *New York Times,* January 26, 1925.

40. Source material for Talcott includes the Edward B. Talcott File, National Baseball Hall of Fame Library, Cooperstown, New York; U.S. Census data; an entry on Talcott in Jay Henry Mowbray, *Representative Men of New York: A Record of Their Achievements* (New York: The New York Press, 1898), 3: 164–165; and certain newspaper articles, particularly a biographical sketch of Talcott published in the *New York Clipper,* July 20, 1893, and obituaries in the *New York Times,* April 7, 1941, and *The Sporting News,* April 17, 1941.

41. As per Mowbray, 165.

42. According to the *Charleston Evening Post,* February 6, 1899.

43. Sources for the personal detail provided on McAlpin include a biographical sketch of Edwin McAlpin in *Sporting Life,* September 3, 1890; U.S. Census data; and newspaper reportage, particularly the obituary published in the *New York Times,* April 13, 1917.

44. As per *History of the 71st Regiment, N.G., N.Y.* (New York: 71st Regiment Veterans Assn., 1919), 453.

45. In 1884, McAlpin was the unsuccessful Republican candidate for a Westchester County congressional seat. Thereafter, he served as president of the Republican League of New York and held the post of New York Republican Party campaign treasurer, in addition to being the mayor of Ossining.

46. Biographical detail on Van Cott was extracted from the extensive newspaper coverage that he received as a prominent NYC politico; U.S. Census data; and a brief sketch of Van Cott in Holice B. Young, *Our Firemen: The History of the New York Fire Departments,* transcribed March 2001 and accessible via http://www.usgen. net.org/usa/ny/state/fire/11/20/ch50pt2.html. Particularly informative was background information published at the time of Van Cott's sudden death amid scandal in October 1904. See, e.g., *New York Times,* October 26–27, 1904.

47. Per Young, Chapter 50, and the *New York Times,* October 26, 1904.

48. For more on the baseball playing Van Cotts, see Peter Morris, et al., eds., *Baseball Pioneers: The Clubs, Players and Cities of the Northeast That Established the Game* (Jefferson, NC: McFarland, 2013), 60.

49. According to *Recreation,* Vol. 12, No. 1, January 1900, 360.

50. John Kieran, "The Brave Days of Old in Baseball," *New York Times,* January 7, 1931.

51. As reported in the *Philadelphia Inquirer*, November 16, 1889. See also, *Sporting Life,* July 26, 1890.

52. As per *Sporting Life,* December 18, 1889.

53. See, e.g., first-person Brunnell columns in *Sporting Life,* November 29 and December 27, 1890.

54. As extrapolated from club ownership data published in *Sporting Life,* October 17, 1891.

55. *New York Herald,* February 10, 1893. Similar sentiments were expressed in the *Philadelphia Inquirer,* February 10, 1893, and elsewhere.

56. For more on the machinations that attended Ward's transfer to New York, see Bryan DiSalvatore, *A Clever Base-Ballist: The Life and Times of John Montgomery Ward* (New York: Pantheon Books, 1999), 348–349.

57. See *Reach Official Base Ball Guide, 1895* ($48,000) and Hardy ($54,000). One newspaper report of the sale estimated that the Talcott group had sold out for only 50 percent of the paper value of its Giant stock, with Talcott strong-arming a reluctant Frank Robinson into going along with the discount price. See *Baltimore Sun,* January 18, 1895.

58. *New York Times,* October 26, 1904.

59. According to *Sporting Life,* June 24, 1896.

60. As per the McAlpin obituary in the *New York Times,* April 13, 1917.

61. As per the Talcott obituary in the *New York Times,* April 7, 1941.

62. As reported in the *Denver Rocky Mountain Post, New York Times,* and *Worcester Daily Spy,* December 25, 1901, and elsewhere.

63. Interestingly, Talcott did not veto the idea of assuming the NL presidency himself. When asked if he would accept the post, Talcott replied, "I don't care to answer that. But it has not been offered to me as yet. Everybody knows the interest I take in baseball. I want to see this muddle straightened out," as per the *Cleveland Plain Dealer,* April 2, 1902. Soon thereafter, the matter was rendered moot when Spalding abandoned the presidency fight and incumbent NL president Nick Young was restored to office.

64. As reported in the *Trenton Evening Times,* April 26, 1939.

65. *New York Times,* April 7, 1941.

66. As per the obituary published in the *Asbury Park (NJ) Press,* April 7, 1941.

67. Hardy, 158.

68. Bill James, *The New Bill James Historical Baseball Abstract* (New York: The Free Press, 2001), 61, and *The Politics of Glory: How Baseball's Hall of Fame Really Works* (New York: Macmillan, 1994), 197.

69. DiSalvatore, 362.

70. Little is known of an elder brother named Jacob (born 1854). Andrew was followed by Isabella (1862–1927) and Daniel (1864–1944), per the Davies family tree chart provided to the writer by the Isabella Freedman Jewish Retreat Center, Falls Village, Connecticut.

71. Per e-mail of CCNY archivist Samuel Sanchez, transmitted to the writer November 8, 2008. When he left CCNY, Freedman ranked 166 out of a class of 200.

72. According to the Freedman obituary published in the *New York Times,* December 5, 1915.

73. See Noel Hynd, *The Giants of the Polo Grounds* (New York: Doubleday, 1988), 69; Mark Alvarez, "The Abominable Owner," *Sports Heritage,* November 1987, 44.

74. See *Sporting Life,* January 26, 1895, and Hardy, 226, n1.

75. *New York Herald,* February 17, 1895.

76. *The Sporting News,* February 5, 1895.

77. See David Stevens, *Baseball's Radical for All Seasons: A Biography of John Montgomery Ward* (Lanham, Maryland: Scarecrow Press, 1998), 183.

78. Late in the 1895 season, Freedman imposed a $200 fine on Rusie for being out of condition. Although the sporting press and Giant fans lined up solidly behind the pitcher's refusal to pay, allegations made by Rusie's wife during acrimonious 1900 divorce proceedings suggest that the grounds for the fine may not have been as capricious as originally supposed.

79. According to A. G. Spalding—a suspect source when it comes to Freedman—the Giants' owner was "so obnoxious to most of those concerned with the game that nobody outside his own following could endure his eccentricities of speech or action. He would apply to other members of the league, in ordinary conversation, terms so coarse and offensive as to be unprintable." A. G. Spalding, *America's National Game* (New York: American Sports Publishing, 1911), 192.

80. On October 12, 1896, Freedman was convicted of assault and given a suspended sentence for punching Edward Hurst, a critical sports columnist for the *New York Evening World,* per an unidentified newspaper clipping in the Andrew Freedman File, National Baseball Hall of Fame Library, Cooperstown, New York. Freedman, however, did not confine his aggressions to local sportswriters. He also had physical altercations with political correspondent Paul Theman, retired umpire Watch Burnham, theatrical agent Bert Dasher, fellow club owners John T. Brush and Harry von der Horst, and any number of Tammany adversaries.

81. Unfortunately for Freedman, a credulous public treated the Dryden satires as factual. Later generations of New York sportswriters did the same, repeating an apocryphal Freedman threat to push Dryden over "the brink of an abscess" and other such nonsense. See, e.g., Frank Graham, *The New York Giants: An Informal History of a Great Baseball Club* (New York: Putnam, 1952), 19.

82. Freedman behaved no better as owner of the New York Mets of the Atlantic League. In mid-season 1896, fellow executives fed up with Freedman's antics expelled the Mets from the circuit. See *Sporting Life,* July 18, 1896.

83. Reportedly $100,000 per year. See David Quentin Voigt, *The League That Failed* (Lanham, Maryland: Scarecrow Press, 1998), 219.

84. *The Sporting News,* July 30, 1898.

85. As subsequently published in the *Boston Globe,* August 20, 1898.

86. See *Sporting Life* editorial, August 20, 1898. In keeping with the times, press criticism of Freedman was frequently expressed in repugnant Jewish stereotypes, with *New York Sun* sportswriter Joe Vila being the foremost exponent. Freedman responded by filing a blizzard of defamation-based lawsuits against the newspaper, all of which he lost. See Stevens, 184–185. See also, Burton W. Boxerman, and Benita A. Boxerman, *Jews and Baseball,* Vol. 1 (Jefferson, NC: McFarland, 2007), 19–26.

87. For more detailed accounts of the Ducky Holmes affair, see Burt Solomon, *Where They Ain't* (New York: Doubleday, 1999), 227–229, and Hynd, 129–130.

88. Mrs. John J. McGraw, 171.

89. Giants home attendance shrunk from a league leading 390,340 in 1897 to 121,384 in 1899.

90. As reported in *Sporting Life,* September 30, 1899.

91. See Seymour, 304–306.

92. Said Freedman, "I have patched up the differences I had with John T. Brush and acknowledge it with pleasure. We will now work on the most friendly terms and will work in harmony for the best interests of the sport." *Sporting Life,* October 14, 1899. For more on the Freedman-Brush rapprochement, see William F. Lamb, "A Fearsome Collaboration: The Alliance of Andrew Freedman and John T. Brush," *Base Ball, A Journal of the Early Game* III, no. 2 (Fall 2009): 5–20.

93. Initially, Freedman acted as liaison between John D. McDonald, the subway's general contractor, and the bankers who financed the project. Thereafter, Freedman was active in virtually every phase—property acquisition, tunnel construction, railway car manufacture, among other things—necessary to make the subway system operational.

94. Although often ascribed to Freedman, the National Base Ball [sic] Trust was almost entirely the brainchild of Brush, who as early as the 1892 season had proposed to Chicago President James Hart that the minor Western League be operated as a trust. See unidentified January 30, 1892, newspaper clipping in the John T. Brush File, National Baseball Hall of Fame Library, Cooperstown, New York.

95. As outlined by Brush in a letter to Freedman, later obtained and published in the *New York Press,* December 11, 1901. For a comprehensive exposition of the Trust, see Hardy, 171–191.

96. In March 1902, New York State Supreme Court Justice Charles Truax sustained Freedman's position on virtually every issue during preliminary proceedings. Shortly thereafter, Spalding resigned his claim to the NL presidency.

97. See Joseph Durso, *Baseball and the American Dream* (St. Louis: The Sporting News, 1986), 64–67; Solomon, 227–231.

98. Whether Freedman was motivated by a sense of obligation to Brush, the desire to thwart Tammany rivals reportedly financing the upstart New York Highlanders club, or for reasons known only to himself is a mystery.

99. From his manor in England, Croker attempted to maintain control of Tammany via trans-Atlantic direction to Freedman and other finance committee loyalists. After new Tammany boss Lewis Nixon resigned in protest, his successor, the shrewd Charles Murphy, cut off this back channel through the simple expedient of abolishing the finance committee and redistributing its responsibilities to Tammany organs under Murphy's control. With Croker's influence now stifled, Freedman was reduced to ceremonial posts and attending Tammany banquets. See *New York Times,* May 22–23, 1902, for more details on the abolition of the finance committee.

100. Notwithstanding the hefty fees charged by Freedman, his administration of the trusts assigned to him was exemplary. The estate of Freedman's most prominent charge, the mentally disturbed millionairess Ida Flagler, posted substantial revenue increases annually under Freedman's care, drawing the commendation of both Mrs. Flagler's legal guardian and the court. See *New York Times,* July 14, 1914.

101. As per an Andrew Freedman Foundation pamphlet, c. 1965, provided to the writer by CCNY archivist Sanchez.

102. As noted in the *New York Times,* February 15, 1915 and various Freedman obituaries.

103. Essentially a high handicap hacker, Freedman once managed to win an 18-hole tourney at White Mountain Golf Club, posting a 100–30 = 70 net score, as per the *New York Times,* September 13, 1913.

104. *New York Times,* December 5, 1915. Similar sentiments were later expressed by prominent New York lawyer and Freedman friend Samuel Untermeyer who stated that, "It is due more to the courage and enterprise of Andrew Freedman than to anyone else that the first subway was built." *Los Angeles Times,* June 18, 1924.

105. A brief 1905 engagement to Elsie Rothschild fell through. Like Andrew, neither Isabella, a benefactress of various Jewish causes, nor Daniel Freedman, a wealthy realtor and minor Tammany functionary, ever married. Shadowy elder brother Jacob, however, may have been survived by an heir named Adelaide. See "Surrogate's Notice" published in the *New York Times,* January 27, 1916. Jacob predeceased Andrew and no connection of his ever came forward to challenge the will. Thus, nothing more is known of Adelaide Gwendolyn Freedman, aka Adelaide Archer.

106. For more on the Freedman will, see the *New York Times,* December 9, 1915.

107. Once known derisively in the neighborhood as "The Home for Poor Millionaires," the Andrew Freedman home is featured periodically in the real estate section of the *New York Times.* See, e.g., July 1, 2008.

108. Sources for the biographical details provided herein include the John T. Brush File, National Baseball Hall of Fame Library, Cooperstown, New York; the John T. Brush and Natalie Brush Gates files maintained by the Indiana Historical Society, Indianapolis; Carlton E. Sanford, *Pioneer Families: The History of the Village of Hopkinton* (Boston: Bartlett Press, 1903); the Brush family tree posted by Vicki Corkhill at http://www.ancestry.com; U.S. Census data; and the profile of Brush by John Saccoman published in *Deadball Stars of the National League,* Tom Simon, ed. (Dulles, Virginia: Brassey's Inc., 2004).

109. John's older siblings were George (1832–1902), Caroline "Carrie" (1840–1874), and Mary (1842–1858).

110. Eliphalet's first wife, Polly Tomlinson Brush, had died in April 1810 giving birth to the original John Tomlinson Brush.

111. This is one of the intimate details of Brush's life revealed by his daughter Natalie in an interview that formed the basis for "The Forgotten Indiana Architect of Baseball" by Rick Johnson, published in the *Indianapolis Star Magazine,* May 4, 1975. The far longer original manuscript of the Johnson article is among the artifacts contained in the Brush file at Cooperstown. The manuscript is an invaluable resource for Brush researchers but must be used with care. Informant Natalie Brush Gates de Gendron was a late-life child and much of what she related about her father was not based on personal remembrance, but upon what others had told her about John T. Brush, some of which was wrong.

112. Johnson, 8–9.

113. The existence of baby Adalaide Brush is noted in both Carlton E. Sanford's history of the Brush family and the Brush family tree posted online by Vicki Corkhill.

114. For more on the When Store, see *The Encyclopedia of Indianapolis,* David J. Bodenhammer and Robert G. Barrow, eds. (Bloomington: Indiana University Press, 1994), 1424–1425.

115. In the 19th century, considerable stigma attached to divorce, particularly for women, and divorcees often identified themselves as widows to census takers.

The Polo Grounds (Lamb)

53

116. A search of newspaper archives by the staff at the Indiana State Library failed to uncover an obituary for Margaret Brush, per e-mail of librarian Kimberly Brown-Harden to the writer, dated September 19, 2012. Stranger still, the Marion County (Indianapolis) Department of Vital Records has no death certificate for Margaret Brush, per e-mail of department officials to the writer, dated October 16, 2012. Thus, nothing is known of the cause or circumstances attending the death of the first Mrs. John T. Brush.

117. According to Natalie Brush, her father's first wife was interred in the Brush family plot for daughter Eleanor's sake. Johnson, 17–18.

118. J. Taylor Spink, "World Series Started with J. T. Brush Fire," *The Sporting News,* October 8, 1939. An informative unpublished profile of Brush by Indianapolis native Guy M. Smith in the Brush file in Cooperstown concurs that Brush's desire to gain the AA franchise was thwarted by Schwabacher. But Natalie Brush maintained that her father was an owner of the Indianapolis AA club when interviewed for the *Indianapolis Star Magazine* feature published in 1975.

119. As per David Wall, "From Basement to Bordello: Fred Thomas and the 1887 Baseball Season in Indianapolis," *Traces Magazine,* publication date unknown. The Wall article in manuscript form was provided to the writer by Brush researcher David Kathman.

120. During his Indianapolis and Cincinnati years, the Brush trademark was a menacing black moustache (that he shaved off around 1905).

121. For more on the Freedman-Brush alliance, see Lamb.

122. A minority shareholder in the new Giants ownership regime was Brush friend and Cincinnati Reds junior partner Ashley Lloyd. But unlike former New York Giant bosses such as Andrew Freedman and Edward Talcott, as well as Joseph Gordon (Mets), and later Frank Farrell and Bill Devery of the New York Highlanders, John T. Brush, an Indiana businessman and one-time delegate to the Republican Party National Convention, would have little, if any, political pull in Democrat-controlled New York City.

123. Brush's malady (locomotor ataxia) was often identified in the press. But its venereal etiology was never mentioned.

124. Brush bore his tribulations stoically, refusing pain-killing medication lest he become addicted. Often unable to sleep, he was given to playing solitaire through the night.

125. As per the *Indianapolis News,* November 27, 1912.

126. For more on this obscure distinction, see David L. Fleitz, "The Honor Rolls of Baseball," *Baseball Research Journal,* no. 34 (2005): 53–59.

127. Hempstead had been a member of an undefeated prep school nine and later played outfield for his class team at Lafayette College.

128. Sources for the biographical details of this profile include the Harry Hempstead File, National Baseball Hall of Fame Library, Cooperstown, New York; U.S. Census data; and assorted newspaper articles, particularly a biographical sketch of Hempstead published in the *Chicago Tribune,* March 1, 1914, and Hempstead obituaries printed in the *Indianapolis News, Indianapolis Star,* and *New York Times,* March 27, 1938.

129. According to sports columnist Harvey Woodruff in the *Chicago Tribune,* March 1, 1914. For less fanciful detail on Harry Hempstead's involvement with his alma mater, the writer is indebted to Diane Windham Shaw, Director of Special Collections and College Archivist, Lafayette College, Easton, Pennsylvania.

130. As reported in *Sporting Life,* November 2, 1902.

131. As per *Sporting Life,* December 23, 1907.

132. As reported in *Sporting Life,* November 23, 1912, and elsewhere.

133. As reported in the *Los Angeles Times,* December 3, 1912. See also, *Sporting Life,* December 21. 1912.

134. As per an undated circa December 1912 *Cincinnati Enquirer* news item preserved in the Harry Hempstead File, National Baseball Hall of Fame Library, Cooperstown, New York.

135. In addition to being a minority Giant owner, Lloyd served as club treasurer.

136. Although Elsie Brush was, legally speaking, Eleanor Brush Hempstead's stepmother, the two women were actually contemporaries, born less than 18 months apart. When John T. Brush died, Elsie and Eleanor were both in their early 40s, as was Harry Hempstead.

137. In granting the Highlanders, who had just lost their leasehold on Hilltop Park, access to the Polo Grounds, Hempstead was reciprocating the accommodation that Highlanders boss Frank Farrell had afforded the Giants the previous year. When fire struck the Polo Grounds in April 1911, Farrell made Hilltop Park available to the Giants while the Polo Grounds was undergoing reconstruction.

138. In his 1923 memoir, McGraw fondly recalled his association with John T. Brush. Harry Hempstead's name was not mentioned. See John J. McGraw, *My Thirty Years in the Game* (New York: Boni & Liveright, 1923).

139. As disclosed in *Sporting Life,* August 15, 1915.

140. As per *Sporting Life,* January 1, 1916.

141. *Ibid.*

142. As quoted in the *New York Times,* December 17, 1915.

143. As per the *New York Times,* January 13, 1916. See also, *The Sporting News,* January 20, 1916.

144. As published in *The Sporting News,* January 20, 1916.

145. H. N. Hempstead, "The National Game," distributed by the National Editorial Service and printed nationwide. See, e.g., *Los Angeles Times,* May 6, 1916.

146. At the behest of club president Hempstead, New York Giant players were often dispatched to Easton to tutor the Leopard nine. An October 1916 exhibition game between the Giants and the Lafayette varsity drew a campus crowd of 1,500, New York winning, 9–0, as per e-mail of Diane Windham Shaw to the writer, September 12, 2012.

147. As reported in the *New York Times,* November 24, 1918.

148. The common view that the Brush family women sold out entirely in 1919 is erroneous. In 1922, Hempstead revealed that he (meaning his wife) was still the third largest Giant stockholder. See *New York Times,* October 26, 1922. Eleanor Brush Hempstead remained a significant Giant stockholder until 1924, when she sold her holdings to a former St. Louis Cardinals co-owner named Anderson for a reported $200,000. See *New York Times,* June 13, 1924.

149. See, e.g., *Chicago Tribune* and *New York Times,* January 15, 1919. Later, Giant historians raised the franchise purchase price to $1.3 million. See Tom Schott and Nick Peters, *The Giants Encyclopedia* (Champaign, Illinois: Sports Publishing, Inc., 1999), 90. Dominant stockholder Stoneham acquired 1,300 shares of club stock. McGraw and McQuade bought 70 shares each.

150. See the *New York Sun,* October 14, 1922; *New York Times,* October 26, 1922; and *The Sporting News,* November 2, 1922.

151. Wife Eleanor Brush Hempstead died at the Hempstead country estate in Irvington, New York, on January 8, 1943. She was 71. Elsie Lombard Brush returned to the stage in matronly roles through the 1930s, and lived until she was 88, passing away in Fort Lauderdale, Florida, in 1957. The last of the Brush family women, twice-divorced spy romance novelist Natalie Brush Gates de Gendron, died in her Manhattan apartment on June 16, 1980, aged 84.

152. Sources for the biographical details on Stoneham include the Charles A. Stoneham File, National Baseball Hall of Fame Library, Cooperstown, New York; U.S. Census data; and the extensive newspaper coverage that Stoneham received during his life. Particularly informative on his early business life is the Stoneham obituary published in the *New York Times,* January 7, 1936.

153. Care must be taken to keep the Stoneham family members straight, as the names *Charles* and *Horace* recur across generations. Our subject is Charles Abraham Stoneham. His younger brother was named Horace Alfred Stoneham, while his second son (and future Giant owner) was Horace Charles Stoneham. Horace Alfred's son, another Charles A. Stoneham, also became a longtime Giant executive, as later did Horace Charles's son, Charles Horace (Pete) Stoneham.

154. Charles's infant daughter Mary would grow up to become the mother of another longtime Giant executive and later National League President Charles Stoneham "Chub" Feeney.

155. See, e.g., *Cleveland Plain Dealer, New York Daily People,* and *New York Times,* May 5, 1905.

156. As quoted in the *Jersey (Jersey City) Journal,* May 8, 1905.

157. As reported by the *New York Times,* May 7, 1905.

158. See "Broker Stoneham Sued by Farmer," *New York Times,* January 16, 1908.

159. The United States Supreme Court defined a bucket shop as "an establishment, nominally for the transaction of a stock exchange business … but really [a place] for the registration of bets and wagers, usually for small amounts, on the rise or fall of the prices of stocks, grain, oil, etc., there being no transfer of the stock or commodities nominally dealt in." *Gatewood v. North Carolina,* 203 U.S. 531, 536 (1906).

160. According to David Pietrusza, *Rothstein: The Life, Times, and Murder of the Criminal Genius Who Fixed the 1919 World Series* (New York: Carroll & Graf, 2003), 129.

161. Besides an Irish-Catholic heritage, Stoneham and McGraw had other things in common, including a love of baseball, horse racing, and New York City night life. Both also had longstanding connections to Arnold Rothstein and a cordial relationship with many in Tammany Hall.

162. Most of the purchase price was supplied by Stoneham, who received 1,000 shares of Giant stock in exchange. The relatively small sums contributed by McGraw and McQuade garnered them 70 shares each.

163. Referring to the recently deceased Tiernan, Stoneham said, "Poor Mike is responsible for my entry into baseball. I am sorry he could not live to see me take control of the Giants club," as per the *Toronto World,* January 22, 1919.

164. See "Better Salaries for All Giants Is Announcement of President Stoneham," *New York Times,* January 24, 1920.

165. Much to the chagrin of Giant management, the Yankees were an even bigger draw. Over one million fans entered the Polo Grounds each season to view AL games from 1919 through 1922. Notwithstanding the substantial annual rent received from the Yankees for access to the Polo Grounds, Stoneham and McGraw forced the Yankees to relocate to their own field (Yankee Stadium) for the 1923 season.

166. See *Springfield (Mass.) Republican,* March 15, 1922, and *New York Times,* April 9, 1922.

167. The allegations of one of these suits, initiated by a Virginia lumber dealer, are presented in the *New York Times,* June 20, 1922.

168. As reported in the *New York Times,* September 1, 1923. Stoneham's connection to Tammany Hall had long insulated him from investigation by local and state authorities but conferred no immunity from Republican federal prosecutors in New York appointed by the Harding and Coolidge administrations.

169. *Ibid.* See also, the *Boston Herald* and *New York Times,* September 2, 1923, for similar remarks by

Heydler and an unnamed NL official who observed that as long as Stoneham maintained his innocence, the league would take no action against him. Stoneham's voluntary resignation was the only possible resolution of the problem at that point.

170. Landis' refusal to speak publicly about the Stoneham situation was reported in the *Boston Herald,* September 5, 1923. For a cogent overview of the situation, see "Stoneham Faces Crisis in Career," *New York Times,* September 9, 1923.

171. News accounts regularly described business partner Robertson as Charles Stoneham's brother-in-law. See, e.g., *Boston Herald,* January 12, 1924, and *New York Times,* January 15, 1924. But genealogical inquiry failed to uncover any marital connection between the Canadian-born Robertson and the Stoneham family.

172. As reported in the *New York Times* and *Springfield (Mass.) Republican,* February 28, 1925, and elsewhere. The charges against Bondy and a Fuller firm cashier had been dismissed midtrial by the court on evidential insufficiency grounds.

173. These civil judgments (such as $2,095 awarded to Robert Harford and $4,782 to Dr. John Duncan) rarely exceeded nuisance amounts for a man of Stoneham's wealth. But the cost of continually defending himself in court was not trivial, and press coverage of the litigation did little to restore Stoneham's reputation.

174. From 1926 through 1932, the New York Giants were the National League's second-best home draw, with attendance figures topped only by the Chicago Cubs. The major leagues' biggest draw, however, was the Babe Ruth-led New York Yankees, playing a long fly ball away from the Polo Grounds in the newly erected Yankee Stadium.

175. The September 24, 1923, heavyweight title bout between champ Jack Dempsey and Argentine challenger Luis Firpo was probably the most famous nonbaseball event ever staged at the Polo Grounds. An estimated 80,000 fans were in attendance to witness the contestants exchange knockdowns before Dempsey posted a thrilling second round KO. During the Stoneham years, the seating capacity of the Polo Grounds was repeatedly enlarged. By 1930, it could hold 56,000 for baseball. See Lowry, 154. Even larger crowds could be accommodated for football, soccer, and boxing.

176. See "Award of $42,827 Is Lost by M'Quade," *New York Times,* January 18, 1934.

177. As reported in the *New York Times,* January 11, 1936.

178. As reported in the *New York Times,* April 2, 1936. A check of the 1930 U.S. Census reveals Charles A. Stoneham living in two separate places: in Jersey City with wife Johanna (Hannah) Stoneham and in Westchester County, New York, with wife Margaret Stoneham and children Russell and Jane Stoneham.

179. As revealed when Margaret Leonard/Stoneham filed suit to have Horace A. Stoneham and Bondy removed from their trustee positions. See *New York Times,* April 16, 1936. See also, Robert E. Murphy, *After Many a Summer: The Passing of the Giants, the Dodgers and a Golden Age in New York Baseball* (New York: Union Square Press, 2009), 32–33.

180. The biographical detail provided herein is derived mainly from material contained in the Horace Stoneham File, National Baseball Hall of Fame Library, Cooperstown, New York, and the extensive newspaper coverage that Stoneham received throughout almost his entire life. Half-sister Mary Alice Stoneham was the daughter of Charles Stoneham by first wife Alice, who died five days after giving birth to her in January 1898. Numerous references that cite Newark as Horace's birthplace are wrong. At the turn of the century, the Stoneham family resided in Jersey City, and Charles's children, including Horace, were born there, not in Newark.

181. Or so Horace told New York sportswriter John Kieran. See "A Presidential Party," *New York Times,* January 20, 1936.

182. See Robert Shaplen, "The Lonely, Loyal Mr. Stoneham," *Sports Illustrated,* May 5, 1958, 75.

183. See John Drebinger, "Giants Transfer Is Held Unlikely," *New York Times,* January 8, 1936, and "Reorganization of the Giants Makes Horace C. Stoneham President of the Club," *New York Times,* January 16, 1936. See also, Shaplen, 75.

184. Shaplen, 76. See also Art Spander, "Game Was Stoneham's Passion and Blind Spot," *The Sporting News,* January 22, 1990, and Robert E. Murphy, "The Real Villain of New York Baseball," *New York Times,* June 24, 2007.

185. Shaplen, 77.

186. The Giants also signed Negro League great and future Hall of Famer Ray Dandridge but, sadly, the aging third baseman never got a shot with the parent club. His time in the organization was spent with their Triple A affiliate in Minneapolis.

187. See, e.g., "Talk of Giants Moving to West Coast Idle Gossip, Says Stoneham," *New York Times,* November 16, 1954. Stoneham assured fans that "the Giants are not planning to vacate the Polo Grounds."

188. Joe King, "Now It's Certain: Giants Will Move After This Year," *The Sporting News,* July 24, 1957.

189. Jack Walsh, "Three's a Crowd in NY, Says Stoneham," *The Sporting News,* July 24, 1957.

190. During his Congressional testimony, Stoneham stated that he "would recommend" franchise relocation to the Giants' corporate board. See "Baseball Is His Life: Horace Charles Stoneham," *New York Times,* July 18, 1957. But given that Horace and his sister Mary Stoneham Aufderher (formerly Feeney) controlled 60 percent of the Giants stock, such a recommendation was tantamount to a command.

191. Quoted in Spander.

192. As reported in the *New York Times,* February 6 and 8, 1958. The criminal charges against Pete

Stoneham were later dismissed following the settlement of a civil suit brought by the deceased's family. See *New York Times,* December 9, 1958.

193. Stoneham had stalled the Bay Area invasion three years earlier, denying a Finley request for permission to let the A's share San Francisco and Candlestick Park. See Hal Lebovitz, "Horace Let Finley's Cat Out of the Bag," *Cleveland Plain Dealer,* July 20, 1963. But Stoneham was powerless to stop relocation of the A's to Oakland.

194. See, e.g., Wells Twombley, "Candlestick Park, the Cancer Ward of Baseball," *The Sporting News,* October 5, 1974; "Piece of Advice for Stoneham: Save Giants by Selling Club," *The Sporting News,* December 28, 1974; and Dave Anderson, "Rose-Colored Glasses for Horace," *New York Times,* March 5, 1975.

195. Neither Horace nor his late mother (Hannah McGoldrick Stoneham had died in 1951) ever acknowledged Charles Stoneham's second "family." After Charles's death in 1936, ex-showgirl mistress Margaret Leonard aka Margaret Stoneham sold the Greenburgh, New York, residence that she had shared with Charles and their children and relocated to California, dying in Beverly Hills in 1989, aged 91. Although ignored by their well-known half-brother, Russell and Jane Stoneham achieved a degree of prominence on their own. Russell married former Miss America Jo-Carroll Dennison (the ex-wife of comic Phil Silvers) and had a fairly successful career as a television director and producer. His younger sister Jane became the second wife of Freeman Gosden, the creator and star of the long-running *Amos 'n' Andy* radio program.

196. The primary source for biographical information on Bennett is the full page obituary published in the *New York Times,* May 15, 1918.

197. According to James Crouthamel, *Bennett's New York Herald and the Rise of the Popular Press* (Syracuse: Syracuse University Press, 1989).

198. *New York Times,* May 15, 1918.

199. *Ibid.* Examples given in the Bennett obituary included yachting, balloon racing, and wilderness exploration. Also, Bennett financed the celebrated expedition that found the lost Dr. David Livingstone in the African bush.

200. Until 1898, Brooklyn and New York were separate municipalities.

201. As per Lowry, 148. The ballpark was razed in March 1889. Today, the location is the site of a Manhattan elementary school, PS 170.

202. Although Coogan later informed U.S. Census takers that he had been born in New York City, the passport application that he submitted under oath on June 28, 1878, declared that he had been born in Ireland, had come to America at about age seven, and was a naturalized U.S. citizen.

203. According to a handwritten statement added by Coogan to his 1878 U.S. passport application, viewable on-line via www.ancestry.com.

204. A large Coogan Brothers sign painted on the side of a brick building at 123 Bowery was still faintly visible in 2005. The pirate Captain Kidd was reputed to have buried treasure on Gardiner's Island.

205. The Edward V. Coogan-Evelynn E. Lynch nuptials, performed by Archbishop Corrigan at St. Patrick's Cathedral, were noted in the *New York Times,* June 22, 1884.

207. As reported in the *New York Times,* October 8, 1888, which calculated that the 9,900 votes that he received had cost Coogan about $10 apiece.

208. Gordon, a Manhattan coal broker, had previously served as president of the New York Mets during that time when the club was owned jointly with the NL Giants. A Tammany Hall stalwart, Gordon was elected to a New York state assembly seat in 1888. But even the influence of a political heavyweight like Gordon was insufficient to save the Polo Grounds.

209. *New York Times,* April 8, 1889.

210. The lease agreement was reported in the *New York Times* and *New York Tribune,* June 22, 1889. But the duration and terms of the lease would soon become matters of dispute between the parties.

211. As reported in the *New York Times,* September 6, 1889. The *Times* estimated that ownership of the New York Giants and Mets had earned John B. Day and his junior partners a $750,000 profit since 1880.

212. As reported in the *New York Times,* February 4 and 5, 1890.

213. See "The Orange above the Blue: Yale's Remarkable Football Record Broken," *New York Times,* December 1, 1893.

214. See *New York Times,* July 1, 1892.

215. As reported in "Coogan Is Bankrupt," *New York Times,* January 1, 1894.

216. *Ibid.*

217. A $12,566.36 judgment lodged by A. A. Anderson, Advertisers, against James and Edward Coogan "formerly dealers in the Bowery under the style of Coogan Brothers" is illustrative. See *New York Times,* January 12, 1894.

218. See "Croker Will Run or Name the Man," *New York Times,* July 22, 1897.

219. As reported in the *New York Times,* December 1, 1897. As mother of Edward's late wife Evelynn, Sarah Lynch was mother-in-law to Edward Coogan, as well as to his brother James.

220. As per the *New York Times,* December 29, 1897. As consideration for title to the Polo Grounds property, Harriet Coogan reportedly paid her mother $2. With her other seven children all sadly dead before

her, Sarah Gardiner Lynch conveyed the remainder of the Gardiner family fortune to Harriet in May 1900, as reported in the *New York Times,* May 1, 1900.

221. See *New York Times,* January 6, 1899. The position of borough president was created when Brooklyn, Queens, North Bronx, and Staten Island were consolidated with Manhattan and South Bronx to form the present New York City in 1898. Peters was the first Manhattan Borough president, Coogan the second.

222. Andrew Freedman acquired the Manhattan Field lease while serving as trustee for the financially ailing Manhattan Athletic Club. When Freedman took control of the New York Giants in 1895, he assumed the lease on both the Polo Grounds and Manhattan Field, lest the latter ballpark fall into the hands of a rival baseball circuit. Among the terms agreed upon in return for the cessation of Freedman hostilities upon fellow NL magnates in October 1899 was league reimbursement of the annual rent that Freedman paid for the Manhattan Field grounds. For years thereafter, first Freedman and then John T. Brush exacted an annual $10,000 tribute for the Manhattan Field rental fee from the NL.

223. The story was featured in Harriet's obituaries when she died in 1947. See, e.g., *St. Petersburg (Fla.) Evening Independent,* December 20, 1947; *Newsweek,* December 29, 1947; and *Time,* December 29, 1947. The snub was popularly attributed to Newport disdain of social climbers, but that seems improbable. The locals were parvenus, robber baron-types who acquired their money in the Gilded Age of the 1870s. But Harriet Coogan was a Gardiner, with a family fortune that dated from the reign of 17th century Stuart kings. Given turn-of-the-century religious antipathies, the Coogans' Catholicism is a more likely cause of their social rejection by the Newport swells.

224. See *New York Times,* May 11, 1911.

225. Provisions of the Polo Grounds lease are detailed by John Hogrogian in "The Polo Grounds Case: Part 1," *The Coffin Corner* 11, no. 6 (1989), and "The Polo Grounds Case, Part 2," *The Coffin Corner* 12, no. 1 (1990).

Early Polo Grounds
Players Who Homered There

ALAN COHEN

In 1881, several clubs, including squads from New York, Brooklyn, Washington, and Philadelphia, formed the Eastern Championship Association. The league struggled, with Washington relocating to Albany, New York, and only four teams finishing the season.

At that time, there was no major league baseball in New York, as the National League had dumped the original New York Mutuals after the 1876 season because they failed to complete their schedule. One of the more successful clubs in the Eastern Championship Association was the New York Metropolitans, who played at the original Polo Grounds. The field actually saw its first use in professional ball on September 29, 1880, when the independent Metropolitans competed against the Washington Nationals, another independent operation.[1] Five days later, in an exhibition game between the Metropolitans and Worcester (then in the National League), the park's inaugural home run was slugged by a player named Walker, most likely Oscar Walker, a first baseman.[2]

The Mets, in early 1880, had been formed by John B. Day and James Mutrie and scheduled most of their home games at the Union Grounds in Brooklyn. At that time, Brooklyn was a separate city and the Brooklyn Bridge had yet to be completed. Thus, Manhattan-based fans could get to the ballpark only via ferry. But John B. Day then learned of a location at 110th Street—property owned by James Gordon Bennett, Jr., of *New York Herald* fame—which, later that summer, became leased to the Metropolitans.[3]

In 1881, the Metropolitans played many of their games against Eastern Association teams. However, they scheduled 60 contests against National League opponents, going 18–42, and they also played games against college teams from Manhattan College, Princeton, and Yale.

The first minor league home run was hit at the Polo Grounds on July 20, 1881. The Metropolitans defeated the Brooklyn Atlantics, 12–8, banging out 14 hits. According to the *Brooklyn Eagle*, Lipman Pike of the Atlantics hit the only round-tripper.[4] However, the *New York Times*, in its coverage, mentioned two home runs by unspecified Met players and failed to mention the one by Pike.[5] An account in the *New York Clipper,* while shedding some light on the subject, left a question mark of sorts. It reported that there were three Met home runs—hit by Lou Say, Mike Muldoon, and Chief Roseman—and noted that Pike's blast came in the ninth inning.[6] But the article in the *New York Herald* set the record straight. The Mets won the coin flip and chose to bat first (this game was played

58

The Polo Grounds hosted many college games, including one between Yale and Princeton played there on Decoration Day (now Memorial Day) in 1882 (collection of Stew Thornley).

well before the home team got to hit last). Lou Say, in the first inning, hit a ball "into the bushes." Three batters later, Roseman connected for his home run, scoring Muldoon ahead of him as the Mets took a 4–0 lead. Muldoon's dinger came in the four-run seventh inning. Although the Atlantics cut the deficit to 12–8 in the ninth inning by virtue of Pike's homer, they could come no closer.[7] The next time the Mets hit three four-baggers in a game at the Polo Grounds would be on April 28, 1962.

Pike, who was at the end of his career, never played in the Polo Grounds as a major leaguer, but during his prime, he had been a home run king in the early days of the National Association, winning the first three titles. Although his combined long ball totals in those years was only 18, he did it in 140 games. His last homers in major league competition were hit in 1877 as a member of the Cincinnati team, where his four round-trippers in 58 games led the National League.

Say got his start in the National Association in 1873 and finished up in the majors in 1884, playing in parts of seven seasons. He had five home runs during his days in the majors, none of which came at the Polo Grounds. Muldoon played in the majors for five seasons, hitting ten four-baggers, none of which occurred at the Polo Grounds either.

James "Chief" Roseman went to the major leagues in 1882, joining Troy of the National League. Troy disbanded at the end of the season and Roseman signed on with the Metropolitans when they joined the American Association in 1883. He had 17 home runs during his major league career, and on July 19, 1884, hit the first of his four Polo Grounds big league blasts. It came off Bobby Mathews of Philadelphia. Roseman thus became the first player to homer in the same ballpark in the minors and the majors.

The next minor league home runs were hit at the Polo Grounds on July 22 by John

Doyle, also of the Metropolitans, and Roseman. Doyle played in three major league games, came to bat 11 times, and failed to go yard.

On July 29, there was a special exhibition—in effect, an "old-timers game." It was played to raise funds to support Dickey Pearce, a player who had started his career long before there was Organized Baseball. Pearce, in 1881, was umpiring and had officiated the first game of the season at the Union Grounds between the Atlantics of Brooklyn and the New Yorks of New York. He used the funds raised to open a bar in Brooklyn. Born in 1836, Pearce had starred with the amateur Brooklyn Atlantics beginning in 1856 (the game commemorated his 25th year in baseball) and played in the majors through 1877, finishing up with the St. Louis team in the National League. That season, Pearce was umpiring in the Eastern Championship Association, mostly in games held in Brooklyn. Other oldsters included Candy Nelson, Lipman Pike, Tommy Bond, Jack Manning, Jim Holdsworth, and Dick Hunt. Pike hit a three-run homer, the only four-bagger of the game, to break a 2–2 tie as the Veterans won, 6–2.

On the afternoon of August 2, the Mets played Boston of the National League and won the game, 9–3, hammering out 18 hits including a ninth-inning home run by Mike Muldoon.[8]

On August 25, the Boston National League team came for a visit and won, 8–2. Two of their players, Ross Barnes and Joe Hornung, each homered that day, both in the eighth inning.[9] Barnes was wrapping up his career, which had begun in 1871 with Boston in the National Association, while Hornung was in the early stages of his and would go on to hit 31 round-trippers in 12 seasons. His eight homers in 1883 were the second most in the National League and included one at the Polo Grounds on September 4 off Mickey Welch of the New York National League team.

On September 26, the Metropolitans and the Cleveland Blues of the National League played a game that was not particularly noteworthy for its outcome (Cleveland won, 8–6) but for the fact that the proceeds were used to benefit victims of fires that had devastated the state of Michigan.[10]

In 1882, the Metropolitans continued to entertain National League teams and formed a "league" with that other National League outcast, Philadelphia. The teams played approximately six times during the course of the season, and there is no record of any home runs being hit during those games.[11] Most of the Mets' games during 1882 were exhibitions against National League squads. In a contest against Troy on August 5, James "Tip" O'Neill homered in a 5–2 Met win.[12] He was, at the time, in his first season of professional ball, but he went up to the majors the following year and played there for ten seasons, spending most of them with the St. Louis Browns of the American Association. His best season, by far, was 1887 when he led the American Association in virtually every offensive category, batting .435 (if his average is adjusted to the current scoring rule that does not count walks as hits, as they were viewed in 1887), scoring 167 runs, and accumulating 52 doubles, 19 triples, 14 home runs, and 128 RBI. Of his 52 career major league homers, two were hit at the Polo Grounds.

On July 19, 1882, Worcester of the National league paid a visit to the Polo Grounds, and Harry Stovey hit a round-tripper for the visitors, who went on to win by a 12–6 count.[13] Stovey played in the major leagues for 14 years and led his league in four-baggers on five occasions. Of his 122 career home runs, two were slugged at the Polo Grounds.

In 1883, major league baseball returned to New York with two clubs. The Metropolitans joined the American Association and, following the resignation of Troy from the

National League, Mutrie, while still maintaining ownership of the Mets, signed the best of the Troy players and entered the National League with the New York team. In relatively short order, there came to be two fields at the 110th Street location. The original one (used since late in 1880) was the Southeast Diamond (aka Polo Grounds I). In May 1883, so as to accommodate the second team, a Southwest Diamond (aka Polo Grounds II) was installed. A canvas fence separated the fields if both were used at the same time.[14] On those occasions when both teams played, the first being Decoration Day, the Mets used the Southwest Diamond.

The Polo Grounds hosted an interesting exhibition in May 1883, when the Metropolitans featuring heavyweight boxing champion John L. Sullivan took the field against a local squad. Sullivan pitched that day, giving up 15 runs, but was credited with the victory as his squad won, 20–15. As a batter, Sullivan had four hits, including a double.[15]

The Mets moved to Metropolitan Park in 1884 but did not last the season there. Metropolitan Park, on the East River, was a temporary facility built on the grounds of an old city dump. A grand total of seven major league homers were hit there before the Mets moved back to the Polo Grounds later in the 1884 season and hosted the National League champion Providence team in a postseason championship series won by Providence.

Steve Brady, Thomas "Dude" Esterbrook, and Chief Roseman of the Metropolitans homered at the Polo Grounds as major leaguers in 1884, and Esterbrook also homered

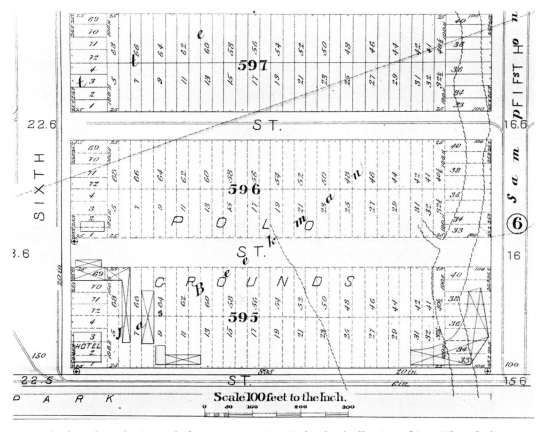

A look at the Polo Grounds from an 1884 New York atlas (collection of Stew Thornley).

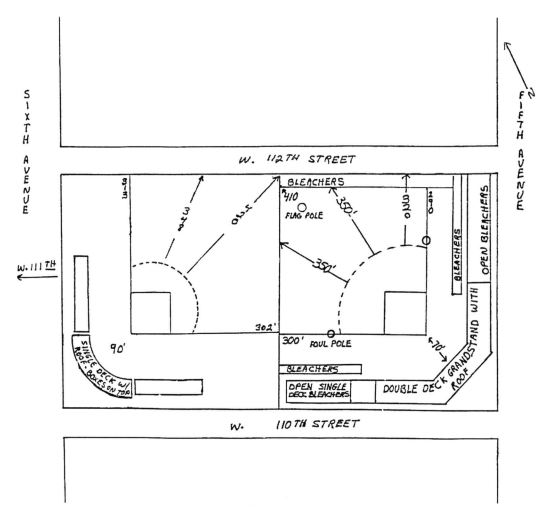

This diagram of the diamonds on the original Polo Grounds was drawn by stadium researcher Larry Zuckerman, who acknowledged that details of the east diamond, on the Fifth Avenue side, are approximate and the arrangement of the west diamond is speculative (although it is known that home plate on the west diamond was toward the southwest corner of the lot with right field to the east and left field to the north) (collection of Stew Thornley).

there three times while a member of the New York National League team in 1885 and 1886. All three men played in the minor leagues for the Mets in 1881 in the Eastern Championship Association, and in 1882, Brady and Esterbrook played with the Mets in the League Alliance.

The Mets moved back to the Polo Grounds during the latter part of the 1884 season and stayed there through 1885, the last season that they used the park. Prior to the 1885 season, owner Day put his best players on the Giants and replaced himself with Mutrie as field manager of the National League team, leading to the Mets finishing in seventh place. During the off-season, the Metropolitans were sold to Erastus Wiman, an entertainment impresario, who moved the Mets to St. George Cricket Grounds on Staten Island for the next two seasons.[16]

The 1888 Giants won the pennant and World Series in the final year of the original Polo Grounds (collection of Stew Thornley).

After the 1888 season, the Polo Grounds facility was knocked down to make way for the completion of a traffic grid, and the next iteration of the Polo Grounds was built near 155th Street, opening on July 8, 1889. While waiting for their new ballpark to be finished, the Giants played at the aforementioned St. George Cricket Club and Oakdale Park in Jersey City. In 1890, the Players League came into existence for one year and included a New York club, also known as the Giants. These Giants played at the fourth version of the Polo Grounds, which was called Brotherhood Park and was located adjacent to the National League ballpark (aka Polo Grounds III) and, after one season in the Players League, became the home of the National League's New York Giants. Following an April fire in 1911, the facility was rebuilt in a matter of weeks and continued to serve the Giants until they moved to San Francisco in 1958.

While waiting for their new building to open, the Giants played at the New York Highlanders' Hilltop Park. However, not long thereafter, the Highlanders, by then the Yankees, took up residence in the Polo Grounds and remained there from 1913 through 1922.

And one other club played at the Polo Grounds in those early years. In 1890, the Brooklyn Bridegrooms (later to become the Dodgers) bolted the American Association for the National League and were replaced in the American Association by an aggregation known as the Brooklyn Gladiators. The Gladiators were a wandering bunch who played at Ridgewood Park (which had been used on Sundays by the American Association club from 1886 through 1889), Polo Grounds III, and Long Island Grounds in Maspeth,

Fans watch the 1905 World Series from the outfield (collection of Stew Thornley).

Queens. But before the end of the season, the Gladiators were without a home and folded their operation.

NOTES

1. John J. O'Malley, "The Mets Open in New York," *Baseball Research Journal* (1980).
2. *New York Times*, October 5, 1880.
3. Noel Hynd, *The Giants of the Polo Grounds* (New York: Doubleday, 1988), 23.
4. *Brooklyn Eagle*, July 21, 1881.
5. *New York Times*, July 21, 1881.
6. *New York Clipper*, July 30, 1881.
7. *New York Herald*, July 21, 1881.
8. *New York Times*, August 3, 1881.
9. *New York Times*, August 26, 1881.
10. *New York Times*, September 26, 1881.
11. *Truth* (New York), September 10, 1882.
12. *New York Herald*, August 6, 1882.
13. *New York Herald*, July 20, 1882.
14. Hynd, 26.
15. *New York Times*, May 29, 1883.
16. Hynd, 38.

Next Stop—Cooperstown

TOM EDWARDS

From the day the New York Giants opened the Polo Grounds on June 28, 1911, until the Mets played the last major league game there on September 18, 1963, there was never a shortage of players, managers, and coaches in the dugouts and umpires on the field bound for the Hall of Fame. In the early years of the iconic ballpark, Giant manager John McGraw had the names Christy Mathewson, Rube Marquard, George "High Pockets" Kelly, and Frankie "The Fordham Flash" Frisch on lineup cards that kept the team competitive. With the Brooklyn Dodgers a long throw from his club's home field, McGraw knew having these stars on the roster of a talented team would be a necessity if he was going to keep the turnstiles spinning at the park on Coogan's Bluff.

On April 17, 1913, the New York Yankees, having left Hilltop Park, became Polo Grounds tenants, making it a two-league venue. During their first 17 years in the American League, the Yankees, known as the Highlanders from 1903 through 1912, did not offer much competition for the rest of the league. But after the 1919 season, that changed with what many consider the biggest deal in baseball history. "The Curse of the Bambino" became a reality when the Red Sox sold George "Babe" Ruth to the Yankees.

The impact the Babe had on the Yankees' attendance, at home and on the road, was significant. Ruth finished the 154-game 1920 season with 54 home runs. The following season, he upped his major league record to an unheard of 59 home runs. Babe Ruth,

John McGraw was the long-time manager of the New York Giants (collection of Stew Thornley).

the New York Yankees, and the Polo Grounds were a perfect fit.

The 1921 and 1922 World Series featured the Giants and the Yankees, which made travel arrangements easy. The National League team earned a World Series championship both years, but John McGraw, having grown tired of the Giants coming in second place in attendance in his own park, made sure 1922 would be the Yankees last season with the Polo Grounds as their home field.

Although the Polo Grounds went back to being a one-team ballpark, the impressive stream of Hall of Fame players that took the field did not slow down. During the Roaring Twenties, John McGraw saw Carl Hubbell, Travis Jackson, Freddie Lindstrom, Ross Mel Ott, Bill Terry, and Ross Youngs in his dugout. With the players other National League teams had on their rosters, the Giants needed all of the top-shelf talent they could get. At that time,

Babe Ruth was well suited to the Polo Grounds. He hit 54 home runs in 1920 and 59 home runs the following season with the Polo Grounds as his home park (collection of Stew Thornley).

the Cubs featured Grover Cleveland Alexander, Kiki Cuyler, Gabby Hartnett, and Hack Wilson. The St. Louis Cardinals were establishing themselves as a club that would give opponents a lot to think about with lineups containing Sunny Jim Bottomley, Chick Hafey, Jesse Haines, and Rogers Hornsby.

Fortunately for the Giants in the 1930s, future Hall of Famers Carl Hubbell, Travis Jackson, Freddy Lindstrom, Mel Ott, and Bill Terry were still taking the field at the Polo Grounds for the home team. When the Pittsburgh Pirates were the visiting team, the New Yorkers had to contend with Heinie Manush, Arky Vaughan, and Lloyd and Paul Waner. It did not get any easier when St. Louis was in town. In the early part of the decade, Jim Bottomley and Chick Hafey were still wearing Cardinal uniforms, and later, Leo Durocher and Enos "Country" Slaughter had been added to the Redbird roster. During the 1930s, the Giants and Cardinals each represented the National League in the World Series three times, and at the Polo Grounds on July 2, 1933, Carl Hubbell pitched 18 innings in a 1–0 win over the Cardinals.

On July 10, 1934, the Polo Grounds became the first National League park to host the All-Star Game. Joe Cronin was the American League manager, and Bill Terry was the National League skipper. Lefty Gomez of the Yankees was the starting pitcher for the American League, with Giant ace Carl Hubbell starting for the senior circuit. Leading off for the American League was Charlie Gehringer, who hit a single. He went to second on an outfield error. Heinie Manush batted second and drew a walk. From there, Hubbell struck out Babe Ruth, Lou Gehrig, and Jimmie Foxx to end the top half of the first inning. The screwball-throwing "King Carl" opened the second inning by fanning Al Simmons and Joe Cronin, which gave him five consecutive strikeouts of players who have a plaque in Cooperstown. The game featured a double steal with Pie Traynor crossing the plate and Mel Ott moving to second, but the American League prevailed by the score of 9–7. The contest was played in two hours and 44 minutes despite the 16 runs, with the National League hitting the only home runs: a solo shot by Frankie Frisch and a three-run blast by Joe Medwick. A crowd of 48,363 saw nine future Hall of Famers starting for the American League and eight for its opponent. It remains one of the classic All-Star Games in baseball history.

On August 1, 1945, at the Polo Grounds, Mel Ott hit his 500th career home run, an amazing and still impressive career accomplishment. The 1940s also witnessed the breaking of the color barrier when Branch Rickey, the Brooklyn Dodgers' president and general manager, signed Jackie Robinson of the Negro American League Kansas City Monarchs.

The Giants integrated, too, and signed a future Hall of Famer: Monte Irvin from the Newark Eagles of the Negro National League. Irvin became part of a team that, during the 1940s, had Ernie Lombardi, Johnny Mize, Mel Ott, and an apparently ageless Carl Hubbell. As was the case with each decade since it opened, the Polo Grounds saw an impressive number of Hall of Fame players leaving the visitors' clubhouse. Billy Herman, Ralph Kiner, Chuck Klein, Stan Musial, and Warren Spahn all played there.

During the 1950s, a number of Hall of Famers played one or more games at the Polo Grounds, including, among others: Hank Aaron, Yogi Berra, Roy Campanella, Joe DiMaggio, Don Drysdale, Monte Irvin, Ralph Kiner, Sandy Koufax, Eddie Mathews, Willie Mays, Johnny Mize, Pee Wee Reese, Phil Rizzuto, Jackie Robinson, Red Schoendienst, Enos Slaughter, Duke Snider, Warren Spahn, and Hoyt Wilhelm. The 1951 season saw the Dodgers establishing a 13½-game lead in August, with Dodger-Yankee World Series programs being printed. But the Giants did not get the memo. They finished the scheduled season with a seven-game winning streak, including a final weekend sweep of the Braves in Boston. On the train home to New York, they got the news that the Dodgers had also won, leaving the teams tied and setting up a best-of-three playoff, which culminated with Bobby Thomson's three-run game-winning homer in the bottom of the ninth of the final contest. An amazing finish to an unforgettable season, it is easily one of the most dramatic moments in Polo Grounds, and baseball, history. The win earned the Giants their sixth World Series matchup with the nearby Yankees.

The 1954 World Series is remembered for a play many consider one of the greatest catches of all time. In the first game, at the Polo Grounds, Vic Wertz of Cleveland hit a shot to deep centerfield. At the crack of the bat, Willie Mays raced back and made an over-the-shoulder catch that is still hard to believe.

Prior to the arrival of the New York Mets, major league baseball had not been played at the Polo Grounds since the final out of the Giants' last home game of the 1957 season. Through that time, only two home runs had been hit into the center field bleachers. Luke Easter did it in a 1948 Negro League game, and Joe Adcock followed that blast five years later for the Milwaukee Braves. During the Mets' inaugural season, Lou Brock did it on June 17, 1962, for the Chicago Cubs, and the very next day, Hank Aaron became the second Braves player to accomplish the feat.

Even the Mets' two years at the Polo Grounds continued the tradition of people bound for Cooperstown. Casey Stengel was the manager then, and Richie Ashburn and Duke Snider were members of the '62 and '63 teams, respectively. Visitors to the Polo Grounds in 1962–1963 included many of the future Hall of Famers who had competed against the New York Giants as well as players such as Lou Brock, Orlando Cepeda, Bob Gibson, Juan Marichal, Willie McCovey, and Ron Santo.

Umpires with careers that earned them a plaque in Cooperstown added to the mix of legendary baseball figures that took the field at the Polo Grounds.

On April 24, 1901, Tom Connolly was the plate umpire in Chicago for the first American League game ever played, and he umpired in the first World Series in 1903. His on-field activity ended at the conclusion of the 1931 season, with the exception of one game that he officiated in 1932. American League president and future Hall of Fame member Will Harridge selected Connolly as the league's first supervisor of umpires, a position he held until 1954. Although most of his career was in the junior circuit, Connolly officiated in the National League from 1898 through part of 1900 and worked games at the previous version of the Polo Grounds. He also umpired at the Polo Grounds in the World Series in 1911, 1913, and 1924.

After 37 seasons of calling balls and strikes and making out and safe calls in the National League, Bill Klem retired at the end of the 1941 season. The most famous of all umpires, Klem worked 18 World Series, including six played in part at the Polo Grounds.

At the age of 22 in 1906, Billy Evans became the youngest umpire in major league history and officiated in the American League through 1927. He made the calls in the Polo Grounds in the 1912, 1917, and 1923 World Series.

Jocko Conlan did not plan on an umpiring career. An outfielder with the Chicago White Sox, he filled in for umpire Red Ormsby, who had been overcome by the heat during a 1935 series between the Pale Hose and the St. Louis Browns. Conlan began his umpiring career in the minors the following year and debuted in the National League in 1941. He retired in 1964 but returned as a substitute umpire for 17 games in 1965.

Al Barlick became a National League umpire in 1940 at the age of 25 and retired after the 1971 season.

Doug Harvey umpired in the National League from 1962 to 1992 and had such an air of authority that his nickname was "God."

Hank O'Day is the most recent umpire to be inducted into the Hall of Fame, posthumously in 2013. He had played for the New York Giants in 1889 and 1890, and he managed in the National League 1912 and 1914, amid an umpiring career that extended from 1884 to 1927. He was the umpire making the call in one of the most memorable games ever at the Polo Grounds on September 23, 1908, the "Merkle's boner" event.

By the Numbers
The Five Polo Grounds Ballparks

RON SELTER

There were five major league ballparks called the Polo Grounds in New York City, starting in 1883 and ending in 1964. They were (1) Polo Grounds I, 1883–1888; (2) Polo Grounds II, 1883 (same site as Polo Grounds I but two different diamonds); (3) Polo Grounds III 1889–1890; (4) Polo Grounds IV, 1891–April 1911; and (5) Polo Grounds V, 1911–1964. Polo Grounds I and II were located in midtown Manhattan, while Polo Grounds III, IV, and V could be found at the far north end of Manhattan very close to the Harlem River. In addition, St. George Grounds was used by the National League (NL) Giants for the first half of the 1889 season during the time that Polo Grounds III was being built.

The New York National League team in the 19th century became known as the Giants. In addition, there was a New York franchise in the 1890 Players League (PL) also called the Giants that built the ballpark that became Polo Grounds IV. That meant there were two major league teams called the New York Giants in New York that season.

A restriction that affected games at all five Polo Grounds was the prohibition of professional baseball on Sundays due to a New York State law, a prohibition that was not lifted until April 1919. A result of this prohibition was the frequent scheduling of doubleheaders on Saturdays, which involved one game in the morning and one game in the afternoon.

Polo Grounds I and II

These two ballparks were located on the same site at Sixth Avenue and 110th Street just north of Central Park at Douglas Circle in midtown Manhattan. Polo Grounds I was built on the southeast portion of the site and was known as the Southeast Diamond, while Polo Grounds II was located in the southwest portion of the site and was known as the Southwest Diamond. The first park was used by the American Association (AA) New York Metropolitans in 1883 and 1884, the National League New York club from 1883 to the end of the 1888 season, and the National Colored League New York Gothams in 1887, as the venue for the Dauvray Cup World Series game between the NL Detroit Wolverines and the AA St. Louis Browns held on October 15, 1887, and for three games

69

of the Dauvray Cup in 1888, when the NL New York Giants opposed the defending AA pennant-winning Browns. Polo Grounds II was used for only about a dozen games in 1883 when other games were being played at the Southeast Diamond, and both parks were used by the Metropolitans during that same year.

Prior to 1886, at both Polo Grounds I and II, there were no fences. It was 180 feet to where small flags marked the foul lines, but this did not mean that it was 180 feet to where a player needed to hit it over the fence for a home run because there was no fence before Opening Day 1886. Starting with the 1886 season, there was a short fence in front of the right field bleachers and another ten-foot-high canvas barrier between the two outfields. Balls rolling under the canvas fence of Polo Grounds I were in play, so outfielders crawled under the fence and then threw the ball over the fence back to the infield.

The site of Polo Grounds I and II had been owned by James Gordon Bennett, publisher of the *New York Herald*, and had been formerly used as a polo field (thus the ballpark's name) by the Westchester Polo Association. The Southeast Diamond opened for baseball use September 29, 1880, with a seating capacity of 12,000, though a second deck of seats was added before the 1883 season. There was a large flagpole in short center field, with a flag saying New York, and there were two diamonds here. The National League and American Association clubs both used the Southeast Diamond until the Southwest Diamond was completed on May 30, 1883. However, the Southwest Diamond, built on top of stinky garbage, was so smelly that the Metropolitans always preferred playing on the Southeast Diamond and would do so whenever they could. In 1883, the Metropolitans played 13 home games at the Southwest Diamond on days when the National League team was playing at the Southeast Diamond and 34 games at the Southeast Diamond on days when the National League team was not scheduled there.

In 1884, the Metropolitans moved to a different ballpark, one not far away on the East River. The following year, the two clubs played all their home games at the Southeast Diamond, with one team playing in the morning and the other in the afternoon on the

The Polo Grounds in 1888, the final year of the original version (collection of Stew Thornley).

A drawing of the original Polo Grounds in the 1880s (collection of Fred Buckland).

days when both clubs were scheduled for games. But this practice ended when the ball-parks burned down in the spring of 1889.

However, even before the fire that destroyed Polo Grounds I and II, the Giants had decided to move after the 1888 season because the city of New York was going to extend 111th Street through the original Polo Grounds (both I and II) site, which would seriously interfere with the playing of baseball. After starting the 1889 season with two games in Jersey City, New Jersey, the NL Giants played at St. George Grounds, a ball-park located in the then separate city of Staten Island, New York, from April 29 to June 14. But they left St. George Grounds and moved to a new park—Polo Grounds III—on July 8.

Polo Grounds I was a below average ballpark for offense in both the National League and the American Association as reflected in runs scored and home runs per game. It appears from a single photo of the park that Polo Grounds I was a relatively small ballpark. Very little is known about the park's dimensions. Therefore, it is not possible to say why the ballpark was moderately below average in runs scored and far below average in home runs per game. The known batting park factors are shown below.

Table 1. Batting Park Factors at Polo Grounds I*

	Runs	Home Runs
1883–1888 National League	92	71
1883–1885 American Association	86	53

* A batting park factor of 100 means a league average ballpark for that time period; a park factor noticeably above 100 means a hitter's park; and a batting park factor noticeably less than 100 means the ballpark favored pitchers.

Polo Grounds III

The next ballpark to be called the Polo Grounds—number III—was generally called Manhattan Field and was located at 155th Street and Eighth Avenue on the northern end of the island of Manhattan. The Giants called the site the New Polo Grounds. Why, if polo was never played at this site, was the ballpark called the New Polo Grounds? Well, the ballpark was new and the Giants wanted fans to know the same team that had played at the original Polo Grounds in midtown Manhattan would be playing at a new site. Later, the "New" portion of the park's name was dropped. The park site and playing field were both narrow and oddly shaped—sort of like a squared-off pear.

The NL Giants played one-and-a-half seasons in this ballpark. In addition to the Giants, the park was used by the American Association Brooklyn Gladiators on June 9 and from July 23 to August 2, 1890. The field was located near the northern tip of Manhattan Island in the southern portion of a low-lying area called Coogan's Hollow. On the north and northeast, behind center field, was the 157th Street alley, then Brotherhood Park, which was used by the Players League for the 1890 season. Home plate and the grandstand were located in the south-southeast part of the park site near the corner of Eighth Avenue and 155th Street. To the west-northwest, on the third base side, was 155th Street, then Coogan's Bluff, where freeloading fans gathered to watch games. On the east, the first base side, and slightly to the southeast was Eighth Avenue.

The grandstand ran from past third base to beyond first base. There were bleachers down both foul lines and a long stretch of outfield bleachers. These shallow wooden outfield stands were situated roughly perpendicular to the home plate-center field axis and ran from about straightaway right field to straightaway left field. At the back of these stands was a wooden fence some 25 feet high on which were mounted advertising billboards. Down in the right field corner was an in-play two-story clubhouse. Later, in 1904, this clubhouse was disassembled and moved to the next-door Polo Grounds IV, where it was reassembled. Relatively far from home plate were uncovered stands in fair territory in left field. According to references in the NL Giants game accounts, these stands were free seats. This ballpark had the steepest and largest embankment ever in major league history, in both center and right fields. On September 14, 1889, Cap Anson of Chicago got an inside-the-park home run when Giant center fielder George Gore could not climb the muddy embankment. The first over-the-fence home run at the park was hit by the Giants' Roger Connor on July 10, 1889. This home run cleared the center field fence, the bleachers, and the 25-foot-high fence at the back of the bleachers by ten feet. This was considered a remarkable feat at the time and went a total estimated distance of 360 feet. During the 1889 season, any player hitting a home run over the center field bleachers was awarded a $100 cash prize.

A large portion of the embankment in right field and center field was removed after the 1889 season and the center field fence was moved back about 40 feet. What remained was a sloping embankment in front of the left field-center field-right field fence. The dirt from the cut-down portion of the embankment was used to fill in the low-lying sections of the outfield (in 1889, flooding in the outfield had been a recurring problem). At the same time, the left field fence was moved back about 35–40 feet. The seating capacity of the ballpark was about 15,000, of which approximately 5,000 was in the grandstand.

Table 2. Dimensions: Polo Grounds III

Years	LF	SLF	LC	CF	RC	SRF	RF
1889	345	367	367	315	315	325	320
1890	375	407	372	346	346	359	336

LF: Left field at the foul pole
SLF: Straightaway left field at 15 degrees off the foul line
LC: Left-center at 30 degrees off the foul line
CF: Center field, meaning dead center
RC: Right-center at 30 degrees off the foul line
SRF: Straightaway right field at 15 degrees off the foul line
RF: Right field at the foul pole

Table 3. Average Outfield Distances: Polo Grounds III

Years	LF	CF	RF	Composite
1889	362	340	335	346
1890	394	364	354	374

Table 4. Fence Heights

Years	LF	CF	RF
1889	6	6	6
1890	6	6	6

The left and right field fences consisted of canvas on posts from the foul lines to the ends of the outfield bleachers. At the front of the outfield bleachers was a wooden fence topped by a short screen.

Table 5. Home Runs by Type at Polo Grounds III

Years	Total	OTF	Bounce	IP	Estimated
1889*	18	14	4	4	0
1890	10	4	0	6	0

* Park opened in July and was used until the end of the season in September
OTF: Over-the-fence (includes bounce)
Bounce: Bounce home runs
IP: Inside-the-park home runs

Table 6. Over-the-Fence Home Runs by Field at Polo Grounds III (Excluding Bounce)

Years	Total	LF	CF	RF	Unknown
1889*	10	3	3	4	0
1890	4	1	1	2	0

* July–September

Table 7. Inside-the-Park Home Runs by Field at Polo Grounds III

Years	Total	LF	LC	CF	RC	RF	Unknown
1889*	4	1	0	1	0	2	0
1890	6	2	0	0	0	4	0

* July–September

Table 8. Batting Park Factors at Polo Grounds III

Years	Runs	HR
1889–1890	91	54

This ballpark was 9 percent below the league average ballpark in runs scored per game. In the year and a half that the ballpark was used by the NL, only 28 home runs were hit, a rate per game that amounted to roughly one-half of the NL rate for 1889–1890. Of these 28 home runs, the home-team Giants accounted for 20 of them. It would appear that the Giants' sluggers Roger Connor and Buck Ewing in 1889 and Mike Tiernan in 1890 were the reasons for the disproportionate share of homers.

Polo Grounds IV

Before the 1890 season, the short-lived Players League built a new ballpark (initially called Brotherhood Park) for the New York PL franchise on the parcel of land immediately north of and adjacent to Manhattan Field (Polo Grounds III). Later the ballpark's name was changed to the Polo Grounds when the NL Giants moved in. Polo Grounds IV was located at Eighth Avenue, West 159th Street, Bridge Park, and West 157th Street. This site was in the northern part of Coogan's Hollow below Coogan's Bluff and was adjacent to and just north of Polo Grounds III. The field of Polo Grounds IV had severe drainage problems, perhaps related to the location having been shown on an 1874 map as underneath the Hudson River, but the park site had been filled in with dirt in the late 1870s. Brotherhood Park, when it opened in April 1890 was, by the standards of the day, of an almost normal size and shape, with the dimensions being 335 in left field, 400 in center field, and 335 in right field.

The Players League New York team was also called the Giants, and their ballpark was named Brotherhood Park, as the organizer of the Players League was the Brotherhood of Professional Base Ball Players. The PL New York Giants that played at Brotherhood Park proved to be far more popular than the NL Giants, who played next door at Polo Grounds III. While the Players League was a success in New York City (the PL outdrew the NL in the Big Apple by better than three to one), the league as a whole agreed to a treaty of sorts with the NL after the 1890 season and ended its operation.

Subsequently, the NL Giants moved from Manhattan Field to what had been called Brotherhood Park for the 1891 season. With not even a trace of originality, the Giants

Polo Grounds IV in October 1910 in a New York City Series game between the Giants and the Highlanders. The double-deck grandstand ends just before the left field corner, though on the other side, the grandstand extends into fair territory in right field (collection of Ron Selter).

renamed the ballpark the New Polo Grounds. This park (Polo Grounds IV; the "New" was soon dropped from the name) and the subsequent one (Polo Grounds V) on this same site were the two ballparks most usually associated with the name Polo Grounds. Also, it should be noted that, contrary to the park's name, polo was never played there.

Midway through the 1890 season, the ballpark had been modified and the foul line distances substantially reduced (335 to 277 for left field and 335 to 258 for right field). As a result, the park acquired its later-to-be-famous horseshoe configuration before it ever became the home of the NL New York Giants.

When it opened in 1890, Polo Grounds IV had a seating structure that consisted of a double-decked wooden grandstand that extended from about third base to about first base and four sets of bleachers: one down the left field line, one down the right field line, one in fair territory in left field, and another in fair territory in right field. There was a clubhouse in straightaway left field and the scoreboard was located in right field near right-center.

After July 1, 1890, Polo Grounds IV was characterized by two distinctive configura-

Polo Grounds IV in the early part of the 1908 season in a photograph taken from the left field end of the grandstand. The left field bleachers and the flagpole in center field are visible. Note all the straw hats and the small section of bleachers in center field. During the second half of the 1908 season, more bleachers were added to fill the entirety of center field (collection of Ron Selter).

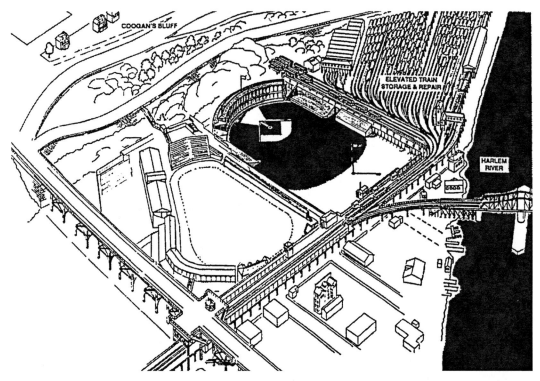

The drawing shows Polo Grounds III and IV. Both stadiums were used during the 1890 season (collection of Stew Thornley).

tion features: the left field and right field stands near the foul lines were parallel to each other and each formed a 135-degree angle with their respective foul lines, and much of the outfield "fence" consisted of ropes on three-foot posts. This portion of the outfield fence extended from the right end of the left field bleachers in roughly straightaway left field near the clubhouse around all of center field to nearly the right field foul line. The clubhouse in left field and the scoreboard in right field were both located behind the ropes. On the other side of the roped off area in center field, carriages were allowed to park, and the occupants of the carriages could watch the game. This curious situation in center field amounted to a bring-your-own-seat arrangement.

At the Polo Grounds IV ballpark, the foul-line dimensions for the 1890s (starting July 1, 1890) were 277 in left field and 258 in right field. The dimensions in the 1890s for left-center, center field, and right-center are more uncertain, but they are known in 1901 and are confirmed by numerous ballpark photos from 1901 to 1908. These dimensions, which were in place at least by 1901 and most likely earlier, were left-center 445, center field 500, and right-center 450.

The home run data in the park's early years throws some light on what the likely dimensions in the 1890s were. During the 1893 season, there were seven over-the-fence home runs to right- or left-center and center field, but during the next season, there were only two OTF home runs hit to center field. In the 1895 season, there were again two OTF home runs hit to center field, while in the next five seasons (1896–1900), center field saw no OTF round-trippers. From this home run evidence, the author concluded that the left-center, center field, and right-center dimensions were markedly increased after the 1895 season. This was a simple feat to accomplish. All the Giants had to do was move the outfield ropes on posts in left-center, right-center, and center field farther back. The new dimensions were estimated to have been the same as in 1901: left-center 445, center field 500, and right-center 450. It is the author's conclusion that the purpose of moving the fence back in left-center, center field, and right-center was to reduce the number of balls hit over or under the ropes that led to a number of in-game disputes.

The effects of these funny fences consisting of ropes on posts in combination with the then existing Blocked Ball Rule were substantial and invited controversy. First, an explanation of the Blocked Ball Rule (Rule 36 from the 1902 Reach Guide), which reads as follows: "A [b]lock is a batted or thrown ball that is touched, stopped, or handled by any person not engaged in the game. Whenever a [b]lock occurs, the umpire shall declare it and the base runners may run the bases without being put out until the ball is returned to and held by the pitcher standing in his position."[1]

Here are some examples of incidents that occurred at the Polo Grounds in the 1890s involving the Blocked Ball Rule and the ropes-on-posts fence:

- May 9, 1893: a home run by George Haddock of Brooklyn where a ball was hit over the ropes in right, and Haddock was awarded a home run on the basis of the Blocked Ball Rule.
- July 19, 1894: Duke Farrell of New York hit a ball that rolled under the ropes in right field and then behind the scoreboard for a bounce home run.
- August 18, 1894: Bill Lange of the Chicago Colts hit a ball into the overflow crowd in right field. The ball was quickly returned to the field (probably with the help of a Giant fan), and Lange was out at home while trying for an inside-the-park home run.
- August 20, 1894: the Giants' Mike Tiernan hit a ball to center field that went into the overflow crowd. The ball kicked back to the Colts' center fielder (Bill Lange) and was returned to the infield. Tiernan was held at third with a triple due to some poor coaching because the ball had not yet been returned to the pitcher as required by the rules.
- August 30, 1894: Eddie Burke of the Giants hit beyond the ropes in right field but had to settle for a triple as the ball was quickly returned to the field.
- June 21, 1895: another ball struck by Eddie Burke to left field hit an on-field policeman and was ruled a bounce home run.
- August 19, 1896: visiting Chicago Colt manager Cap Anson refused to accept a ground rule for that day's game that made hits over the ropes home runs. During the game, Mike Tiernan of the Giants whacked a ball over the right field ropes into the overflow crowd. The ball was handled by an out-of-uniform Colt player in the crowd, who fumbled the ball in attempting to return it to the field. A Giant fan in the overflow crowd then picked up the ball. The Colt player tussled with the fan, retrieved the ball, and threw it to the Colts' right fielder, who returned it to the infield, and Tiernan wisely stopped at third.

Because of these and other incidents involving the ropes-on-posts fence and the Blocked Ball Rule, the Giants, late in the 1896 season, established a park ground rule that made all balls hit over the ropes home runs, while balls hit under the ropes could continue to be returned to play (subject to the Blocked Ball Rule). For the 1897 season, this ground rule was modified to make all balls hit over or under the ropes home runs.

At the time that the Temple Cup was played after the 1894 season, the grandstand had been extended to points halfway between first base and third base and the foul poles. Before the 1904 season, the wooden bleachers in the fair area in left field were torn down and rebuilt with no additional seating. At the same time, the right field bleachers were extended further towards right-center, which resulted in an increase in the capacity of this section from 4,000 to 6,000, and the two-story clubhouse from Manhattan Field was disassembled and moved to Polo Grounds IV. This new clubhouse was located behind the ropes in right-center. By the 1905 season, the grandstand had been extended down the left field and right field lines about two-thirds of the distance to the foul poles. This expansion increased the capacity of the ballpark to 22,000. During the 1908 season, the grandstand was extended in left field and right field to the foul poles and additional bleachers built in left-center, center field and right-center, which caused the capacity to reach 26,000 by July 1908 and 28,500 by October of that year. Before the 1910 season, the final expansion of the ballpark occurred when the double-deck wooden grandstand was extended into fair territory in right field, replacing a portion of the bleachers in right.

Polo Grounds IV, like all of the prior Polo Grounds ballparks, was built of wood. But as Boy Scouts already knew, and baseball owners of that era were slow to learn, wooden structures burn. Only two games into the 1911 season, disaster struck early in the morning of April 14. A fire broke out that destroyed the entire wooden grandstand and a small portion of the wooden right field bleachers near the right field end of the grandstand. Early press reports (the morning papers of April 14) of the ballpark being completely destroyed were exaggerations. Actually about 90 percent of the outfield bleachers survived the fire. Specifically, nearly all of the right field bleachers, all of the left field and center field bleachers, and the clubhouse/office building survived. These last structures were separated by gaps from the burning grandstand. The Giants moved, in a manner of speaking, in with their neighbors—the American League (AL) Yankees—and played the next three month of their 1911 schedule at nearby Hilltop Park. The Polo

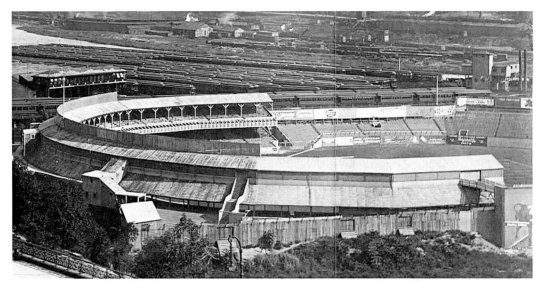

The Polo Grounds that was destroyed by fire in 1911 (shown above) had the same shape as the one that replaced it (collection of Stew Thornley).

Grounds grandstand and the right field bleachers were rebuilt during the 1911 season in steel and concrete, becoming the Classic ballpark Polo Grounds V.

The Basis of Polo Grounds IV's Configurations and Dimensions

When the ballpark opened in April 1890, it had rather conventional, for the 1890s, dimensions as shown below. In the middle of the 1890 season, substantial changes were made in the park's dimensions when the left field distance was reduced to 277 feet and the right field distance to 258 feet. During the remaining life of the ballpark (1890–1910), the configuration of the stands and playing field changed a number of times. From photos of the ballpark, it was determined that the wooden double-deck grandstand was extended at least twice. Based on home run research, it is known that the fair area right field bleachers were in place during the 1890 season and the left field bleachers by the 1892 season. In 1904, the grandstand extended only a short ways past the infield, and the fair area right field bleachers were expanded for the 1907 season.[2] During the 1908 season, both the grandstand and the outfield bleachers were expanded. So, by October 1908, the double-deck wooden grandstand now extended to the foul poles. Then, before the 1910 season, the portion of the right field bleachers adjacent to the right field corner were dismantled and replaced by an extension of the double-deck wooden grandstand into fair territory in right field.

The dimensions of the playing field were based on three principal sources: the book *Green Cathedrals*,[3] an 1893 Sanborn Fire Insurance Co. map,[4] and a 1909 Sanborn Fire Insurance Co.[5] map. The dimensions for Polo Grounds IV were left field: 277, center field: 400, and right field: 258, as of July 1890. These dimensions remained unchanged until 1896 when the ropes-on-posts portion of the outfield fence was moved back in left-center, right-center, and center field. The dead center field dimension became an awesome 500 feet. Game accounts and park photos were used to determine the extent of the ropes-on-posts center field fence and when it was removed in 1908 to permit the construction of more outfield bleachers.

At about the midpoint of the 1908 season, the building of additional sets of outfield bleachers reduced the center field dimension from 500 to 433. Photos of the ballpark were used to modify the single-segment center field fence shown on the 1909 Sanborn map, as the photos showed the actual alignment of the fence to have consisted of three segments. The middle center field segment was a diagonal that was perpendicular to the home plate-center field axis that was the same alignment as shown on the 1909 map. On both sides of this middle center field segment were sections that angled towards left-center and right-center respectively. The dimensions derived from the scale used on the Sanborn map were consistent with the 1909 listed dimensions in *Green Cathedrals*. This meant the deepest points in the ballpark (left- and right-center) were not as great as shown on the 1909 Sanborn map. That map was modified to produce a ballpark diagram for midseason 1908–1910. All subsequent ballpark dimensions for midseason 1908–1910 were derived from this diagram. From research into home runs hit at the Polo Grounds, it was learned there were home runs hit over or under the ropes in the outfield in every season from 1896 to midseason 1908.[6]

Table 9. Dimensions

Years	LF	SLF	LC	CF	RC	SRF	RF
April–June 1890	335	362	375	400	365	338	335
July 1890–1895	277	362	375	400	365	338	258
1896–June 1908	277	381	445	500	450	359	258
July 1908–1910*	277	377	445	433	404	348	258

* In addition, the ballpark was used for two regular-season games in 1911 before the fire of April 14.

Table 10. Fence Heights

Years	LF	CF	RF
April–June 1890	0–35*	0–3**	0–6***
July 1890–1895	0–4	0–3**	0–6
1896–June 1908	0–25	0–3	0–15
July 1908–1910	10	8	8

* The 35-foot-high portion was the section nearest the foul pole; the rest of left field was zero-three.

** The zero-three-foot heights were the outfield sections with the ropes on posts.

*** The six-foot-high section was canvas on posts from the foul area right field bleachers into fair right field.

Table 11. Average Outfield Distances

Years	LF	CF	RF	Composite
April–June 1890	360	385	344	363
July 1890–1895	349	385	325	353
1896–June 1908	370	474	359	401
July 1908–1910	370	434	356	387

Capacity: 16,000 (1890), 18,000 (1894), 20,000 (1904), 22,000 (1905), 26,000 (July 1908), 28,500 (October 1908), 30,000 (1910)
Park site area: 7.4 acres
Deadball Era run factor (1901–1910): 100 (Rank: NL 8)

The Impact of the Park's Configurations and Dimensions on Batting

In the park's early years (1890–1895) Polo Grounds IV was a slightly below-average park for runs scored (runs batting park factor was 98) but noticeably above average for home runs (park factor 126). Another surprising finding: despite the huge distances in left- and right-center (both more than 440 feet in 1895–1908), the Polo Grounds IV was a below-average park for triples as shown by the triples park factor (82 for 1901–1908 and 89 for 1908–1910). This can be explained because of the ballpark's unique configuration. Since the park had such short dimensions in both the left field and right field corners, teams played their corner outfielders more towards center field which cut down on triples and inside-the-park home runs (IPHR). The scarcity of IPHR to left field and left-center at the Polo Grounds after 1900 (only 3.2 per season in 1901–1910), is difficult to understand. The average left field distance was greater than the average right field distance at the park, yet IPHR were far more numerous to right field/right-center than to left field/left-center. The data on home runs and batting park factors for Polo Grounds IV are shown below in five tables.

Table 12. Home Runs by Type at Polo Grounds IV

Years	Total	OTF	Bounce	IP	Estimated
1890–1892	137	46	6	91	20
1893–1895	138	67	12	73	5
1896–1900	122	99	12	23	1
1901-E 1908	213	130	50	88	3
L 1908–1910	97	37	3	60	0

E 1908: April–June
L 1908: July–October
Bounce: Bounce home runs
IP: Inside the park
OTF: Over the fence (includes bounce)

Table 13. Over-the-Fence Home Runs by Field at Polo Grounds IV (Excluding Bounce)

Years	Total	LF	CF	RF	Unknown
1890–1892	40	7	0	12	21
1893–1895	55	12	7	30	6
1896–1900	87	29	0	55	3
1901-E 1908	80	12	0	65	3
L 1908–1910	34	16	0	17	1

Table 14. Inside-the-Park Home Runs by Field at Polo Grounds IV

Years	Total	LF	LC	CF	RC	RF	Unknown
1890–1892	91	28	12	27	6	14	5
1893–1895	79	16	10	24	5	13	2
1896–1900	23	5	1	8	0	9	0
1901-E 1908	88	10	5	41	5	26	1
L 1908–1910	60	5	12	24	11	7	1

Table 15. Batting Park Factors at Polo Grounds IV, 1890–1900

Years	Runs	HR
1890–1895	98	126
1896–1900	94	85

Table 16: Batting Park Factors at Polo Grounds IV, 1901–1910

Years	BA	OBP	SLUG	2B*	3B*	HR*	BB**
1901–1908	101	101	102	102	82	172	96
1909–1910	100	99	99	87	89	135	95

* Per at bats
** Per total plate appearances (at bats + base on balls + hit by a pitch)

Polo Grounds V: New York American League 1913–1922, National League 1911–1957, 1962–1963

Polo Grounds V, built because of the April 14, 1911, fire that destroyed the grandstand and a portion of the right field bleachers of Polo Grounds IV, was one of the earliest Classic parks and is the one most associated with the name Polo Grounds. Later in the second decade of the Deadball Era, the ballpark was officially renamed Brush Stadium (after the owner of the Giants, John T. Brush). However, the name change never stuck and the park was still referred to by both the press and the fans as the Polo Grounds.

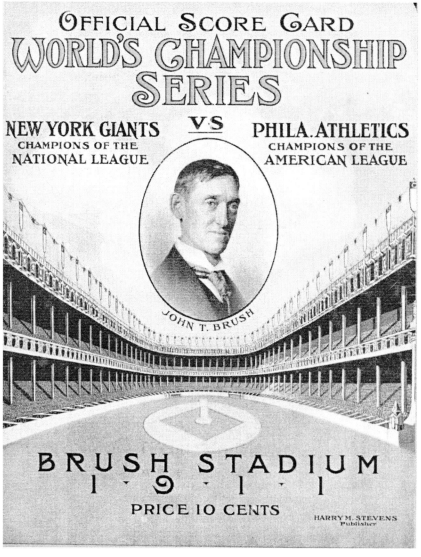

The rebuilt Polo Grounds in 1911 was originally known as Brush Stadium (collection of Stew Thornley).

Polo Grounds V stayed in continuous use by the NL until the Giants moved to San Francisco after the 1957 season and then saw two more seasons of major league games, 1962 and 1963, when the NL expansion team, the Mets, played there while Shea Stadium was being built.

The new steel-and-concrete double-deck grandstand of Polo Grounds V was built on a foundation that included steel piles driven 20–40 feet below the surface to bedrock[7] and was extended from the left field foul pole to beyond the right field foul pole—about 50–60 feet into fair territory in right field. Between the right field end of the grandstand and the right field bleachers there was an in-play gap some 15–20 feet in width. Note that this grandstand, including the wing in fair right field, had no second-deck overhang. By June 28, 1911, the lower section of the grandstand was complete and allowed the Giants to return to the Polo Grounds. The capacity of the ballpark at this time was 16,000 seats in the lower deck plus the undamaged and rebuilt outfield bleachers for a total of about 26,000. Construction work in the upper deck of the grandstand continued for the rest of the season. Additional seating was added in stages, such that by the start of the 1911 World Series in October, the permanent capacity had reached 34,000. For the World Series itself, several thousand temporary seats—called circus seats—were added in the outfield. These sections were 20 feet deep and their usefulness can be seen from the attendance at Game One of the Series: better than 38,000 in a ballpark with a permanent capacity of 34,000. Capacity in the center field bleachers was increased in 1917 by the removal of the green canvas screens that had been used as batter's backgrounds,[8] which allowed total seating capacity to become about 36,000. The Yankees used the Polo Grounds for three games in 1912 and moved permanently there from Hilltop Park at the start of the 1913 season, where they stayed as tenants of the Giants for ten years.

There were prohibitions on playing Sunday professional baseball in the entire state

The "new" Polo Grounds, in 1913. Eventually the grandstands were extended into center field (collection of Stew Thornley).

The Polo Grounds in 1917. This version varied only slightly from the expanded version, which was completed by 1923 (collection of Stew Thornley).

of New York until early in the 1919 season. After 1915, Brooklyn considered scheduling Sunday home games at Harrison Field in Newark, New Jersey, some ten to 15 miles away, but such plans never materialized. One reason was that the International League Newark team had the territorial rights. During the 1907–1914 period there were two innovative professional Sunday baseball games that took place in New York City. One, held on July 4, 1909, was a charity function at Washington Park III in Brooklyn to aid newsboys, and the other, held on April 21, 1912, at the Polo Grounds, was to aid survivors of the sinking of the Titanic. Both games skirted the prohibition on Sunday professional baseball by charging no admission. Instead, fans bought a program at the usual admission price. Finally in 1919, the New York state legislature passed a bill, signed by the governor on April 19, 1919, legalizing Sunday professional baseball.[9] The first completely legal major league Sunday baseball games in New York City were played on May 4, 1919.

Was Sunday baseball a success? The response was tremendous! Brooklyn hosted the Braves at Ebbets Field before 22,000 fans, while 35,000 watched the Giants play the Phillies at the Polo Grounds.[10] These were the largest regular season crowds at both ballparks to that date.

The Polo Grounds did not reach its final configuration until after the end of the Deadball Era. Expansion on the ballpark began in November of 1922 and the work continued well into the 1923 season. Both the north (left field) and south (right field) double-deck grandstands were extended towards center field, and new concrete bleachers were constructed in the now far-distant center field area on both sides of the new center field alcove. This produced the park's famous bathtub shape, which in combination with the alcove, were the park's most distinctive features. A new clubhouse was located at the far end of the alcove and was reached by the players via the field, which was also the postgame exit route for many of the fans. There were in-play bullpens in both left-center and right-center. As they were located 430 plus feet from home plate, they had no effect on the play of the game. Night games started at the ballpark in 1940 after light towers were built atop the double-deck grandstand. The ads on the outfield walls were removed starting with the 1948 season, when the Giants signed a deal with Chesterfield Cigarettes to be the exclusive advertiser at the ballpark.

The Giants left New York for San Francisco after the 1957 season and the Polo Grounds was not used from 1958 through 1961, with the last major league use of it being by the expansion NL team, the Mets, in 1962 and 1963. The ballpark was demolished in 1964 and the site now contains four 30-story apartment buildings called the Polo Grounds Towers. An ironic fact: the wrecking ball that knocked down the Polo Grounds was the same one that demolished Ebbets Field.

The Basis of the Polo Ground's Estimated Configurations and Dimensions

When the ballpark was rebuilt after the April 14, 1911, fire as Polo Grounds V, the principal dimensions of the prior ballpark (Polo Grounds IV)—277 in left field, 433 in center field, and 258 in right field—remained the same. The only change was to a portion of right field where the right field bleachers began. These dimensions were used with the 1909 Sanborn map of the ballpark site to derive a Polo Grounds V ballpark diagram. The 1909 map had a defect in it that showed all of the center field fence as being a diagonal that ran perpendicular to the home plate-center field axis. The error was corrected from photos that revealed the fence to have been composed of three segments, a center portion that was perpendicular to the home plate-center field axis, one angled toward left-center, and one towards right-center. All subsequent ballpark dimensions for 1911–1922 were derived from this diagram.

The second configuration of Polo Grounds V (1923–1964) varied only slightly over the next 38 seasons. Unlike typical major league ballparks at that time that were mostly rectangular in shape, Polo Grounds V had left field and right field fences that were parallel to each other and met their respective foul lines at 135 degrees. As a result, the frequent movement of home plate towards center field or towards the backstop did not change the left field or right field foul line dimensions; only center field, left-center, and right-center were altered. A curious footnote about this ballpark is that the marked outfield dimensions in left field, right field (away from the foul lines, as there were never marked dimensions at the foul poles), left-center, and right-center were never updated. This did not mean that all of the above dimensions were unaffected by moving home plate, only that the marked distances were never revised. In fact, only the dimensions at the foul lines, straightaway left field, and straightaway right field never changed after 1923.[11]

One noticeable alteration in the actual center field dimension occurred for the 1931–1933 seasons, the 1938–1939 seasons, and the 1948 season when a three-foot fence or berm was in place at the front of the alcove between the two sections of center field bleachers.[12] The center field dimension at Polo Grounds V has been listed in various ballpark books and baseball guides as anywhere from 430 to 505 feet over the 1923–1963 seasons, showing that it has not been possible to eliminate all the differences for all the years among the various sources. So, the following tables provide the best estimates. However, one thing is clear: the changes in the center field dimension had virtually no impact on the play of the game as all of the center field distances were beyond the reach of nearly all hitters.

Table 17. Dimensions (Calculated from Park Diagrams)

Years	LF	SLF	LC	CF	RC	SRF	RF
1911–1922	277	377	419	433	431	367	258
1923–1929, 1946–1947, 1952, 1954, 1963–1964	279	393	445	483	445	367	258
1930, 1943, 1945, 1946	279	393	452	490	452	367	258
1931–1933, 1938–1939, 1948	279	393	442	430	442	367	258
1934–1937, 1953	279	393	445	480	445	367	258
1940–1942, 1944, 1949–1951	279	393	468	505	468	367	258
1955–1957, 1962	279	393	437	475	437	367	258

Table 18. Fence Heights

Years	LF	CF	RF
1911–1922	10–16	10–20*	11–12
1923–1930	10–16	10–8.5**	11–12
1931–1933, 1938–1939, 1948	10–16	3–8.5	11–12
1934–1937	10–16	10–8.5**	11–12
1940–1964	10–16	10–8.5**	11–12

* The 20-foot height was the canvas batter's background until May 1917
** Excludes clubhouse at back of alcove (60 feet high)

Table 19. Average Outfield Distances

Years	LF	CF	RF	Composite
1911–1922	368	434	358	387
1923–1929, 1946–1947, 1952, 1954, 1963–1964	367	445	368	393
1930, 1943, 1945–1949	369	452	370	397
1931–1933, 1938–1939, 1948	367	437	368	390
1934–1937, 1953	366	442	367	392
1940–1942, 1944, 1949–1951	372	472	373	406
1955–1957, 1962	365	443	366	391

Capacity: 26,000 (estimated; June 28, 1911), 34,000 (October 1911), 36,000 (May 1917), 43,000 (April 1922), 54,000 (October 1923), 55,000 (1926), 56,000 (1930), 53,856 (1937), 56,000 (1940), 54,500 (1947), 56,000 (1953), 55,137 (1957), 55,000 (1962)
Park site area: 7.4 acres
Deadball Era run factor: AL: 101 (Rank: AL 10); NL: 93 (Rank: NL 14)

The Impact of the Park's Configurations and Dimensions on Batting, 1911–1930

The double-deck expansion in left field and right field occurred before and during the 1923 season. At the start of that season, the double-deck stands were in place in most of fair territory in left field but were still under construction towards left-center. The bottom of the left field second deck was 34 feet above the field level. There was no overhang in right field, but in left field, the upper deck extended 22.5 feet beyond the lower deck. Because of the 135-degree angle between the left field foul line and the left field stands, the overhang down the left field line amounted to 29 feet. At the straight-away left field point (15 degrees off the foul line), the overhang, as measured on a line

Construction during the 1923 season extended the grandstands in left and right field (collection of Ron Selter).

from home plate to the stands, was 46 feet. The maximum effective overhang was at a point (at 18 degrees off the foul line where the left field wall started to curve towards center field) and was located to the right of straightaway left field. The overhang here amounted to a staggering 58 feet along the flight path of a ball hit into this area of the stands.

Detailed data on home runs to left field at the Polo Grounds were compiled for the 1923–1930 seasons. In these eight seasons 383 OTF home runs were hit to left field. There were 133 home runs that went into the left field stands—upper or lower deck not specified. Of the 250 OTF home runs to left with data on where they landed, 217 went into the upper deck (including off the façade of the upper deck) and only 27 went into the lower deck. Six home runs to left went completely over both decks. It is the author's opinion that many—perhaps as much as half—of the home runs knocked into the upper deck in left field would have been catchable fly balls if no overhang had existed.

Because the Polo Grounds was such a good ballpark for home runs, it acquired in the press and among fans the reputation as a hitter's park. A well-known example: Hall of Famer New York Giant Mel Ott slugged nearly two-thirds of his 511 round-trippers at

The upper deck in left field hung over the lower deck by more than 20 feet (collection of M. Frank).

his home park. For the 1911–1930 period, Polo Grounds V had home run park factors that were always above 100 and as high as 209. So for dingers, Polo Grounds V was certainly a hitter's park.

For batting average, it was quite a different story. In the 1923–1930 seasons, the NL as a whole hit .293 at home and .282 in road games, a difference of 11 points. This home vs. road variance (about 4 percent) was typical for major league seasons for 1901–1957. How did the New York Giants do at the Polo Grounds as opposed to road games? The following table answers this question.

Table 20. New York Giants Team Batting Averages, 1923–1930

Year	Home	Road
1923	.294	.296
1924	.292	.307
1925	.281	.285
1926	.278	.278
1927	.301	.293
1928	.288	.298
1929	.280	.303
1930	.313	.324

In 1930, the New York Giants had the highest major league team batting average (.319) ever achieved since 1900, despite hitting in what was in fact a poor hitter's ballpark!

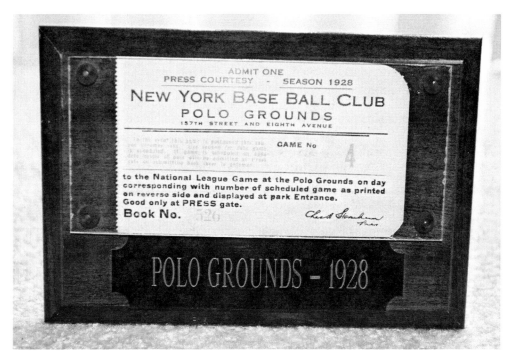

A Polo Grounds season pass in 1928 (collection of Tom Edwards).

One offensive category that Polo Grounds V was not conducive to was triples. The average batting park factor (1911–1930) for triples was 82. What is curious is that the usually triple-friendly dimensions to left-center and right-center (a minimum of 419 in left-center and 431 in right-center) were much larger than at nearly all other AL or NL ballparks in this time period. The answer is that the unique shape of the Polo Grounds with very short dimensions at the foul lines (277/279 in left and 258 in right) led to the corner outfielders playing over towards left-center and right-center and thus being able to cut off more balls hit in the gaps.

The data on home runs and batting park factors for Polo Grounds V in 1911–1930 are shown below in five tables.

Table 21. Home Runs by Type at Polo Grounds V

Years	Total	OTF	Bounce	IP
1913–1919 (AL)	300*	234*	1	65
1911–1919 (NL)	269	211	4	60
1920–1922 (AL)	325	295	0	30
1920–1922 (NL)	243	202	1	41
1923–1930 (NL)	896	832	0	64

* Includes one home run in three 1912 games
Bounce: Bounce home runs
IP: Inside-the-park home runs
OTF: Over-the-fence (includes bounce)

Table 22. Over-the-Fence Home Runs by Field at Polo Grounds V (Excluding Bounce)

Years	Total	LF	CF	RF	Unknown
1913–1922 (AL)	233*	88	0	144*	1
1911–1922 (NL)	268	104	0	163	1
1923–1930 (NL)	832	361	0	461	10

* Includes one home run in 1912

Table 23. Inside-the-Park Home Runs by Field at Polo Grounds V

Years	Total	LF	LC	CF	RC	RF	Unknown
1913–1922 (AL)	65	2	5	23	16	19	0
1911–1922 (NL)	82	2	10	22	27	20	1
1923–1930 (NL)	64	3	16	20	17	4	4

Table 24. Batting Park Factors at Polo Grounds V: Deadball Era, 1911–1919

Years	BA	OBP	SLUG	2B*	3B*	HR*	BB**
1913–1919 (AL)	99	100	100	90	73	209	103
1911–1919 (NL)	98	98	97	91	77	138	100

* Per at bats
** Per total plate appearances (at bats + base on balls + hit by a pitch)

Table 25. Batting Park Factors at Polo Grounds V: Lively Ball Era, 1920–1930

Years	BA	OBP	SLUG	2B*	3B*	HR*	BB**
1920–1922 (AL)	96	97	100	78	98	156	101
1920–1922 (NL)	97	99	101	85	67	192	109
1923–1930 (NL)	96	97	97	77	78	134	100

* Per at bats
** Per total plate appearances (at bats + base on balls + hit by a pitch)

The Impact of the Park's Configurations and Dimensions on Batting, 1931–1963

For the 1931–1941 seasons, the effect of Polo Grounds V on batting was very similar to the period prior to 1923–1930. Park factors for batting average, on-base percentage, doubles, and triples were all below average. During World War II, the park factors show the Polo Grounds had become a very average ballpark in terms of batting. The use of mostly lesser-skilled replacement players during the war years made ballpark differences largely unimportant. After World War II, the uniqueness of the Polo Grounds as a hitter's park for home runs and below average in nearly all other offensive categories became less pronounced compared to the prewar figures. Since there were no substantial changes in the configuration of the Polo Grounds in the postwar period, changes in the other NL ballparks had to have been the cause of the Polo Grounds becoming less exceptional. In fact, in the park's final two seasons (1962 and 1963), the park factor for triples was 31 percent above the league average. This historically unprecedented result was due to many of the other NL parks becoming multiangular or semicircular in shape instead of the rectangular shapes typical of earlier parks in the 20th century. The result of these configuration changes was shorter distances to left-center and right-center, which reduced the number of triples in these parks. This result illustrates how batting park factors are relative, not absolute, measures of the effects of ballpark configurations on batting.

Batting Park Factors at Polo Grounds V, 1931–1963

Table 26. Batting Park Factors at Polo Grounds V: Lively Ball Era, 1931–1963

Years	BA	OBP	SLUG	2B*	3B*	HR*	BB**
1931–1941	95	97	101	61	80	192	102
1942–1945	100	100	100	96	100	107	98
1946–1957	97	97	103	70	99	143	101
1962–1963	97	101	108	84	131	148	108

*Per at bats
** Per total plate appearances (at bats + base on balls + hit by a pitch)

NOTES

1. *The Reach Official American League Base Ball Guide 1902* (Philadelphia: A. J. Reach Company, 1902).
2. *New York Times*, April 30, 1907.
3. Philip Lowry, *Green Cathedrals: The Ultimate Celebrations of All 273 Major League and Negro League Ballparks Past and Present* (Reading, Massachusetts: Addison-Wesley, 2006), 188–189.
4. Sanborn Fire Insurance Co. Map, New York City 1893, Section 256.
5. Sanborn Fire Insurance Co. Map, New York City 1909, Map No. 68.
6. *New York Times*, game accounts, 1896–1908.
7. *New York Times*, May 19, 1911.
8. *New York Times*, May 31, 1917.
9. Charlie Bevis, *Sunday Baseball: The Major Leagues' Struggle to Play Baseball on the Lord's Day, 1876–1934* (Jefferson, NC: McFarland, 2003), 194.
10. *Ibid.*
11. Sanborn 1909.
12. Bill Shannon and George Kalinsky, *The Ballparks* (New York: Hawthorn Books Inc., 1975), photo 146.

Polo Grounds Seating, Dimensions and Design

JOHN PASTIER

New York has been the nation's largest and most prosperous city for as long as formalized baseball has been played there, so it is natural to think that it would be home to some of the sport's largest, most patronized, and best-arranged accommodations. This has been true at times, but not always, and the Polo Grounds, in one or another of its six incarnations, has both met and fallen short of these yardsticks.

The original 1883 wooden ballpark constructed on polo fields at Fifth Avenue and 110th Street was a double-decked structure. This was a cutting edge technology at the time and seems to have been the first of its type built for baseball.[1] The final 19th-century bearer of the name, located about two and a half miles farther north and labeled Polo Grounds III by researchers, was also double decked.

Double-decking was a way to improve seating quality and quantity: first, by providing an all-encompassing elevated perspective of the field and increasing the number of seats near the infield, and second, by fitting more seats into building sites constrained by tight city street grids. Thus, double-decking was a useful tool for both achieving high seating capacity and improving the quality of those seats.

Seating Capacity and Attendance

It is not known—nor will it probably ever be known—exactly how many seats Polo Grounds III had. For a big game, it was able to hold nearly 25,000 fans in fixed seats and standing on the field. However, it is known that the grandstand was arranged in an impressively sweeping, nearly semicircular form, that its wooden structure was heavily reinforced with metal braces, and that there were bleachers in the outfield adjoining a zone in deepest center field where the upper classes could watch the game from their horse-drawn carriages. (Was there ever another ballpark where the upper crust occupied the most distant vantage points?)

Two games into the 1911 season, the grandstand of Polo Grounds III burned down overnight. The Giants' owner, John T. Brush, vowed to rebuild bigger and better than ever and rushed to erect a replacement, using Henry B. Herts, a New York theater architect

Opening Day in 1888 at the original Polo Grounds (collection of Stew Thornley).

of Herts and Tallant, and the Osborn Engineering Company, a Cleveland structural firm with fireproof ballpark experience, as his designers. The new park, boasting a steel skeleton and reinforced concrete foundations and seating tiers, opened just a little over eight weeks after the fire. It was less than half complete, with a 6,000-seat single-decked unroofed fireproof grandstand and adjoining wooden bleachers in left field, holding about 10,000, that had survived the fire. Its premature opening game drew only approximately 10,000 fans, but construction continued throughout the season, and by mid–October, enough seats were in place to accommodate a record World Series crowd of 38,281.

On many levels, Brush's swift replacement effort was a striking demonstration of big-city ambition. It produced the largest ballpark in the largest city for the best National League team of its time. A dozen years later, under Charles Stoneham's ownership, it underwent a massive expansion to about 53,000 seats.[2] Again, it will probably never be known what its exact seating capacity was, but a clue can be found by examining how many spectators passed through its turnstiles during the period that it served the Giants and compare that to its contemporaries.[3] The total does not include millions more who attended prizefights, college and professional football games, soccer games, religious gatherings, and other nonbaseball events, nor does it include two million patrons of Mets games. Here are the major league parks with at least 30 million paying customers through the end of the 1957 season:

Table 1. Baseball Attendance at the Most Patronized
Classic Parks through 1957[4]

City	Park	Period	Attendance (millions)	Team Seasons[5]	Attendance per Season
New York	Yankee Stadium	1923–1957	47.181	35	1,348.0 K
New York	Polo Grounds	1911–1957	45.577	56.6	805.2 K
Detroit	Briggs/Tiger Stadium	1912–1957	41.198	46	895.6 K
St. Louis	Sportsman's Park	1909–1957	38.543	82	470.0 K
Brooklyn	Ebbets Field	1913–1957	37.186	45	826.4 K
Philadelphia	Shibe Park	1909–1957	35.874	78.4	457.6 K
Chicago	Wrigley Field	1916–1957	34.924	42	831.5 K
Chicago	Comiskey Park	1910–1957	32.150	47.6	675.4 K
Boston	Fenway Park	1912–1957	31.212	46	678.5 K

Measured by total attendance, the Polo Grounds was the busiest National League park between 1911 and 1957 and was second in the majors to Yankee Stadium during that period. Using average attendance per season, it ranked in fifth place after Yankee Stadium, Tiger Stadium, Wrigley Field, and Ebbets Field (which was a much smaller venue), respectively.

Establishing its exact seating capacity is impossible, but it seems safe to say that up until the Giants' abandonment of New York at the end of 1957, the largest ballparks, measured by estimated peak capacity, were Cleveland Municipal Stadium (78,000),[6] Yankee Stadium (70,000), Tiger Stadium (56,000), the Polo Grounds (53,000), Comiskey Park (51,000), Wrigley Field (46,000), and Forbes Field (43,000). These estimates are

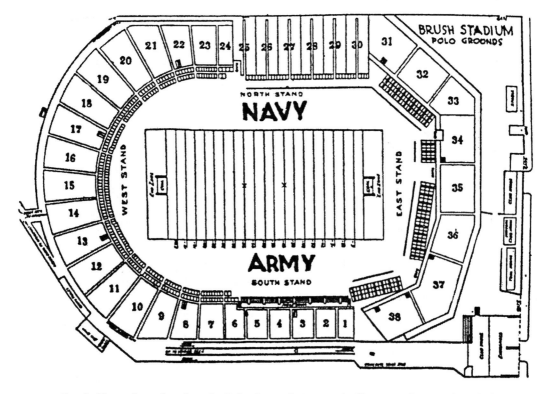

Football was first played at the Polo Grounds in 1913 (collection of Stew Thornley).

based on peak crowds for various types of games—World Series, All-Star, opening day, doubleheaders, night games, and day games—and on figures published in five baseball and general reference sources. The Polo Grounds is the most puzzling one to gauge because, despite four credible sources independently stating that it had 56,000 seats, the Giants broke the 50,000 barrier at World Series and All-Star games only twice in 21 opportunities, and averaged a surprisingly low 43,945[7] for those gold-standard dates.

Thanks to the stadium's large playing field and oblong form, it was very well suited for football, both in capacity and shape, and could accommodate 24 temporary seating sections holding about 8,000 fans, thus reaching or exceeding the 60,000 mark after the 1922–1923 expansion. There are reports of professional- and college-game crowds as high as 80,000 and 75,000 in the 1920s and 1930s, but those figures are almost surely inflated. Whatever its exact number of seats, the Polo Grounds' capaciousness was obvious and was the greatest in the National League for almost, if not all, of its life.[8] Give it an "A" for baseball and football seating quantity. But what about quality? Was its seating layout well planned for game action and well designed for spectators?

Basic Layout, Its Antecedents and Its Effects

Here the assessment is not as favorable. The 1911 fire was an opportunity to correct serious basic flaws in the ballpark's layout that had existed for 20 years, but John Brush was in poor health (he was confined to a wheelchair and had only a year and a half more to live) and speed of rebuilding and reoccupancy was obviously a priority. Sheer size and a limited sprinkling of cosmetic detail[9] were also among his goals. In haste, he chose to perpetuate three by-then old-fashioned design ideas embodied in the burned-down park—the semicircular shape of the grandstand, the home plate shape of fair territory, and very short foul lines—rather than assessing the situation afresh and considering seating and field layouts that were better shaped to the needs of the sport and creating an external civic gesture. (Examples of the latter were the newly opened parks in Philadelphia, Pittsburgh, and Chicago, and one on the drawing boards in Brooklyn.) He also chose to retain the 10,000-seat wooden bleachers that survived the fire, rather than reshape and replace them with fireproof construction. That process would occur a dozen years later, under different ownership, and in competition with the Yankees, who, thanks to Babe Ruth, had begun to outdraw the Giants and were building the biggest and grandest stadium in the sport just a half mile away in the Bronx.

The Polo Grounds' three final incarnations (1891–1911, 1911–1922 and 1923–1964, all located at 157th Street and Eighth Avenue) had the most unusual field and seating layout of any permanent major league ballpark. It took the form of an old-fashioned bathtub, and, paradoxically, was a home run paradise despite having one of the largest outfields ever. While its shape was unusual, it was not totally unprecedented. Philip Lowry has described Chicago's West Side Park (1885–1892) as "bathtub shaped, narrow and long, just like the Polo Grounds."[10] One or another of its three main shape components was also found in several other 19th-century and early 20th-century parks.

The first of these—the practice of laying out fair territory in the shape of home plate—may be as old as the very idea of installing fences around a playing field. Pictorial evidence strongly suggests that the Union Grounds in Brooklyn, the first enclosed ballpark (1862), took this shape. "Playing Parlor Base-Ball," a tabletop mechanical baseball

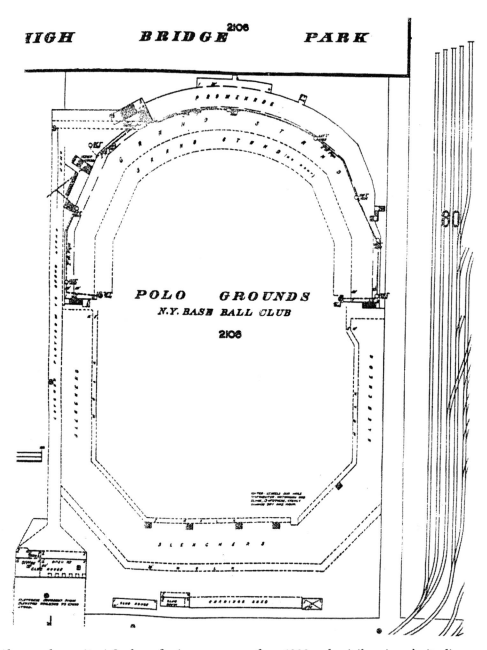

Above and opposite: A Sanborn fire insurance map from 1909 and a civil engineer's site diagram from 1911 indicate the similarity in appearance with the wooden ballpark that was rebuilt with steel and concrete (collection of Stew Thornley).

game patented in 1868[11] by F. C. Sebring, has both its fair territory and its own overall outline shaped like home plate. This suggests that the pentagonal field form was already common in the real world. Known or probable 19th-century examples include Baltimore's Madison Avenue grounds[12]; Chicago's Lake Park, Lakefront Park, and West Side Park; South End Grounds I, Boston; Messer St. Grounds, Providence; Lloyd Street Grounds

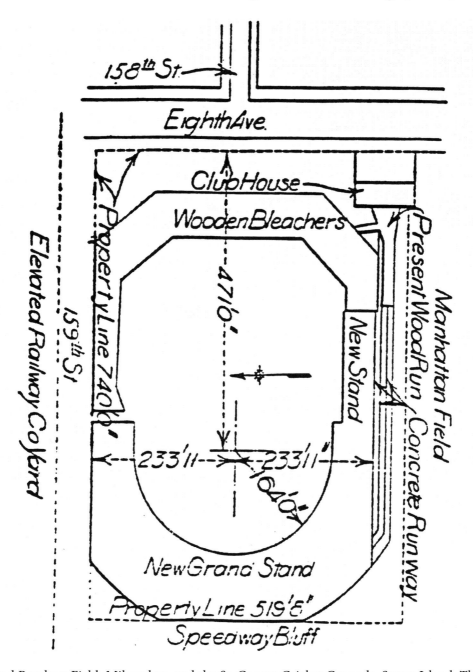

and Borchert Field, Milwaukee; and the St. George Cricket Grounds, Staten Island. The practice continued into the postwar era of the 20th century, with the original version of St. Petersburg's Al Lang Field (1947).

However, there were two major drawbacks of pentagonal fields. First, the shape was not conducive to outfield seating—the Polo Grounds was the only known park of this form that left room for seats in fair territory in left and right, and then only at the price of producing very short foul lines, and having many of those seats face center field rather than the infield.

Table 2. Outfield Characteristics of Pentagonal Ballparks[13]

City	Park	Year	Site Width	LF Dist.	CF Dist.	RF Dist.	Max. Dist.	Seats in LF?	Seats in CF?	Seats in RF?
Buffalo	Riverside Park	1879	299'	210'	410'	210'	436'	No	No	No
Chicago	Lakefront Park II	1884	272'	180'	300'	196'	326'	No	No	No
Chicago	West Side Park I	1885	307'	216'	?	216'	?	?	?	?
Milwaukee	Borchert Field	1891	380'	267'	395'	267'	417'	No	No	No
Milwaukee	Lloyd St. Grounds	1901	419'	295'	450'	295'	496'	No	No	No
New York	Polo Grounds V	1911	520'	279'	433'	258'	439'	Yes	Yes	Yes
St. Petersburg	Al Lang Field	1947	426' (est.)	n.a.	n.a.	300' (est.)	n.a.	No	No	No

The second basic element was its semicircular main grandstand. More than a century ago, this shape was used in several wooden ballparks, including Buffalo's Olympic Park, Boston's handsomely double-decked Grand Pavilion (a.k.a. South End Grounds II) of 1888,[14] and Brooklyn's Eastern Park of 1891. In the early decades of the 20th century, minor league and collegiate parks such as Bosse Field in Evansville, Indiana, and the City College of New York's Lewisohn Stadium employed the form.[15] In the second half of the 20th century, the semicircular shape was expanded to a full circle and a tsunami of round stadia flooded the sports world, starting in Washington, D.C., and spreading to New York, Atlanta, Cincinnati, St. Louis, Pittsburgh, Houston, Arlington (Texas), Oakland, Seattle, and Tampa Bay. Shaped and scaled to accommodate the ultimately incompatible geometries of baseball and football, this genre of stadium is almost unanimously considered the historic low point of ballpark design.

The third element—extremely short foul lines—was a product of 19th-century Deadball Era thinking and practice. Because balls of the time could not be hit very far, sub-300-foot outfield dimensions were fairly common and not necessarily deemed problematic. Only when they measured less than 200 feet, such as in Chicago's White Stocking Park (1883–1884), were they considered in need of prompt correction.[16] In that case, a league-wide rule was adopted the next year, defining the minimum dimension for an over-the-fence home run as 210 feet. This first decree was quite permissive, but as balls became livelier (and were replaced more frequently) and home runs increased, the minimums rose over time. The Giants left the Polo Grounds shortly before the latest minimum was established, but it should have been in effect when the Mets used the park in 1962 and 1963.

Table 3. Evolution of Minimum Distance for Over-the-Fence-Home Runs

New Minimum Distance	210'	235'	250'	325'	250' with 320' preferred[17]
Season That Rule Took Effect	1885	1892	1926	1959	Date unknown; rule is current

The regression embodied in the present rule is puzzling. Many of today's fences fall short of the current 320-foot foul line minimum, whether through grandfathering (Fenway Park, 302 and 308 feet), nostalgia (Yankee Stadium II, 314 and 318 feet),[18] a yen for quirkiness (Houston, 315 feet), seating encroachment into the field area (Tampa Bay, 315 feet), or a genuine property-size limitation (Baltimore, 318 feet, and San Francisco, 309 feet).

Quality of Seating and Spectator Experience

As long established as these three elements may have been in baseball history, there is no evidence that they made for a good ballpark, either singly or combined. Nevertheless, even before the 1911–1912 reconstruction was complete, *Engineering Record* lauded the

Polo Grounds' round grandstand end, claiming that "[t]his stadium is unique in baseball park design in that the main portion, back of the diamond, is a true semicircle. The usual arrangement is to follow the lines of the diamond, making the stands parallel thereto, allowing the foul lines to extend about 300 feet each way, then to draw the bleachers in toward the outfield. The semicircular form makes the foul lines a little shorter, but gives all the spectators a direct view of the diamond."[19]

These confident observations were either uninformed or disingenuous. They ignored the round predecessors mentioned above and dramatically understated the prevailing foul line dimensions of the day. The Polo Grounds' foul lines were not just "a little shorter," but rather 74 feet shorter to left and 72 feet shorter to right than the average of the other major league parks used in 1911. They were the shortest home run distances to be found in any ballpark built expressly for major league use between 1895 and the present day. The "direct view of the diamond" (meaning that most of the grandstand seats faced a point about midway between the pitching rubber and second base), while praiseworthy in itself, came at a steep price: a huge foul territory and abnormally distant views from the infield seats to the bases. Furthermore, most of the seats beyond the semicircle faced center field rather than the infield, producing uncomfortably twisted necks and torsos.

The round home plate end of the grandstand produced an excessive foul area and long viewing distances (especially to the bases and a little beyond) for fans occupying what should be prime infield seats. Comparing foul territory measurements at the three classic New York ballparks quantifies the problem: The minimum viewing distance from the front row to home plate was a reasonable 69 feet at the Polo Grounds, a foot more than at Ebbets Field, and 11 feet less than at Yankee Stadium—so far, so good. But the measurements for seats closest to first and third base tell a less rosy tale. At the Polo Grounds, the minimum distance to the bases was a daunting 97 feet, nearly two-and-a-half times the 39-foot figures for the other two parks. All in all, the weighted-average figure for the foul zone around the Polo Grounds infield was 87 feet, compared to just 53 feet at Ebbets Field and 55 feet at Yankee Stadium—more than 60 percent greater than the more intimate New York parks. Closeness to the infield action was clearly not a feature at Coogan's Hollow. Measuring viewing distances from home plate to the midpoint of the upper deck during the first two dozen years of the fireproof era provides a more broadly based comparison.

Table 4. A Chronological Listing of Upper Deck Viewing Distances at Early Fireproof Parks of the Deadball Period, 1895–1919[20]

Distance to Home Plate	*Park, City and Year the Upper Deck Was Built*
100'	Baker Bowl, Philadelphia, 1895[21]
118'	Shibe Park, Philadelphia, 1909[22]
128'	Sportsman's Park, St. Louis, 1909[23]
125'	Forbes Field, Pittsburgh, 1909
105'	League Park, Cleveland, 1910
129'	Comiskey Park, Chicago, 1910
105'	Griffith Stadium, Washington, 1911[24]
132'	Polo Grounds, New York, 1911[25]
135'	Crosley Field, Cincinnati, 1912
113'	Ebbets Field, Brooklyn, 1913
118'	Average excluding the Polo Grounds

Here the Polo Grounds ranks ninth out of ten in upper-deck seating proximity to the plate, 14 feet farther than the others in the sample, even though this calculation does not take into account the park's undue viewing remoteness at the corner bases.

Some Roads Not Taken

The 1911 fire could have been a blessing in disguise, giving Brush the opportunity to commission quarters having greater intimacy, more adequate foul lines, a less extreme field shape, and a greater degree of fire safety. At least four types of alternative field geometries were possible.

One design direction would have been to keep the principle of a semicircular grandstand, but clear the site completely by tearing down the wooden bleachers and extending the foul lines to meet the park's outer walls (producing roughly 330-foot foul lines) and build fireproof stands parallel to the foul lines, beginning at about the 350- or 360-foot point. They could have continued until a 410-to-430-foot depth, where a 45-degree turn or a curved connection would join them in dead center. This approach would reduce the left-center and right-center dimensions slightly and roughly match the late 1911 seating capacity. If the outfield bleachers were partially or completely double decked, the 1911 capacity would have increased.

Another direction would have been to treat the outfield as suggested above and lay out the seating in foul territory not as a semicircle, but in straight line segments (with the possibility of a tight curve behind home plate), as was the practice of almost all the other new parks of the period. By bringing the infield seats much closer to the bases, this approach would be better than the first, since there would be no real benefit to building a new semicircular grandstand.

A third direction would be to demolish all the surviving seating structures, creating a completely clean slate, and rotate the field 45 degrees so that the foul lines would be parallel to the property lines and aligned with the adjacent street grid. Every new park of the period, other than the Polo Grounds, employed this type of alignment. This would allow one outfield wall of good height, 340 feet deep, with no seats behind it, located in left field to avoid sun problems, and produce a seating capacity of about 50,000. That would be 50,000 good seats, intimate around the infield, and with the farthest outfield seats being about 60 feet closer to the plate than the design that was actually implemented.

The fourth would have been to buy or lease a portion (say, a strip 50 or 100 feet wide) of the old Manhattan Field site immediately south of the Polo Grounds' right field. This extra property would allow for improvement of each of the other alternatives above by providing planning flexibility and room for more seating. Direction number three, for example, would be capable of holding 55,000 to 60,000 baseball seats, depending on the desired size of the bleachers.

John Brush's Architectural Patronage

But nothing remotely like those scenarios ever took place. Had John Brush been in better health and less pressed for time, he might have been just the right person to pull an exemplary piece of architecture out of the ashes of 1911. His credentials as a patron of ballpark architecture were as strong as anyone's in the business. In 1902, as owner of the

Cincinnati Reds, he had retained architect John G. Thurtle of Kansas City and Indianapolis to design the Palace of the Fans, the most structurally advanced and stylistically evolved[26] venue in baseball at the time. Philadelphia's Baker Bowl, built in 1895, was the first largely fireproof ballpark,[27] but Cincinnati's Palace raised the bar. Unlike Philadelphia's, its structure was reinforced concrete, an even more thoroughly fire-resistant technology than the exposed steel-framed structural systems that would become standard in the new big league parks built between 1895 and 1932.[28] Designed in a pedimented Beaux Arts classical mode, The Palace was richly detailed and technically innovative. Sadly, it was torn down after a decade[29] because its 12,000 seat capacity had become inadequate[30] and defied expansion.[31] Economics had trumped beauty and structural permanence, and the grandest ballpark of baseball's first six decades was replaced in 1911. It would be 43 years before the big leagues had another all-concrete park.[32]

Although Brush was unable to match his Cincinnati architectural success in upper Manhattan, he did attempt something interesting and unprecedented in 1911. In addition to assigning the up-and-coming Osborn Engineering Company of Cleveland the role of designing and structural engineers, he also brought in Henry B. Herts, a prolific and

The rebuilt Polo Grounds had decorative façades (collection of Stew Thornley).

highly successful Broadway theater architect, to contribute to the undertaking. Brush presented this part of the project as an unabashed triumph: "The decorations are a step in advance of the past or the present age in exterior adornment and represents the taste and skill of the best designers,[33] sculptors and artists in the country."[34] It was a laudable and imaginative move, but, despite Brush's enthusiasm, not a successful one. Writing in an architectural journal, Herts candidly refers to the ballpark as a "very utilitarian structure."[35] His role was limited to providing some exterior decoration. He was not asked to develop an appropriate and coherent expression for the ballpark or to devise an architectural style supportive of the engineering. To put it bluntly, his job was to spread a little icing on Osborn's cake. His stucco ornamentation took three forms: semiabstract bas-reliefs on the end of the right field grandstand wall, invisible to most people in the seats; repeating symbolic bas-reliefs facing the field on the lower parapet of the upper deck and the frieze of the roof; and dozens of sculptures of eagles, wings folded, perched on the inner edge of the roof. This outdoor ornament was not up to the level of his theater work, either in visual sophistication or quality of materials. Furthermore, it soon began to deteriorate, crumbling and falling to the ground in small pieces. None of it survived the expansion of 1922–1923.

Other seating and playing field configuration problems arose or were made permanent when the park was expanded dramatically after the 1922 season. The pre-expansion arrangements were a working-class nirvana—about 15,000 of its 38,000-or-so seats (roughly 40 percent)—were affordable bleachers. The new layout slashed the proportion and absolute number of cheap seats dramatically to about 4,400[36] out of a stated 54,500, or about 8 percent in an era when the other parks averaged about 15 percent. Furthermore, not all of these seats were actually usable, since wooden batting backdrops blocked views of the field from the seats in lower rows of bleachers abutting the notch in dead center field. The *New York Herald Tribune* summed up the situation candidly: "As a matter of fact, bleacher seats will be provided at the Polo Grounds only because traditions require that a baseball park should have bleachers."[37]

The outfield walls and seats, which were too close to the plate in the foul corners and too far away in the central segment of the outfield, were not reshaped during this window of opportunity. The major leagues' shortest 20th-century foul lines were locked permanently into place rather than rectified.

In fact, the left field foul line was further truncated by the installation of the notorious upper deck overhang, which shortened the horizontal home run dimension by 29 feet at the foul line, and as much as 44 feet in straightaway left. The following table gives an idea of how teams of that era dealt with—or did not deal with—substandard fence dimensions.

Table 5. Mitigation Measures for Short Foul Lines in Classic Parks

Ballpark	Short Field	Length	Wall Height	Combined Dimension[38]	Forego Seats	Install High Wall and/or Screen
Polo Grounds	Right	258'	11'	269'	No	No
Polo Grounds	Upper Deck	250'	37'[39]	287'	No	No
Polo Grounds	Left	279'	17'	296'	Partial[40]	Medium-High Wall
Yankee Stadium	Right	296'	4'	300'	No	No
Yankee Stadium	Left	301'	4'	305'	No	No
Forbes Field	Right	300'	28'	328'	No	Screen

Ballpark	Short Field	Length	Wall Height	Combined Dimension	Forego Seats	Install High Wall and/or Screen
Baker Bowl	Right	280'	50'	330'	Yes	Both
League Park	Right	290'	45'	335'	Yes	Both
Ebbets Field	Right	297'	38'	335'	Yes	Both
Sportsman's Park	Right	310'	33'	343'	No	Screen
Fenway Park	Left	308'	37'	345'	Yes	Wall
Griffith Stadium	Right	320'	31'	351'	Yes	Wall[41]

The Giants had the worst problems with short home run distances, yet, except for the Yankees, did the least to remedy them. As a result, their park was tied with Baker Bowl as the softest home run touch in the 20th century. But the Phillies at least did what they could to address their park's inadequate dimensions by not locating seats where there was no room for them and by building a wall and screen that some sources list as high as 60 feet, but which photos suggest was about ten feet shorter.

Of course, the Polo Grounds had not only some very short home run dimensions but also some very long ones. The three New York stadiums led the pack in feast-or-famine dimensions.

Table 6. Greatest Home Run Distance Disparities Within Pre–World War II Parks

City	Ballpark	Shortest Home Run Distance	Longest Home Run Distance	Absolute Difference	Percent Difference[42]
New York	Polo Grounds	258'	483'	225'	87.2%
Brooklyn	Early Ebbets Field	300'	500'	200'	66.7%
Cleveland	League Park	290'	467'	177'	61.0%
New York	Yankee Stadium	296'	461'	165'	55.7%
Pittsburgh	Forbes Field	300'	462'	162'	54.0%
Philadelphia	Shibe Park	307'	468'	161'	52.4%
Saint Louis	Sportsman's Park	270'	422'	152'	56.3%
Cleveland	Municipal Stadium	320'	470'	150'	46.9%
Detroit	Tiger Stadium	325'	467'	142'	43.7%
Philadelphia	Baker Bowl	272'	412'	140'	51.5%
Pittsburgh	Exposition Park	380'	515'	135'	35.5%
Philadelphia	Baker Bowl	280'	412'	132'	47.1%
Chicago	Wrigley Field	327'	447'	120'	36.7%
Washington	Griffith Stadium	320'	426'	106'	33.1%
Brooklyn	Late Ebbets Field	297'	399'	102'	34.3%

Seating Issues

The 1922–1923 expansion produced a jaw-dropping maldistribution of seats whereby the greatest number of grandstand seating rows—54—were located in left-center and right-center upper-deck Siberia, ranging from 435 feet from the plate to as much as 600 feet. Among the classic parks, only Yankee Stadium, with a 25 percent greater seating capacity, approached these numbers. The others' most distant seats were on average about 135 feet (about 23 percent) closer to the plate than those two. Among sports facilities of any size and length of service, only the Los Angeles Coliseum, a sprawling single-deck bowl designed for football and track holding as many as 100,000 spectators, pressed into service as a temporary baseball venue between 1958 and 1961, had more distant seats. A similar superstadium, Cleveland Municipal, also scaled for football more than baseball, had last-row seats closer to home plate (about 521 feet in the grandstand and 549 feet in the bleachers) than did the Giants' park. It is safe to say that in light of the excessive viewing distances around its infield and throughout most of its outfield, the Polo Grounds was the least intimate permanent baseball venue in the long history of the national pastime.

Table 7. Most Distant Seats From Home Plate in Classic Parks

Ballpark	Average Maximum Distance	Maximum Bleacher Distance	Maximum Grandstand Distance
Polo Grounds	586'	574'	600'
Yankee Stadium	529'	572'	485'
Average of Parks Below	451'	478'	423'
Fenway Park	514'	539'	490'
Comiskey Park	484'	495'	473'
Tiger Stadium	481'	507'	455'
Sportsman's Park	472'	476'	469'
Ebbets Field	470'	473'	467'
Griffith Stadium	450'	404'	495'
Forbes Field	437'	384'	490'
Wrigley Field	428'	471'	386'
Shibe Park	427'	490'	365'
League Park	419'	475'	363'
Crosley Field	414'	442'	386'
Braves Field	375'	454'	296'
Baker Bowl	372'	436'	307'

In the semicircle behind home and the bases, where one would expect to find the most lower deck seating rows, there were 44 to 48, or six to ten fewer than in the center field grandstands. Adding to the puzzlement, the stands that ran east-west joining these two zones were quite shallow. In right field, they held about 22 rows, while in left, only about 14. Due to the left field overhang, the upper-deck dimensions and row counts were equal. It seems as though the Giants' owners and designers were pursuing as high a capacity as possible, putting seats wherever there was room, rather than where they would be most useful. Another symptom of the flawed seating layout was described by writer Robert Creamer, who found that "in the upper decks, people in right field could not see the right fielder, and people in the left field could not see the left fielder."[43] In fact, many people in the left field lower deck would also have had difficulty seeing the left fielder.

In the fall, the Giants' second-string baseball home magically turned into a Heisman-candidate football stadium. Temporary seats beefed up the lower deck to about 90 feet deep along the sidelines—nearly doubling the right field rows and nearly tripling the number in left while producing good field proximity. Those seats, about 7,500 in number, also boosted the Polo Grounds' football capacity above 60,000, highly desirable for a sport that traditionally plays to bigger crowds than baseball, albeit less frequently.

The Polo Grounds' outfield grandstands were so deep (136 feet) that they needed four separate rows of structural columns to support them, creating an unprecedented three-dimensional array of view-blocking posts. The home plate seating zone had similar but less severe issues. Creamer noted that "the Polo Grounds [was] a terrible place to watch a ball game…. Some seats … are behind several posts simultaneously, particularly those in the rear of the lower stands behind the dugouts. Watching a game from there is like watching it through a picket fence, and the people who sit there sway back and forth continuously during a game, first one way to get a glimpse of the pitcher winding up—as the batter disappears behind a post—and then the other way, abruptly dismissing the pitcher to watch the batter swing."[44]

All these viewing problems grew out of a questionable planning decision in 1891, which was set in concrete, as it were, in 1911 by a rushed decision, probably on Brush's part, to perpetuate the semicircular form of the burned grandstand and the inadequately sized foul lines, without sufficiently analyzing all the pros and cons of that strategy.

The net result of all these conditions was probably the worst seating layout of any permanent ballpark, one that would be perpetuated for 48 seasons.

And Yet …

The listing of the Polo Grounds' problems and flaws could go on for quite a bit longer, but such an exercise would eventually become pointless. The worst ballpark experiences (and there are several that are worse than what the Polo Grounds had to offer) are still better than none at all. All but one of the half-dozen games that I saw there took place during the day under a bright sun, with rich colors, crisp shadows, and balmy temperatures. I was young and with friends. The grass, like almost all major league grass, was impressively lush in a way that was not remotely hinted at in an era of black-and-white television. Bart Giamatti was fond of pointing out that "paradise" derives from a Persian word for an enclosed green space, and with its high seating decks and clubhouse completely cradling the field, the Polo Grounds certainly met his definition. How many tens of millions of others, unaware of his observation, have nevertheless experienced something very similar?

NOTES

1. Reliable information regarding 19th-century baseball venues is difficult to come by. The first Polo Grounds opened on May 1, 1883, and had two decks. The assumption here is that the upper deck was part of the initial construction, and not a later addition. Four days later, Chicago's double-decked Lakefront Park II opened. Other early wooden second decks include Philadelphia Base Ball Park's (1887), Boston's splendid South End Grounds II (1888) and Congress Street Grounds (1890), Brooklyn's Eastern Park (1890), Polo Grounds IV (1891), and Chicago's West Side Grounds (1893).

2. Despite the impressive size of the expanded Polo Grounds, it was trumped by Yankee Stadium, which opened that year.

3. This data is also somewhat imprecise since attendance at many early games was estimated.

4. 1957 is chosen as the end point since it marked the Giants' and Dodgers' final seasons in New York.

5. Several parks in this period were home to two teams and/or were used for less than full seasons in certain years, so the number of team seasons may differ from the number of years the park was in use.

6. Municipal Stadium does not appear in the table because it hosted too few games to reach the 30 million threshold by 1957.

7. Author calculation.

8. Between 1915 and 1922, Braves Field may have had more seats, but this is uncertain because there is a great divergence between the Boston ballpark's published capacity estimates and its big-game attendance patterns.

9. This detailing included low Italian marble slab partitions defining lower and upper deck box seat boundaries and a somewhat fussy appliqué of symbolic cement bas-relief decorations on the roof edge, upper deck parapet, and the end wall of the right field grandstand. The bas-reliefs soon began to deteriorate and, along with the marble dividers, were removed before or during a major expansion a dozen years later.

10. Philip Lowry, *Green Cathedrals: The Ultimate Celebration of Major League and Negro League Ballparks* (New York: Walker, 2006), 49.

11. Patent #74154, February 4, 1868.

12. James Bready, *The Home Team* (Baltimore: n.p., 1958), 51.

13. The number of examples is limited due to the scarcity of hard data and informative imagery.

14. Strictly speaking, this structure was not a full semicircle, but it was a true circular arc of about 120 degrees.

15. The latter facility was about a mile from the Polo Grounds and was built just four years later.

16. The park's dimensions were 180 feet to left, 300 feet to center, and 196 feet to right. Several individual, team, and venue home run records were set there in 1884, after which the team moved to larger quarters.

17. "Major League Baseball 2016 Official Rules," http://mlb.mlb.com/mlb/official_info/official_rules/objectives_1.jsp.

18. The Yankee Stadium site was large enough to easily allow 320 foot foul lines, but the club wanted to duplicate the dimensions of the 1976 predecessor park, which in turn differed from those in effect for the first half-century of the 1923 original stadium's existence.

19. "The Stadium for the New York Baseball Club," *Engineering Record* 64, no. 5 (July 29, 1911): 126–127.

20. These distances were compiled by the author over a period of about 12 years beginning in 1989. Data sources included direct measurements, scaling, and calculations from architects' working drawings; published cross-sections; interviews with stadium architects; and as-built surveyors' drawings.

21. Scaled and calculated from diagram on "Clem's Baseball," http://www.andrewclem.com/Baseball.php.

22. *Ibid.*

23. *Ibid.*, with some modification based on the architect's diagram.

24. Calculated from an Osborn Engineering working drawing.

25. Calculated from an Osborn Engineering site diagram and working drawing.

26. One might argue that Boston's Grand Pavilion, a.k.a. the South End Grounds, was baseball's greatest architectural accomplishment. The Boston and Cincinnati baseball palaces were yin and yang: one wooden and the other concrete, one energetically picturesque and the other serenely classical, one combustible and the other not. But both departed the baseball scene far too soon.

27. Ironically, it witnessed two fires, since only the grandstand was steel, while other portions were built of wood.

28. Brush himself insisted on a reinforced concrete framework in the interest of fire safety. The Palace's predecessor, Redland Field, also owned by Brush, had burned down even though its structure was partly steel.

29. Thus, the Palace of the Fans was both the first grand architectural monument of its type and the shortest-lived permanent major league park in history.

30. During the fireproof building boom in the first dozen or so years of the 20th century, seating capacities took a sudden jump, in part because steel construction permitted larger grandstands than did wood framing.

31. Its prime seating zone, the unusual raised "opera boxes," was small and could not be enlarged without extensive demolition and reconstruction.

32. Baltimore Memorial Stadium in 1954.

33. If "designers" includes architects, then one can easily deflate Brush's claim by pointing out a simple fact: Frank Lloyd Wright, still almost universally deemed America's finest architect 150 years after his birth, was in the middle of his career in 1911.

34. John T. Brush, "Evolution of a Baseball Grandstand: A New Era in the Development of the National Game," *Baseball Magazine* VIII, no. 6 (April 1912): 3.

35. Henry B. Herts, "Grand Stand for the Polo Grounds," *Architecture and Building* XLIV, no. 11 (November 1912): 457.

36. Bill Shannon and George Kalinsky, *The Ballparks* (New York: Hawthorn Books Inc., 1975), 248. Other published figures range from 3,900 (Tygiel) to 5,500 (*New York Times*), while seemingly credible seating diagrams show room for 3,000 or 4,280 bleacherites. The average of the five data points is 4,216.

37. *New York Herald*, November 21, 1922.

38. Horizontal home run distance plus fence height.

39. The 37-foot figure refers to the bottom of the overhanging upper deck, rather than to a high wall.

40. Left field had about eight fewer seating rows than right, but this was not adequate to stem the flood of home runs. And the left field upper deck had a full complement of seats, overhanging the lower deck by about 29 feet.

41. This high wall was also built to block views of the game from neighboring row houses, a problem that affected several other contemporary parks, just as it does today at Wrigley Field.

42. Difference divided by shortest dimension.

43. Jules Tygiel, *Extra Bases: Reflections on Jackie Robinson, Race, and Baseball History* (Lincoln: University of Nebraska Press, 2002), 154.

44. *Ibid.*

Black Baseball
at the Polo Grounds

Part I: Notable Players, Teams and Performances
BY TOM EDWARDS

The history of the Negro Leagues has interested me for many years. During a baseball event in San Diego in the 1980s, I asked Buck O'Neil if it bothered him that he did not get to play with and against some of the best players in the world because of his race. I remember his answer as clearly as if he said it yesterday: "How do you know I didn't?" What a great reply. And some of those outstanding black players that O'Neil implied that he had played against participated in games held at the Polo Grounds.

A doubleheader featuring two black teams and a team of white minor league all-stars at the Polo Grounds produced highlights on September 19, 1937. The first game matched the Dominican Republic All-Stars, which had Satchel Paige as its pitcher, against a picked squad of black players, most of whom were from the Negro National League (NNL). For the latter team, Schoolboy Johnny Taylor took the mound. Taylor, a Connecticut native, had been with the New York Cubans of the NNL the previous two years and in 1937 was pitching for the Savitt Gems, a semipro team in Hartford, Connecticut.

Taylor and Paige matched scoreless innings through seven, but in the bottom of the eighth, Jim West of the Philadelphia Stars launched a two-run homer off Paige to put the picked squad in front. In the ninth, Taylor retired George Scales, Spooner Palm, and James "Cool Papa" Bell for a no-hitter. By winning the first game, the Negro Stars qualified to play the white minor leaguers, one of whom was 45-year-old Ray Schalk.

On September 17, 1946, the first game of the Negro League World Series was played at the Polo Grounds. It was a best-of-seven format that featured the Negro American League (NAL) Kansas City Monarchs and the Negro National League Newark Eagles. After the first inning, it was 1–0 Kansas City, but Newark tied the game in the bottom of the sixth. Then, in the seventh inning, Satchel Paige singled and eventually scored the winning run for the Monarchs. Unlike current fall classics, Negro League championships were held in ballparks that were not always the home field for either team.

The Monarchs were one of the most successful teams in Negro League history with championships that went back to the 1920s. Manager Frank Duncan's team had NAL batting champion Buck O'Neil at first base and Chico Renfroe at short, the man who backed

Buck O'Neil with Tom Edwards, who had the chance to meet O'Neil in the 1980s (collection of Tom Edwards).

up Jackie Robinson prior to Robinson breaking the color barrier in Organized Baseball. Satchel Paige, Hilton Smith, James LaMarque, Ted Alexander, Ford Smith, and Steve Wylie took the mound for the Kansas City team, with Paige and Hilton as well as center fielder Willard Brown later being inducted into the National Baseball Hall of Fame.

Unlike the Monarchs, the Eagles were not a frequent Negro League World Series team, but their owner, Effa Manley, and their manager, Biz Mackey, both 2006 National Baseball Hall Fame inductees themselves, had three other future Hall of Famers on their team: Leon Day, Larry Doby, and Monte Irvin.

When the New York Giants were on the road, the Negro National League New York Cubans played their home games at the Polo Grounds. For team owner Alejandro "Alex" Pómpez, it was their home field for a number of years in the 1940s. Pómpez owned the Cubans from 1935 until 1950 and in 1924 helped organize the first Negro League World Series. From 1946 to 1948, he was the vice president of the Negro National League. His 70 years in the game included scouting for the New York and San Francisco Giants.

The Cubans frequently had strong teams. In 1935, they won the second-half title but were defeated four games to three by the Pittsburgh Crawfords in the playoff for the league championship. The ace of the Cubans' pitching staff was Martín Dihigo, a Hall of Famer who many long-time baseball followers consider among the greatest players of all time. During the 1941 season the Cubans were the second-half winner, but fell in the league playoff, three games to one, to the first-half winner, the Homestead Grays. In 1947, the Cubans, led by future major league star Minnie Miñoso, won the pennant and defeated the Negro American League's Cleveland Buckeyes in the World Series. The following year, the Cubans became the only Negro League team with a formal agreement with a major league franchise; they were a farm team for Horace Stoneham's New York Giants.

In 1948, the final Negro League World Series was held, as by this time the top black players were moving into the now-integrated National and American leagues. By 1951, Willie Mays had gone from the Birmingham Black Barons to the New York Giants after stops in the minors at Trenton and Minneapolis. Hank Aaron, Roy Campanella, and Ernie Banks were among the Negro League stars who followed Jackie Robinson and Larry Doby to the majors and the integration of the game effectively brought an end to what many had called blackball.

Part II: The New York Cubans BY RORY COSTELLO

From 1944 until they became defunct after the 1950 season, the New York Cubans of the Negro Leagues called the Polo Grounds home. This short but intriguing segment of the stadium's history revolves around the club's owner, Hall of Famer Alex Pómpez.

During the 1920s and 1930s, Pómpez was involved with the numbers racket in New

From 1944 to 1950 the New York Cubans played at the Polo Grounds (collection of Stew Thornley).

York, and so he became a target of special prosecutor Thomas Dewey. As a result, the Cubans did not operate during the 1937 or 1938 seasons; Pómpez hid out in Mexico for a portion of this time. Meanwhile, his team's former home was demolished in 1938. That was Dyckman Oval, in the Inwood neighborhood of Manhattan, about two miles north of the Polo Grounds.

The Cubans returned to play in the Negro National League (NNL) in 1939—but they did not have a park of their own. As author Neil Lanctot wrote, they scheduled their rare home games at Yankee Stadium, sharing the park with the New York Black Yankees. Pómpez tried to lease Ebbets Field in Brooklyn but encountered opposition from the management of Dexter Park (located in Woodhaven, Queens), home of the Brooklyn Bushwicks, a fast semipro team that often played Negro League clubs. The Cubans were rightly viewed as a competitive threat.[1]

Lanctot added that the Polo Grounds "had also remained largely off-limits, a situation that Eddie Gottlieb and Yankee Stadium officials seemed uninterested in changing." Gottlieb, a promoter and booking agent, had been assigned by the NNL in 1937 to book all independent games for league teams on the East Coast.[2] However, the Cubans did play at least one game at the Polo Grounds in 1943, as part of a four-team doubleheader on May 30.[3]

"In 1944, however," Lanctot continued, "Pómpez succeeded in leasing the park for several dates without the involvement of Gottlieb, achieving such success that the Cubans would soon gain permanent residency, scheduling more than 20 dates at the Polo Grounds in 1945."[4]

According to Adrián Burgos, Jr., author of *Cuban Star*, the definitive Pómpez biography, the announcement of a lease deal for the Polo Grounds with Horace Stoneham, owner of the New York Giants, came in the first week of June 1944.[5] It is not entirely clear how Pómpez made this breakthrough, but he and other NNL executives were sick of the Yankee Stadium situation and Eddie Gottlieb's role. Lanctot also suggests that the Giants saw how much the Yankees were making on Negro League games during World War II and wanted in on the action.[6] Indeed, Stoneham and his club benefited greatly from their ties with Pómpez—especially in the long run.

Actually, the Cubans had already opened their 1944 season at the Polo Grounds. Before 12,000 fans on May 21, they defeated the Black Yankees, 6–4.[7] Judging from newspaper accounts, the Cubans played more than just several games at their new home in 1944. One exciting contest came against the Homestead Grays, starring the great Josh Gibson, on July 15. Gibson had two homers—described as a "mighty clout in the right-field stands" and "a whistling line drive into the left-field stands"—plus a triple. However, a fierce electrical storm that ripped up trees and tore down building structures halted the game in the ninth inning with the score tied 5–5.[8]

The '44 Cubans had quite an array of talent. At first base was the captain, Dave "Showboat" Thomas, who got a tryout with the Brooklyn Dodgers the following spring. Gil Garrido from Panama was the second baseman. His son, also named Gil, played in the major leagues from 1964 through 1972. The shortstop was Horacio "Rabbit" Martínez, acclaimed as the slickest gloveman in the Negro Leagues in that era. At third base was Héctor Rodríguez, a Cuban who eventually played one season in the majors with the Chicago White Sox in 1952. In the outfield were two veteran Latino stars: Pancho Coimbre from Puerto Rico and Juan "Tetelo" Vargas, the greatest Dominican player of his time. They were then aged 35 and 38, respectively, but still commanded much of their skill.

Alongside them was Claro Duany, a fine Cuban player. The pitching staff included Dave "Impo" Barnhill, Pat Scantlebury (a Panamanian who made it to the majors briefly in 1956), Barney Morris, and Luis E. Tiant, father of the big-league star of the 1960s and 1970s.

Even with this roster, the Cubans finished well behind the Grays in 1944, but that December, Joe Bostic, sports editor of the *People's Voice*, told Pómpez that he had a gold mine with the Polo Grounds as a home field.[9] At least in 1945 that held true; by one report, home attendance was 300,000 that season.[10] That came despite a cluster of rainouts and injuries, plus the loss of Cuban talent to big-league organizations. Another prominent black sportswriter, Wendell Smith of the *Pittsburgh Courier*, described Pómpez's woes in a funny column from June 1945.[11]

That year, Pómpez added burly catcher Rafael "Ray" Noble, who later became a member of the Giants' pennant-winning team in 1951. He brought in still more strong players in 1946, including Orestes Miñoso, later known as "Minnie," who played third base. The shortstop in 1946 was Silvio García, who pushed Rabbit Martínez over to second base. Still, the Grays remained the power in the NNL in 1945, and the Newark Eagles—starring Larry Doby and Monte Irvin—succeeded them.

Finally, in 1947, the Cubans brought Pómpez his first pennant in his 30 years in the Negro Leagues. After an inconsistent start, they surged in the second half of the season. New York then defeated the Cleveland Buckeyes, champions of the Negro American League (NAL) or West in the Negro League World Series. The Series was held in a string of different stadiums; Game One at the Polo Grounds ended in a tie because of rain.

A couple of months before, on July 29, another meaningful Negro League game took place at the Polo Grounds: the second of the two East-West All-Star games that year. The West won, 8–2, but that game held a more enduring significance. Pómpez had invited a number of major league executives. "Most declined, but Stoneham showed up, and their friendship deepened. Stoneham would forgive Pómpez his rent when he couldn't pay."[12]

The 1948 season was the last for the Negro National League. The Cubans therefore joined the Negro American League in 1949. In January of that year, the *New York Age* wrote: "Pómpez has had a rough time financially for the past two years. His world champions in 1947 weren't moneymakers, and playing every Sunday in 1948 in either Yankee Stadium or Polo Grounds was definitely a losing proposition. Perhaps no club owner in baseball has ever gone through an entire season losing at the gate every Sunday as did Pómpez and his New York Cubans last year and survive. He, however, is going to give it one more trial this year and is making extensive plans to have an outstanding club to match the strong competition that will be encountered in the new league."[13]

Adrián Burgos also described how following the 1948 season, Pómpez—strapped for cash—entered a working agreement with the Giants. The Cubans became an informal Giant farm team, and the first transactions between the clubs occurred in June 1949. Pómpez sold player-manager Ray Dandridge, Ray Noble, and Impo Barnhill to the Giants for $21,000.[14] It was the beginning of the end for the Cubans.

Pómpez, though, stuck it out through the 1950 season. That May, Dan Burley of *The New York Age* wrote, "Alex Pómpez ... has been the 'Noblest Roman of them all' in refusing to quit the game in the face of stupendous losses." Burley described the owner's optimism vividly: "Pómpez has an abiding faith in his people and in the destiny of organized Negro baseball.... That is why he has willingly lost a fortune trying to keep the game alive.... The fact that colored patrons deserted him and the other owners for the new varieties of Negroes in major league uniforms hasn't deterred him one bit in his deter-mination to sell a strong Negro league to the public…. 'If Rube Foster did it, I can too,' he told me."[15]

That year, the Cubans had another future major leaguer on their roster: Edmundo "Sandy" Amorós, whose racing catch in Game Seven of the 1955 World Series was crucial in the only fall classic that the Brooklyn Dodgers ever won. While playing for Pómpez, the little Cuban (then aged just 20) hit at least one notable homer at the Polo Grounds. Pitcher Sam Williams had promised to knock Amorós down before the game and sailed a fastball dangerously close to the batter's head. Sandy then held up his end of the pregame exchange by belting one into the second deck.[16]

As Burgos wrote, though, more deals with the Giants could not quite make the team profitable, and slashing ticket prices for games at the Polo Grounds did not stimulate attendance.[17] It was too much even for Pómpez to endure, and the weary owner pulled the plug on the New York Cubans.

Pómpez then moved into scouting for the Giants, a job he held as late as 1971. His integral role in bringing black and Latino talent into the organization—and more broadly, the major leagues—is evidenced by such names as Mays, Marichal, Cepeda, Irvin, and Alou.

NOTES

1. Neil Lanctot, *Negro League Baseball: The Rise and Ruin of a Black Institution* (Philadelphia: University of Pennsylvania Press, 2004), 148.

2. *Ibid.*, 148, 111. Eddie Gottlieb was also a vital contributor to the game of basketball, becoming a member of that sport's Hall of Fame in 1971.

3. "Cubans in P.G. Clash," *Brooklyn Eagle*, May 29, 1943.

4. Lanctot, 148.

5. Adrián Burgos, Jr., *Cuban Star: How One Negro-League Owner Changed the Face of Baseball* (New York: Hill and Wang, 2011).

6. E-mail from Neil Lanctot to Rory Costello, November 6, 2014.

7. "Negro National League Officially Opens Season at Polo Grounds before 12,000 Fans," *New York Age*, May 27, 1944.

8. "Grays, Cubans Tied; 'Satch' Blanks Barons," *Pittsburgh Courier*, July 22, 1944.

9. Wendell Smith, "The Sports Beat," *Pittsburgh Courier*, December 28, 1944.

10. Al Buck, "Negro Loop Slaps Back with Raid on Outlaws," *The Sporting News*, March 7, 1946, 2.

11. Wendell Smith, "Smitty's Sports Spurts," *Pittsburgh Courier*, June 23, 1945.

12. James S. Hirsch, *Willie Mays: The Life, The Legend* (New York: Simon & Schuster, 2010), 283.

13. Curtis A. Leak, "NY Cubans Lining Up Local Tilts," *New York Age*, January 22, 1949.

14. Burgos, 182–183.

15. Dan Burley, "Will This Be Negro Baseball's Comeback Year?," *New York Age*, May 20, 1950.

16. Brent P. Kelley, *"I Will Never Forget": Interviews with 39 Former Negro League Players.* (Jefferson, NC: McFarland, 2003), 178. For a picture of Amorós as a New York Cuban, see *The Kingston Daily Freeman*, August 23, 1950.

17. Burgos, 184.

The Boys of the Polo Grounds
Youth Baseball, 1944–1958

ALAN COHEN

On September 28, 1946, one of the greatest pitching duels in the history of the Polo Grounds took place. Prior to the big leaguers taking the field that day, a contest was held to decide the New York City Sandlot Championship. Nineteen-forty-six marked the second year in which the New York *Journal-American* sponsored contests between the teams in the leagues comprising the *Journal-American* Sandlot Alliance. One of the foremost leagues in this union was the Queens-Nassau Alliance, which was represented by the 34th Avenue Boys with its star pitcher, Ed "Lefty" Ford. They were challenged by the Bay Ridge Cubs from Brooklyn and their ace pitcher, Lou DeAngelis.

For three innings, not a hit was allowed. Then, Bay Ridge broke through for a single in the fourth and another one-bagger in the ninth but could not get a runner across the plate against Ford, who struck out the side three times en route to an 18-strikeout performance. Meanwhile, DeAngelis tossed a no-hitter for ten innings, but Ford led off the bottom of the 11th with a double and came around to score the winning run in the 1–0 contest.[1] For his heroics, Ford was selected as the game's Most Valuable Player (MVP), and one week later, he was signed by the Yankees for a $7,500 bonus. His next game was as a professional, and the rest is history, as Ed "Whitey" Ford went on to a Hall of Fame career in the Bronx.

The New York *Journal-American* in 1946, at the urging of sports editor Max Kase, sponsored the inaugural Hearst Sandlot Classic. Hearst newspapers from 12 cities across the country sent players to New York to face the New York *Journal-American* All-Stars. In that first year, it was known as the Hearst Diamond Pennant Series.

The Hearst syndicate was not the only publishing group in the country to be involved in youth baseball. In 1944 and 1945, *Esquire Magazine* had sponsored the *Esquire* All-American Boys Baseball Game at the Polo Grounds. Boys 16 and 17 years old were selected from around the country, with most states being represented, and then divided into East and West squads.

In 1944, the managers were none other than Connie Mack (East) and Mel Ott (West), with Mack's coaches being Al Simmons and Roy Mack, and Ott's being Carl Hubbell and Bubber Jonnard.

The West Squad included a catcher from Tilden, Nebraska, named Richie Ashburn, who would return to the Polo Grounds often during his major league career, covering the expansive center field at the old ballpark. Ashburn wore number 1 and was somewhat

Managers and coaches in the Esquire's All-American Boys Baseball Game at the Polo Grounds in 1944. Left to right: Mel Ott, Virgil Jester, Billy Pierce, and Connie Mack (collection of Alan Cohen).

frustrated that Ott did not include him in the starting lineup. His father, Neal, encouraged his becoming a catcher to facilitate his move to the big leagues. He also encouraged him to hit from the left side to take advantage of his speed. At the *Esquire* game, East manager Connie Mack suggested that Richie become an outfielder. Not long thereafter, he did move to the outfield, and, 18 years later, he finished his Hall of Fame playing career back at the Polo Grounds with the 1962 New York Mets.

Prior to the first *Esquire* game, there were festivities that kept the large crowd entertained. Featured were Abbott and Costello, actors Dana Andrews and Jay C. Flippen, baseball clown-prince Al Schacht, and the Gene Krupa Band. The umpires were George Barr of the National League and Bill Grieve of the American League. Red Barber and Harry Wismer broadcast the game over a national radio network.

Ott stated, "The All-American Boys Baseball game is a great contribution in the nation in wartime. This game takes me right back to the days when I was a youngster playing baseball on the corner sandlot. I am very proud that *Esquire* has invited me to be a manager of one of the All-American Boys Baseball teams."[2]

Mack added, "Please accept my sincere thanks for the appointment to manage the Eastern team in the All-American Boys Baseball game sponsored by *Esquire*. I deem it a privilege to aid such a worthy cause as the 'living memorial" fund and will contribute what I can to help the boys and baseball as a whole."[3]

A crowd of 17,803 watched as the East team shut out the West team, 6–0. The pitching star of the East team, Billy Pierce, known as "Mr. Zero" due to his numerous shutouts, tossed six scoreless innings for the win and was named the MVP.[4] Pierce then signed with the Tigers and pitched for them in parts of the 1945 (he took the mound in ten games during the season and got a World Series ring) and 1948 seasons before being traded to the White Sox, where he blossomed. In 13 years with Chicago, he went 186–152 with a 3.19 ERA, was named to seven All-Star teams, and led his league in wins (20 in 1957), strikeouts (186 in 1953), and ERA (1.97 in 1955). At age 35, when it looked like he was slowing down, Pierce was traded to San Francisco and his 16–6 record was vital as the Giants won the 1962 National League pennant.

Pierce was a Detroit native and played on the sandlots with a team known as the Owls, for which his father, a druggist, was one of the team's sponsors. Billy overcame wildness to become a successful high school pitcher. As Pierce tells the story: "In 1944, I went to New York for the *Esquire* amateur all-star game. I had never thought about being a major leaguer—I was taking Latin and physics in anticipation of becoming a doctor—but after going to the Polo Grounds and Ebbets Field, I got more of a feeling of what it would be like. The Tigers were my favorite team, and I signed with their head scout, Wish Egan, when I was still 17. I finished classes on March 15, joined the Tigers (for spring training), and then came back in June and got my diploma."[5]

In addition to Ashburn and Pierce, Ervin Palica and Virgil Jester made it to the majors, and 19 of the 29 participants in the game went on to play professionally.

The 1945 *Esquire* game at the Polo Grounds produced Curt Simmons, who would go on to star with the Phillies and the Cardinals. Managers were Babe Ruth (East) and Ty Cobb (West). At the time, Simmons had just completed his sophomore year of high school and was only 16. "His mound prowess earned him selection to an American Legion all-star game in Shibe Park in Philadelphia, where he struck out seven of the nine hitters he faced in three innings."[6] From there, it was on to New York, where he emulated Ruth. He pitched the first four innings, allowing one earned run and then switched to the outfield for the final five innings, tripling and driving in a teammate during a three-run ninth-inning rally as his East team came from behind to win, 5–4.

Six players in addition to Simmons made it to the majors. They included Davey Williams, Bob DiPietro, Jack Dittmer, Vern Morgan, Herbert Plews, and John Thomas.

DiPietro remembered a scene during practice when Babe Ruth was frustrated with one of his players in the batting cage. "He [Ruth] grabbed the bat from one of the players and told the kid, 'Get the hell out of the batting cage. You aren't worth shit as a hitter.' He said, 'Carl [Hubbell], groove a few of 'em here. Let me show them how to hit.' Carl Hubbell was pitching! I look back. Cobb, Ruth, Hubbell, and what did I get? Zip [for autographs]! Ruth hit six balls into the stands. It was the damnedest exhibition I'd seen. And he was in a sweat suit. But he had that great swing. Of course, the Polo Grounds, it was very short down both lines, but he hit a good drive to center field. He put on a show; it was great."[7]

The last *Esquire* game was held at Wrigley Field in Chicago in 1946, the same year that the first Hearst Sandlot Classic was held at the Polo Grounds.

The Hearst Sandlot Classic: Founders, Managers, Personalities

In 1946, sportswriter Max Kase of the *New York Journal-American* created the Hearst Sandlot Classic, an annual event featuring a team of New York All-Stars against a team of U.S. All-Stars that was held at the Polo Grounds through 1958. But beginning in 1959 and continuing through 1965, the game was played at Yankee Stadium, since following the move of the Giants to San Francisco, the Polo Grounds was effectively abandoned.

As a sidelight, Kase would go on to great fame and a Pulitzer Prize when he broke the story of the basketball fixing scandal involving City College of New York, Long Island University, and New York University in 1951.[8]

The Sandlot Classic had the backing of William Randolph Hearst who, early on, stated: "This program will be conducted in all Hearst cities from coast to coast. The purpose of the program will not be to develop players for [O]rganized [B]aseball, but will be designed to further the spirit of athletic competition among the youth of America."[9]

Just getting into the game was no easy task. Hearst Newspapers throughout the country sponsored tournament and all-star contests to determine candidates who would go to New York.

Newspapers that were involved included the *Boston Record-American, Milwaukee Sentinel, Pittsburgh Sun-Telegraph, San Francisco Examiner, Los Angeles Herald-Express, Baltimore News-Post, Seattle Post-Intelligencer, Detroit Times, Albany Times-Union, Chicago Herald-American, Oakland Post-Enquirer* and *San Antonio Light*.

The epicenter of baseball in America was New York City. During the first 12 years of the Hearst Classic, there were three major league teams in The Big Apple. From 1947 through 1958, at least one New York team was in the World Series, and in seven of those years, the entire Series was played in New York. And in The City that Never Sleeps, the best youngsters honed their skills on the sandlots in any number of leagues.

The involvement of the *Journal-American* in boys baseball began in 1945 with support from the Police Athletic League (PAL), Catholic Youth Organization (CYO), Kiwanis, New York City Baseball Federation, and the Queens-Nassau Alliance. Heading up the program was Ethan Allen, a former outfielder who had compiled a .300 batting average during a 13-year career with six major league teams. He later coached at Yale for 26 seasons, from 1943 through 1969, and one of his players was George H.W. Bush.

"All they need is a little encouragement, and they'll be playing it as well as I ever did."[10] Those words were spoken by Walter James Vincent "Rabbit" Maranville in 1949 at Yankee Stadium. Three years earlier, the scope of the sandlot program was increased. Maranville succeeded Allen as director, and the first Hearst Sandlot Classic, bringing in boys from around the country, was held. The New York team was selected from tryouts conducted in the leagues that comprised the *Journal-American* City Sandlot Alliance, with Maranville as its manager, in addition to running the program.

Maranville began his major league career in 1912 with the Boston Braves and played in the majors for 23 years. An exceptional middle infielder, he still holds the all-time record for assists with 8,967. As his career wound down, his defensive skills were as good as ever. In 1930, at the age of 38, he led the league's shortstops in fielding percentage, and two years later, he moved to second base and duplicated the feat. Not considered a great hitter, he nevertheless ranks 19th all-time with 177 triples. As noted in his obituary in the *New York Times*, "he established himself as one of the greatest little men [he stood only 5'4"] that baseball has ever known and also endeared himself to followers of the national pastime as an outstanding personality."[11] Of his defense, it was stated that "his ground-covering ability was amazing, he had sure hands and a strong, accurate throwing arm and he supplemented his mechanical talents with unrivaled dash and verve."[12]

Maranville arranged clinics for youngsters in the New York area under the tutelage of players, coaches, and managers from the three New York major league squads. Although sentiment did play a role in his election to the Hall of Fame in 1954 (he had died just prior to the voting), he was named on 62.1 percent of the ballots the preceding year. His stellar defense during 23 major league seasons was the most significant factor in his election, although the electors also were aware of his involvement in the youth program.

Arthur Daley of the *New York Times* was an ardent supporter of Maranville. Noting the star infielder's off-the-field escapades (he definitely enjoyed a good time), Daley wrote: "There was a certain amount of irony in the fact that the Rabbit's later years were spent in doing an extraordinarily fine job in promoting sandlot baseball for the *Journal-American*. He was helping and inspiring the kids, although he would have shuddered in horror if any of them had ever followed his [off-the-field] example. But maybe there was not so much irony in his job at that. The Rabbit was always a kid himself, a Peter Pan who didn't want to grow up."[13]

George Vecsey of the *New York Times* set off a firestorm of sorts when he stated in 1989 that Maranville's two greatest attributes were longevity and good deeds as the sandlot ambassador for a newspaper chain with many Hall of Fame electors.[14] Within a couple of weeks, a deluge of letters appeared on his desk. The Rabbit, indeed, was worthy of the Hall of Fame.

After Maranville died suddenly from a heart attack in January 1954 at the age of 62, Al Simmons took over. Simmons, a Hall of Famer, got his start playing sandlot ball as a youngster in Milwaukee and managed in the Classic for two years until his untimely death in 1956,[15] when George "Snuffy" Stirnweiss became the director. Snuffy had played with the New York Yankees from 1943 through 1950 and won the American League batting title in 1945. After Stirnweiss' tragic death in a railroad accident, Tommy Holmes assumed leadership in 1959, when "The World Series of Kids' Baseball" was moved to Yankee Stadium.

Kase enlisted Ray Schalk and Oscar Vitt to lead the U.S. All-Stars. Schalk managed the team through 1948, but he stepped aside after three years because his contract as baseball coach at Purdue did not allow him to engage in any outside activities. At the time he left, he said that he "liked being around the kids and the biggest kid of all, Rabbit Maranville."[16] Vitt took over the head job, ably assisted by such luminaries as Max Carey, Charlie Gehringer, and Lefty Gomez and stayed with the program until illness forced him to step aside in 1962, at which time Eddie Joost took over.

Vitt played with the Detroit Tigers from 1912 through 1918 and the Boston Red Sox from 1919 through 1921. He went on to a successful managerial career, spending 11 years in the Pacific Coast League and leading the Hollywood Stars to three consecutive league championship finals from 1929 through 1931. During the 1936 and 1937 seasons, he compiled a 197–110 record with the Newark Bears of the International League, winning the league championship in the latter year. He then managed Cleveland from 1938 through 1940. However, though he had a winning record and led his teams to three first-division finishes—two thirds and a second—there was major dissension among a number of his players, and he was let go after the 1940 season. He retired in 1942 following a two-year stint in the Pacific Coast League and turned to youth baseball, running the *San Francisco Examiner's* baseball school beginning in 1946.

Frank Graham of the *Journal-American* said this of Vitt: "As a young fellow playing ball with the Tigers and the Red Sox, Oscar Vitt was full of zing. Now in his fifties, graying and wearing spectacles, he is—you guessed it—full of zing. The kind of guy who, if he lives to be a hundred or more, will not change. You know why the kids like him so much. He has the gift of remembering his own youth. He doesn't have to tell that to the kids with whom he works. They know it just by looking at him and listening to him. The mistakes they make on the field are the mistakes he made long ago, and he doesn't attempt to conceal it from them."[17]

Fifty-seven of the young men who played in the Hearst Classic at the Polo Grounds made their way to the major leagues, including three Hall of Famers. In the 1957 World Series, five participants could trace their starts to the Hearst Classic. And one player from those Polo Grounds games managed a World Series champion.

Hearst Sandlot Classic, 1946

The inaugural Hearst game was played on August 15 and set the bar for the visitors. Included in the players' package were seats to a Yankee–Red Sox game, a day at Long Island's Jones Beach, a reception at the residence of New York's mayor, a trip around Manhattan Island by boat, a Broadway play—that year it was *Showboat*—a trip to West Point, a steak dinner at the Bear Mountain Inn, accommodations at the Hotel New Yorker, and an opportunity to perform in front of major league scouts and meet with major league players.

The game was won, 8–7, in 11 innings by the New Yorkers in front of 15,269 fans, and nine players would go on to perform in the big leagues.

The first ball was thrown out by New York City mayor William O'Dwyer, and officiating was the dean of umpires and reigning National League umpire-in-chief, Hall of Famer Bill Klem, who was assisted by Butch Henline and Dolly Stark.

The game went into extra innings when Brooklyn's Chris Kitsos, with two outs in the bottom of the ninth, singled in two runs to knot the score at 7–7. He was on third in the second half of the 11th inning and scored on a wild pitch for the game-ender. Kitsos signed with the Dodgers and spent five years in their minor league system before being drafted by the Chicago Cubs after the 1951 season. The Cubs called up the shortstop in 1954, and, on April 21, he was inserted as a defensive replacement in the eighth inning after a struggling Ernie Banks had been pulled for a pinch-hitter. He handled two ground balls flawlessly, returned to the dugout, and never re-emerged. His major league career was over.

The starting pitcher in that first Hearst game for the U.S. All-Stars was Herb Adams from Chicago. He signed with his hometown White Sox in 1947 as an outfielder and batted .405 in his first minor league season with Class D Madisonville, Kentucky. He then played parts of three seasons with the Sox before his major league career concluded in 1950 at the age of 24.

The first player to get a hit in the contest was the MVP of the game: Dimitrios Speros

"Jim" Baxes of Mission High School in San Francisco, who could easily be mistaken for Joe DiMaggio, to whom he bore an uncanny physical resemblance. Not only did he come from the same city as the Yankee Clipper, but he also adopted Joe's batting style.[18] The first of his three hits was a fourth-inning double that led to his team's getting into the scoring column, taking a 1–0 lead. Each of his other hits, both singles, factored in rallies that accounted for all of his team's runs. Although the U.S. All-Stars lost, he was clearly the star of the game. Baxes was signed by Brooklyn in 1947 and finally made it to the majors in 1959, where he got into 11 games with the Dodgers before being traded to Cleveland and playing 77 games for the Tribe. In 280 major league at bats (all in 1959), he hit .246 with 17 homers and 39 runs batted in.

Billy Harrell, who also appeared in the 1946 game, was the first player of color to perform in the Hearst Classic, less than a year before major league baseball was integrated. Because of Harrell's participation, heavyweight champion Joe Louis bought 1,000 tickets for the game, and these tickets were distributed by the *Amsterdam News* to children in Harlem.[19]

Harrell grew up in Troy, New York, and attended Siena College, where he also played basketball. He was so appreciated during his time at Siena that the school held a special night in his honor on February 14, 1952. Later that year, he was signed to a contract with the Cleveland Indians, and over the next three years, he starred in the minors at Cedar Rapids (where he had a .325 batting average), Reading (.330), and Indianapolis (.307) before playing with the Tribe in parts of the 1955, 1957, and 1958 seasons. He made his last major league stop in Boston in 1961. In the big leagues, he batted .231 with eight home runs and 26 RBI.

As a junior at Waltham High School in 1946, Norman Roy began his season with a no-hitter against Middlesex and followed it with a one-hitter, striking out 15, but his team lost to Watertown, 1–0.[20] On July 2, 1947, he signed with the Boston Braves organization, and after accumulating a 27–13 record during three years in the minors, he spent the 1950 season with the Braves in Boston, going 4–3. His career in the majors ended at the age of 21, but he returned to the minors in 1951, playing in one game that year and two more the next year.

Billy Loes was signed by the Dodgers on August 20, 1948, for a bonus estimated at $22,000.[21] He split the 1949 season between Class B Nashua and Class AA Fort Worth, posting a 16–5 record. In 1950, now with the Dodgers, he saw very little activity, getting into ten games and pitching a total of 12⅔ innings. After a year in the military, he returned to Brooklyn and achieved a 50–25 record over the next four seasons. He was sold to Baltimore early in 1956 and finished his career with the Giants in 1961.

Jimmy Mangan, a catcher from San Francisco, signed with the Pirates in 1949 and made it to the big leagues in 1952. Over the next few years, he shuttled back and forth between the majors and minors, getting into a total of 45 major league games during three seasons and finishing his career in Organized Baseball with the San Antonio Missions of the Class AA Texas League in 1958.

Earl Smith signed with the Pirates in 1949 but found himself stuck in their minor league system for far too long. In 1955, he finally got to the parent club and wore number 21 for five games, garnering one hit in 16 at bats. On April 29, he played his last game, and number 21 was reassigned by the Pirates for the last time—to Roberto Clemente.

The career of Paul Schramka was even shorter. Prior to the Hearst Game, he had completed his freshman year at the University of San Francisco and had excelled in the Hearst Diamond Pennant Series All-Star Game held at Borchert Field in Milwaukee. He then became the starting center fielder and the first batter in the game in New York, where he grounded out twice before tripling off the right field wall in his five-inning stint. Signed by the Chicago Cub organization in 1949, he began the 1953 season with the parent club, wearing uniform number 14. However, he appeared in only two games and never came to the plate. And, thus, number 14 went to Ernie Banks.

1947

> "The Hearst papers would have us on the move for every minute [of our stay in New York]. [They would have us] in the spotlight on this famous old Manhattan island, showing us off, and promoting the game for all it was worth, and each of us loved every minute of the astronomical, All-American week!"
>
> —U.S. All-Star center fielder Bobby Hoeft[22]

The agenda was similar to that of 1946 with a couple of additions that made the trip more memorable. At West Point, the boys met with All-American footballers Doc Blanchard and Glenn Davis. A busy agenda was expanded to include a tour by Joe DiMaggio of the clubhouse at Yankee Stadium.

The boys were taken on the Yankee team bus to the fights at Madison Square Garden, where they had ringside seats. Trips to the mayor's residence and the amusement park at Coney Island followed, and they saw *Annie Get Your Gun,* starring Ethel Merman, on Broadway. On the eve of the game, the boys went to Radio City Music Hall, where they viewed *The Bachelor and the Bobby Soxer,* which was in its world premiere at the theater. The stars of the movie, including a grown-up Shirley Temple, were seated two rows in front of the Hearst teams.

The class of 1947 produced nine major leaguers. Playing for the U.S. team, which won a lopsided 13–2 decision, were three men who would be reunited in the 1960 World Series—Gino Cimoli, Dick Groat, and Bill Skowron, whose inside-the-park homer was the first round-tripper in the short history of the Hearst Classic. The 31,232 spectators—the most to ever attend a Hearst game—saw a golf and baseball exhibition by Babe Didrikson Zacharias, an appearance by boxer Rocky Graziano, and a performance by the Clown Prince of Baseball, Al Schacht, who had also performed at the 1946 Hearst game. The icing on the cake was one of the last public appearances by the game's honorary chairman, Babe Ruth. The Bambino took his seat in the bottom of the second inning and was accorded a standing ovation that stopped the game.

Left-handed pitcher Don Ferrarese represented Oakland and was selected the game's MVP. In high school, he was undefeated and struck out an average of two batters per inning.[23] He earned the trip to New York by excelling in the annual all-star game at the Oakland minor league ballpark, where he hurled all nine innings, had 12 strikeouts, and was credited with the win,[24] and he did so well during practice sessions in The Big Apple that he was chosen to start in the Hearst Classic. There, he pitched three hitless innings and struck out six batters in gaining the victory. After the game, he was carried off the field to the clubhouse in center field by Cimoli and Reno Cheso. He also got to meet Babe Ruth, who had throat cancer and was barely audible but who asked to speak with the game's MVP. Ferrarese made his major league debut with Baltimore in 1955 and played with five teams over the course of eight years, posting a 19–36 record.

More known for his basketball feats in high school, Gino Cimoli played baseball only in his senior year. But he batted .607 and was selected for the Hearst squad. He then was signed by the Brooklyn Dodgers and his first year in Organized Ball was in 1949 when he split his time between Nashua, New Hampshire, and Montreal. Seven years later, he made it to the majors and was selected for the National League All-Star team the following season.

When the Dodgers and Giants moved to the left coast in 1958, Dodger manager Walt Alston had Cimoli bat leadoff during the Dodgers visit to Seals Stadium in San Francisco for the first West Coast game. After 1958, Cimoli was traded to St. Louis, and from there it was on to Pittsburgh, where he was a member of the 1960 championship team ("They set all the records, but we won the game"). By 1962, he was with Kansas City, and for the combined 1962 and 1963 seasons, his 26 triples were the best in the majors. He retired after the 1965 season and took a job with UPS.

On October 17, 1989, San Francisco was experiencing a severe earthquake. Cimoli and his friend Big Ed Silva turned their UPS truck into an ambulance, with Cimoli entering one of the homes along Scott Street and saving a woman who had been trapped on the third floor. He helped out other victims as well, traveling throughout the Marina area.[25]

Dick Groat represented Pittsburgh in the Hearst Classic by virtue of his performance in the *Pittsburgh Sun-Telegraph* All-Star game at Forbes Field on August 5. He went into the Sun-Telegraph Game in Pittsburgh as a defensive replacement and singled in his first at bat. Then, with his team trailing by three runs and runners on first and second, he tripled to close the gap and scored the tying run in the top of the eighth inning, at which point the game was called due to darkness.[26]

As Groat stated: "I was fortunate enough to be one of two players picked to represent Pittsburgh both as a junior and a senior in high school in Hearst All-Star games in New York. That's how I knew I had special talent. Scouts saw me both years, but I turned them down when they offered me contracts after I graduated. As much as my father wanted me to play major league baseball, he wanted all his kids to get college diplomas before doing anything else."[27]

Groat went to Duke, where he earned consensus second-team All-American status in basketball his junior year in 1951, when he set an all-time collegiate scoring record with 831 points. The following season, he was a unanimous first-team All-American and was chosen the United Press Player of the Year.

In baseball, Groat batted .386 and was named to the American Baseball Coaches Association (ABCA) All-American team in 1951. That summer, he was offered a contract by Branch Rickey of the Pirates but elected to return to Duke for his senior year, where he became an ABCA All-American again and helped his team to advance to the College World Series in Omaha. With Groat getting three hits, the Blue Devils trounced Oregon State, 18–7, in their Series debut. But losses to Penn State and Western Michigan ended the team's dream of a national championship.

On June 14, 1952, Groat signed with Pittsburgh, joining the Pirates at the Polo Grounds on June 17 and seeing his first action the next day. He hit a team-leading .284 in 95 games and was third in the Rookie of the Year balloting. In 1960, he won the batting title with a .325 average, was selected for his second All-Star team, and was voted the

National League's MVP, as the Bucs won their first pennant since 1927 and their first World Series since 1925. He stayed with Pittsburgh through 1962, batting .300 or more on three occasions, and then played with the St. Louis Cardinals from 1963 through 1965—during which time he was the starting shortstop on the Birds' World Series championship team in 1964—the Philadelphia Phillies from 1966 until June 22, 1967, and the San Francisco Giants for part of the 1967 season.

Bill Skowron, known to his legion of fans as "Moose," hailed from Chicago. He signed with the Yankees in 1949 and tore things up on the farm. In 1952, at Kansas City, he hit 31 homers with 134 RBI and a .346 batting average, but believe it or not, the powers that be made him stay there another year, where he began the 1953 season with an 18-game hitting streak. The following year, he was called up and played with the Yanks for nine years. Then, between 1963 and 1967, he was a member of the Los Angeles Dodgers, the Washington Senators, the Chicago White Sox, and the California Angels, and finished his career with 211 homers.

Harry Agganis of Classical High School in Lynn, Massachusetts, represented Boston on the 1947 U.S. team, signed with the Red Sox organization in 1952 after completing his studies at Boston University, and played with the parent club in 1954 and 1955. He was en route to a promising career when he was hospitalized with pneumonia on May 16, 1955. He was released and returned to the lineup for two games in early June, raising his average to .313. In pain caused by a blood clot in his right calf, he was again hospitalized on June 5. On June 27, the blood clot moved to his chest, causing a massive pulmonary embolism that killed him. He was only 26.

Rudy Regalado, who got his love for baseball from his father, was from Glendale, California, and appeared in 91 games with the Indians from 1954 through 1956, batting .249. After the Hearst Classic, Rudy stayed in school and played for legendary coach Rod Dedeaux at the University of Southern California, going to the College World Series. He later served in Japan and Korea during the Korean conflict. Upon his return to the United States, he was signed by scout Cy Slapnicka and given a $10,000 bonus by the Cleveland Indians.[28] He was part of Cleveland's 1954 American League championship team and returned to the Polo Grounds for the 1954 World Series, becoming the only Hearst alum to appear in that Series, where he went 1-for-3, with a pinch hit in the fourth game, as the Indians fell to the Giants.

New York's Bob Grim, who pitched in the Classic after completing his junior year of high school, went on to success with the Yankees, winning the Rookie of the Year Award in 1954 with a 20–6 record. Grim saw action in two World Series, was named to the All-Star team in 1957, and finished his eight-year major league career with a 61–41 record. In that 1957 season, pitching exclusively as a reliever, he was 12–8 with a career-best 2.63 earned run average, which helped him to finish 16th in the MVP balloting.

Brooklyn's Hy Cohen attended Thomas Jefferson High School and played on the Brooklyn sandlots. Following his junior year of high school, he was encouraged to try out for the *Journal-American* All-Stars by one of the newspaper's sportswriters, Al Jonas. Prior to the Hearst game, Babe Didrickson borrowed Cohen's glove when she performed her pregame exhibition. Cohen's father, who did not know much about baseball, was at the game and was seated right next to Babe Ruth. He neither recognized the Bambino nor knew who he was. Upon completing high school, Cohen was signed by Paul Krichell of the New York Yankees for a bonus of $750, but he was drafted by the Chicago Cubs following the 1949 season. After going 62–45 in five minor league seasons, he got the call from the parent club in 1955. Seven games, 17 innings, and no decisions later, he was back in the minors, where he pitched until 1958, compiling an overall minor league record of 100–77.

1948

Baseball lost Babe Ruth on August 16, 1948, and the Hearst game on August 26 was played in his memory. Joe DiMaggio stepped in as honorary chairman, and each of the players received an autograph from the Yankee Clipper. Dick Groat's one vivid memory of his games in New York was standing outside in the rain, across from St. Patrick's Cathedral, during Ruth's funeral. Prior to the game, one tribute featured Al Schacht doing his pantomime of the Babe's called shot in the third game of the 1932 World Series, and Robert Merrill brought tears to everyone's eyes with his rendition of "My Buddy."[29] On hand was the former submarine commander Johnny Sylvester, who was 11 years old when the Babe made his fabled hospital visit in 1926—a visit which was said to have saved the young man's life.[30] On his deathbed, Babe made provisions in his will that 10 percent of his estate was bequeathed "to the interests of the kids of America."[31]

The game was won by the U.S. All-Stars as they came from behind to take an 8–7 lead in the eighth inning, and they went on to win 9–7.

Tom Morgan represented Los Angeles, played center field, and went two for three. After the game, he made a decision. "Right then and there I decided I had to play in New York, if I ever could prove myself good enough and that I had to do it as a Yankee. So when I got back home, I didn't waste any time fooling. Five or six other scouts had been talking to my folks about me, but I signed right up with Joe Devine of the Yankees."[32] That signing took place in the spring of 1949 and he went 29–17 during his first two minor league seasons. Such success earned him a rapid promotion to the majors, where he had a 9–3 record for the 1951 World Champions. He stayed with the Yanks through 1956 and then performed for three other clubs before finishing his career with the Los Angeles Angels, achieving a 67–47 won-lost record.

The 1948 U.S. squad included a catcher from Detroit who would return to the Polo Grounds often during his major league career. Hobie Landrith is best known, perhaps, as being the first pick of the New York Mets in the expansion draft after the 1961 season, but his first national exposure had been in the *Esquire* Game in Chicago in 1946. After arriving in New York for the 1948 Hearst Classic, his services were needed for an American Legion championship game in Detroit. The Hearst folks were worried that if he returned to the Motor City, he might miss the game in The Big Apple. However, he did indeed make it back to New York and was the starting catcher for the U.S. All-Stars. He then signed with the Cincinnati Reds organization prior to the 1949 season, and first appeared in the big leagues in 1950, where he spent parts of 14 years, usually as a backup catcher, before playing his last game with Washington in 1963.

Also on the squad was the second half of the first pair of brothers to graduate from the Hearst Classic to the major leagues. Mike Baxes came to the game from San Francisco's Mission High School and signed on with the Phoenix Senators of the Class C Arizona-Texas League in 1949. A batting average of .322 with 196 hits, including 39 doubles, got him noticed. By 1951, he was playing at Class B Yakima, where he batted .318 with 37 doubles. After two years in the military and another two years with the San Francisco Seals in the Pacific Coast League, he was traded to the Kansas City Athletics and made his major league debut in 1956. In parts of two major league seasons, he got into 146 games and batted .217.

1949

Joe DiMaggio once again served as honorary chairman of the Classic in 1949, when the game was held two days after the anniversary of the death of Babe Ruth. DiMaggio read a message to youngsters as Ruth was remembered. Musical performances were provided by Romolo de Spirito from the Metropolitan Opera, singing "My Buddy," and Susan Wayne from the Broadway stage, singing the national anthem.

The game was won by the U.S. All-Stars by a 7–6 count, as the New Yorkers were unable to maintain an early five-run lead. The best pitching performance of the night came from a fellow who travelled cross-country for the game, and five players from this contest went on to play in the majors.

Bobby Will of Berwyn, Illinois, represented Chicago at the Hearst Classic and was named the game's Most Valuable Player after driving in three runs with a single and a double. His double in the sixth inning scored the first two runs for the U.S. All-Stars and his bases-loaded single in the seventh inning plated two more and tied the game, 5–5. The tie was broken when the next batter drove in the final two tallies with a single. Will attended Mankato Teachers College in Minnesota and Northwestern University. He signed with the Cubs in 1954 and first made it to the majors in 1957, appearing in 70 games. In 1959, he played the full season at Class AAA Fort Worth, batted .336, and was named the American Association's MVP. The next three years, he was with the Cubs for the whole season. In June 1963, he was dispatched Salt Lake City, and he finished up at Jacksonville in the International League in 1964.

Representing Seattle in the 1949 game was Gene Conley, who had just completed his freshman year at Washington State College. He had been selected to participate in the Hearst Game after the sixth annual State vs. Seattle doubleheader in Seattle on July 25. Former major league pitcher Monte Stratton made the selection after the player dubbed "double-shorty" by Stratton had banged a two-run homer and pitched the final $5\frac{1}{3}$ innings, giving up only two hits. His homer was the first ball hit out of the park in the six-year history of this All-Star game.[33] Gene made the two-day trip by rail from Pasco, Washington, to New York City accompanied by a reporter from the *Seattle Post-Intelligencer*.

Conley entered the game in the fourth inning and, in three frames, allowed no hits, struck out six, and was credited with the win as the U.S. All Stars came back from a 5–0 deficit to defeat the New York squad, 7–6.[34] In the bottom of the sixth inning, Conley walked a man, who was sacrificed to second by the opposing pitcher, but he struck out the final batter of the inning to keep the score at 5–3 and set up Will's heroics.

At Washington State College, Gene excelled in both baseball and basketball but left after his sophomore year and was signed by the Boston Brave organization in August 1950,[35] debuting with the parent club in 1952. He got off to a very poor beginning, losing each of his three starts and was sent back to the minor leagues. In 1954, he rejoined the Braves, who by then had moved to Milwaukee. In his first two years in Brew City, he went 25–16 and was named to two All-Star teams. In 1959, he was traded to the Phillies, for whom he went 12–7 and was selected for his third All-Star team. His major league career ended with the Red Sox in 1963.

Conley played against a 1957 Braves teammate in the 1949 Hearst Classic. Years later, that player, who was on the New York squad, regretted that he did get an official at bat against Conley in the Hearst game. He had come up against Conley in the sixth inning and sacrificed.

Frank Torre entered the game to pitch with one out in the sixth, but he gave up the decisive four runs in the next inning and was charged with the loss. Torre represented the Cadets Baseball Club of Brooklyn's Bay Ridge League in the Hearst game. In 1951, he was signed as a first baseman by Honey Russell of the Braves and made his major league debut in 1956, after batting .327 with Toledo during the previous season. He played, along with Conley, on the Milwaukee pennant winners in 1957 and 1958, and hit .300 (three for ten) with two home runs and three RBI as the Braves defeated the Yankees in the 1957 World Series. Sharing first base duties with Joe Adcock through 1960, Torre was sent to Vancouver of the Pacific Coast League for the 1961 season. In December of that year, he was sold to the Phillies and finished his career in the City of Brotherly Love in 1963. His last game at the Polo Grounds was on June 23, 1963, and for his career, he batted .273.

Jim Marshall, representing Los Angeles, was a big first baseman who was signed by the Chicago White Sox in 1950. His travels took him to six different minor league locales before he finally made it to the majors in 1958 with Baltimore. In the big leagues, he played with five teams in as many years. From Baltimore, he went to the Chicago Cubs, where he saw action in 134 games, and the Giants, for whom he got into 119 games. By 1962, he was with the original New York Mets. He was then sent to the Pirates for Vinegar Bend Mizell, which proved to be his last stop. For his career, he batted .242 in 410 games. After his playing days, he managed for 14 seasons in the minors and majors, spending three years with the Cubs and one with the A's.

Pete Naton hailed from Flushing, New York, and caught for the New York team. He signed with the Pittsburgh Pirates on June 12, 1953, and made his major league debut four days later. In all, Naton appeared in six major league games in 1953 and went two for 12. He was sent back to the minors in 1954 and spent the next five seasons toiling in the bus leagues.

1950

In 1950, the Hearst players, when not practicing, toured West Point, seeing the newly unveiled statue of General Patton, watched ballgames, and went to a Broadway show, *Where's Charley?*, featuring Ray Bolger.[36] The 1950 game was the highest-scoring affair in the 20 years of the Classic as the U.S. All-Stars won 13–11.

Tony Bartirome from Pittsburgh was selected to play first base for the U.S. Stars. His hometown Pirates signed him to a contract, and he was in the majors two years later, appearing in 124 games for the last-place Bucs. It would be his only major league season, after which, he was drafted and spent two years in the Army. When he returned from the Army, he played in the minors and then spent 22 years as a trainer, 19 of them as the head trainer for the Pirates from 1967 through 1985.

In a workout before the 1950 game, Charlie Lau from Detroit deposited a pitch from San Antonio's Ray Glau into the right-field seats at Yankee Stadium, where the practice was held.[37] Lau signed with the Tigers and eventually made it to the majors in 1956. He played 11 seasons, compiling a fairly unremarkable .255 batting average. However, after his playing days, Lau became a successful hitting coach, working with such stars as George Brett and Hal McRae during his years at Kansas City.

1951

The 1951 Hearst game included Jersey Joe Walcott giving a two-round boxing exhibition against actor Jeff Chandler as part of the pregame festivities. Not only did Walcott appear, he donated $500 to the cause after winning the money on a television quiz show, *Break the Bank*. His donation was matched by Yankee great Phil Rizzuto, and Walcott himself purchased 1,000 tickets to the game, to be used by area youngsters.[38]

The U.S. Stars were managed by a trio of veterans, including Oscar Vitt, Lefty Gomez, and Charlie Gehringer. They won the main event by a score of 9–2 to give them their fifth consecutive win in the classic.

The game's MVP hailed from Baltimore and had just completed his sophomore year of high school. At 16 years, seven months, and 20 days, he was one of the youngest players ever to play in the Hearst Classic. Al Kaline was accompanied to New York by *Baltimore News-Post* writer Frank Cashen, who would go on to work with the Baltimore Orioles as general manager. Cashen later orchestrated the ascendancy of the New York Mets during the 1980s and had the unique distinction of hiring and firing Hearst alums as Met managers.

Kaline's performance in the Hearst game came as no surprise. As a high-school freshman in 1950, he had been named to the Maryland All-State team. At the start of his American Legion season in 1951, he had gone 14-for-17. He went two for four in the Hearst Classic with a single and an inside-the-park homer that sailed over the center-fielder's head. In the field, he was equally adept, making five good plays and gunning down a runner at third base.[39]

In 1960, longtime U.S. All-Star manager Ossie Vitt remembered, "I could tell he was one of the best prospects I'd ever seen the first time I saw him. He had those wrists with a snap in them, the poise, hustle, and attitude, and how he could throw and run."[40]

Kaline was signed to a bonus when he completed high school in 1953 and, due to the bonus rule in effect at the time, went straight to the Tigers, making him one of five Hearst alumni to sign bonuses and go directly to the major leagues. The bonus rule of 1953 was structured to tie players signing for bonuses in excess of $4,000 to the major league team for a period of two years. But the experience did not prove beneficial to most of the young men involved. Kaline's success far exceeded that of each of the other "Bonus Babies" who had played in the Hearst game.

Kaline was embraced by his teammates and the Tiger organization. It was obvious that he was a superlative fielder, and his hitting came around. Like with so many others, fate intervened and gave Kaline his big chance. An off-season injury to regular right fielder Steve Souchock kept him out of the lineup, and Kaline was the only right fielder left. The Tigers were going no place, and manager Fred Hutchinson played Kaline. As Don Lund said, "Although he started slowly, he gained confidence, enhanced his skills, and finished with a fine year. Al used the bonus rule to his advantage and had a minor-league experience in the major leagues. The rest is history."[41] That history included 22 years with the Tigers, a batting championship in 1955 at age 20, 16 All-Star Game appearances, 10 Gold Gloves, and election to the Hall of Fame in 1980.

John "Tito" Francona, who represented New Brighton High School and Pittsburgh, signed with the St. Louis Browns and went on to play 15 years in the big leagues.

Gerald Davie was sent east by the *Detroit Times* and on the eve of his selection for the trip won both ends of a doubleheader. He signed with the Tigers in 1952 and went 17–3 for Class D Jamestown in his first minor league season. After two years in the military and another four years in the minors, he started the 1959 season with the Tigers. There, he had a 2–2 record with a 4.17 ERA in 11 games and was sent back to the minors in June. He would never return to the majors.

1952

In 1952, the New York squad won 5–4 in 11 innings, and three players in that game made it to the majors.

Bobby Locke represented the Pittsburgh area but was not the initial selection. He took the place of Rudy Filek,[42] who was disqualified for being past the age limit. Locke signed with Cleveland in 1953 and, in 1956, was at Class A Reading, where he posted an

The Polo Grounds hosted the Hearst Sandlot Classic from 1946 to 1958 (collection of Stew Thornley).

18–9 record. In 1959, he started the season at San Diego in the Pacific Coast League and was called up to the Indians in June. Over the course of ten years, he shuttled back and forth between the majors and minors, wrapping up his career in the majors in 1968 with the California Angels. As a big leaguer, he had a lifetime record of 16–15.

Tony Kubek did not sign right away, as he was still in high school when the game was played in 1952. At 16 years and ten months he was the youngest player on the field that evening. He did not play baseball in high school because his school had dropped the sport, but he gained great experience playing sandlot ball and caught the eye of Lou Maguolo, a scout for the New York Yankees.[43] Charlie Gehringer, the former Detroit Tiger infielder, was coaching the U.S. All-Stars and helped young Kubek with his fielding. Kubek went back to Bay View High School in Milwaukee and signed with Maguolo and the New York Yankees in 1954. The bonus rule was in effect, and Kubek's father, who had played with the minor league Milwaukee Brewers during the 1930s, suggested that he sign for a smaller amount and get some minor league experience.

Kubek's first spring training with the Yankees was in 1954, where he met the old professor, Casey Stengel, while taking the customary postworkout lap around the playing field at St. Petersburg, Florida. Stengel called out to him, "Kubek" and Tony had no idea what would come next. But Stengel told him that he remembered Tony Sr. and how the team tried to make Tony's father pull the ball more, something that he promised not to do with the younger Kubek. Tony made his debut with the Yankees in 1957 and spent nine years in the Bronx, being named American League Rookie of the Year his first season and playing on three All-Star teams. However, he is perhaps best known for taking a ground ball to the throat in Game Seven of the 1960 World Series and was rushed to the hospital after the play. The following day, he had two visitors from the Pirates. They were Bill Virdon, whose ground ball had struck Kubek, and Dick Groat, who had played in the Hearst Games in 1947 and 1948.

Ralph Mauriello, a native of Brooklyn, moved to North Hollywood, California, at a young age and represented Los Angeles in 1952. He pitched two innings in relief, striking out three, and was signed by the Dodgers. His journey through the minor leagues began in Class C Santa Barbara in 1953, and by 1955, he had worked his way up to Mobile in the Class AA Southern Association, where he went 18–8 with a 2.76 ERA.[44] He finally appeared in three games with the Los Angeles Dodgers at the end of the 1958 season, which was the beginning and end of his major league career. His won-lost record was 1–1, with his lone triumph coming against the Chicago Cubs on September 19 when he started and pitched 7⅔ innings in a 5–1 Dodger victory.

1953

Always on the lookout to promote the event, the organizers booked the Harlem Globetrotters to play an exhibition against a team led by George Mikan of the Minneapolis Lakers prior to the 1953 game. Attendance ballooned to 29,480, one of the highest in the history of the event, and the Trotters won 59–48. Then, the U.S. Stars won the game that counted, 5–1.

Reno Bertoia represented Detroit in the 1953 Classic. He was born in Italy, and his family came to Windsor, Ontario, when he was 22 months old. Starring at Assumption High School in Windsor, he played sandlot ball in both that city and the city that he represented, before signing with the Tigers right after the Hearst game and making his major league debut on September 22, 1953. In his first at bat, he faced the legendary Satchel Paige, then pitching with the St. Louis Browns, and struck out. Reno spent most of his time on the Tigers bench, a victim of the bonus rule, but in 1957, he got off to a great start, had a nine-game hitting streak at one point, and, on May 16, was batting .398 after hitting safely in 22 out of 24 games. However, his productivity tapered off and he was sent to Washington prior to the 1959 season. With the Senators, he had the best year of his career in 1960, batting .265 in 121 games. He finished his time in the majors with Detroit in 1962.

Frank Leja was perhaps the "poster child" for the bonus-rule catastrophe. He represented Boston in the 1953 Classic. A scholar-athlete, he stood 6'4" and weighed 210 pounds, and while in high school, he played baseball, football, basketball, and soccer. In his senior year, he batted .432, hitting safely in each of this team's 21 games, so after graduation, he was courted by several teams, with the Giants, Braves, and Indians being cited for tampering. He signed with the Yankees for an estimated $60,000, but over the next two years, Leja sat on the Yankees' bench. He got into a total of only 19 games and had one hit in seven at bats. His return to the majors with the Angels for a brief stay in 1962 was frustrating, with him going hitless in 16 at bats. His dream ended at Class AAA Toronto in 1963. As a minor leaguer, he banged out 164 homers, including 30 in 1961, when he also had an International League-leading 98 RBI, but his potential was not fulfilled.

Jim Small was signed to a bonus after he graduated high school in 1955 and went straight to the Tigers. His best season was 1956 when, in 58 games, he batted .319, but he started only 19 of those games, and his major league career ended in 1958 at the tender age of 21. He then went to the minors, where he played through 1962. In his final season, at Albuquerque in the Texas League, he showed "what might have been," batting .317 with 13 homers and 82 RBI in 127 games. But it was too late.

1954

The 1954 game was played in chilly weather in front of 9,143 spectators. Bill Monbouquette, representing Boston, won MVP honors, as the U.S. team triumphed 5–3. Monbo, celebrating his 18th birthday, struck out five of the six batters he faced and went on to a successful career with the Red Sox and three other teams, pitching 11 seasons, having a 114–112 record, and being named to three All-Star teams. His best year was 1963 when he went 20–10 and displayed excellent control with 174 strikeouts against only 42 walks. Defensively, he did not make an error and led the league in putouts among pitchers that season with 31.

Five others from the 1954 game made it to the majors.

Barry Latman at the age of 18 hurled a perfect game for Fairfax High in 1954, the first one in a decade in the Los Angeles school system, which helped him to be named the Los Angeles All-City Player by the Helms Athletic Foundation. He also impressed major league scouts and was offered bonuses by several clubs. However, he declined these offers and accepted a baseball scholarship from the University of Southern California.[45] Eventually signed by the Chicago White Sox, he pitched six years in the majors and compiled a 59–68 record, going 8–5 for the 1959 team when it won the American League pennant.

Jim McAnany, also from Los Angeles, signed with the White Sox and had the best year of his career in 1959, batting .276 in 67 games.

Gary Bell was the first San Antonio player to make it all the way to the big leagues. He started in youth baseball at age 13 with the YMCA in San Antonio. His next stop was American Legion ball in 1953, after which he was signed by the Cleveland Indians and made it to the majors in 1958. Over the course of his 12 major league seasons, he had a 121–117 record and was named to three All-Star teams.

Ted Sadowski, a pitcher who represented Pittsburgh in 1954, signed with the Washington Senators in 1955 and debuted in the majors with them in 1960, the Senators' last season in the nation's capital. He then accompanied the team to Minnesota in 1961, played in parts of three seasons, appeared in 43 games, and had a 2–3 record.

Fred Van Dusen is not known by many baseball fans. He performed well in the practices leading up to the Classic and was recognized by manager Al Simmons as a top player going into the game.[46] In his senior year at New York's Bryant High School, he batted .521 with ten home runs and 57 RBI in 22 games and garnered "Most Valuable Schoolboy Player" honors.[47] He was signed by the Phillies on August 20, 1955, at which time, he had 14 offers, two of which included bonuses, but he elected to play for Philadelphia for a lesser amount,[48] staying with the parent club only through the end of the season before heading off to the minors.[49] He made his major league debut on September 11, 1955, at Milwaukee, when he came up as a pinch hitter in the top of the ninth with one out and the Phillies trailing the Braves by a 9–1 count. In his only plate appearance, he was hit by a pitch, and he never came to bat in the majors again.

1955

In 1955, Hurricane Connie put a damper on things, and the game was stopped after four and a half innings with the New Yorkers winning 4–3.

One of the participants on the New York squad was Herman Davis from Brooklyn's Boys High School, who, as a sandlotter, played for manager Clarence Irving's Bisons in the Kiwanis League when the team won the New York State championship that year. Tommy Davis (as he was better known) was courted by both the Yankees and the Dodgers, but the Dodgers had a trump card. Jackie Robinson called Davis, and, not long thereafter, Al Campanis signed the youngster for $4,000, the maximum allowable without his being forced to spend two years on the major league roster (and bench), and he was off to Hornell in the Class D PONY League, where he batted .325. The following season at Kokomo in the Class D Midwest League, he played for former Dodger Pete Reiser, who instilled values in the young Davis that would prove most helpful at his next minor league stop.[50]

Davis spent the bulk of the 1958 season with Victoria in the Class AA Texas League, where he had a full season's dose of a racism that he had not experienced in his days as a Brooklyn sandlotter. Nevertheless, he had his third consecutive .300 season, batting .304 and earning himself a late season call-up to Montreal of the International League. Davis made his first big-league appearance for the Los Angeles Dodgers on September 22, 1959, and went on to win batting championships in 1962 and 1963, being selected to the National League All-Star team both years. In 1962, not only did he lead the National League in batting with a .346 average, he also led the league in hits (230) and RBI (153—

still a Dodger record). An injury in 1965 set him back, but he reemerged as a designated hitter in the 1970s with Baltimore. Over the course of his 18-year career, he batted .294 and amassed 2,121 base hits.

Ted Schreiber grew up in the Marine Park section of Brooklyn and attended James Madison High School. In the Hearst game, he batted leadoff and had one hit. He then went to St. John's University and was signed by Frank "Botts" Nikola of the Red Sox in 1958. At the end of the 1962 season, he was drafted by the Mets and spent the 1963 season back at the Polo Grounds. On September 18, 1963, in the last game ever played at the Polo Grounds, Ted was the last batter, grounding into a double play as the Mets lost 5–1 to the Phillies. In the last game of the season, at Philadelphia, the Mets were trailing 13–4 when Schreiber was put in as a defensive replacement. He caught a foul pop-up for the final out in the bottom of the eighth inning. This was followed by the Mets going quietly in the ninth inning, and the game, the season, and Schreiber's major league career were over.

1956

The 1956 game, which the New Yorkers won 5–1, featured six future major leaguers. The youngsters attended a Giant-Pirate game at the Polo Grounds, saw the film *High Society* at the Radio City Music Hall, and took the Circle Line boat tour around Manhattan.

The New York squad was chosen by George Stirnweiss, in his first year at the helm, and Steve Ray, baseball coach at James Monroe High School. They took the early lead and went on to defeat the U.S. All-Stars in front of 16,634 spectators. The U.S. Stars featured several heavy hitters and sent five players to the majors, but the New Yorkers had the pitching to keep the invaders from mounting a significant threat.

The only New Yorker to play major league ball attended New Hyde Park High School on Long Island and represented the Queens-Nassau Alliance. He singled and scored his team's second run in the Hearst game and, after the contest, returned to Manhattan College, where he received his degree. Chuck Schilling signed with the Boston Red Sox organization in 1958, made it to the big leagues in 1961, and played at Fenway from 1961 through 1965. Once his playing days had ended, Schilling worked as an engineer for seven years, then made a career switch and taught mathematics at the Selden Middle School on Long Island for 24 years.[51]

Although the New York squad won the game, it would be a player from Los Angeles who would steal the show and another player from Los Angeles who would have one of the longest major league careers of any of the Hearst players.

The first of the pair had been named the California player of the year after pitching two no-hitters en route to a 12–0 record in his senior season at Mark Keppel High School in Alhambra. During the course of his high-school career, Mike McCormick went 34–4, and he put together a 49–4 record in American Legion baseball. In his final year of Legion ball, he pitched three no-hitters, including a perfect game in which he struck out 26 of the 27 batters he faced. He punched his ticket to The Big Apple, striking out nine consecutive batters in the all-star game in Los Angeles.[52] In New York, with his team trailing, he pitched the last two innings and fanned each of the six batters he faced, garnering MVP honors.

McCormick signed with the Giants for a bonus said to be somewhere between $50,000 and $65,000 and, since the bonus rule was still in effect, went directly from the Polo Grounds to the Polo Grounds.[53] During his first two years with the Manhattanites, he had only seven starts but saw more action when the team moved to San Francisco. He led the National League with a 2.70 ERA in 1960 and was named to the All-Star team that season and in 1961. After the 1962 season, he was traded to Baltimore and then Washington before returning to the Giants in 1967 for his best year ever. He went 22–10 with a 2.85 ERA and was selected as the National League Cy Young Award winner. His major league career ended in 1971, and he finished with a 134–128 won-lost record in 16 seasons.

The other Los Angeles representative was given much hype by Morrey Rokeach in the *Journal-American*, but as is often seen, a player does not live up to the hype. Rokeach said that the "heavy-thumping centerfielder is the big conversation piece among the managers, scribes, and scouts." Manager Oscar Vitt said the kid "got the same quick reflexes and wonderful wrist action that characterized Al Kaline."[54] In the game itself, that kid, Ron Fairly, corralled a fly ball in center field in the first inning and gunned down Jimmy Pappas, who had tried to score after tagging up at third. He went on to attend the University of Southern California and played for Rod Dedeaux in USC's Bovard Field, where the dimensions suited Ron's left-handed swing.[55]

Following two years at USC, Fairly signed with the Los Angeles Dodgers for $75,000. He was sent to the minors (the bonus rule was no longer in effect) for a brief spell before coming up to the Dodgers late in the 1958 season. He batted only .238 for L.A. in 1959 and spent most of 1960 at Class AAA Spokane, batting .303. That season, Spokane was a powerhouse, featuring the likes of Willie Davis, and the team won their pennant by 11½ games. Fairly returned to the majors to stay in 1961. Over the course of his 20-year career, he batted .266 with 1,919 hits and was named to two All-Star teams.

San Antonio's representative was Joe Horlen, who first appeared in the San Antonio–South Texas All-Star game in 1955. Horlen played American Legion ball and pitched for Dan's Café in a Sunday beer league, earning his slot in the Texas All-Star game. After the Hearst Classic, Horlen went to college at Oklahoma State and, in his junior year, pitched well enough to lead his team to the national championship in the College World Series. Shortly thereafter, he was inked to a contract that included a $30,000 bonus by Jack Sheehan of the Chicago White Sox.[56] Horlen made it to the majors in 1961 and spent 12 years there, 11 with the White Sox. His best season was 1967 when he went 19–7, led the league with a 2.06 ERA, and finished second in the Cy Young balloting.

Russ Gibson represented Boston in the Hearst game. The catcher had scholarship offers from several colleges and had just completed his junior year in high school when he traveled to New York. He was scouted by Jumping Joe Dugan of the Red Sox while in high school and signed with Boston's head scout, Neil Mahoney, after graduating in June 1957.[57] Over the next ten seasons, he took the grand tour of the Red Sox farm system before suiting up on opening day in 1967 for the parent club. As Gibson recalled, "The biggest thrill for me was the first game I ever played in the majors, and that was at Yankee Stadium."[58] Few players have had such a debut. In his first two games against the Yankees in New York, he went five for 12. In the initial outing, he caught a near no-hitter by Bill Rohr that was broken up with two outs in the ninth inning by an Elston Howard single on a 3–2 pitch. In his next start, he caught 18 innings. He ended the month of April with a .300 average, but it was downhill from there. Gibson played six years in the majors, from 1967 through 1972. After the 1969 season, the Red Sox traded him to San Francisco, where he finished his career.

One of Detroit's representatives in 1956 was Larry Foster. The final elimination game for choosing players for that year's Hearst Classic was held on a muddy track in Ann Arbor, Michigan. There, Foster pitched his team to a 1–0 victory. In the Hearst game, he broke up a no-hitter with a bunt single in the sixth inning and pitched two hitless frames in relief. He signed with Detroit in 1958 for $35,000 after spending two years at Michigan State, and on September 13, 1963, he made his major league debut, pitching two innings in relief as the Tigers lost 10–0 to the Twins. It was his only big league appearance. After his baseball days ended, he returned to his studies and received his degree from Michigan State in 1965. He went on to become a Lutheran minister, serving as a pastor at Grace Lutheran Church in Lansing for six years and 18 years at the parish in Whitehall, Michigan.[59]

1957

The crowd of 14,867 was treated to a home run hitting contest between Joe DiMaggio, Mickey Mantle, and Willie Mays, and the first pitch was thrown out by New York governor W. Averill Harriman. Harriman said, "I am delighted to attend this game which is part of a constructive and character building program which benefits so many of our youth in New York and throughout the nation."[60]

The adage of "good pitching beats good hitting" was appropriate as the New Yorkers shut out the invaders 4–0. The MVP was 17-year-old Tommy Hunt, who struck out five in four innings of work and, on the Sunday evening after the Saturday night Hearst Game, appeared on the *Ed Sullivan Show* with Mrs. Lou Gehrig.

Ron Brand, heralded as "another Pee Wee Reese," came to the Hearst game from North Hollywood High School in the San Fernando Valley. He, Dick Nen, and John B. Old of the *Los Angeles Herald-Examiner* traveled by prop plane to New York, where Brand and Nen roomed together and spent their $9-per-day meal allowance wisely. The U.S. All-Stars that year went to Radio City Music Hall and saw the Rockettes, the movie *Silk Stockings,* and a young comic by the name of Jonathan Winters. In the game, Brand came in as a substitute and walked in his only plate appearance.

He signed with Pittsburgh in 1958. Then, one day in early 1961, he was working out at North Hollywood Park in California when fate arrived in the way of a stranger. An older man who had played some minor league ball and spent a year in Japan took the 21-year-old Brand under his wing and put him through a six-week regimen of workouts focusing on all elements of the game. Later, during Brand's first major league season, the Pirates were playing in Los Angeles, and Ron heard a familiar voice. It was the voice of the man who had turned his career around: Don Bussan. A very modest fellow, Bussan did not ask Ron for a ticket but instead paid his own way into the ballpark, having Brand's success as his reward.

Nen, who played at Los Angeles Harbor Junior College and California State University, Long Beach, signed with the Dodgers in 1961 and played that season for Reno in the California League. He batted .351 with 32 homers and 144 RBI and made it to the majors in 1963, getting into seven games at the end of the season for Los Angeles. He was traded to Washington prior to the 1965 season and retired after the 1970 season with a career batting average of .224.

Al Moran represented Detroit and played shortstop for the U.S. All-Stars. He was signed by the Boston Red Sox and bounced around their minor league system for five seasons before being traded to the New York Mets in the deal that brought Felix Mantilla to Boston. In 1963, he was back in the Polo Grounds and played 119 games for the Mets. Early in the 1964 season, he was sent back to the minors, having played his last major league game on May 10, 1964.

1958

The 1958 game was won by the New York All-Stars, 9–1. The kids, during their stay in New York, took the customary trip to West Point and Bear Mountain, and the entertainment included a trip to the Roxy Theater, where they saw the film, *Windjammer*. They also saw the Aquacircus at the Flushing Meadows Amphitheater on the site of the 1939 World's Fair.[61]

Four players from this game made it to the major leagues.

Ron Santo was the starting catcher for the U.S. team and his hitting display in the practice leading up to the game was beyond impressive. Four of his first five swings were for homers. But there was more to Santo than just slugging round-trippers. A star infielder in his early years of high school, he caught as a senior, and that fall, he was signed to a bonus estimated at $25,000 by the Chicago Cubs. One of their scouts, Dave Kosher, had been watching Santo since his sophomore year in high school, and he, with Cub head scout Roy "Hardrock" Johnson, corralled Santo for their club. After his signing, Santo was converted back to third base in his Texas League days. He made his major league debut with the Cubs in 1960, less than two years after playing in the Hearst Classic, and had a 15-year major league career, during which he was named to nine All-Star teams and batted .277 with 372 home runs. His posthumous election to the Hall of Fame occurred in 2012.

In his senior year of high school, Santo was a man of all positions. He moved behind the plate for the first time but was not stuck there, becoming the starting shortstop against West Seattle on May 16, and using his bat to help his team build a 7–0 lead. But West Seattle staged a comeback, and Santo was summoned to pitch. He induced the first batter to hit into a 1–2–3 double play and the next batter to ground out, stopping the rally and preserving a 7–4 win.[62] Thus, it was somewhat fitting that he was named to the All-City team this time around as a utility player.

Santo was the catcher for the Seattle team in the annual All-Star doubleheader in Seattle and did the unthinkable, for Santo anyway. In the seventh inning of the second game, he drew a walk and stole second, third, and home (as part of a double steal). He had two hits, was named the game's MVP, and was en route to New York.[63]

Less than two years later, on June 26, 1960, he played in his first game with the Cubs.

Joe Torre, who started the 1958 Hearst game on the bench for the New York team, went on to stardom with the Braves and Cardinals, but it took some time. Torre was a bona fide hitter for the Brooklyn Cadets, but he was significantly overweight and was not considered major league material at either first or third base. His older brother, Frank, who provided the money for Joe to attend St. Francis Prep in Brooklyn, convinced him that his only way to the majors would be as a catcher, and he made the switch. Within a year, he was signed by the Milwaukee Braves. He appeared very briefly at the end of the 1960 season, getting a hit in his first major league at bat, and the following year, he batted .277, finishing second in the Rookie of the Year balloting.

In nine seasons with the Braves, he was named to five consecutive All-Star teams (1963–1967) and won the Gold Glove in 1965. After the 1968 season, he was traded to the St. Louis Cardinals, with whom he went on to four more All-Star teams (1970–1973) and, after slimming down before the 1971 season, was selected the National League MVP, when he led the league in batting average (.363), hits (230), total bases (352), and RBI (137).

He retired as a player during the 1977 season with a career batting average of .297 and 252 home runs. He then took over the managerial reins of the New York Mets. After five disappointing years managing the Mets, he returned to the Braves for three seasons, leading Atlanta to a divisional championship in 1982. He managed the Cardinals from 1990 through 1995 before moving on to the Yankees in 1996. During his 12 years with the Yanks, his teams made it to the postseason every year, winning ten divisional championships, six American League pennants, and four World Series, while compiling an 1173–767 record. He left the Yanks after the 2007 season and managed the Dodgers to divisional championships in 2008 and 2009, before retiring from managing at the end of the 2010 season and taking a position as an executive vice-president in the office of the Commissioner of Baseball. But his proudest accomplishment has been the work that he has done with the Safe at Home Foundation for battered children.

On December 9, 2013, he received word that he had been elected to the Hall of Fame.

John Boccabella, who played third base and batted cleanup for the U.S. team, became a fixture behind the plate with the Montreal Expos. The Marin High School star represented the San Francisco area in the 1958 Classic by virtue of his performance in the *San Francisco Examiner*'s Baseball School's All-Star game. In that contest, he had a single, a double, and a homer as his North All-Star team won 5–0 against the San Francisco All-Star squad.[64] After the Hearst game, he resumed his studies at Santa Clara University and, upon graduation, was signed by scout Ray Perry of the Chicago Cubs organization for $25,000.[65] For six years, he shuttled back and forth between the majors and the minors, getting into a total of 146 games with the Cubs. Then, prior to the 1969 season, he was selected by Montreal in the expansion draft and spent five seasons with the Expos before finishing his career with the Giants in 1974.

West Virginia, for the first time, was represented in the regional game played at Forbes Field in Pittsburgh by a second baseman known as "the erstwhile Flemington Flash."[66] Of his performance in that game at Pittsburgh, it was said, "this 170-pounder is a slick fielder and consistent hitter who surprises with a long ball. He collected three hits Wednesday, took part in a double play and easily made the standout play of the day. On a ball that looked like a sure Texas-Leaguer, Paul Popovich ran after it with his back to the infield, jumped in the air for it and, after losing his balance, and falling to the ground, held the ball for a sensational putout."[67] Popovich went to West Virginia University for two years before signing with the Chicago Cubs in 1960 for a $42,500 bonus. He first appeared in a Cubs uniform in 1964 and played in the majors for 11 seasons, with his best year being 1969 when he batted .312.

In San Antonio, the Wrambling Wrecks disabled veterans group sponsored the San Antonio-South Texas All-Star event in conjunction with the *San Antonio Light*. They provided seats free of charge to area orphans, used proceeds to support veterans in need, and sent two players to the game in New York. Harold Scherwitz of the *San Antonio Light* covered the games in Texas for many years, and although his comments were made about the players in those San Antonio games, they really apply to all those youngsters who took the field at the Polo Grounds. "They're a classy bunch. And the same enthusiasm that had kids playing on the sandlots from daybreak to dark in grandpa's time spurs this bunch on. These kids will tell you there's nothing wrong with it [baseball]—as long as there's a chance to play it. Just being around youngsters blossoming into peak performers on the diamond is refreshing—every last one of them going out every moment, all of them straining to the last ounce to win, and to show to good advantage before a panel of major league scouts."[68]

Notes

1. "34th Avenue Nine Takes Met Crown with 1–0 Victory: Ed Ford Outstanding Star of 11 Inning Test at Polo Grounds," *Long Island City Star Journal*, September 30, 1946.

2. Game scorecard.

3. Game scorecard.

4. Louis Effrat, "East's Nine Wins in Boys' Game, 6–0," *New York Times*, August 8, 1944.

5. Danny Peary, *We Played the Game: 65 Players Remember Baseball's Greatest Era—1947–1964* (New York: Hyperion, 1994), 48.

6. C. Paul Rogers, III, "The Day the Phillies Went to Egypt," *Baseball Research Journal* 39, no. 2 (Fall 2010): 9.

7. Nicholas Diunte, "Bob DiPietro," SABR BioProject, http://sabr.org/bioproject.

8. "Max Kase is Dead; Sports Editor, 75," *New York Times*, March 20, 1974.

9. Jack Conway, Jr., "Ten Sandlot Tasks Set," *Boston Daily Record*, July 14, 1953.

10. John Drohan, "Stengel Sees Yanks Destiny's Tots," *Boston Traveler*, July 5, 1949.

11. "Maranville Dies; Noted Shortstop," *New York Times,* January 6, 1954.

12. *Ibid.*

13. Arthur Daley, "Sports of The Times," *New York Times*, January 7, 1954.

14. George Vecsey, "Sports of the Times," *New York Times*, January 11, 1989.

15. "Al Simmons Funeral Held at Church of His Boyhood," *Milwaukee Sentinel*, May 29, 1956.

16. John Drohan, "Shots of Tribal Third Sacker Elliott Taken by Lew Fonseca for Educational Film," *Boston Traveler*, August 6, 1949.

17. Frank Graham, "Graham's Corner," *New York Journal-American*, August 17, 1949.

18. Barney Kremenko, "Star of Stars: Baxes, Coast Sandlotter, Steals Show at Big Game," *New York Journal-American*, August 16, 1946.

19. "Negro on Hearst Sandlot Nine; Louis Tix for Free," *The Amsterdam News*, August 3, 1946.

20. Fred Foye, "Newton Favored in Suburban Field: Waltham Nine Still Contender Despite Coach's Pessimism," *Boston Traveler*. May 2, 1946.

21. Jack Lang, "Schoolboy Phenom Loes Sells Himself to Rickey for 22 Grand," *The Sporting News*, September 1, 1948, 7.

22. Bobby Hoeft, *When Baseball Was Fun: A Baseball Memoir* (Xlibris, 2002), 57.

23. Al Jonas, "Ferrarese, V. P. Winner, Puts College Ahead of Ball Career," *New York Journal-American*, August 14, 1947.

24. Gene Perry, "Ferrarese, Fingeroid Voted Winners of P-E's N. Y. Trip," *The Oakland Post-Enquirer*, June 23, 1947.

25. Tom Fitzgerald, *San Francisco Chronicle*, May 7, 1990, and Interview with Lorraine Vigli.

26. Bill Heyman, "Hopper and Groat Win All-Star Berths: Players Shine as Teams Tie, 7–7," Pittsburgh Sun-Telegraph, August 6, 1947.

27. Danny Peary, *We Played the Game: 65 Players Remember Baseball's Greatest Era, 1947–1964* (New York: Hyperion, 1994), 157.

28. Steve Johnson, "Rudy Regalado" in *Pitching to the Pennant: the 1954 Cleveland Indians*, ed. Joseph Wancho (Lincoln: University of Nebraska Press, 2014), 110–112.

29. Lewis Burton, "Fans Honor Babe as Met. Stars Bow, 9–7" *New York Journal-American*, August 27, 1948.

30. Al Jonas, "U.S. Aces in Drill: 35,000 Expected at Sandlot Classic," *New York Journal-American*, August 22, 1948.

31. "Babe Left 'Kids' Share in Estate," *New York Journal-American*, August 23, 1948.

32. Hugh Bradley, "All-Star Yankee: Sandlot Classic Set Goal for Morgan," *New York Journal-American*, August 7, 1951.

33. "Gene Conley Named Top Boys' Player," *Seattle Daily Times*, July 26, 1949.

34. "Conley Hurls All-America Team to Polo Grounds Win," *Walla Walla Union Bulletin*, August 19, 1949.

35. "Big Gene Conley Signs with Boston Braves," *Walla Walla Union Bulletin*, August 11, 1950.

36. "Hearst Nine Due to be Selected," *San Antonio Light*, August 22, 1950.

37. "Glau May Pitch in New York Game," *San Antonio Light*, August 20, 1950.

38. "Walcott to Box on Benefit Show for Sandlot Kids," *The Syracuse Post-Standard*, July 27, 1951.

39. Al Jonas, "U.S. Stars Defeat New York Team in Sandlot Classic," *The Sporting News*, August 15, 1951, 28.

40. Morrey Rokeach, "Vitt Picks Hearst Stars: Kaline, Loes, Among Grads of Sandlot Tilts," *New York Journal-American,* August 14, 1960.

41. Brent Kelley, *Baseball's Biggest Blunder: The Bonus Rule of 1953–57* (Lanham, Maryland: Scarecrow Press, 1997), 34–37.

42. "Filek, Stoernell Stand Out in Annual Sandlot Classic: Merchant Stars Collect Seven Hits; Ronnie Gray Strikes Out Five," *The Mount Washington (PA) News*, August 8, 1952.

43. Joseph Wancho, "Tony Kubek," SABR BioProject, http://sabr.org/bioproject.

44. Vincent Johnson, "Mauriello, Bonus Hurler, Pays Off Dodgers on Farm," *The Sporting News*, August 3, 1955, 31.

45. Ralph Berger, "Barry Latman," SABR BioProject, http://sabr.org/bioproject.

46. Morrey Rokeach, "New York All-Stars Power-Packed in Sandlot Classic," *The Sporting News*, August 11, 1954, 21.

47. "Gifts for N.Y. Schoolboy Stars," *The Sporting News*, July 6, 1955, 21.

48. Art Morrow, "Who's Mayo? Philly Knows Now," *The Sporting News*, August 31, 1955, 4.

49. Art Morrow, "Phillies Line Up 44 Phenoms for Force-Fed Diet," *The Sporting News*, February 8, 1956, 20.

50. Andrew Paul Mele, *The Boys of Brooklyn: The Parade Grounds—Brooklyn's Field of Dreams* (Bloomington: Author House, 2008), 155–159.

51. *Ibid.*, 258.

52. Warren Corbett, "Mike McCormick," SABR BioProject, http://sabr.org/bioproject.

53. "Giants pay $50,000 for L. A. Prep Hurler," *San Diego Union*, August 30, 1956.

54. Morrey Rokeach, "Coast Slugger Looks Fine in Sandlot Drills," *New York Journal-American*, August 20, 1956.

55. Paul Hirsch, "Ron Fairly," SABR BioProject, http://sabr.org/bioproject.

56. Gregory H. Wolf, "Joe Horlen," SABR BioProject, http://sabr.org/bioproject.

57. Tom Harkins, "Russ Gibson," SABR BioProject, http://sabr.org/bioproject.

58. Ed Linn, *The Great Rivalry: The Yankees and the Red Sox, 1901–1990* (Boston: Houghton Mifflin Company, 1991), 259–260.

59. Richard Tellis, *Once Around the Bases: Bittersweet Memories of Only One Game in the Majors* (Chicago: Triumph Books, 1998), 227–38.

60. Morrey Rokeach, "Governor Harriman to Make First Pitch at Hearst Sandlot Classic." *New York Journal-American*, August 15, 1957.

61. Morrey Rokeach, "U.S. Stars Due This Week for Hearst Classic," *New York Journal-American*, August 17, 1958.

62. Bob Schwarzmann, "Garfield, Ballard Gain City Baseball Final," *Seattle Times,* May 17, 1958.

63. "Santo Named Best Player in Prep Game," *Seattle Times,* June 10, 1958.

64. Jim Gilmartin, "Boccabella Wins All-Star Honors," *(San Rafael, CA) Daily Independent Journal*, July 7, 1958.

65. "Marin's Boccabella Signs with Cubs; $25,000 Bonus," *(San Rafael, CA) Daily Independent Journal*, June 10, 1963.

66. *(Morgantown, WV) The Dominion News*, July 30, 1958.

67. Andrew Dugo, "Popovich, Kuntzler Picked for Hearst All-Star Game," *Pittsburgh Sun-Telegraph*, August 8, 1958.

68. Harold Scherwitz, "Want to get in on an evening of real fun? Make the All-Star Game," *San Antonio Light*, July 22, 1958.

White Circled Targets Drawn in Crayon

The Untold Story Behind
the Tragic Shooting of Bernard Doyle
at the Polo Grounds

DAN VANDEMORTEL

If you were young and Irish in the 1920s and dreamed of a sports career, you were offered only two tickets to punch: boxing and baseball. Football and basketball were in their infancies, while golf and tennis were restricted to more privileged whites at country clubs and colleges. Genetics limited to a rarefied few those diminutive enough to be horse jockeys.

Bernard Doyle did not meet the freakish requirements necessary for equestrian activities. But he was as Irish as the bogs. Born in Lowell, Massachusetts, on August 8, 1896, he was the first of eight or nine children raised by an Irish father from Kells (County Meath) and a Welsh mother of Irish parents, both of whom had immigrated to America in 1895 and 1890, respectively.[1] By 1910, his family had moved to Rockland County, north of New York City.[2] Around that time, he dropped out of or was removed from the eighth grade, exiting school early like some of his siblings, as many children did a century ago, to fend for himself and his family at assorted blue-collar jobs.[3] Answering the call of World War I, he served in the Navy and was stationed in England.[4] By 1920, at age 23, he had settled with his 21-year-old New Jersey-born wife, Margaret, in West Hoboken/Union City, New Jersey, where he toiled as a carpenter for the Erie Railroad and quietly raised a family during the Roaring 20s with the birth of his son, Bernard Jr., and daughter, Eileen.[5] All in all, a relatively unremarkable life. Except, his new home offered something most other American communities could not: a short train ride to the New York City mecca of boxing and baseball.

Doyle entered the ring at an early age, perhaps boxing professionally.[6] His record and career arc are uncertain. Yet assuredly through schoolyard scrapes, street altercations, ring exploits, and access to watching legends such as Jack Dempsey hammering inside the ropes, the blue-eyed, 5'9" and compactly-built youngster vigorously scratched the boxing itch, at least as a cherished hobby, more likely for his ticket to grander dreams.[7]

As many Irish and other immigrants turned to boxing, in nearby North Bergen, New Jersey, Irish lad Joe Braddock ascended the ranks the fastest. And soon springing up beside him was boxing-world-named "Barney" Doyle, who, after becoming the head trainer in a hard-boiled Jersey City basement doubling as headquarters for the Irish-American Ath-

138

letic Club, translated his gym rat ring intensity into catching Braddock's rising star as his manager.[8] Regarded by one boxing historian as an "ambitious, truculent small-timer," he fit well in a city of Irish, Italian, and German immigrants governed by a Democratic political machine with a reputation for "corruption, skullduggery, and political ledgermain."[9] Through sweat and guile he guided Braddock to the state Welterweight Championship in 1923.[10]

Doyle received the boxing equivalent of a supernova-hot tech stock split when Joe's younger brother, James, soon donned the gloves and blew through the state's amateur ranks like a whirlwind. With James now a fixture at the Jersey City basement, the skid was greased for Doyle to manage him in a career that began to exceed his brother's. In 1925, James won amateur titles in two weight divisions via three knockouts in a 48-hour span. At that moment, the Braddocks ruled Irish boxing circles, with Doyle the king of a potential dynasty.

After his third knockout, James was awarded an expensive watch, which Doyle carried for months, showing it off to any Northern New Jersey reporter who would pay attention.[11] "Jimmy did the fighting and Barney did the talking" became the saying of the day.[12] As James' biographer Ludwig Shabazian colorfully described: "Doyle, always in the hair of sports editors, now began to appear on the other side of the rail more frequently than ever. What was more, he gave evidence of prosperity: he was now ALWAYS smoking cigars. 'We just won another championship,' he would start. Braddock's ordinary victories usually meant an effusion of some twenty minutes for Barney; but championships always meant a panegyric oration that lasted anywhere from an hour to two hours, with no words barred."[13]

Unquestionably, Doyle, almost 30, had two tickets in hand to the Big Time. Until, that is, hubris and frustration took over head smarts and loyalty. While James was winning his amateur championships, Joe, who had turned professional, signed to fight local rival Anthony Lake. Joe picked up an early solid lead, but in the fourth round he got sloppy, succumbing to blows that rendered him unconscious. Rather than going to Joe's aid, Doyle, believing his protégé had ignored his advice, fled the arena in a huff. As Joe revived, his brother informed him that Doyle had stormed away. Once the cobwebs wore off, Joe continued to work with Doyle, as his contract stipulated, but he never forgot the slight and determined that he would manage James himself when his brother turned professional. When that moment came in 1926, Joe and another manager took over James's career. Doyle was exiled from the Braddock camp, joining a long list of casualties in boxing's history of subterranean transactions.[14] "There were some Irish attitudes to this stuff," his grandson quipped.[15]

In one quick, argumentative moment, the Braddock train had left the station, leaving Doyle to inhale fumes. "Terribly upset" over his termination, he nonetheless stayed with boxing as a trainer at local clubs and perhaps even managed again, although that is unconfirmed and would not have taken place in the limelight.[16] More likely, in the confined 1920s boxing world when matches were all-consuming and "you could go see your neighbor fight, or your grocer's son, or your daughter's beau," Doyle's ringside abandonment may have irrevocably branded him, correctly or incorrectly, as a manager you could not rely on.[17] James, meanwhile, later overcame injuries and financial deprivation to become the world heavyweight champ from 1935 to 1937. His life was memorialized by director Ron Howard's 2005 *Cinderella Man*, winner of three Academy Awards.

Stripped of boxing fame, Doyle assumed a markedly lower-profile life in various northern New Jersey locations, eventually becoming a Railway Express freight sorter on the New Jersey docks.[18] He was well respected and determined, and he continued to follow boxing and smoke cigars, so much so that his brother used the nicotine extracted from Doyle's cigar box to spray his flowers in order to keep bugs away.[19] By 1950, he and his wife, a licensed practicing nurse, had sold their house and were seeking an apartment in northern Hudson County. In the interim, Doyle moved to Fairview, his wife to friends in West New York, while his son lived on his own and his daughter attended nursing school.[20]

Amidst the vagaries of life in boxing and beyond, Doyle's other love persisted: baseball. It is unlikely he played the game beyond the sandlots, but he did somehow become an ardent Giants fan and attended the team's home games at the Polo Grounds as often as possible.[21] He also met his wife through her brother, who was a baseball fan.[22] Recently retired due to a heart condition, and with time on his hands as the July 4 holiday approached in 1950, he made plans to see a game with Bernard Jr.[23] When his son could not attend, he promised a former neighbor and friend from his boxing training days, Otto Flaig of nearby Union City, that he would take Flaig's 13-year-old son, Otto Jr., to a Giants home game.[24] Doyle had recently become interested in the boy, teaching him boxing and helping him "keep his nose clean and away from the police" as a favor to his father, so a trip to the Polo Grounds fit the bill perfectly.[25] Plans were made to go to the Friday, June 30, contest but were postponed when Doyle discovered this to be a night game. Instead, he bought tickets for the Tuesday, July 4, twin bill when the struggling 33–34 Giants would take on the 36–29 Brooklyn Dodgers, just two-and-a-half games out of first place.

After attending early Mass and hurrying through breakfast, the burly Doyle left his residence at 8:30 a.m., wearing a straw hat with a brim to cover thinning brown hair, his trademark cigars—remnants of a bygone era—stuffed in his white long-sleeved shirt pocket.[26] He picked up Flaig, who had barely slept due to adolescent pregame excitement.[27] Upon arrival and purchase of a ten-cent program, Doyle and Flaig trekked to the upper left-centerfield grandstand, section 42, row C, unreserved seating area, adjoining the bleachers on the eastern Eighth Avenue side of the park. After switching their seats, possibly to aid Flaig's sight line, Doyle sat down snugly in seat 3 while the skinny, sandy blond, freckle-faced boy in dark pants and a white T-shirt plunked down in seat 4 to his right with room to spare.[28] Scattered clouds meandered overhead with no precipitation, sealing a typical summer day of temperatures and humidity in the high 70s with "just enough of a breeze to keep the flies away," according to *Newsday*.[29]

About an hour before the game's start, many of the still arriving 49,316 crowd "bellowing its noisy admiration" over that era's modern Mets-Yankees subway series equivalent—likely with cheers and boos—watched the Dodgers take the field for warm-ups.[30] Among the Brooklyn players participating that day were future Hall of Famers Jackie Robinson and Roy Campanella, as well as Don Newcombe, all having recently broken baseball's color barrier, all scheduled to start in the first game. Doyle and Flaig, facing home plate, had a perfect view of the action and, rising over the horseshoe shaped oval grandstand, Coogan's Bluff, and the row of apartment houses on Edgecombe Avenue sitting above it. In an almost Norman Rockwellian scene, at 12:30 p.m. on our nation's birthday, Doyle turned, program in hand, to say something to his young companion.

The Harlem neighborhood resting on Coogan's Bluff and beyond that Doyle glimpsed was no longer the one of his youth at the Polo Grounds. When he was Flaig's age, central Harlem was 90 percent white in a city 98 percent white beyond greater Harlem.[31] But, while Doyle grew up and entered a volatile orbit around the boxing world, Harlem dramatically transformed in one of the largest internal demographic shifts in American history. Previously confined in the South by slavery, sharecropping indebtedness, civil rights abuses, and society-induced ignorance of life beyond the Mason-Dixon line, blacks began fleeing toward New York City and other industrial centers when the supply of cheap white immigrant labor was cut off just as defense-related manufacturing was ramping up to meet World War I needs. By 1920, this influx, uncertain neighborhood economic conditions, and related white flight led to central Harlem becoming 32.4 percent black.[32] A decade later, that number exploded to 70 percent in a city still 98 percent white beyond greater Harlem, part of the overall movement of roughly 1.6 to over two million blacks from the South toward northern cities from 1910 to 1930.[33]

With so many blacks funneled into such a dense area, black culture, finally free to express itself after years of denial and oppression, flowered. The soon-dubbed Harlem Renaissance of the 1920s showcased one of the greatest artistic, philosophical, and musical explosions in American history. Neighborhood residents then and in subsequent years presented a roll call still awe-inspiring today: entertainers Paul Robeson and Cab Calloway, civil rights leaders W.E.B. DuBois and Roy Wilkins, literary icons Langston Hughes and Ralph Ellison, future Supreme Court justice Thurgood Marshall, and many more.

The neighborhood of choice for these notables and those with similar aspirations, especially along Edgecombe Avenue, became known as "Sugar Hill" for the "sweet life" it offered its residents. One apartment building alone at 409 Edgecombe housed Marshall, DuBois, and Aaron Douglas, the "father of black American art."[34] As the 1930s gave way to World War II, another building at 555 Edgecombe accommodated so many celebrities such as Robeson, Duke Ellington, Lena Horne, Coleman Hawkins, and boxer Joe Louis, that it is now a National Historic Landmark.[35]

Despite these successes, parts of Harlem were becoming increasingly mired in problems. The second wave of the Great Migration rapidly transformed the nation's black population after the Depression. With five million more blacks scattering outward over the next few decades, a southern race, once the nation's most rural, converted into urbanites, trending toward 1960 when almost 75 percent of blacks would reside in cities, 90 percent of them in northern cities.[36] Harlem reflected this shift, with central Harlem climbing to 89.3 percent black in 1940 and 98 percent in 1950, even though the city remained lily-white at 94 percent beyond greater Harlem.[37] Many arrived unskilled and illiterate to a neighborhood of about 400,000 blacks living in a space designed for 75,000 people.[38] As Claude Brown described in *Manchild in the Promised Land*, his seminal memoir of being a black Harlem teenager at mid-century, "these migrants were told that unlimited opportunities for prosperity existed in New York and that there was no 'color problem' there…. To them, this was the 'Promised Land' that Mammy had been singing about in the cotton fields for many years."[39] Instead, after fleeing flawed but stable Southern social and religious orders, these migrants arrived at a Northern ghetto best described by author Richard Wright as a "teasing torture."[40] Discrimination, consignment to employment in the economy's lowest rungs in white-owned businesses, comparatively atomized existences, and substandard, segregated housing opportunities awaited their fantasies and prospects.

For many, The Promised Land of the old spirituals became an economic and societal mirage. In 1938, Wright observed that the glamour of black opportunity was "overlaid with shadows of tragic premonition," which proved prescient.[41] Quality jobs at credible wages were difficult, often impossible to obtain. With money scarce, prostitution and gambling rose up to fill in the cracks. The streets, even the roofs, once a source of social connection, in many areas drifted toward the dangers of drugs and theft. As World War II concluded, Harlem was becoming, as Ralph Ellison later described, "the scene and symbol of the Negro's perpetual alienation in the land of his birth" and, for many "displaced persons of American democracy," the "scene of the folk-Negro's death agony."[42]

As ghetto life and black cultural successes simultaneously spread into white society's consciousness, steps were made toward accommodation; others veered backward toward segregation. Baseball itself was part of this conundrum. Jackie Robinson broke the color barrier in the major leagues in 1947. The Giants followed suit two years later with outfielder Monte Irvin and third baseman Hank Thompson. Still, unwritten quotas limited the number of blacks per team, often the positions they could play, and how they were dealt with when injured or slumping. By 1950, only five of 16 teams had integrated.[43] Full integration by all clubs was nine years distant, hiring of a black manager was a quarter-century away, and the concept of a black general manager or owner was preposterous.

Nothing better illustrated the distance America's racial divide had to progress in conjunction with baseball's hold on its collective imagination than the *Saturday Evening Post*'s handling of a Polo Grounds cover painting for its April 22, 1950, issue. That edition featured a Rockwellian scene of expectant fans along the left field foul line grasping for a foul ball as a player approached the railing, the foul ball tantalizingly beyond his reach. Doyle's grandstand seating area was artistically rendered in the background. Every fan was white, in stark contrast to the mixed race attendance at a real Giant game.

The portrayal, though, was not by Rockwell. And if even if it had been, blacks would have been absent since he had already been advised by the *Post*'s editor to never include them in his work because "it makes people uneasy."[44] Rather, the painting was by artist Austin Briggs, who in his original cover inserted portraits of himself, his daughter, his son, and his family's beloved black maid, Fanny Drain, into the frame. When Briggs delivered his cover to the *Post*'s Philadelphia office, however, the editors quickly instructed that he would have to paint Drain out of the picture. Furious, Briggs broke the painting over his knee and walked out, never regretting his act or repenting his anger. The *Post* reacted by hiring another Rockwellian cover artist to repaint Briggs's original, mimicking everything down to composition and tonality, minus the erasure of Drain in favor of a hefty, Bernard Doyle–like middle-aged man with a handkerchief on his head for sun protection.[45]

The editorially sanctified *Post*'s whitening of American virtue, however, did not eradicate the changing 1950 demographics and behavior just beyond the Polo Grounds. A volatile street culture of crime, drugs, and gangs was just beginning to rush up to another level with the advent of heroin.[46] Lamenting deteriorating portions of Harlem, Langston Hughes wrote poignantly of "dark, unpleasant houses with steep stairs and narrow halls, where the rooms are too small, the ceilings too low and the rents too high…. The house is full of roomers. Papa and mama sleep in the living room, the kids in the dining room, lodgers in every alcove and everything but the kitchen is rented out for sleeping."[47] Although such overcrowding and underprivileged means did not strangle the tonier areas of Sugar Hill, spillage from these conditions meant some of the famous names from the past were no longer in residence.

One person who did reside, at 515 Edgecombe, one of the Hill's less fancy apartment buildings, was 53-year-old Marie Belld. Born in 1897 in North Carolina, she left school after the sixth grade and later married circa 1917. By 1930, she was living in New York City in a six-story apartment building at 211–215 Edgecombe Avenue. But her husband was no longer with her, having separated through some avenue good or ill, near or far.[48] She worked as a servant for a private family, was literate, and rented a unit for about $842 (modern equivalent) per month, possibly half her take-home pay, in which she housed two residents: a 21-year-old nephew from North Carolina and a Virginia-born lodger.[49]

By 1940, married but still unattached, she was living four blocks north at 764 St. Nicholas Avenue, a four-story apartment building in which she lived with a family of seven, her great-nephew, and 15 other roomers of scattered ages and relationships. She worked as a part-time maid earning at times just $3,600 (modern equivalent) a year.[50] At some point prior to or during 1950, she relocated ten blocks north to the top floor of a six-story apartment building at 515 Edgecombe, joining an unknown nexus of family and lodgers.

What is known is that her great-nephew, 14-year-old Robert Mario Peebles, then called her apartment home, having been born in New York and coming to stay with her circa 1937 when he was 19 months old, shortly after his parents separated.[51] Belld sacrificed to give Robert a solid upbringing, working long hours at times at domestic work and using her savings to send him to a private nursery school, where he stayed from ages two to eight. However, her hours were inconsistent and unstable. And a frequently fluctuating cast of poorly educated, economically deprived, and on-the-go lodgers surrounding her would have added to that instability, especially as viewed through a youngster's eyes.[52] After an illness cut back on her work stamina and savings, she was forced to transfer Robert to a public school where he did not adjust so well. In 1947, he was referred by a Harlem church rector to the Lafargue Clinic, founded the year before as Harlem's first out-patient mental health care clinic.[53] Volunteer medical professionals and social workers evaluated and counseled him for various issues, including being a "school problem" and for intermittent sleepwalking suffered since the age of six or seven, one incident so pronounced that he told Belld he was "going to look for his mother."[54]

Wearing tortoise-shelled black glasses and considered undersized, Peebles was a somewhat nerdy-looking student at nearby Edward W. Stitt Junior High School.[55] Belld helped him obtain afternoon jobs delivering packages for neighborhood grocery stores. In his free time, among other activities, he read comic books featuring Superman, Batman and Robin, Green Arrow, and other superheroes.[56] But he also smoked cigarettes and was beginning to exhibit a Harlem rap sheet at odds with his recognized intelligence and pleasant speaking manner.[57] On two separate occasions, he was arrested for burglary and having a homemade gun.[58] May 5, 1950, brought an arrest for grand larceny involving automobile theft, in which he was found guilty of the reduced charge of juvenile delinquency.[59] And sometime in the afternoon or evening of July 4, while on probation, he burglarized a nearby house, stealing $73 (modern equivalent).[60]

A sense of unease, of change, gripped Harlem and the nation that day and over the holiday weekend, as unpleasant news encroached on all fronts. President Harry Truman had just ordered U.S. ground troops to assist South Korea's overwhelmed forces in repelling North Korean invaders. Winston Churchill spoke of imminent holocaust at the hands of the Soviet Union's Red Menace. General Dwight Eisenhower warned of world enslavement. Approximately two-and-a-half million New Yorkers left the city for the weekend, replaced by two million folks from the hinterlands, scurrying that contributed to a record 466 four-day national traffic death toll.[61] In search of good news, fans headed to the Polo Grounds for a timeless Dodgers-Giants matchup, for some patriotic bunting to cover the green stands, and a slice of Americana that would assuredly drown out everything harsh, whether a continent away or a bluff nearby.

At the moment Doyle turned to Flaig, two Brooklynites near Doyle heard a "loud popping noise, like a blown-up paper bag bursting."[62] Flaig heard it, too. Suddenly, he saw Doyle slump forward, blood pouring out of his nose, ears, and mouth and onto the clothing of a man seated in front of them. As Doyle drifted over onto him, Flaig attempted to straighten him only to see that he too was now covered in blood. "Wha—what's the matter?" he stammered.[63] Doyle neither moved nor responded.

Thinking Doyle had suffered a heart attack, Flaig summoned an attendant, who notified the police. At some point, a nearby fan identifying himself as a physician examined Doyle and said, "That man's dead," before disappearing back into the crowd.[64] Despite the fan's pronouncement, there was no panic, no hurried evacuation. Few fans took immediate interest, either focusing on the pregame festivities or, if distracted by Doyle, assuming that he had taken ill.[65]

As a police sergeant arrived, an ambulance was called from Harlem Hospital. By this time, 16-year-old Ed Drohan from Yonkers, sitting with his brother and father about 10 to 15 rows in front of Doyle, became aware of a growing "commotion of people's attention being turned toward [Doyle]."[66] He looked backward and to the left, seeing Doyle covered in blood, "like a red mask down his face."[67] He also saw a cadre of about seven to nine cops arriving upon the scene, comprising part of a mixture of ballpark employees, a doctor, and medical orderlies.[68] As the hospital personnel showed up and noted a bullet entry wound, Doyle was pronounced dead.[69] The blood likely covered most or all of a small hole near his left ear, in which a slug was partially visible.[70] Eventually, he was taken away, covered on a stretcher, a sudden victim passing through a crowd of strangers, forever unaware that his unremarkable yet attentive switching of seats had probably saved a 13-year-old boy's life.

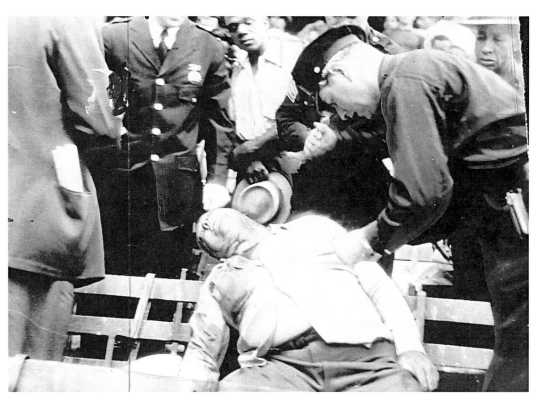

Bernard Doyle slumped in his seat after being shot, while a black spectator looks down with concern (collection of Dan VanDeMortel).

A 2014 *Sports Illustrated* retrospective, quoting 1950 *New York Daily News* coverage, reflected in astonishment that after Doyle's removal the game went on as scheduled, with fans flocking to the two unoccupied seats.[71] It also was incredulous at Flaig, who, according to the *News*, complained that the detectives' questions were making him miss the game. "I've been dreaming about this game for a month," he grumbled.[72] The *New York Herald Tribune* likewise lamented how fans "kept their eyes on the diamond, as death, the master dramatist, brushed past them unnoticed," failing to diminish the value of a seat.[73]

Hindsight, whether hours or a millennium later, casts a harsher light on the Giant fan base than is warranted. Ed Keele, sitting with his brother and uncle one row behind and about four to five seats to the right, thought Doyle died naturally, even after his uncle spoke with the attending police, who initially theorized Doyle had suffered a massive cerebral hemorrhage.[74] Drohan likewise concurred with the *New York Times* that few seemed to know what had happened to Doyle, shooting or otherwise.[75] If anything, he felt there was a somewhat remorseful vibe in the crowd at first, before it eased into nonchalance as the innings ensued. The police seemed to be perplexed, too, he reflected, since if there had been any inkling of foul play or a continuing danger, they would have had their guns drawn and "cleared out that place in a hurry."[76] He felt it was "in the nature of the New York mind not to leave," and there was no reason to do so based on crime knowledge, fear, or instructions from officials.[77] The crowd felt sorry for Flaig, he added. The boy did not scream or cry as he was led away after answering questions from a "swarm" of detectives, but Drohan noticed he "seemed bewildered": a state incongruous with some press accounts but which aligns with common sense and a look at his frail, somewhat bedraggled frame as photographed later while in police custody.[78] The *Carolina Times* even went so far as to describe Flaig as "horrified," certainly a more understandable reaction.[79] In 2016, Flaig's son surmised his father would have been "shocked" by the experience; any report to the contrary sounded inaccurate and would have been "someone trying to sell newspapers [more] than anything else."[80] As for the *Daily News*-conjured visions of callous fans jostling for the unattended seats, a stark rebuttal was offered by a press photo showing the seats unoccupied at some point after the shooting.[81]

Meanwhile, action on the diamond continued unabated, giving little cause for concern or an explanation for Doyle's sudden fatality. Giant shortstop and captain Alvin Dark said there was no talk of it on his team's bench. The Dodgers were in the know a bit more, but not by much. Robinson spoke of early rumors of the incident among his teammates and that they talked more about the shooting than baseball once radio details offered by Hall of Fame announcer Red Barber were confirmed after the game, uneasy that they might be targets on the diamond.[82] Doyle's 83-year-old father blissfully watched the game at home on television, uninformed by the announcers of his son's death. As far as most fans were concerned, the only violence at hand was the near fistfight that erupted at one point between reliably bellicose Giant manager Leo Durocher and Dodger outfielder Carl Furillo.[83] At a time even before portable transistor radios, news travelled at a snail's pace.

While the Giants and Dodgers split the twin bill, Doyle's body was taken to a nearby police station, where it was examined by Chief Medical Examiner Thomas Gonzales. His analysis revealed Doyle had been shot over the left temple, the bullet ranging downward and lodging on the other side of his skull.[84] No powder burns or skin breaks were found around the bullet hole.[85] Radio news of the shooting brought one of Doyle's brothers, and later Bernard Jr., to the station, where they confirmed identification before the body was removed to the morgue.[86] One can only imagine the devastating shock, the sense of dislocation, to Doyle's family upon hearing the news, especially considering his daughter's wedding was just a month or two away.[87]

After the examination, the police were presented with a logistical nightmare: how do you find the killer(s) of a man inside the Polo Grounds with no eyewitnesses, no audio or video evidence to hint at the shot's origin, and no clue who might have pulled the trigger? And, given that even Doyle's family was mystified by the shooting, what was the motive?

Assistant Chief Inspector Conrad Rothengast immediately assigned detectives to the scene to find out. His team spread out inside the Grounds and searched buildings and vacant areas outside of it, questioning several boys playing in the bushes along Coogan's Bluff. A few hours later, they discovered an undischarged .22 "high speed" cartridge in a wooded area of the Bluff behind a Highbridge Park playground, strengthening a developing theory that the shooting was an accident.[88] Rothengast told reporters he believed the fatal bullet was fired from that location, travelling almost a half mile to reach the upper tier stands before landing on a downward trajectory. His team and uniformed policemen combed the park until 10:00 p.m. to determine whether any additional bullets had been fired.[89]

A view from Doyle's seat. 515 Edgecombe is the smaller apartment building directly above third base (collection of Dan VanDeMortel).

At 12:30 a.m., police rounded up about a dozen boys in the area for questioning. One admitted owning two .22 rifles and a long-range .22 pistol with two bullets in the magazine, which were found in his top-floor apartment on Edgecombe Avenue. There were a dozen additional bullets in the boy's home, some similar to the ones found along the Bluff.[90] Up on the roof, police found five .22 Short shells: four rusty, one clean. The roof's parapet was also pocked by bullets.[91] When questioned, the youth maintained he was playing in the streets when Doyle was killed and that he used rifles for target practice. With some dots beginning to connect, the authorities released the other boys and arrested Robert Mario Peebles for juvenile delinquency regarding gun possession in violation of the antiweapons Sullivan Law and questioned him throughout the night.[92] His great-aunt Marie was also arrested, held on $2,500 bail on a charge of violating the Sullivan Law by harboring concealed weapons.[93] "The kid brought them in. I didn't know they were there," she was quoted as saying to reporters or police in one press account.[94]

Frustratingly, as night turned into day, the dots began to separate. Doyle's autopsy revealed that he had been struck by a .45 missile—not a .22—discharged from an automatic pistol.[95] Thrown for a loop, Rothengast assigned 40 additional detectives to cover the Grounds and to examine the grass, shrubs, and bushes along the park and in Highbridge Park. They also searched nearby buildings for evidence. Overall, 1,200 persons, including 150 youths, were questioned, with efforts continuing until darkness neared. Thirty detectives continued to question residents along Edgecombe Avenue, and half a dozen boys were brought in for questioning. Nevertheless, a full day's work yielded no gun and no clues.[96]

Aware of the forensic setback, Peebles held firm. Rothengast found him "'cocky' and non-cooperative."[97] According to police, when questioned about the shooting, Peebles denied involvement, replying, "You've got me but you haven't got the gun. You've got a tough row ahead of you."[98] He would only admit to often using the roof for target practice. Despite his intransigence, he was still considered a suspect in the shooting and was charged with juvenile delinquency for gun possession, a more serious charge not available due to his being under 15 years old.[99] He was arraigned and remanded to the Youth House in lower Manhattan for continued questioning and a court hearing the following week.[100] With a background investigation unearthing no known enemies of Doyle, the police were now considering the shooting a freak accident originating from outside the park since an inside shot would have exited through Doyle's head.[101]

On Thursday, the police broadened their search. With Doyle's seat as an apex, a surveyor measured a large triangle within the 1,660-yard range detectives felt the bullet might have travelled: a 30-block section containing hundreds of apartment dwellings.[102] Forty detectives continued their sniffing efforts in Coogan's Bluff, Highbridge Park, and surrounding areas for a .45 shell or weapon. Members of the police Youth Squad joined the hunt, mingling with boys playing in Highbridge Park in hopes of picking up some leads. Even more residents of Edgecombe Avenue were questioned. Peebles continued to provide nothing, except admitting he once owned a .38 revolver of foreign make before it had been taken away from him by Belld.[103] As the investigation shut down near midnight, questioning of 1,000 persons that day had turned up zilch.

Early the following afternoon, the dam broke. After days of questioning led by Detective Lieutenant Thomas McCabe, Peebles suddenly and unexpectedly confessed to the shooting. According to police, Peebles admitted he had a .45 automatic pistol with one bullet in its chamber, which he had found in Central Park about six months previously and had kept hidden in his basement until that Tuesday. Heading to the roof, he held the pistol at a 45-degree angle elevation, then pulled the trigger "in Fourth of July exuberance," later returning the weapon to the basement and flushing the shell down a toilet.[104] He claimed he had no intention of firing a shot into the Polo Grounds. From where he stood beside a shelter enclosing the roof's stairway, police stated he was unable to see the park, since a five-foot-high parapet surrounding the roof prevented him from firing downward.[105] Peebles was unaware until about half an hour after the shooting that the bullet had struck someone in the ballpark. He learned this from a woman on Edgecombe Avenue who heard it on a radio broadcast. Frightened, he went back to the basement, removed the unloaded gun from its hiding place, and took it to Highbridge Park, where he threw it away behind a public swimming pool, down a precipitous slope toward the Harlem River Driveway.[106] In further questioning, he admitted that between the time of the shooting and his arrest he also stole money from a house on 159th Street, near St. Nicholas Avenue.[107]

After writing and signing a brief confession at 2:30 p.m., Peebles was taken, later that afternoon, to the spot where he discarded the weapon. According to police, when they asked him along the way if he felt relieved after confessing, he replied, "I certainly do."[108] Once at the scene, he pointed well-attired authorities upward to a bluff about 100 feet high in Highbridge Park, about 150 feet west of the Harlem River Driveway, which overlooked a wooded, rugged terrain covered with undergrowth, rocks, and high grass. A newspaper photographer snapped him pointing upward at this moment, capturing him with cropped hair, his trademark glasses, dark pants, a sweater vest, and a white, wide-lapelled, long-sleeved shirt under it rolled up to his elbows, unbuttoned to midchest: a portrait more akin to an astronomy student locating Mars than a perpetrator indicating a gun's whereabouts.[109]

After the shutter closed, Peebles reenacted the weapon-tossing scene at the top of the bluff, using a stone about the same weight as the gun. Detectives and Park Department employees focused their search at the pinpointed scene before calling off their efforts hours later, stationing two patrolmen to guard the area overnight.[110] The next day, more than 120 police officials used a mine detector, long poles, and sticks to shake trees and search bushes, rock crevices, and high grass in the area.[111] Despite these and other efforts, the gun was never found. Police hypothesized it might have been picked up by a passerby at some point.[112]

The web of intrigue surrounding Peebles and his guns broadened the following week. On July 15, Mary Elizabeth Crum, 26, and William Mitchell, 36, both from Harlem, were arrested and charged with the February purchase for Peebles of one of his .22 rifles. By mid–August, Crum was still in jail in lieu of $500 bail, while Mitchell was free on the same bail. Both awaited trial in the Court of Special Sessions, the result of which is unknown. In addition, a warrant for failure to appear in court was out for a third person involved in procuring the rifle: Robert Thomas, 29, also from Harlem. Available records do not confirm his apprehension or conviction.[113]

At some point after Peebles's confession, Belld returned home.[114] On July 11 in Felony Court, she waived a hearing before Felony Court Magistrate Frederick Strong on a misdemeanor charge of harboring the three .22 weapons without a permit and was continued on bail for trial in Special Sessions. The disposition of her potential conviction and sentencing is unknown. She continued living in New York City and died in November 1985.[115]

Despite witnessing Doyle's death and narrowly escaping his own, Otto Flaig spoke infrequently of the shooting and went on to lead a solid, structured life, perhaps in an effort to rectify, to control the chaotic world he had been subjected to at such an early age. He remained a Giants fan until the team moved to San Francisco, then switched to the Mets. After completing high school and earning all-state honors in baseball and basketball despite being only 5'8", he served four years in the Marines Corps. His father wanted him to become a fireman, a position in which he would reliably receive public gratitude. His Marine Corps experience coupled with an interest in police work and the secure income it would provide, however, prompted Flaig to become a cop. He started his career at a part-time security detail in which he broke up bar fights in a tough Transfer Station-Union City neighborhood where there were "two bars on every corner."[116] He moved on to various New Jersey police departments, becoming president of the Bergen County Police Chiefs Association. In 1967, he joined the Teterboro force, becoming its chief in 1974. Residing in Little Ferry, he died of a chronic liver ailment in 1992 at age 55, on the day he was scheduled to retire due to a police force consolidation, and was survived by a wife and two children.[117] "He wasn't big, but there was a presence about him. He never yelled, but if he raised his voice you knew there was something serious going on," his son recalled.[118]

The Doyle family, likewise, continued living in Northern New Jersey and did their best to move forward from the tragedy. Within 36 hours of the shooting, according to her grandson, Margaret was visited at her home by two "suits," likely lawyers, from the Giants who induced her to "sign a paper saying she wouldn't sue the stadium or make any trouble."[119] The offer of a very low-cash settlement, if anything, was conducted before Bernard Jr. could arrive to participate in the discussion, which "hacked him off for the rest of his life."[120] With no life insurance policy in effect to financially ameliorate her husband's death, Margaret lived within her means, regularly attended church, remained widowed, and continued working as an in-home nurse for the elderly and terminally ill until close to her death in 1979. "It doesn't cost anything to be kind" was the most valuable life lesson she passed along to her children.[121] Like Flaig, she rarely talked about the shooting.[122] Bernard Jr., a World War II Navy veteran, scrapped plans to join the monastery and instead obtained a teaching degree in order to always have income to assist his mother. He remained single and taught at northern New Jersey high schools until his death in 1974.[123] Eileen married, worked as a nurse, had four children, and lived in northern New Jersey until her death in 2005. She also did not frequently dwell upon her father's death. But as her daughter, Maria, recalled, "She always liked everyone close and accounted for on the fourth of July. She wasn't overprotective, but there was always that sense, that fear, at that time. It's like 9/11, when you get that phone call you'll never forget."[124]

As for Peebles, freedom proved as elusive as the missing gun. He remained in the all-boy Youth House, a Lower East Side detention home for delinquent boys remanded by the courts for confinement and diagnostic study, described as "a cross between a Y.M.C.A. branch and a jail" in another classic black 1950s coming-of-age account, *Out of the Burning*.[125] Held in a single, barless cell—perhaps with a roommate—he awoke at seven to make his bed and sweep his room every other day, then was marched by social-worker guards to the cafeteria for breakfast. Afterwards, per Claude Brown, also held there around this time, Peebles would have been able to "play pool, basketball, checkers, go swimming, fight, and do a lot of other things."[126] Perhaps he received visitors on weekends. Escaping to "home" or another sanctuary was virtually impossible as the windows were gated and the doors always locked. He was surrounded by a mixture of races he would potentially live with in a future location(s) at the rate his future was heading. Three years later, another undersized youth with oversized aggressiveness would also briefly call this location home: Lee Harvey Oswald.[127]

For the better part of a month, his case dragged along in Children's Court pending continued investigation by authorities. In a closed July 11 hearing, he was described as "nervous but quiet."[128] At a later hearing on July 26, an attending social worker observed that Peebles came across as a "bad actor" who "got caught in several lies," perhaps "trying to establish an alibi" due to being on probation for his prior offenses.[129] Even more problematic, his best friend, 16-year-old Arnold Henderson, testified that Peebles had a .45.[130] On August 3, Justice Juvenal Marchisio found Peebles guilty of juvenile delinquency regarding illegal ownership of the three .22-caliber weapons and ammunition found in his apartment. A separate charge for possession and discharging of the .45 was dismissed for lack of evidence. The 47-year-old judge committed Peebles to the State Training School for Boys at Warwick for an indeterminate term.[131]

Thus concluded one of the more bizarre incidents in Polo Grounds lore. Not to mention the only occurrence of a fan being killed inside a major league park by a shot fired from outside.[132] A gun-loving youth on the fast track to nowhere, in a moment of patriotic fervor, fired off a random shot with a one in a million trajectory that accidentally killed someone from a different state and a different time. His confession said as much. With black youth about 53 percent of all juvenile delinquency cases in Manhattan, another Harlem crime had been cleared off the books, with society all the better.[133]

Not so fast. Peebles's actions as reported and adjudicated could be the truth, or at least most of it. But that is improbable. Lafargue Clinic co-founder Dr. Fredric Wertham was "not at all convinced" that Peebles was guilty of the shooting.[134] And decades of legal developments and more advanced societal views regarding black-on-white crime lead a probing modern eye to open several doors that diminish assumptions of guilt.

Looking backward, one must view Peebles's case through the prism of 1950. At midcentury, whatever he did or did not do occurred in a time before legislation, court decisions, and civil disobedience ended legally sanctioned segregation. And if one associates the horrible pre-civil rights treatment of blacks as something perpetrated by men in white robes, a rigged economic system, and recalcitrant governors in backwater Southern enclaves, how does one rationalize central Harlem being overcrowded and 98 percent black that year in a city 94 percent white beyond greater Harlem? Or similar situations in other cities around the country? In such a reality, the *Saturday Evening Post's* editor was only doing what most Americans and their baseball teams were perpetrating: relegating blacks to a confined, legally unprotected second-class status where they could eat, breathe, shit, live, die, kill each other, whatever, just as long as the national 89.5 percent white population did not have to be made "uneasy" by the "Negro" minority.[135]

Nationwide white press coverage of the shooting reflected this mindset. The widest, loudest trumpeting of notes that now ring discordantly was *Time's* comparison of the "freckled" Flaig in contrast to the "row of dingy apartment houses on Coogan's Bluff," specifically targeting Peebles's "dirty yellow apartment house."[136] No other account then or now differentiated the Sugar Hill area with other parts of Harlem, reporting instead by omission the historical inaccuracy that the entire neighborhood was unsafe, to be avoided at all costs. But as mid-century Harlem resident and current award-winning chronicler Terry Mulligan recently affirmed, Harlem was a mixture of good and bad. It all depended upon which blocks and areas you were talking about and who you were talking about. Some areas and families were crime ridden, mired in collapsed social structures; others were full of talented or capable or fortunate people getting by. As for

Sugar Hill, it was still considered a residence for well-to-do blacks. The idea of someone along Edgecombe Avenue firing off a gun toward the Polo Grounds would have come as a surprising aberration to many Hill residents and other Harlemites.[137]

The other flawed journalistic sound came from a damning failure of investigative reporting by the white press. The fatal bullet passed directly over the press box on its way to striking Doyle, and so did many facts and reporting standards. Laughably, some accounts could not even get Peebles's name correct, referring to him as "Howard" Peebles, which leads one to wonder if the reported name of "Mario" is correct.[138] Their ability to genealogically classify Belld was even more scattered, referencing her as his grandmother, his aunt, his great-aunt, his great-grandaunt, and his great-great aunt.[139] Intellectual laziness was also rampant. Then or later, Peebles was never tracked down for an interview or the subject of analysis in the absence of one. Belld, too, was neither interviewed nor considered. Also, at least one attorney represented Peebles, but he was never quoted or mentioned in available press accounts.[140]

Likewise, if any white journalist visited 515 Edgecombe to explore its roof to sift through the police's version of events, no one mentioned it. When the police explained that Peebles suddenly and unexpectedly asked for a pencil and wrote his confession without coercion or coaching, the press reverentially transcribed their words as Biblical pronouncements.[141] From arrest to sentencing, and decades later by reporters relying on police-fed stories of the time, Peebles received a benefit of no doubt befitting the "colored boy," "Negro boy," "gun happy youth," and even "dangerous psychopath" labels under which he was often cast.[142]

Only the black press displayed a hint of nuance and attempted to close loopholes open to this day. The *Carolina Times*, the paper which noted Peebles's nervous courtroom demeanor, referred to the shooting as a "tragic case."[143] James Hicks of the *Washington Afro-American* took matters a step further, noting that "many questioned the veracity of [Peebles's] confession, pointing to the fact that the measured distance from the roof of 515 [Edgecombe] to the seat occupied by Doyle in the Polo Grounds was 1,120 feet, or more than 372 [*sic*] yards away."[144] These critics contended that a .45 bullet would not kill someone at such a distance, and perhaps not even be able to travel that far. Police meanwhile countered that it would, maintaining its ballistics showed that death was possible from such a distance as reconstructed, despite supplying data indicating that it was "highly improbable."[145] Although the U.S. Army Ordnance manual of the time indicated the range of a .45 weapon was "approximately 1,955 yards," it listed no performance data pertaining to the efficacy of surface penetration beyond 250 yards.[146]

Hicks also called into question the police's determination regarding Peebles's inability to have seen the Polo Grounds when firing due to facing a five-foot parapet surrounding the roof. His examination of the roof revealed five narrow slits, about eight inches wide and sloping downward about two feet, through which someone of Peebles's height could have seen the Polo Grounds directly ahead. Building superintendent Alfred Smith guided Hicks on a tour of the roof, where they observed white circled targets drawn with crayon along the parapet. The parapet and other parts of the roof were pock-marked with bullet holes, some of which may have been from the target practice Peebles admitted to. A housing on the dumbwaiter of the apartment was also shot through by a bullet.[147]

Unfortunately, Hicks's probing efforts were read only by his limited black readership. The rest of the country was offered a wildly inaccurate International News "How Fan Was Shot" photo from 515 Edgecombe's rooftop vantage point, showing a *white adult male* firing from the *front edge* of the roof at a *90-degree angle*, arms raised as if he were holding a *rifle*, with a marked bullet trajectory line indicating a *straight shot* toward Doyle's seat.[148]

Modern examination exposes further room for questioning of police and press reporting of the shooting. First, consider the .45. It seems unlikely that Peebles was walking through Central Park during winter time and—oh, blessed miracle!—a gun suddenly appeared for snatching and safekeeping. A more plausible explanation, if he actually had it, was that it was given to or illegally purchased for him, that he hid it for a contact of his, or that he stole it. Assuming for argument's sake the random chance of Peebles finding the gun, his later tossing it away to a densely wooded spot where over 120 police officials never found it further stretches statistical probability. Even the police were "inclined to believe [Peebles] was lying about where he disposed of the gun."[149] Imagining what happened to the weapon easily leads to Peebles possibly giving it away for hiding, selling or trading it, returning it to its original owner(s), or perhaps hiding it somewhere for retrieval once his case blew over. Belld also could have assisted him in disposing of it. Indeed, she is the ultimate wild card. Her professed unawareness of Peebles's .22 weapons is either a lie to cover up more intimate knowledge or involvement, or a tacit admission that she had lost complete control of her household, unconcerned or, more likely, overwhelmed by Peebles's fervent collecting of firearms under her roof. Even New York's black press judged her as being "on the delinquent side of the adult ledger," albeit acknowledging her attention to her great-nephew's activities may have been distracted by the "pressing problems of making a living and keeping the home intact."[150]

Secondly, if Peebles fired the fatal shot, did he really do so accidentally out of holiday exuberance? Police told the Associated Press the day after the shooting that the bullet was probably fired "by someone celebrating Independence Day or by a person with a depraved mind," opening the possibility that this holiday explanation was fed to Peebles for later confession.[151] He certainly would have known that the Polo Grounds, including its outfield and grandstands, was clearly visible from the Edgecombe side of his roof. And, even if the parapet blocked his view from most angles, only the front of the building contained slots, an architectural signal that the Polo Grounds resided just beyond view. Perhaps a target practice shot went awry? Perhaps a fit of adolescent rage, fantasy, or stupidity led to a shot toward the park intended merely to scare or confuse people? Perhaps drugs or horsing around with a friend impaired his aim or common sense, or caused the gun to go off accidentally? A few news stories left these and other possibilities open, stating Peebles fired "without reason" or "for the fun of it," "trying out the gun" after feeling "an impulse."[152] Also open is the reason why after learning of his shot's impact, then allegedly flushing the spent shell down a toilet and taking the .45 to Highbridge Park for disposal, Peebles decided to burglarize money from a nearby house. The more understandable choice for a "guilty" youth would be to maintain a low profile, to avoid any additional transgression that could potentially alert authorities. Whether by impulse or deliberation, engaging in burglary right after accidentally killing someone would be a curious, unlikely decision, if that indeed was the chain of events.

Thirdly, how linear were the dots connecting the shooting to Peebles? Initial evidence attributed Doyle's death to a .22 weapon when a .22 bullet was discovered along the Bluff. Although that theory was later rebuffed by the autopsy's disclosure of death due to a .45 bullet, by then the die may already have been cast for the youngster. A 2011 *Napa Valley Register* retrospective on the shooting claimed that police received a break in the case via a phone call from a "credible source" who snitched on Peebles. The informant, one of the Bluff's residents, "had seen it all and gave the play-by-play account of what would be a case closed within a matter of days."[153] A citation for this assertion, though, was

"How Fan Was Shot": the misleading nationally-distributed news photograph showing the Polo Grounds from the alleged shooter's perch (collection of Dan VanDeMortel).

inexcusably absent, its author later only able to offer that it "probably" came from an unrecalled and unavailable newspaper account.[154] This scenario also does not conform to Claude Brown's account of meeting Peebles when they were at Warwick together: "It was a jive tip, but there were a whole lot of cats [at Warwick] on humbles.... He was telling me one day how they sent him up there on a humble. He said when this guy had gotten shot in the Polo Grounds, they started looking in all the houses on Edgecombe Avenue, and that's where he lived. They started looking for guns and stuff. They had a house-to-house search for guns. And they found a .22 rifle in the house. The man had been shot with a .45[,] but they blamed it on him."[155]

In other words, he took the fall on a suspect b.s. tip, but did his time in a cool, unassuming manner.[156] And this occurred after Arnold Henderson was shown a .45 at a police armory and then testified that Peebles had one.[157] However, if Henderson was truthful, did he or some other snitch actually see Peebles fire from the roof? Was he/she with Peebles at the time? Or, did he/she merely see or hear of Peebles target practicing at other times and suggest to police that they should investigate him stemming from that activity? Did he/she have a grudge against Peebles? Or did he/she "drop the dime" on him to save his/her own skin, as a social worker attending Peebles's hearing reported that "the detectives probably had something on him and forced him" regarding Henderson?[158] Maybe Peebles "took one for the team" rather than being labeled a snitch by friends, schoolmates, street contacts, or someone else lodging in his apartment or building. Even police accounts conflict with the snitch's chain of events as he/she told the *New York Herald Tribune* that Peebles was "seen on Coogan's Bluff about the time of the shooting," not specifically on the roof.[159] Amidst this confusion, the fact-of-life equation of "Kids and guns don't mix," as offered by Doyle's granddaughter, is all that is certain.[160]

Lastly, questions can be raised about Peebles's confession as reported. Why did it come so quickly and unexpectedly given that the police had no gun to pin him to the shooting? Did they lie about or stretch particulars, bluffing him into confessing? The police's account that the confession was obtained without coercion or coaching confirms nothing: If the opposite were true, it would hardly be a procedure that authorities would admit unless struck by overwhelming incompetence. Indeed, circa July 15, Belld told a social worker that detectives had told Peebles that if he confessed they would let her out of jail, even going so far as to let him call home to verify this was the case.[161] Detectives later disclosed at Peebles's hearing that they had reminded him that his "old aunt" was in a jail, gave him $21 (modern equivalent), and talked with him in the Youth House without the presence of a social worker or custodian.[162]

Even the absence of coercion or coaching does not discount that a false or inaccurate confession was possibly given. World-renowned confession expert Richard Ofshe and others have written and lectured extensively on the nature of confessions, explaining that false testimony is often given in times of "exhaustion or mental impairment."[163] Given his arrest after midnight, disrupted sleep patterns or deprivation would easily be possible, especially when aided by extensive questioning. And, while described as intelligent, Peebles was just 14, streetwise beyond his years, but still going solo against a team of experienced interrogators. His verbatim "laboriously scrawled" confession conveys how mismatched the intellectual sparring between him and detectives may have been over time.[164] And two additions suggest less than full autonomy while writing at the Youth House with only a detective for company:

> I fired 45 cal. aut at 12:30 o'clock 7/4/50. I threw the gun in park south of High Bridge pool toward river. Robert Peebles, 515 Edgecombe Avenue, New York 32, N.Y.C.
> P.S. Gun was found in Central Park about six months ago. Kept in basement until Fourth of Julia. There was only one shell in gun when was found and stayed in until was fired.
> Pebbles.
> Got gun from basement. Took it into park. As I always threw shell in toilet."[165]

Guilty or innocent, in August, Peebles headed on a 75-minute bus ride to the Warwick school in rural Orange County, about 50 miles northwest of his apartment. Outside his bus window, amidst wooded hills and cow pastures, awaited a 740-acre, 40-building campus built and dedicated in the early 1930s to resemble the well-maintained elite private schools of New England. Red-brick buildings enclosed a large mall. Athletic fields, a sparkling lake, and the Ramapo and Catskill Mountains in the distance gave the surroundings a resort-like vibe. He arrived with eight to twelve other boys on a Friday and disembarked at a reception center for a six-week orientation. A new uniform awaited: gray corduroy pants, blue denim shirt, and sneakers, with a navy pea jacket, knitted watch cap, and clumpy work shoes for outdoor wear. After a haircut was administered to conform him to the other boys, he was later shut up for the night in a barless cell similar to Youth House. The windows were sealed by heavy mesh, with wooden slats preventing them from being pulled up or down more than a few inches.

At reception, he was isolated from the rest of Warwick's population and given a series of physical and mental examinations. Behind-the-scene evaluations were in progress as to which of the four quadrangles of sixteen, identical two-story L-shaped cottages he would be assigned to upon release: alphabetically-labeled housing ranging from A1-A4 to four D cottages where the older and bigger boys were kept.

Recreational activities such as ping-pong, reading, band practice, letter writing, a trip to the gym or lake, and radio listening were available. Religious services took place every Sunday. He was awoken every day at 6 a.m. and confined to bed by 10 p.m. with lights out and virtual silence—no city traffic, no voices in the hallways, only the insects in summer and the nightly snoring of bunkmates for company.

Anytime Peebles was taken out of reception, older "runners" from the D section accompanied him. Various trainers instructed him on how to behave in the cottages. While awaiting processing, he would have had ample time to ponder his fate, his future cottage mates, even rumors of fights and home-made knives he could have heard about in Youth House.

Once reception concluded, per Brown, Peebles landed in A4, the "crazy cottage" housing "rapists, murderers, and perverts": "the most brutal cats, and everybody knew it." This account, though, is sharply contradicted by Shirley Leinweber, the wife of one of Warwick's senior supervisors at the time, who claims the A cottages housed younger, well-behaved boys.[166] And it is possible housing assignments were more unstructured than either of them described.[167] Wherever he was placed, Peebles and the other roughly 400 boys on campus required a pass to go anywhere. If they 'breezed" too far or wide, or tried to run away into the countryside, they encountered no walls or fences but instead area men with runners on "breeze duty" who were tasked with finding them. Everyone had school to attend or a job to do in a group: working in a bakery, along the roads, on a farm, in the laundry or kitchen, or in other chores geared to inculcate responsibility.[168] Trusted boys could get a job in one of the administrative offices or program buildings, which is where most of the well-behaved younger kids worked and Peebles was assigned for a time.[169] Older kids were more apt to be runners, taking younger boys around to workplaces, sponsors, or social workers.

Each cottage housed boys on the first floor dormitory style, with an open wing of about 20 bunk beds and the other wing containing 12 individual rooms for those who earned privileges.[170] On the second lived the cottage "parents" who watched over everything and provided assistance and counseling. Per Brown, Peebles was assigned to a "Mrs. Washington," about 55, who had a gang of boys who mopped the halls and swept up in the detail building.[171] He would have performed other clean up and maintenance duties in other areas on a rotating basis.

Mingling with the overall population, Peebles encountered kids roughly 12–16 of mixed races from southeastern New York State, the majority of which were blacks from the greater New York City area. Homosexuals were housed in a separate cottage. Again per Brown, almost everyone was a "real criminal" who knew how to pick locks, cross wires in a car to start it without keys, pick pockets, roll a joint, and cut drugs.[172] This would have been Peebles's entire contact with the world for the first 12 weeks, until he was allowed to go home for a visit. After that, assuming his privileges were not revoked for bad behavior, he could go home for a three-day visit from Friday to Monday every eight weeks. Anyone wishing to visit him at Warwick would have been allowed in every Sunday.

If Peebles misbehaved, two potential punishments awaited him. First would be "working on the Burma road," which involved a repetitious cycle of pushing a wheelbarrow full of stones on a dirt path, unloading and reloading them, and pushing the wheelbarrow back to its starting place.[173] More serious repeated violations would have meant being sent for a two-year stint to the more strict "Annex" New Hampton Reformatory Farms, 14 miles north of Warwick.

Like Peebles, most of his cottage mates had never served time before. Many also did not mind the lack of connection to home as they had no stable home to return to. As Brown observed, "One place was just as good as another. For them, Warwick was just one more place until the next stop, which would probably be Coxsackie or Elmira or [some upstate New York prison] like that."[174]

Ordered about, cared for, and watched over like a hawk, Peebles's regimented life passed with one day similar to the next. The high-profile Polo Grounds shooting made his presence stand out, but Leinweber remembers him as a quiet boy, perhaps due to being a bit sullen or defeated, as some boys were.[175] Either due to good behavior or school overcrowding, two years later he was released.[176] At that time, despite society's best intentions at the rural school, the recidivism rate for Warwick alumni being arrested was near 80 percent.[177]

Oddly, Peebles's next reported movements involved a run-in with crime on the receiving end. Post-Warwick, at some point Peebles moved to Troy, New York, an industrial city across the Hudson River from Albany, the state capital. On March 31, 1957 at the city's YMCA, where a "Robert Peebles" matching his description had been working as a desk clerk for five months, two men about 19 years old ordered him at gunpoint to clean out the desk register and a small safe in an adjoining room, then to put the money in a bag. After the safe was opened and emptied, they tied and gagged Peebles so that any effort to free himself tightened the bounds and a noose around his neck. A few minutes after the thieves fled with about $3,600 (modern equivalent), he attracted attention by banging his feet against a wall and was discovered by a fellow employee.[178]

After this scare, Peebles's life settled for a time. He moved on to an office worker position at Troy's Rensselaer Polytechnic Institute, where he lived near and on campus.[179] Circa 1958 he married his wife, Patricia, a New York Telephone Company operator, and the couple had two children.

Despite this promising domesticity, Peebles proved unable to defy the odds of Warwick's grim recidivism rate. June 8, 1959 brought an arrest on a warrant from the Troy police for breaking into a general merchandise store and stealing four weapons. He was taken into custody at a southern Harlem hotel, where he lived and possessed, among other arms and ammunition, a shotgun and two pawn tickets for two guns later found at separate New York City pawn shops. He claimed to have purchased all guns the previous October from a man named "Jenkins" and selling one of them to a stranger. Police stated the two guns had been pawned under the name "Robert Carter," which Peebles was living under at his hotel. Asked by police about his penchant for guns, Peebles replied, "I'm a hunter."[180] Authorities returned him to Troy, where he was held at the Rensselaer County Jail. A month later, charges of burglary and grand larceny regarding these weapons were dropped due to insufficient evidence. However, he continued to be held for an undefined time by the Troy Children's Court, which issued a warrant for his arrest for non-support of his wife and two children, then residing in a second-floor apartment in one of four nine-story buildings comprising the Taylor Apartments public housing project.

After this time, Peebles was and remains elusive. The following year a fire was reported in his family's apartment, but only his wife was mentioned as tenant.[181] Two years later, living in the same apartment but unaware of her husband's whereabouts, she filed for divorce, which was likely granted.[182] Peebles's movements, positive or negative, after that time are unknown. He could be dead, although that status is unconfirmed.[183]

Beyond several days of national press coverage, the Doyle shooting oddly had little immediate effect on the sporting public. In 2014, *Sports Illustrated* looked back in amazement at the "pandemonium, chaos, and legislation" that failed to emanate from Doyle's death but which would likely occur today.[184] And its aim was not off the mark. Consider 2013, when the San Francisco Giants, 2,700 miles and a different sport away, heightened ball park security measures in the aftermath of the Boston Marathon bombing.

More amazing and unasked, however, is imagining the national conversation that would take place regarding race relations and police accountability if a similar high-profile incident happened today. Such a dialogue did not happen in 1950. Instead, another troublesome black youth was tossed into the system with a sigh and relief. Time moved on. The following summer, 20-year-old rookie Willie Mays made his way to the Polo Grounds, residing in Harlem with a protective landlady a few fly balls away from the field and from 515 Edgecombe Avenue. Three years later, the Giants would win the World Series, aided by Mays making an outfield catch that humbled Cleveland Indians dreams and which would have been visible from 515 Edgecombe's roof.

Yet, the tragedy loomed as a signpost warning. In 1958, Giants owner Horace Stoneham, citing poor attendance, parking shortages, a deteriorating ballpark, and a declining neighborhood as evidenced by the shooting, would uproot Doyle's team to San Francisco. The following decade led to the demolishing of the Polo Grounds to make way for public housing.

For Peebles, references to his life pre- and post-shooting portray many failed opportunities for rehabilitation and redemption. They codify an early life consumed by disadvantage, bad choices, and bad luck: perhaps aided by boredom and frustration, definitely enhanced by an inability for self-examination and self-correction amidst reduced prospects dragging him and many of his generation downward. After visiting Warwick in 1945, former First Lady Eleanor Roosevelt was "bothered by the question of what factors made for so-called 'bad children'" and why there were so many more black than white ones housed there and at similar institutions. Her concerns, unfortunately, are still relevant.[185]

If Peebles's great-aunt Marie was alive today perhaps she would cry out with words similar to Richard Wright's: "We watch strange moods fill our children, and our hearts swell with pain. The streets, with their noise and flaring lights, the 'taverns, the automobiles, and the poolrooms claim them, and no voice of ours can call them back."[186] But, her voice was never publicly heard, instead relegated to a lifetime of unexpressed remembrance over a confounding Independence Day gun shot that snatched a child from her home. Sadly for her great-nephew–separated from parents themselves separated, living at a formative age in a tough, alien northern world with a southern relative–the race of life had placed him well behind the starting line. As *Manchild for the Promised Land* achingly asked, "Where does one run to when he's already in the Promised Land?"[187] Peebles may never have found the answer, instead wandering aimlessly along troubled Harlem streets and over roofs, where Ellison wrote, "The most surreal fantasies are acted out."[188]

Bernard Doyle suffered from one of those fantasies. Once again, his life changed instantly at a sports event. This time irrevocably at a baseball park, in a unforeseen, shocking death unwitnessed by his family but always memorialized by a press photograph of him slumped backward in his seat while a black spectator looked down on his corpse with concern.[189]

Author's Acknowledgments

I owe heartfelt gratitude to Bernard Doyle's surviving family: granddaughters Maria Atti and Judy Baldwin, grandson Ralph Atti, and great-nephew Keith Hermann. They graciously answered questions about a relative they sadly never had a chance to meet. I hope this essay provides some truth, explanation, and questioning toward a death that has lacked context and defied reason. I echo this same hope to Otto Flaig's son, Christopher.

As this essay neared completion, I was introduced to University of Georgia associate professor of contemporary American literature Christopher Pizzino. Chris became interested in the shooting and Peebles through research into Lafargue Clinic co-founder Dr. Fredric Wertham's 1950s crusade against comic books. We independently concluded that Peebles was quite possibly not guilty of the shooting and that he certainly was not guilty according to the slipshod, historically-reported version.

Stew Thornley provided unwavering editorial support and encouragement. Additional tips of the cap go to Kenneth Manyin and Leslie Cassidy for research and editorial assistance, and to Harlem chronicler Terry Baker Mulligan for helping me understand mid-century Harlem in context. Gary Mintz of the New York Giants Preservation Society connected me with many people with knowledge of the Polo Grounds and the shooting. Christine Filippelli of the Troy, New York, library helped me track Peebles and his wife from 1957 to 1962. And Sue Gardner of the Albert Wisner Public Library in Warwick, New York, aided my understanding of the Warwick Training School for Boys.

NOTES

1. "Youth Questioned in Death at Game," *New York Times*, July 6, 1950; 1900 U.S. Census; 1910 U.S. Census; Maria Atti, phone interview, July 22, 2016; Bernard Doyle World War I Draft Registration Card.
2. 1910 U.S. Census.
3. 1940 U.S. Census; Ralph Atti, phone interview, July 22, 2016.
4. LUD (pseudonym for Ludwig Shabazian), "When Barney Talked Everyone Listened," *Hudson Dispatch*, July 9, 1977.
5. 1920 U.S. Census; 1940 U.S. Census.
6. Steve Rushin, *The 34-Ton Bat: The Story of Baseball as Told Through Bobbleheads, Cracker Jacks, Jockstraps, Eye Black, and 375 Other Strange and Unforgettable Objects* (New York: Little, Brown and Company, 2013), 254, is the only available source that cites boxing professionally. Doyle's family does not corroborate this.
7. Ralph Atti; Bernard Doyle World War I and II Draft Registration Cards.
8. Michael DeLisa, *Cinderella Man: The James J. Braddock Story* (Wrea Green, United Kingdom: Milo Books Ltd., 2005), 21.
9. De Lisa, *Cinderella Man*; Thomas F. X. Smith, *The Powerticians* (Secaucus, New Jersey: Lyle Stuart Inc., 1982), 24.
10. DeLisa, *Cinderella Man.*
11. *Ibid.*
12. LUD.
13. Ludwig Shabazian, *Relief to Royalty: The Story of James J. Braddock, World's Heavyweight Champion* (Union City, New Jersey: Hudson Dispatch, 1936), 26.
14. Shabazian, 32–33; Jeremy Schaap, *Cinderella Man: James Braddock, Max Baer, and the Greatest Upset in Boxing History* (New York: Houghton Mifflin Company, 2005), 29–32; LUD.
15. Ralph Atti.
16. *Ibid.*; LUD; Maria Atti.
17. Schaap, 29–30.
18. Maria Atti.
19. Ralph Atti.
20. "Fan Shot to Death (How?) in Polo Grounds," *San Francisco Chronicle*, July 5, 1950; "Youth Questioned in Death at Game"; "Mystery Bullet Kills Baseball Fan in Midst of Crowd at Polo Grounds," *New York Times*, July 5, 1950; Maria Atti.
21. "Mystery Bullet Kills Baseball Fan," *Spokesman-Review*, July 5, 1950.
22. Judy Baldwin, phone interview, July 25, 2016.
23. *Ibid.*

24. 1940 U.S. Census; "Grandma, Boy Held in Park Slaying," *New Journal and Guide*, July 8, 1950; Jay Maeder, "Line of Fire Independence Day, 1950," *New York Daily News*, August 30, 1998; Ralph Atti.

25. Ralph Atti.

26. "Mystery Shot Kills Fan at Polo Grounds," *Miami Daily News*, July 5, 1950; "Boy Quizzed in Killing of Baseball Fan," *San Mateo Times*, July 5, 1950; "Seat 3, Row C," *Time*, July 17, 1950; Ed Keele, October 18, 2010, comment on Timothy Williams, "A Stairway to Sports History From the Polo Grounds," *New York Times*, February 19, 2008.

27. Maeder.

28. "Seat 3, Row C"; Rushin, 251; "Mystery Shot Kills Fan at Polo Grounds," *San Francisco Examiner*, July 5, 1950. Christopher Flaig, phone interview, August 4, 2016; Keith Hermann, phone interview, July 20, 2016; Maria Atti.

29. "The Weather Throughout the Nation," *New York Times*, July 5, 1950; "Mystery on Coogan's Bluff," *Newsday*, July 5, 1950.

30. "Mystery Shot Kills Baseball Fan in Crowd of 49,000," *Chicago Tribune*, July 5, 1950.

31. Andy Beveridge, "Harlem's Shifting Population," *Gotham Gazette*, September 2, 2008.

32. *Ibid.*; James Paul Allen and Eugene James Turner, *We the People: An Atlas of America's Ethnic Diversity* (New York: Macmillan Publishing Company, 1988), 147; Jacob Lawrence, "Claude Brown, Manchild of the Promised Land" slide presentation, Long Beach City College, http://itdc.lbcc.edu/oer/hum7socsc7/presentations/BrownManchild/BrownManchild-notes.html (accessed on January 13, 2019).

33. *Ibid.*; Jonathan Gill, *Harlem: The Four Hundred Year History from Dutch Village to Capital of Black America* (New York: Grove Press, 2011), 215. *See also* Great Migration (African American), http://en.wikipedia.org/wiki/Great_Migration_%28African_American%29 (accessed on January 13, 2019).

34. David Gonzalez, "In Sugar Hill a Street Nurtured Black Talent When the World Wouldn't," *New York Times*, January 22, 2010.

35. *Ibid.*; 555 Edgecombe Avenue, http://en.wikipedia.org/wiki/555_Edgecombe_Avenue (accessed on January 13, 2019).

36. Lawrence.

37. Beveridge.

38. Ralph G. Martin, "Doctor's Dream in Harlem," *New Republic*, June 3, 1946.

39. Claude Brown, *Manchild in the Promised Land* (New York: Simon & Schuster, 1999), 7.

40. James T. Campbell, *Middle Passages: African American Journeys to Africa, 1787–2005* (New York: Penguin, 2006), 275.

41. Guilds' Committee for Federal Writers' Publications, Inc., *New York Panorama* (New York: Random House, 1938), 151.

42. Ralph Ellison, "Harlem is Nowhere," *Harper's Magazine*, August 1964.

43. Jonathan Fraser Light, *The Cultural Encyclopedia of Baseball* (Jefferson, NC: McFarland, 2005), 486.

44. Austin Briggs, "Norman Rockwell Lives," *New York Review of Books*, November 16, 2000.

45. *Ibid.* It is no longer on display: "From Polo Grounds to Cooperstown—via Westport," Dan Woog blog, May 8, 2013, http://06880danwoog.com/2013/05/08/from-polo-grounds-to-cooperstown-via-westport/ (accessed on January 13, 2019).

46. Brown, 99.

47. Langston Hughes, "Down Under in Harlem," *New Republic*, March 27, 1944.

48. 1930 U.S. Census; 1940 U.S. Census.

49. *Ibid.* The average rent for Harlem residents at the time was about $827/month (modern equivalent), about half of average take-home pay. Gill, 231.

50. 1940 U.S. Census.

51. *Ibid.*; "Boy, 14, Admits Firing .45 Pistol at Time of Polo Grounds Killing," *New York Times*, July 8, 1950; Fredric Wertham, M.D., *Seduction of the Innocent* (New York: Rinehart & Company, Inc., 1953), 7.

52. Per 1940 census records regarding the 22 persons Belld and Peebles lived with at 764 St. Nicholas Avenue: The "family" hailed from the British West Indies and five states, nine were under 18, all nine persons who worked were employed in low-paying service or domestic jobs, and only three had beyond an eighth grade education.

53. *See generally* Gabriel N. Mendes, *Under the Strain of Color: Harlem's Lafargue Clinic and the Promise of an Antiracist Psychiatry* (Ithaca: Cornell University Press, 2015).

54. Wertham, 7–8.

55. "Boy Admits Firing Polo Grounds Death Bullet," *Traverse City Record-Eagle*, July 13, 1950; "Judge Sends Peebles to Youth House Pending Polo Grounds Shooting Probe," *New York Amsterdam News*, July 15, 1950.

56. Wertham, 8; Comics allegedly belonging to Peebles, stored in the Fredric Wertham Papers collection at the Library of Congress ("Wertham Papers"). Dr. Wertham's *Seduction of the Innocent* ("*SOTI*") and other warnings of the alleged dangers of comic books on children led to a Congressional inquiry on the topic and the 1954 creation of the Comics Code to regulate comic books' tone and topics. As co-founder of the Lafargue Clinic, Wertham had intimate knowledge of Peebles's treatment there. In *SOTI*, Wertham asserted that Peebles's comic book reading of violent and salacious topics contributed to his delinquency issues. Critics have poked

holes in Wertham's sometimes overreaching or fabricated conclusions regarding comic books' harmful effects. Consequently, this essay relies on portions of *SOTI*'s background on Peebles but avoids attributing his behavior to comic book reading. As Wertham wrote best in *SOTI*, "Evidently in [Peebles's] case there was a constellation of many factors" explaining his behavioral problems." Wertham, 7.

57. "Boy Admits Firing Polo Grounds Death Bullet"; Fredric Wertham, M.D,. notes of phone call with Dr. Hilde Mosse, July 12, 1950 (Wertham Papers).

58. "Slaying Mystery Takes New Turn," *Spokesman-Review*, July 6, 1950.

59. "Boy, 14, Admits Firing .45 Pistol at Time of Polo Grounds Killing."

60. "Boy, 14, Admits Shot Killing Fan at Polo Grounds," *New York Herald Tribune*, July 8, 1950; Vivienne Cheatham (Quaker Emergency Service Readjustment Center) letter to Fredric Wertham, M.D., July 27, 1950 (Wertham Papers).

61. Maeder.

62. "Fan Shot to Death (How?) in Polo Grounds"; "Mystery Bullet Kills Baseball Fan in Midst of Crowd at Polo Grounds"; Charles McHarry and Henry Lee, "Shot Dead at Polo Grounds; Mystery Bullet Kills Giants Fan," *Daily News*, July 5, 1950.

63. "The Random Bullet," *Newsweek*, July 17, 1950; "Mystery Shot Kills Fan at Polo Grounds," *Long Beach Independent*, July 5, 1950; Flaig.

64. "Mystery Shot Kills Baseball Fan in Crowd of 49,000"; "Mystery on Coogan's Bluff."

65. "Mystery Shot Kills Baseball Fan in Crowd of 49,000."

66. Ed Drohan, phone interview, September 10, 2014.

67. *Ibid.*

68. *Ibid.*; "Mystery Shot Kills Fan at Polo Grounds," *Miami Daily News*.

69. "Search Widens in Death of Man at Polo Grounds," *New York Herald Tribune*, July 7, 1950; David Pincus, "A Man Was Once Shot at an MLB Game and Play Went On," *Sports Illustrated*, June 13, 2014.

70. "Mystery Bullet Kills Baseball Fan"; "Mystery Shot Kills Baseball Fan in Crowd of 49,000"; "Bullet Kills Spectator at Polo Grounds," *Galveston Daily News*, July 5, 1950.

71. Pincus.

72. *Ibid.*

73. "Death at the Ball Game," *New York Herald Tribune*, July 6, 1950.

74. Keele; "Mystery Shot Kills Fan at Polo Grounds."

75. "Mystery Bullet Kills Baseball Fan in Midst of Crowd at Polo Grounds."

76. Drohan.

77. *Ibid.*

78. *Ibid.*; "Arrives for Questioning," *Hanover Evening Sun*, July 6, 1950; "Mystery on Coogan's Bluff."

79. Negro Woman and Nephew Held in Murder of Polo Grounds Fan, *Carolina Times*, July 15, 1950.

80. Flaig.

81. "Death Takes Seat at Polo Grounds Double-Header," *New Journal and Guide*, July 15, 1950.

82. "Mystery Bullet Kills Baseball Fan in Midst of Crowd at Polo Grounds"; "Boy Quizzed in Shooting," *Reading Eagle*, July 5, 1950; "Mystery on Coogan's Bluff."

83. "Line of Fire Independence Day, 1950"; "Mystery on Coogan's Bluff."

84. "Mystery Shot Kills Fan at Polo Grounds"; "Mystery Bullet Kills Baseball Fan in Midst of Crowd at Polo Grounds."

85. "Fan Shot to Death (How?) in Polo Grounds."

86. "Mystery Bullet Kills Baseball Fan in Midst of Crowd at Polo Grounds"; Judy Baldwin; Ralph Atti.

87. Maria Atti; Judy Baldwin. Due to the tragedy, the wedding was postponed until December 30, 1950.

88. *Ibid.*; "Youth Questioned in Death at Game."

89. "Mystery Bullet Kills Baseball Fan in Midst of Crowd at Polo Grounds."

90. *Ibid.*; "Youth Questioned in Death at Game"; "Boy, 14, Admits Shot Killing Fan at Polo Grounds"; "Mystery Shot Kills Baseball Fan in Crowd of 49,000."

91. "Youth Questioned in Death at Game"; "Boy Quizzed in Killing of Baseball Fan."

92. "Boy Quizzed in Killing of Baseball Fan"; "Grandma, Boy Held in Park Slaying."

93. "Slaying Mystery Takes New Turn"; "Ball Fan's Death Blamed on Youth," *Lewiston Daily Sun*, July 8, 1950.

94. "Youth Freed in Slaying at New York Polo Grounds," *New Journal and Guide*, July 8, 1950.

95. "Youth Questioned in Death at Game."

96. ".45 Pistol, Not Rifle, Killed Fan at Polo Grounds; Boy, 14, Held," *New York Herald Tribune*, July 6, 1950.

97. *Ibid.*

98. *Ibid.*

99. "14 Year Old Admits Firing Pistol Near Polo Grounds," *Daytona Beach Morning Journal*, July 8, 1950; "Boy, 14, Admits Shot Killing Fan at Polo Grounds."

100. ".45 Pistol, Not Rifle, Killed Fan at Polo Grounds; Boy, 14, Held"; "Slaying Mystery Takes New Turn."

101. ".45 Pistol, Not Rifle, Killed Fan at Polo Grounds; Boy, 14, Held"; "Search Widens in Death of Man at Polo Grounds."

102. "Search Extended in Mystery Death," *New York Times*, July 7, 1950.
103. *Ibid.*
104. "Boy, 14, Admits Firing .45 Pistol at Time of Polo Grounds Killing"; "Boy, 14, Admits Shot Killing Fan at Polo Grounds"; "Line of Fire Independence Day, 1950"; "Confession Lifts Mystery of Polo Grounds Slaying," *New Journal and Guide*, July 15, 1950.
105. *Ibid.*
106. *Ibid.*; "Police Suspend Gun Hunt in Polo Grounds Killing," *New York Herald Tribune*, July 9, 1950.
107. "Boy, 14, Admits Shot Killing Fan at Polo Grounds."
108. *Ibid.*
109. "Boy Confesses Firing Shot Into Polo Grounds," *New London Connecticut Evening Day*, July 8, 1950; "Boy, 14, Admits Shot Killing Fan at Polo Grounds"; "Boy, 14, Admits Firing .45 Pistol at Time of Polo Grounds Killing."
110. "Boy, 14, Admits Firing .45 Pistol at Time of Polo Grounds Killing"; "Boy, 14, Admits Shot Killing Fan at Polo Grounds."
111. "Boy, 14 Admits Shot Killing Fan at Polo Grounds"; "Police Suspend Gun Hunt in Polo Grounds Killing."
112. "Pistol Search Continues," *New York Times*, July 9, 1950; "Police Suspend Gun Hunt in Polo Grounds Killing."
113. "3 Held in Arms Inquiry," *New York Times*, July 16, 1950; "Still Hunting for Death Gun," *New York Age*, August 19, 1950; "Man Sought in Gun Sale to Boy Who Killed Fan," *New York Herald Tribune*, July 20, 1950.
114. Dr. Hilde Mosse letter to Fredric Wertham, M.D., July 15, 1950 (Wertham Papers).
115. "Held in Ball Park Death," *New York Times*, July 12, 1950; "Trial of Boy Who Killed Giant Fan is Postponed Again," *Carolina Times*, July 22, 1950; "Fan Slaying Suspect Held," *Washington Afro-American*, July 25, 1950; Marie Belld obituary, http://crestleaf.com/p/50ba9636651a69e4d4c265e2/marie-belld.
116. Flaig.
117. *Ibid.*; "Otto Flaig, 55, Teterboro Police Chief," *The Record*, August 3, 1992.
118. Flaig.
119. Ralph Atti. This information was passed down to Atti by his mother and uncle.
120. *Ibid.*
121. *Ibid.*; Maria Atti.
122. Judy Baldwin.
123. Ralph Atti.
124. Maria Atti.
125. Ira Henry Freeman, *Out of the Burning: The Story of a Boy Gang Leader* (New York: Crown Publishers, Inc., 1960), 115.
126. Brown, 60.
127. Freeman, 115; Brown, 60–64; Vincent Bugliosi, *Reclaiming History: The Assassination of President John F. Kennedy* (New York: W.W. Norton & Company, 2007), 531–536.
128. "Trial of Boy Who Killed Giant Fan Is Postponed Again"; "Polo Grounds Boy Killer Nervous," *Philadelphia Tribune*, July 18, 1950.
129. Cheatham letter to Wertham.
130. Fredric Wertham, M.D., notes of phone call with Vivienne Cheatham, July 29, 1950 (Wertham Papers).
131. "Boy Suspect Committed," *New York Times*, August 4, 1950.
132. Robert Gorman, phone interview, October 11, 2014. Robert Gorman and David Weeks, *Death at the Ballpark: More Than 2,000 Game-Related Fatalities of Players, Other Personnel and Spectators in Amateur and Professional Baseball, 1862–2014* (Jefferson, NC: McFarland, 2015).
133. Ira Rosenwaike, *Population History of New York City* (Syracuse: Syracuse University Press, 1972), chapter 6.
134. Unpublished Fredric Wertham, M.D., letter to *New York Amsterdam News*, July 24, 1950 (Wertham Papers).
135. Beveridge.
136. "Seat 3, Row C."
137. Terry Baker Mulligan, phone interview, October 10, 2014. *See generally* Terry Baker Mulligan, *Sugar Hill: Where the Sun Rose Over Harlem* (St. Louis, Missouri: Impulse Press, 2012).
138. Mario was a very unlikely first or middle name for a black youth born 1935–1936.
139. This article cites Belld as Peebles's great-aunt since many key references classify her as such.
140. Cheatham letter to Wertham. William Hatfield was identified as Peebles's attorney. Prominent defense attorney James D. C. Murray was also identified, but his relationship to Peebles is unclear.
141. "Boy, 14, Admits Shot Killing Fan at Polo Grounds"; "Boy, 14, Admits Firing .45 Pistol at Time of Polo Grounds Killing."
142. "Grandma, Boy Held in Park Slaying"; "Mystery Shot Kills Fan at Polo Grounds," *Miami Daily News;* "Boy, 14, Admits Shot Killing Fan at Polo Grounds"; "Polo Grounds Slaying," *San Francisco Chronicle*, July 8, 1950; "The Random Bullet"; Ev Parker, "Death at the Ballpark," *Napa Valley Register*, August 5, 2011.

143. "Trial of Boy Who Killed Giant Fan Is Postponed Again."

144. James Hicks, "Distance Held Too Great," *Washington Afro-American*, July 11, 1950; *see also* "Polo Grounds Fan Killing Solved? Still Hunt Pistol," *New York Age*, July 15, 1950.

145. Hicks; "Slaying Mystery Takes New Turn"; ".45 Pistol, Not Rifle, Killed Fan at Polo Grounds; Boy, 14, Held."

146. Hicks. Note: A .45 pistol's range may be just 1,660 yards. *See* "Search Widens in Death of Man at Polo Grounds"; ".45 Pistol, Not Rifle, Killed Fan at Polo Grounds; Boy, 14, Held."

147. Hicks.

148. "Boy Shot Fan in Ball Park," *Milwaukee Sentinel*, July 8, 1950.

149. "Polo Grounds Fan Killing Solved? Still Hunt Pistol."

150. "An Unsolved Problem," *New York Amsterdam News*, July 15, 1950.

151. "Slaying Mystery Takes New Turn."

152. "Polo Grounds Slaying"; "Trial of Boy Who Killed Giant Fan is Postponed Again"; "The Random Bullet"; "Seat 3, Row C."

153. Parker.

154. Ev Parker, phone interview, October 3, 2014.

155. Brown, 136.

156. Urban Dictionary, http://www.urbandictionary.com.

157. Wertham notes of Cheatham phone call.

158. *Ibid.*

159. ".45 Pistol, Not Rifle, Killed Fan at Polo Grounds; Boy, 14, Held."

160. Maria Atti.

161. Mosse letter to Wertham.

162. Cheatham letter to Wertham.

163. "False Confessions Expert Richard Ofshe," http://www.falseconfessions.org/experts/49-richard-ofshe; Richard Ofshe, discussion with author, November, 1997. As of 2016, 28 percent of convictions overturned by DNA evidence have involved false confessions.

164. "Boy, 14, Admits Firing .45 Pistol at Time of Polo Grounds Killing."

165. *Ibid.*; "Boy, 14, Admits Shot Killing Fan at Polo Grounds"; Cheatham letter to Wertham.

166. Brown, 128–142; Leinweber's husband was one of Warwick's senior supervisors in the Upper Staff building and D cottages in 1950–1952. She recalls the older, more disruptive youths were housed in the D cottages. Shirley Leinweber, phone interview, May 10, 2016.

167. Ken Stewart (Warwick social worker, 1960–1968), phone interview, August 9, 2016.

168. *Ibid.*

169. Leinweber.

170. Donna Schuler. New York State Training School for Boys. Ancestry.com March 19, 2005 message board, http://boards.ancestry.com/localities.northam.usa.states.newyork.counties.orange/5819.1.1.2/mb.ashx.

171. Brown, 136. This name could be a pseudonym. Leinweber.

172. *Ibid.*, 138.

173. Freeman; *see generally* 177–208, 235–39, 254–55 for background regarding the Warwick school.

174. Brown, 140.

175. Leinweber.

176. "Ballpark Slayer Faces New Charge," *New York Times*, June 9, 1959.

177. Freeman, This rate was 80% in 1947 but improved to 40% by 1960.

178. Normand Dault, "Weekend Thefts Also Net $5,600," *Troy Record*, April 1, 1957; "Troy Detectives Seek Clues in Weekend Holdup, Burglaries," *The Times Record*, April 1, 1957.

179. Troy City Directory, 1957 and 1958.

180. "Ballpark Slayer Faces New Charge"; Milton Lewis, "'50 Slayer of Ball Fan Held as Shotgun Thief," *New York Herald Tribune*, June 9, 1959; "Peebles Still Likes Firearms," *New York Amsterdam News*, June 20, 1959; John J. McNamara, "Ex-Trojan Charged With Grand Larceny of Firearms," *Troy Record*, June 9, 1959.

181. "Mattress Burns in Taylor Apts.," *Troy Times Record*, Feb. 20, 1960. Also, only his wife was listed at this address in the 1960–1962 Troy City Directories.

182. "Ballpark Slayer Faces New Charge"; "Nab Former Trojan for Gun Thefts," *Troy Times Record*, June 9, 1959; "Free Peebles on Burglary, Still Held," *Troy Record*, July 7, 1959; Legal Notice, *Troy Record*, March 30, 1962.

183. Efforts to ascertain Peebles's death or lack thereof proved frustratingly elusive.

184. Pincus.

185. Eleanor Roosevelt, *My Day*, June 30, 1945, The Eleanor Roosevelt Papers Digital Edition (2008), https://www.gwu.edu/~erpapers/myday/displaydoc.cfm?_y=1945&_f=md000064.

186. Wright, Richard. *12 Million Voices* (New York: Thunder's Mouth Press, 1988), 136.

187. Brown, 8.

188. Ellison.

189. *See* assorted press coverage of the shooting.

Voice of the Giants
Russ Hodges

STEW THORNLEY

Russ Hodges was known by New York baseball fans as the broadcasting voice of the Giants. However, his "The Giants win the pennant!" call of Bobby Thomson's home run to capture the 1951 National League flag brought him lasting recognition to many beyond New York and San Francisco.

Hodges was born in Dayton, Tennessee, in 1910 and moved to Danville, Kentucky, when he was very young. As a ten-year-old, he became the water boy for Danville's Centre College Praying Colonels football team. However, soon after, his family relocated to Covington, Kentucky, across the Ohio River from Cincinnati.

Hodges took a liking to one of the Reds' stars, Edd Roush; the penchant was strong enough that when Roush was traded to the New York Giants in 1927, Hodges kept his allegiance with the player and became a Giant fan.

More than 20 years later, Hodges also became an announcer for his favorite team. In the meantime, he had a varied life and career. He went to the University of Kentucky on a football scholarship, got hurt, and ended up in the press box, working as a spotter and being given the chance to announce the games.

Then, while attending law school at night at the University of Cincinnati, Hodges began his involvement with radio. He passed the bar but stuck with radio, a career that took him to Rock Island, Illinois; Chicago; Charlotte, North Carolina; Washington, D.C.; and finally New York.

In 1945, Hodges worked with Mel Allen on New York Yankee baseball broadcasts and also announced college games and those of the New York Yankees of the All-American Football Conference.

Four years later, Hodges moved across the Harlem River from Yankee Stadium to the Polo Grounds and began his long affiliation with the Giants. The following season, he was teamed with Ernie Harwell, and the two split the final game of the 1951 playoff series between the Giants and Brooklyn Dodgers. Harwell started and finished on television, handling the radio broadcast in between, with Hodges doing the opposite.

When Thomson hit his three-run homer with one out in the last of the ninth, Harwell said he immediately blurted, "It's gone," before regretting the phrase, fearful that the drive might fall short of the fence.[1]

Hodges stated he did not remember what he said, and his now-famous soliloquy

Hodges did not have to travel far when he moved from the Yankees to the Giants in 1949. The Polo Grounds and Yankee Stadium were across the Harlem River from one another. This 1940s photograph of the Bronx (with Yankee Stadium in the foreground) and Upper Manhattan shows the George Washington Bridge in the background (collection of Stew Thornley).

might have been lost to him and others if not for a Dodger fan named Lawrence Goldberg. Goldberg taped the final inning of the radio broadcast, but not for the benefit of Hodges or anyone connected with the Giants. His desire was to record a disappointed Hodges calling the final out in a Brooklyn victory. However, when the result turned out differently, Goldberg was good-hearted enough to send Hodges a copy of the recording. Hodges said he sent Goldberg $10 to show his gratitude.

Thus, Hodges was able to relive his call of the play, along with fans for decades to come:

> Bobby Thomson up there swinging. He's had two out of three, a single and a double, and Billy Cox is playing him right on the third base line. One out, last of the ninth, Branca pitches. Bobby Thomson takes a strike called on the inside corner.... Bobby hitting at .292. He's had a single and a double and he drove in the Giants' first run with a long fly to center. Brooklyn leads it, 4 to 2. Hartung down the line at third, not taking any chances. Lockman without too big of a lead at second, but he'll be running like the wind if Thomson hits one. Branca throws. There's a long drive! It's going to be, I believe! The Giants win the pennant! The Giants win the pennant! The Giants win the pennant! The Giants win the pennant! Bobby Thomson hits into the lower deck of the left field stands! The Giants win the pennant! And they're goin' crazy! They're goin' crazy! Heeey-yoh! I don't believe it! I don't believe it! I do not believe it! Bobby Thomson hit a line drive into the lower deck of the left field stands and this great place is goin' crazy! The Giants! Horace Stoneham has got a winner! The Giants won it by a score of 5 to 4, and they're picking Bobby Thomson up and carrying him off the field![2]

The iconic call has echoed in various forms in other sports broadcasts of big moments, announcers channeling Hodges' excitement with some variation of his "The Giants Win the Pennant!" theme.

Although he had a memorable call with Thomson's home run, Hodges was noted by Jimmy Powers in *The Sporting News* in 1950 as an announcer with "no overly cute remarks. He doesn't get hysterical. He just goes along, furnishing an excellent workaday account of the happenings on the field below."[3]

Powers quoted Hodges, who provided insight on his style: "The fans don't want too many details. They want pertinent facts—not what a star's mother-in-law did last Thursday night at a church supper in Alarm Clock, Iowa. Even official record books are beginning to get cluttered up with trick records … Most Home Runs Hit on a Rainy Monday … Most Innings Pitched with the Wind Southwest by South … Most Pop Flies Caught Near Third Base Box Occupied by Platinum Blondes. How silly can you get?"[4]

The same season that Powers wrote this piece, Hodges and Mel Allen received *The Sporting News* awards as the outstanding play-by-play broadcasters for 1950 in the National and American leagues, respectively.[5]

With the Giants, Hodges became close to the team's young star, Willie Mays. He reportedly often helped Mays with money or advice, and over the years, he was the one person, besides Willie, to witness every one of Mays' home runs as they reached milestones as well as a National League record.

When the Giants moved to San Francisco after the 1957 season, Hodges went west with them and called the games with new partner Lon Simmons.

Hodges retired from broadcasting after the 1970 season,[6] still current with seeing every one of Mays' 628 career homers at that point. He did some public relations work with the Giants and planned to fill in on broadcasts. Thus, he was present for home runs struck by Mays on April 6 and 7 in San Diego. However, the next day he was back home, making a speech at a banquet in Mill Valley, California, when Mays slugged a grand slam.

According to writer Jerome Holtzman, Hodges listened to the call of the shot on a transistor radio brought by a man sitting next to him at the banquet and he commented, "I actually could hear the home run. I was thrilled because it put the Giants ahead. Outside of that, I felt no emotion at all."[7]

Holtzman went further to report that "[s]everal days later, Mays saw Hodges and said to him: 'Well, you finally missed one.' Replied Hodges: 'I'll be around to see you hit many more.'"[8]

There is no indication of whether Hodges saw the home runs hit by Mays on April 10—probably not since the game was in St. Louis—or April 17 in San Francisco.

Holtzman visited Hodges on April 18 and got his thoughts on finally missing a Mays home run. The next day Hodges died of a heart attack. Willie Mays was one of the pallbearers at his funeral.

"No radio man was better loved by the athletes he associated with," wrote Wells Twombly in *The Sporting News*.[9]

Nearly ten years later, Hodges had a posthumous honor when he was named the recipient of the National Baseball Hall of Fame's Ford Frick Award.[10]

NOTES

1. Curt Smith, *Voices of the Game: The First Full-Scale Overview of Baseball Broadcasting, 1921 to the Present* (South Bend, Indiana: Diamond Communications, Inc., 1987), 65.

2. "Bobby Thompson [*sic*] HR—Three Different Calls," https://archive.org/details/BobbyThompsonHr-threeDifferentCalls (accessed on July 15, 2017), and "Baseball—An Action History: Bobby Thomson's Home Run To Win the Pennant for the Giants in 1951 (Russ Hodges Announcing)," *Take Me Out to the Ball Game*, Sony Music Entertainment, 1958.

3. Jimmy Powers, "The Powerhouse," *The Sporting News*, August 2, 1950, 12.

Willie Mays hitting in the Polo Grounds. Mays hit 660 home runs in his career, and Russ Hodges was there for the first 630 of them (collection of Stew Thornley).

4. *Ibid.*
5. "Named as Majors' Top Broadcasters," *The Sporting News,* September 27, 1950, 11.
6. Pat Frizzell, "Hodges, Voice of Giants for 22 Years, Retires," *The Sporting News,* November 28, 1970, 41.
7. Jerome Holtzman, "Hodges Missed No. 631," *The Sporting News,* May 8, 1971, 11.
8. *Ibid.*
9. Wells Twombly, "The Homer of the Century," *The Sporting News,* May 8, 1971, 7.
10. "Hodges Winner of Frick Award," *The Sporting News,* March 8, 1980, 36.

When the Circus Came to Town

The New York Mets at the Polo Grounds, 1962–1963

Scott Ferkovich

Born as a National League expansion team, the New York Mets were scheduled to play their first season in 1962 at the Polo Grounds. Yankee Stadium had been another option, but Yankee owner Dan Topping was not too keen on the idea of having the upstart franchise as his tenant. He floated the idea of the Polo Grounds instead, and the Mets took the bait. The ancient ballpark in upper Manhattan, left for dead by the Giants after they played their final game there in 1957 before rushing to San Francisco, had suddenly been given a new life.

But it was nothing more than a stopgap arrangement; a slick modern stadium for the Mets was being erected in Queens, with every hope of being ready by Opening Day, 1963. Delays pushed back the inaugural game of the new stadium until 1964, which meant that the Mets played in the Polo Grounds for two summers.

After having sat idle for four years, the old ballpark was in need of a sprucing up. Among the list of improvements were new lights, a new bat rack, a new water cooler, and a new paint job. The finest Merion blue replaced the crabgrass that had invaded the playing surface. Lubrication had been applied to the squeaky pulleys in the ancient manual scoreboards in left and right field. A stadium club also opened up. And a new American flag was run up the pole, this one with 50 stars, replacing the old one that had only 48, Alaska and Hawaii having been admitted to the Union since the last time a National League baseball game had been played at West 155th Street and 8th Avenue. The final price tag of $250,000 (although some accounts go as high as $400,000) was more than the cost to build the place nearly half a century before.

The question on the minds of most every baseball fan in New York was where the Mets would finish in 1962. Stengel had a quick answer: "In Chicago, on September 30."[1]

The truth was, even Stengel did not know what to expect. "This team is strangers with strangers."[2] He guessed that 70 wins might be a realistic possibility. *Sports Illustrated* pegged them for eighth place in the ten-team National League.

Stengel, who in a previous life had won ten American League pennants and seven World Series as the manager of the New York Yankees, put it bluntly: "Of course, Mantle and Maris would help my managerial ability."[3] But as the Mets' skipper, he would have to make do with the likes of Elio Chacon and Chris Cannizzaro.

The Mets' first game of the season was a loss to the St. Louis Cardinals at Busch Stadium. With their 0–1 record in tow, Stengel's men reopened the Polo Grounds on April 13, a damp, chilly day, typical for New York City for that time of year. By coincidence, their opponent was the Pittsburgh Pirates, the same team that had beaten the Giants on that emotional final day in 1957.

To welcome New York's newest team on Opening Day, 1962, a parade snaked its way down the Great White Way to City Hall, hailed by 40,000 in the street. At the Polo Grounds, New York mayor Robert Wagner threw out the ceremonial first pitch. The Mets were introduced to loud cheers, the loudest being reserved for Stengel and for Gil Hodges, the 36-year-old former Brooklyn Dodger who had been reduced to bench duty. The National Broadcasting Company featured the contest for its national telecast, with Joe Garagiola and Bob Wolff doing the chatter. Stengel, who began his playing career with the Brooklyn Dodgers in 1912, and suited up for the Giants in the early 1920s, gazed toward the vast outfield where he had once roamed. "I chased a couple Babe Ruth hit out there," he muttered. "Almost killed me."[4]

To many, it seemed just like old times, maybe too much so. One fan declared, "You have to love baseball to come out on a day like this. But I'm a Giant fan and I had to come. I hope the Giants—I mean the Mets—do real good."[5]

Thirty minutes before the contest was set to start, Stengel locked himself out of his office, where he had left his team's lineup card on his desk. As luck would have it, however, the door was eventually opened, the lineup card was rushed down to the umpires at home plate, and the game began. In the top of the first, the Pirates' Dick Groat, facing the Mets' Sherman Jones, grounded out to shortstop Felix Mantilla for out number one, and it was official: the Polo Grounds was once again open for business.

In the fifth inning, Richie Ashburn accounted for the first Met run at the Polo Grounds when he lined a single, scoring Jim Marshall. Frank Thomas hit the first Polo Grounds home run in Mets history, a solo shot in the sixth. But in the end, New York lost that first game by a score of 4–3, bringing their record to 0–2. It had quickly become obvious that Stengel's men were in for a long season.

For the 12,447 fans in attendance, the outcome was almost secondary. That seemed to be the prevailing theme for most of that summer of '62: It did not matter so much whether the Mets won or lost. There was a giddiness at the Polo Grounds that transcended the play on the field. Having been jilted by the Giants and the Dodgers, fans of National League baseball who had refused to join hands and root for the Yankees finally had a team they could call their own.

Unlike the stodgy, corporate atmosphere at Yankee Stadium, where fans were customers (or, even worse, *clientele*), a Polo Grounds crowd was a more festive lot, which made sense, seeing as so many of them were transplanted Ebbets Field denizens, that most eccentric of species. Sportswriter Joe King made the observation, "Ebbets Field was the expression of a neighborhood for the underdog (long before the great Dodgers) and baseball. To that extent, the Flatbush faithful are the spiritual mentors of Mets fans, and, of course, many of the old Dodger rooters are present."[6] But even Stengel marveled at the typical Mets congregation. "Ebbets Field? Never like this."[7] The Mets lost a major league record 120 games that first season in 1962, but make no mistake about it, the Polo Grounds was a fun place to be and to watch a baseball game.

Cavernous Yankee Stadium could never have bred such crowds. But the Polo Grounds had a folksy, time-worn quality to it that meshed perfectly with the Mets and their fans. Along with its odd bathtub shape, its low overhanging upper deck brought the paying multitudes closer to the action and was conducive to shouting, whether to berate opposing players or (less often) to congratulate a fine Met play. "Part of the charm of the Polo Grounds," pointed out Pulitzer Prize-winning journalist Jimmy Breslin, "is the fact that a man pitching a game can, without turning his head, listen to fans in the right-field [sic] stands ask each other for matches. They are exactly 254 feet away."[8]

Following a particularly excruciating loss, even by Met standards, Stengel asked reporters, "Did you hear those fans yelling for our players?" There had only been about 9,000 fans in the stands, but the passion at the Polo Grounds had been clearly felt by the Old Perfessor. "The way those people yelled, our players ought to play better," Stengel added, "and you can be sure they will."[9]

The players had an inspiration in Stengel himself. After the first Met win at the Polo Grounds, the 72-year-old manager celebrated by trotting from the dugout to the clubhouse in deepest center field, 475 feet away. Witnesses timed the trek at two minutes flat, but most agreed that Stengel would have done better if he had not stopped to take half a dozen bows along the way.

"We had blue collar [sic] fans," noted Ron Hunt. "There weren't a lot of suits and ties in the Polo Grounds."[10]

Gene Woodling, veteran of five Yankee World Series winners, then finishing out his career with the Mets, marveled at the team's supportive fans: "I've played in lots of places, but never have I seen anything like the fans at the Polo Grounds. You hit into a double play, or strike out with men on base, and as you go to your position, you expect to get chewed out real good. But what do they do? They clap their hands, and they say, 'Okay, Gene, we'll get them next time!' They're amazing people."[11]

Met fans were not only verbal, however. They were also literate. The banner craze was the most visible manifestation of fan-player interaction at the Polo Grounds. It all started with a few individuals from New Jersey who had taken a liking to Met player Rod Kanehl. On Opening Day of 1962, a banner (really a bedsheet with painted lettering) was spotted in the upper left field stands: "LEONIA, N.J., LOVES HOT ROD KANEHL."

This seemed strange to the rest of the Mets. Kanehl, after all, was a career minor leaguer from Kansas. When questioned how he could have a fan base in Leonia, New Jersey, Kanehl retorted, "My fame preceded me."[12]

The use of banners caught on, and soon the Polo Grounds was awash with fans holding up all variety of inscribed bedsheets and poster boards:

"LET'S GO METS!"
"PRAY!"
"WE DON'T WANT TO SET THE WORLD ON FIRE—WE JUST WANT TO FINISH NINTH."

At first, the Mets' management was not sure what to make of all the banners. Taking their cue from the Gestapo, they went so far as to confiscate several of the less-positive bedsheets. This made for bad public relations, and in time, the Mets held a Banner Day at the Polo Grounds, but the bedsheets still did not sit well with Met president and general manager George Weiss. "These people ... these noisy people with their bedsheets[.]Where do they come from? Why don't they keep quiet?"[13] Indeed, Met fans, who came to be referred to as the "New Breed," were anything but quiet, routinely bringing bugles and cherry bombs to the Polo Grounds, along with their bedsheets.

Clearly, Weiss did not get it. Among the Mets 120 losses in 1962, 58 of them came at the Polo Grounds, so Met fans needed to make their own fun somehow. One married couple went a bit too far, however. When neighboring fans began to wonder what the two were doing beneath their bedsheet, stadium security was quickly alerted. It was discovered that the amorous couple had been attempting to get physical in the privacy beneath the sheet; they were made to exit the ballpark and find a room. "But we're married," the woman protested, "and we're Met fans."[14]

The biggest draws those first two seasons at the Polo Grounds were, of course, the Los Angeles Dodgers and the San Francisco Giants. A total of 55,704 nostalgic fans jammed their way in when the Dodgers made their first appearance in 1962, a Memorial Day doubleheader. It was the largest crowd at the Polo Grounds in two decades. The Giants came to town next; the three-game series drew 118,845. On July 1, more than 37,000 witnessed a 17–3 thrashing at the hands of Los Angeles, and the next day a Giant doubleheader brought in 35,463. Another crowd in excess of 33,000 saw the Mets rally in the eighth inning to beat San Francisco on August 22, and the home team beat L.A.'s Don Drysdale two days later in front of 39,741. The biggest Polo Grounds crowd in 1963 was a May 5 doubleheader against San Francisco that drew 53,880, while the highest attendance against Los Angeles was 46,184 for a twin bill on the 18th of August.

In any discussion of the worst baseball teams of all time, the New York Mets of 1962 and 1963 rank at or very near the top. They are the shining example by which all other bad teams are compared. They followed up their 120-loss last-place season with a record of 51–111 in 1963, again finishing in the National League cellar. In 1962, they were an astonishing 60½ games behind the pennant-winning Giants, 18 games behind the ninth-place Chicago Cubs, themselves losers of 103.

The Mets were putrid in all phases of the game, ranking at the bottom in team batting average, earned run average, and fielding percentage in 1962, and again the next year. In '62, their pitching staff featured two 20-game losers (Roger Craig and Al Jackson), a 19-game loser (Jay Hook), a 17-game loser (Craig Anderson), and a hurler who went 1–12 (Bob L. Miller). The club lost its first nine games in 1962 and also endured losing streaks of 17 and 13 games. They did not start any better in 1963, losing their first eight, and at one point lost 15 in a row, and later 11 straight.

But the Mets of those years have not entered baseball folklore merely because they were historically atrocious. After all, the 2003 Detroit Tigers, themselves losers of 119 games (an American League record), have never inspired love and affection the way the 1962 Mets did. With the latter, it was as much about the process as it was the result. As Stengel put it, "The Mets have shown me more ways to lose than I even knew existed."[15] Hook agreed: "We lost games every way there was to lose them and I think we made up a few."[16]

The New York Mets had resurrected a grand old ballpark loved by many, but it seemed a cruel fate that the baseball gods had inflicted upon the Polo Grounds. Its grassy diamond, on which legends such as Christy Mathewson, Bill Terry, Mel Ott, Carl Hubbell, and Willie Mays had once cavorted, was now overrun by the likes of Choo Choo Coleman, Harry Chiti, Ed Bouchee, and Marv Throneberry.

Marvelous Marv was the poster child of the Mets in 1962. Throneberry stories abound, perhaps none of them more famous than the tale of what occurred in the first inning of a doubleheader versus the Chicago Cubs at the Polo Grounds on June 17. In a familiar scenario, the Mets trailed early, down 4–0 before they had even batted. In the bottom of the first, with runners on first and second, Throneberry hit a smash off the right field wall. Both runners scored, and Throneberry chugged into third with a triple. But not so fast, said Ernie Banks, the Cubs' first baseman, who called for the ball and stepped on first base. Umpire Dusty Boggess thumbed Throneberry out, claiming that he had missed the bag at first. Marvelous Marv was out (although the two runs still counted).

Stengel bolted out of the dugout to protest, but before he could get started, second base umpire Stan Landes headed over and told Casey, "I hate to tell you this, Casey, but he missed second base, too." Nonplussed, Stengel looked down at Throneberry at third. "Well, I know he touched third base because he's standing on it."[17]

Writer George Vecsey points to that day as the beginning of the legend of Marvelous Marv. Only about 13,000 fans were in the stands. "In fact," Vecsey wrote nearly a decade later, "there are probably 200,000 people who claim to have been in the Polo Grounds that afternoon. This happens very often with historic contests."[18]

Then there was catcher Choo Choo Coleman, whom nobody was exactly sure how he got his nickname, including Coleman himself. In a radio interview, Mets play-by-play announcer Ralph Kiner asked Coleman, "Choo Choo, how did you get your nickname?"

Coleman, not the talkative type, answered, "Dunno."

Kiner, not about to give up so easily, came back with, "Well, what's your wife's name—and what's she like?"

Choo Choo replied, "Her name is Mrs. Coleman—and she likes me."[19]

Left-handed pitcher Al Jackson was said to have the best stuff of anybody on the Mets' staff. Despite his 8–20 record in 1962, he was named to the Topps All-Rookie team. But in the opening game of a June 17, 1962, doubleheader against the Chicago Cubs, he was part of history when Lou Brock hit a homer off him that landed in the center field bleachers at the Polo Grounds. The blast was estimated to have travelled between 460 and 470 feet. Only one other major league player had ever hit a ball into that section of the Polo Grounds before: Joe Adcock, who did it as a member of the Milwaukee Braves in 1953. As with every other Met hurler, the Polo Grounds years were rough ones for Jackson. "We just had a very poor ballclub," he said later, "and there wasn't nothing great going to happen in 1962."[20]

The night following Brock's blast, Hank Aaron became a member of the exclusive club, when he hit a drive off Hook that landed in the bleachers for a home run. According to Hook, before the at bat, "Casey came out to the mound and said, 'Hook, pitch him outside and make him hit to center field.' I threw a low outside fastball and he hit it 600 feet to center field."[21]

Roger Craig, a talented pitcher who deserved a better fate, lost 24 in 1962 and 22 the following year. As the old baseball adage goes, you have to be pretty good to be allowed to lose that many games. "You can't win the game," Craig said. "You go out there knowing that. So you try harder. Try too hard, it usually turns out…. I want a raise next year. I'm going to pitch over 220 innings for this team before the season is over, and I want to get paid for it."[22]

The most star-crossed Met, however, may have been Hobie Landrith. A 32-year-old veteran of 12 big-league seasons, Landrith had been a serviceable backup catcher for four teams. But he certainly was not the type of player that an expansion club should waste their first-round draft pick on, which is exactly what the Mets did. Stengel tried to justify the decision at the time: "You have to have a good catcher or you'll have a lot of passed balls."[23] Landrith played in only 23 games for New York in 1962 (with three passed balls) before being shipped to the Baltimore Orioles (to complete an earlier deal in which the Mets had acquired Throneberry).

Venezuelan Elio Chacon was a good field, no-hit second baseman, and a certified ladies' man who reportedly owned 18 suits and 23 pairs of shoes. According to Rob Gardner, a teammate of Chacon's in the minor leagues, "He had a cousin in every town we went to. I could never figure out how he could have so many cousins. And they were all women. That was really weird. He had no male cousins."[24]

Ed Kranepool was pegged as the cornerstone of the Mets' franchise. One Yankee scout said of him, "There stands the best 18-year-old hitter I've ever seen in my time in baseball."[25] Rod Kanehl felt the same way about Kranepool, until he saw him actually play in a game. "When Kranepool tried out with us at the Polo Grounds," he remembered, "he was hitting balls out of the park. He was pulling the ball and hitting it to center field. Then he came up to the big leagues and he a was Slapsy Maxie."[26] Kranepool played a total of 18 years in the majors, all with the Mets (including two World Series), retiring after the 1979 season with a lifetime .261 batting average. But he never hit more than 16 home runs in a season.

On September 23, 1962, the Mets beat the Cubs in a contest that everybody supposed was to be the absolute final game at the Polo Grounds. Only about 10,000 misty-eyed folks bothered to show up, and they were rewarded with a 2–1 New York victory, pulled out in the bottom of the ninth when a single by Frank Thomas scored Choo Choo Coleman to break a 1-all tie. After the game, Stengel took one final walk from the dugout to the clubhouse in center field (not trotting this time), as "Auld Lange Syne" echoed throughout the old ballpark. Attendance for the year, boosted by the visits of the Dodgers and Giants, had been a pleasant surprise and, at 922,530, was actually better than that of five other teams in the National League. By the end, the Polo Grounds, according to writer Harold Rosenthal, was "like some 90-year-old person suffering from arteriosclerosis."[27]

And, just as Stengel had predicted, the Mets finished their season in Chicago, on September 30. Aided by a triple play, the Cubs put the visitors out of their misery, handing them their 120th loss.

As the 1963 season approached, it had become clear that the new Mets stadium in Flushing Meadows would not be ready until at least July. Said Rosenthal, "The ghosts will dance around the old 'graveyard' for a few months this spring and summer, then will depart forever."[28] The final Opening Day at the crumbling Polo Grounds was April 9, 1963, in front of 25,049 fans. "They made it so we could play in it," Kranepool said. "It was painted, but it was dark. The clubhouse was terrible, and the conditions there were strange. It wasn't easy to get to. We were looking forward to moving into Shea."[29] Upkeep and maintenance at the doomed ball yard had virtually ceased. George Vecsey called the place "rusted-out and pigeon-befouled."[30]

General manager Weiss believed his team would be in its new digs no later than August. "We would like to get away from the Polo Grounds and be set in our new home as quickly as possible."[31]

July turned into September, with the new stadium in Queens still not fully functional. "The green barn," as writer Roger Angell referred to the Polo Grounds, continued to hang on for the entire 1963 season.[32] On September 18, only 1,752 hardy souls braved the overcast, drizzly day to see the final National League game at the old ballpark, which brought the final season attendance to 1,080,808. The Philadelphia Phillies prevailed, 5–1, though the Mets' Jim Hickman hit the last home run, a shot off Chris Short in the fourth inning.

Craig Anderson, the starter and loser for New York, was not even aware of the significance of the event. "Nobody said anything to me," he recalled decades later. "It's funny, but I don't remember any fanfare of its being the last game at the Polo Grounds."[33] That was perhaps because the stadium had already been closed twice before, following the 1957 and 1962 seasons. To those on hand that final day in 1963, it may have simply been a case of "been there, done that."

Baseball writer Red Smith, who had also covered the last Giant game in 1957, had a sense of déjà vu as Met pinch-hitter Ted Schreiber grounded into a double play to end the game and finally put the Polo Grounds to rest. "On the last day," he wrote, "the team and the customers and the script were tired."[34] Indeed, in the words of a *New York Times* reporter, "hardly anyone cared."[35]

NOTES

1. William J. Ryczek, *The Amazin' Mets, 1962–1969* (Jefferson, NC: McFarland, 2008), 5.
2. "Casey Stengel Talks About the Mets," *The Sporting News*, April 4, 1962, 34.
3. Ray Gillespie, "Diamond Facts & Facets," *The Sporting News*, April 11, 1962, 18.
4. "Fans Cheer Mets, Boo Mayor at Old Polo Grounds," *Pittsburgh Post-Gazette*, April 14, 1962.
5. *Ibid.*

Top: The yearbook from the final season of the Mets at the Polo Grounds. *Bottom:* A ticket stub from one of the last games at the Polo Grounds (collection of Tom Edwards).

6. Joe King, "Ol' Perfessor Never Heard Such Din as Mets Fans Muster," *The Sporting News*, May 11, 1963, 7.

7. *Ibid.*

8. Jimmy Breslin, *Can't Anybody Here Play This Game?* (Chicago: Ivan R. Dee Publisher, 2003), 71.

9. Joe King, "Surrender? Casey's Just Started to Fight," *The Sporting News*, May 9, 1962, 2.

10. Ryczek, 59.

11. Dick Young, "Young Ideas," *The Sporting News*, September 1, 1962, 12.

12. George Vecsey, *Joy in Mudville* (New York: The McCall Publishing Company, 1970), 49.

13. *Ibid.*, 58.

14. *Ibid.*

15. Michael Lichtenstein, *Ya Gotta Believe!: The 40th Anniversary New York Mets Fan Book* (New York: St. Martin's Press, 2002), 85.

16. Ryczek, 50.

17. Robert Creamer, *Stengel: His Life and Times* (Lincoln: University of Nebraska Press, 1996), 300.

18. Vecsey, 66.

19. *Ibid.*, 76.

20. Ryczek, 17.

21. *Ibid.*, 47.

22. Breslin, 74.

23. Peter Morris, *Catcher: The Evolution of an American Folk Hero* (Chicago: Ivan R. Dee Publishers, 2009), 295.

24. Ryczek, 29.

25. *Ibid.*, 63.

26. *Ibid.*, 64.

27. Harold Rosenthal, "Torpedoed Ship That Refuses to Sink—That's the Polo Grounds," *The Sporting News*, February 9, 1963, 13.

28. *Ibid.*

29. Ken Belson, "Memories of Polo Grounds on Anniversary of Final Opener," *New York Times*, April 9, 2013.

30. *Ibid.*

31. Barney Kremenko, "Weiss Confident Mets Will Unveil Arena in August," *The Sporting News*, May 11, 1963, 7.

32. Roger Angell, "A Clean, Well-Lighted Cellar," *The New Yorker*, May 30, 1964.

33. "Mets Players Recall Final Game in the Polo Grounds, September 18, 1963," http://www.examiner.com/article/mets-players-recall-final-game-the-polo-grounds-september-18–1963 (accessed on September 7, 2014).

34. David M. Jordan, *Closing 'em Down: Final Games at Thirteen Classic Ballparks* (Jefferson, NC: McFarland, 2010), 70.

35. *Ibid.*

Memorable Games

Metropolitans 4, Nationals 2: September 29, 1880
BY RICHARD HERSHBERGER

The first professional baseball game played in Manhattan took place on September 29, 1880, between the Metropolitan Club of New York and the National Club of Washington. This late a date is remarkable. Organized baseball had arisen among New York clubs a quarter-century previous, and openly professional baseball had been played for over a decade. So why did it take so long to reach Manhattan? The explanation lies in geography and economic and social history.

The geography of New York City (meaning, in this era, the island of Manhattan) tended against professional baseball within its limits. The city grew from the south end, gradually spreading up the island. Within the developed area there were no good locations for a professional ball ground, for the simple reason that any suitable lot could be more profitably developed for other purposes. There were suitable lots above the line of development, but inadequate transportation infrastructure for spectators to easily get to them. It was cheaper and easier to take a ferry, crossing either the Hudson River to Hoboken or the East River to Brooklyn.

Many clubs based in New York City played in Hoboken or Brooklyn. The first ball fields enclosed by a fence—a necessary condition for charging admission—were constructed in Brooklyn. This had the proper balance of enough population density (both those residing in Brooklyn and visiting from New York) to support large paying crowds, with land values low enough that baseball exhibitions were an economically rational use of the land. The most prominent New York nine was the Mutual Club. It played in Hoboken in the amateur era and then moved to the Union Grounds in Brooklyn in the professional era.

Baseball in Manhattan was further delayed by the general economic Depression of 1873–1879. Indeed, professional baseball went into general decline. The National League, founded in 1876, had a high turnover of club failures in its early years, with vacancies filled by bringing in outside clubs. The nadir was the summer of 1880. The National League had its full complement of eight members, but there were only two other fully professional clubs in existence.

This general decline does not explain why such a large metropolis as New York could not support a professional club. The Mutuals collapsed late in the 1876 season. The Hartford club stepped in and played the 1877 season in Brooklyn, but they too failed and were not replaced. A similar process occurred in Philadelphia, leaving the two largest metropolises in the country without professional—much less major league—baseball clubs. Their long histories with baseball worked against them. They both had baseball establishments, which were inflexible and often corrupt. Advances in both playing and business techniques occurred elsewhere, leaving the New York establishment unable to compete. Professional ball's absence acted like a farmer leaving a field fallow, giving it time to renew itself. This allowed a new generation, and the more forward-looking of the previous generation, to create a new establishment unburdened by the past.

The baseball recovery began late in the season of 1880. In August, the Nationals and the Rochester Club scheduled a series of games in Brooklyn. This would prove visionary, but the decision was one of desperation. Recent history had shown the metropolis to be a baseball dead zone, but both clubs were in dire straits and prepared to try anything. They played three days in a row, beginning Wednesday, August 11. The first game drew only three or four hundred spectators, but attendance increased with each successive game.

This caught the attention of the dormant New York baseball community. Several respectable nines sprung up, recruiting from the ample supply of inactive players. Most were ephemeral organizations, essentially pick-up teams that would not outlast the season. Two men, however, saw potential for something more substantial.

These were John B. Day, a cigar manufacturer, baseball fan, and unaccomplished player, and James Mutrie, an experienced professional player and manager, if not at the top level. Day provided the capital and Mutrie the baseball know-how. Day's genius was in recognizing that he was in the right place at the right time. Baseball was reviving in New York, with no established club holding the public's loyalty. Furthermore, the time had come for professional ball to be played on Manhattan. Railroad infrastructure had developed such that paying spectators could easily reach a site beyond the edge of development.

An eminently suitable parcel was available immediately beyond the northern end of Central Park and easily reached by no fewer than four rail lines. This property was owned by James Gordon Bennett, son of the founder of the *New York Herald*. He was a member of the Manhattan Polo Association, which had been using it for several years. Day leased the ground, its use to be divided between the polo club for two days a week and Day's new Metropolitan Baseball Club for four days. Sunday, of course, was off limits, both being respectable organizations.

By acting quickly to set up a ball club on a permanent basis, Day could gain control of the New York market. But the venture came with risk. Setting up the club on a permanent basis meant investing capital in salaries and real-estate improvements. Should the baseball revival prove illusory, this capital would be lost.

The improvements were substantial, with facilities not only for polo and baseball, but also for track and field sports ("athletics" in the vocabulary of the day) and football, with a grandstand capable of holding a thousand spectators and encircled by a fence to ensure payment for entry.

Mutrie recruited the new Metropolitan team as the Polo Grounds were being prepared, rapidly putting together a credible nine. On September 15, they opened a series of warm-up games in Brooklyn and Hoboken against some of the new ad hoc collections, winning eight of nine games, most of them easily.

However, the occasion of the opening game of the new Polo Grounds called for more substantial competition than a glorified pickup team. This was the National Club of Washington. The Nationals were an established team, the second of that name. The original Nationals had been the premier Washington club in the 1860s, most famous today for being the first eastern club to tour the West (what is now called the Midwest) in 1867. But they faded away in the early professional period. The second Nationals were founded in 1877. This was an inauspicious time to be getting into professional baseball, and it is a testament to their management that they rode out the darkest years. Their prospects were excellent in the fall of 1880. They had good reason to believe that they would be inducted into the National League for 1881 and were making the investments to be competitive at that level. And they provided the Metropolitans with the perfect balance: They were decent competition while being beatable, still fielding their lineup of 1880.

The afternoon of the game opened well. Some 2,000 to 2,500 spectators showed up. Though tiny by modern standards, and small by the standards of just a few years later, this was a very good crowd in 1880. Matters took a turn for the worse when the Nationals were late. Play was advertised for 3:30 p.m. By 4:00, some of the crowd was beginning to leave and a scrub game was being organized. But the Nationals finally arrived, and play began at 4:20 with the Metropolitans batting first. The game was everything that could be asked for given the late start. The leadoff batter opened with a triple and scored two outs later on a ground ball through the second baseman's legs. The score was tied 2–2 after two innings. Then, the Metropolitans scored two runs in the top of the fifth, and the game was called on account of darkness in the sixth, for a 4–2 victory for the home club.

This win was followed by two more over the Nationals the next two days. These early triumphs set a good tone, and it was fortunate that they were played when they were. The end of September closed out the National League season and opened the October barnstorming season. The following Monday, the decidedly mediocre Worcester club came into town and beat the Metropolitans, 7–3. The Metropolitans would go on to win against National League clubs about one game in three. They were not yet ready for the big time, but their future was bright. Unfortunately for the Nationals, they faced a bleaker future. The National League chose the new Detroit club over them and proceeded to find a thin excuse to steal away the Nationals' best players. This broke the club, and it finally collapsed the following summer.

The new Polo Grounds would prove a financial bonanza. The Metropolitans could limit their travel and their travel expenses, and let other teams come to them and to large crowds. They managed to do this for the next two seasons, but this strategy had run its course by 1883. Both the National League and the new American Association courted Day, and he managed the neat trick of playing both sides and getting a franchise in both leagues.

With two franchises and only one team, Day signed the players of the defunct Troy team en masse, combined the Metropolitan and the former Troy players into one pool, and divided them up again, assigning the better half to the National League club. He sold the American Association half a few years later, and it lasted only a few years beyond that. He kept the National League side for a decade until he succumbed to a later economic depression and was forced to sell.

The National League club was, of course, the Giants, while the American Association side maintained the old Metropolitan name. Because of this difference, some moderns dismiss the connection between the Metropolitans of 1880 and the Giants of today. But this way of thinking is misguided. The Metropolitans of 1880 fathered the Giants every bit as much as they did the Metropolitans of 1883. Or better, to choose a different biological metaphor, they underwent mitosis, splitting into two. The 1880 season was a watershed year in professional baseball, with not only its entry into Manhattan but also the creation of one of its storied franchises.

New York Giants 2, St. Louis Browns 1: October 16, 1888
BY BILL LAMB

In October 1888, the atmosphere at New York Giants headquarters was a mixture of exhilaration and foreboding. Club founder John B. Day and his junior partners were celebrating their first National League pennant and looking forward to the Giants' postseason match against the St. Louis Browns, the standard-bearers of the rival American Association. But the championship playoff, not yet called the World Series, could have been the last sporting event conducted at the Polo Grounds, the handsome ballpark erected for the Giants only seven years earlier. City officials, bowing to the demands of residents of the tony Central Park North neighborhood, had adopted a traffic improvement plan designed to eliminate the ballpark by running a street extension through the outfield. Only rearguard action by Day's lawyers had forestalled condemnation, and the Polo Grounds' long-term prospects looked bleak.

For the next fortnight, however, such cares would be shelved, so that all concerned could focus their attention on the championship contests. The match featured two of late 19th-century baseball's most formidable nines. The Giants (84–47) had finally succeeded in supplanting arch-rival Chicago atop the National League standings and featured a lineup that boasted no fewer than six future Hall of Famers: Buck Ewing, John Montgomery Ward, Tim Keefe, Roger Connor, Jim O'Rourke, and Mickey Welch. The Browns (92–43), meanwhile, were the class of their circuit, having just cruised to a fourth consecutive American Association title. On the field, team fortunes were guided by captain-first baseman Charlie Comiskey, who had league batting champ Tip O'Neill, rising outfield star Tommy McCarthy, Arlie Latham, Silver King, and other AA worthies at his disposal. The play of the Browns, however, was often overshadowed by the antics of club owner Chris von der Ahe, the flamboyant saloonkeeper who bankrolled the franchise and often drove Comiskey to distraction. It was von der Ahe, for example, who agreed to the best-of-ten-games championship arrangement and the disadvantageous format that placed the first six games in the East, four at the Polo Grounds, and one each in Philadelphia and Brooklyn, before the match relocated to St. Louis.

Rain fell steadily on the morning of October 16, putting the opener in jeopardy. But by noon, skies had cleared and liberal application of sawdust made the Polo Grounds playable. Unhappily, the morning weather and an erroneous wire service report that the game had been postponed affected the gate. Only about 4,800 made their way through the turnstiles. That assemblage included local politicians, various baseball executives, and a sizable contingent of players, led by the redoubtable King Kelly. Late arrival of the umpiring crew of John Kelly (National League) and John Gaffney (American Association) pushed the first pitch back to after 3:00 p.m. When it finally commenced, the game pitted the cream of each league's pitching ranks against one another. The Giants' Tim Keefe had punctuated a 35–12 season with a 19-game consecutive win streak, a major league record for a season (tied by Rube Marquard in 1912) that stands to this day. Keefe, originally an underhand righty, had excellent stuff, thrown from a variety of pitching-arm angles. He relied on deception, and his out pitch was the game's first great changeup. For the regular season, Keefe led the NL in wins, winning percentage (.745), ERA (1.74), strikeouts (335), and shutouts (8). His opposite number had been equally dominant. The less-celebrated Silver King (born Charles Koenig) had gone 45–20 for the Browns and led the AA in wins, ERA (1.63), innings pitched (584), and shutouts (6). The onus to perform well lay heavy on King, as Nat Hudson (25–10), the Browns number-two pitcher, had skipped the postseason to return home to Chicago.

Neither Keefe nor King disappointed in Game 1, each holding the opposition to a mere three hits (although present-day baseball references credit the Giants with only two safeties, rather than the three hits published in contemporaneous newspaper box scores). The Giants broke the scoring seal in the bottom of the second. Roger Connor singled to center leading off. Called upon to sacrifice, John Montgomery Ward dropped a bunt toward third and beat the throw to first. Both runners then advanced a base on a King wild pitch. Connor tagged up and scored on Mike Slattery's fly to center, but Ward was thrown out trying to reach third by Brown center fielder Harry Lyons, effectively ending any further threat.

St. Louis promptly responded in the top of the third. With one out, Arlie Latham walked. He stole second while Yank Robinson was striking out and continued to third on a poor throw by Giant catcher Buck Ewing. Tip O'Neill then knotted the score at 1–1 with a two-out single.

The Giants tallied the decisive run in their half of the frame, scoring without the benefit of a base hit. With two out, Mike Tiernan walked. On the next pitch, he set out for second. The throw of Brown catcher Jack Boyle sailed into center field, where the ball also eluded Lyons. Tiernan came all the way around to score, making the score 2–1 in the Giants' favor. And there it would stay, as neither team mustered another scoring threat.

Keefe's victory over King in Game One was a harbinger of results to come. Keefe defeated the Browns' ace in Game Three as well as Game Five, on his way to posting a 4–0 playoff record. By the end of Game Eight, the championship had been decided in New York's favor, six wins to two. St. Louis won the final two meaningless and sparsely-attended playoff contests to complete the series. By October 27, the New York Giants had captured their first baseball world championship, providing a fitting sendoff for the original Polo Grounds in the process. Before the ensuing season began, the ballpark was razed.

New York Giants 1, Boston Beaneaters 0 (13 innings): May 12, 1890 BY JOEL RIPPEL

During his 13-year major league career, Mike Tiernan proved himself to be one of the top home run hitters of the National League.

The left-handed-hitting Tiernan, who spent his entire career with the New York Giants, slugged 106 home runs and led the National League in home runs twice. At the time of his retirement in 1899, his career total was only 32 shy of the existing major league mark of 138 (held by Roger Connor, whose record stood from 1895 to 1920).

In 1890, his fourth season with the Giants, Tiernan hit a league-leading (and career high) 16 home runs. And one of those round-trippers had the unique distinction of being cheered simultaneously by fans in two ballparks and was called "one of the most spectacular in history."[1]

The Giants, who had won back-to-back National League titles in 1888 and 1889, had gotten off to a slow start in 1890. Through the games of May 11, they were in last place with a 5–10 record. Tiernan, just one of two regulars in 1889 who did not sign with the New York team in the rival Players League for the 1890 season, was an early-season bright spot for the club.

Tiernan took a .303 batting average into New York's home game against Boston on May 12. On the mound for the Beaneaters was rookie (and future Hall of Famer) Kid Nichols. Nichols, who was 20, and Giant rookie (and another future Hall of Famer) Amos Rusie, who was 19, matched scoreless innings until Tiernan provided the heroics in the 13th.

In the top of the eighth inning (the home team had the option of batting first at that time), Tiernan singled with two outs and stole second. But Nichols ended the threat by retiring shortstop Jack Glasscock.

The game remained scoreless through 12 innings. Nichols struck out Rusie to open the top of the 13th, bringing Tiernan to the plate. Tiernan's eighth-inning single was just one of three hits Rusie had allowed up to that point.

After Tiernan fouled off the first pitch, a new ball was put into play. Newspaper accounts differ slightly on what happened next.

One account reported, "He hit a foul, and then a new ball [was provided]. The first ball was too far away for the batter, but the next one was just right."[2]

Another account said, "He had knocked a foul and a new ball was thrown out. He hit the first one pitched."[3]

A third account said, "Two balls were pitched to Tiernan, and a new ball came into the game. Tiernan met it squarely on the end of his bat."[4]

Whether it was the second or third pitch of the at bat can be debated, but the result cannot. Tiernan lined a tremendous drive that cleared the center field fence for a home run to give the Giants a 1–0 lead. After Tiernan's home run, Nichols retired Glasscock and Dude Esterbrook. In the bottom of the 13th, Rusie put down the Beaneaters in order to complete his three-hit shutout victory.

The game was "the best that has been seen in New York and it has been a long time since one so good was played in the United States."[5]

Tiernan's home run not only stirred the 687 fans in attendance at the Polo Grounds, it brought cheers from the fans of the adjacent Brotherhood Park—the two ballparks were separated by an alley—where, by coincidence, a Players League game between New York and Boston was being played at the same time. "Never before in the history of the game have the same number of people shown so much enthusiasm on a ball field.... Even the people who were at the Brotherhood game, and who were watching the League game at the top of the fence, made a great demonstration. And why not? Tiernan had done what few people ever believed could be accomplished. The ball struck the fence of Brotherhood Park."[6]

According to one newspaper account, Tiernan's home run was not the only thing that made the game memorable. "Another thing about the game. It was the finest contest ever played by two professional teams, and will go down to record as such, not on account of the number of innings played, but because of the wonderful work done by the pitchers and the brilliant fielding."[7]

Tiernan would go on to hit .304 with 59 runs batted in and a league-leading .495 slugging percentage for the Giants in 1890. But the Giants could do no better than finish sixth in the National League with a 63–68 record—24 games behind the first-place Brooklyn Bridegrooms.

Tiernan retired in 1899 with a .311 lifetime batting average, including a career-high .369 in 1896, and a number of years later, renowned sportswriter Tim Murnane, a former major leaguer himself, pointed out that the star hitter should be remembered for his defense as well: "In looking back over the history of the game for great outfielders, one invariably picks the men who worked in the center garden, yet some of the most remarkable workmen the game has produced played the other outfield positions. Among the latter were Andrew Leonard, Joe Hornung, [and] Hardy Richardson, in left; Sam Thompson, Tom McCarthy, and Mike Tiernan[,] in right. All worked without a mitt or glove of any kind and were the true artists of the game."[8]

When he passed away at the age of 51 in 1918, Tiernan was remembered as "one of the best players of his day. At the plate, he had a fine eye and a splendid follow-through swing. His fielding was phenomenal and his base running very fine."[9]

Notes

1. "Tell Tales of Mike Tiernan," *The Sporting News,* November 28, 1918, 2.
2. "Sports of Springtime. The Base-Ball Field," *New York Post*, May 13, 1890.
3. "Tiernan's Home Run Won It," *New York Times,* May 13, 1890.
4. "Tiernan Was Tired," *Boston Globe,* May 13, 1890.
5. "Sports of Springtime. The Base-Ball Field."
6. "Tiernan's Home Run Won It."
7. "Tiernan's Home Run Won It."
8. Tim Murnane, "Modern Methods," *Sporting Life,* June 19, 1909, 19.
9. "Tell Tales of Mike Tiernan," 2.

New York Giants 1, Chicago Cubs 1: September 23, 1908
By Norm King

The National Football League (NFL) is replete with famous games that have titles attached to them. Every serious football fan knows that the 1958 NFL championship match between the New York Giants and the Baltimore Colts became known as "the greatest game ever played," and that the 1974 playoff tilt between the Oakland Raiders and the Miami Dolphins lives on as "the sea of hands game."

Baseball history, on the other hand, gives titles to moments of glory or ineptitude rather than whole games. The third game of the 1951 playoff between the New York Giants and the Brooklyn Dodgers is known for Bobby Thomson's "shot heard 'round the world," and there was the famous "Snodgrass muff," a fly ball dropped by Fred Snodgrass of the Giants in the final game of the 1912 World Series.

The New York Giants had a long history of famous moments. One of the earliest occurred on September 23, 1908, at the Polo Grounds and it has gone down in baseball lore as "Merkle's boner."

Here is the scenario. By September that year, the Giants, Cubs, and Pittsburg Pirates were involved in a pennant race so tight that any of the three could be in first place on one day and third place the next.[1] On September 23, the Giants (87–50) and the Cubs (90–53) were in a dead heat with the Pirates (89–54) one game back. On that date, the Giants and Cubs met in the third game of a crucial four-game series at the Polo Grounds. The Cubs had swept a doubleheader the previous day, winning 4–3 and 3–1.

Jack Pfiester, who went 12–10 with a 2.00 earned run average that year, started for the Cubs, while Hall of Famer Christy Mathewson, who would finish the season at 37–11 with a 1.43 ERA, went to the hill for New York. The game was scoreless until the top of the fifth, when Joe Tinker hit a home run off Mathewson to put the Cubs up, 1–0.[2] The Giants tied the game in the sixth on a single by right-fielder Mike Donlin that scored second baseman Buck Herzog. Neither team scored in the seventh or eighth, or the top of the ninth for that matter. The Giants took their turn in the bottom of the inning with a chance to win the game and take a one-game lead on the Cubs.

Center fielder Cy Seymour led off by grounding out to Johnny Evers at second. Third baseman Art Devlin followed with a single. With one out and one on, perhaps the most critical play of the game occurred when left fielder Elwood "Moose" McCormick hit a grounder to Evers that had double play written all over it. Evers tossed to Tinker, forcing Devlin at second, but in a move that probably brought a tear to the eye of Giant manager John McGraw, Devlin slid hard into second, preventing Tinker from completing the double play.

Merkle was up next. It should be noted here that Merkle was a 19-year-old rookie at the time; he appeared in 15 games in 1907 and had only 41 at bats in all of 1908. This game marked his first start in the major leagues and it only occurred because regular first baseman Fred Tenney woke up that morning with a case of lumbago.

As he entered the batter's box, Merkle had gone 0-for-2 with a walk. With two strikes on him, the youngster smacked Pfiester's third pitch down the right field line for a single, allowing McCormick to run all the way to third. Shortstop Al Bridwell was up next. Pfiester threw; Bridwell swung and hit a line drive up the middle. McCormick scored from third and Merkle, on his way to second, stopped running before he reached the base. The rest, as they say, was pandemonium.

Merkle's action was understandable. Fans were allowed onto the field after games at the Polo Grounds, and team locker rooms were in center field. To get to the clubhouse, a player would have to run past the fans, many of whom wanted to talk to or congratulate the players—if the team won. It was common practice in that type of situation for a player to forego the formality of touching the base he was running to and start hightailing it to the showers.

But while that may have been the custom, it is not the rule. Rule 4.09 says that a run shall not count if the runner advances to home when the third out is made by a force play, in this case, at second. Evers knew that and even though fans were all over the field, he shouted at Cubs center fielder Solly Hofman to throw him the ball so he could touch the bag for the force play on Merkle, thus negating the run. What actually happened next is impossible to say with certainty because accounts vary and no video evidence exists of the event. This explanation is as good as any:

"Once it [the ball] was thrown in, it might have been intercepted by Giants pitcher Joe (Iron Man) McGinnity, who was coaching third base that day, and McGinnity might have lost it to charging Cubs players or thrown it into the stands, where the Cubs retrieved it, possibly by decking a fan in a bowler hat," wrote Tim Layden in *Sports Illustrated*. "Then again, the recovered ball might not have been the one that Bridwell struck."[3]

Fans flocked to the field after games, which caused players to leave quickly. In the case of Fred Merkle, the exit was too quick (collection of M. Frank).

At any rate, Evers grabbed somebody's ball and touched second, setting off an argument amidst rioting fans in which the Cubs claimed that Merkle was out. The two umpires needed to make a decision and required police protection to get to an area under the grandstand to consult. Second base umpire Bob Emslie had fallen down to avoid getting hit by Bridwell's smash, and so did not see anything. The call was home plate umpire Hank O'Day's to make, and he called Merkle out.

Most people do not realize that O'Day and the Cubs were involved in this type of situation just a few weeks earlier. On September 4, the Cubs were playing the Pirates when Pittsburg rookie Warren Gill did not touch second base when a run scored. O'Day was umpiring on his own that day and was watching the runner from third cross the plate when Evers got the ball and touched second. O'Day told Evers he did not see the play at second, so he could not call it. The Cubs made a formal protest but National League president Harry Pulliam upheld O'Day's call.

Calling Merkle out should have ended the inning, but the game should have continued. However, it was getting dark and the field was full of ornery fans, so the umpires stopped the game on account of darkness and declared it a tie. Pulliam, who was at the game, upheld their decision. It would be replayed in its entirety at the end of the season if it were needed to decide the pennant winner.

It is incorrect to say that this game cost the Giants the pennant. In fact, the two teams met the next day, with the Giants winning 5–4 and taking a one-game lead over the Cubs. McGraw's men just could not pull away from the Cubs, despite winning 11 of their last 16 games, and, when the season ended on October 7, the two teams were tied atop the standings. They met again on October 8 at the Polo Grounds, with the Cubs winning 4–2 to take the pennant and to go on to defeat the Detroit Tigers in the World Series.

The saddest part of the game was its effect on Merkle. He went on to have a highly respectable 16-year major league career and had a lifetime .273 batting average. He played in five World Series, although he was on the losing side each time. Neither McGraw nor his teammates blamed him for what happened, and they considered him a highly intelligent player. Nonetheless, he got stuck with the nickname "Bonehead," a sobriquet that followed him for years. He was managing a minor league team in 1929 and quit abruptly when somebody called him the name. He ended his association with baseball permanently in 1936 when some unnamed minor leaguer "used the 'B' word" while Merkle was umpiring an exhibition game between the bushers and the Washington Senators.[4]

After 14 years away from the game, Merkle surprised his family in 1950 by accepting an invitation to an Old Timer's Day at the Polo Grounds. When he was introduced, the fans gave him a loud ovation.

"Merkle and the fans made peace with one another," wrote Keith Olbermann. "The pain was relieved, the blame absolved."[5]

NOTES

1. In 1891, the U.S. Board of Geographic Names eliminated the "h" from all American localities that had "burgh" at the end of their names. Pittsburgh got its "h" back in 1911.

2. Tinker hit six home runs that season, good enough for fourth place among National League home run leaders.

3. Tim Layden, "Tinkers to Evers to Chance. .. to Me," *Sports Illustrated*, December 3, 2012.

4. Cait Murphy, *Crazy '08: How a Cast of Cranks, Rogues, Boneheads and Magnates Created the Greatest Year in Baseball History* (New York: HarperCollins, 2007), 295.

5. Keith Olbermann, "The Goof That Changed the Game," *Sports Illustrated*, September 29, 2008.

The Polo Grounds in 1908, the year of "Merkle's boner" (collection of Stew Thornley).

New York Giants 1, New York Yankees 0: October 13, 1921 BY T.S. FLYNN

The day after the Red Sox sold Babe Ruth to the Yankees, the *New York Times* decreed, "Manhattan's fondest dreams of having a World Series at the Polo Grounds between the Giants and Yankees now becomes a tangible thing, and that is the big event which New York fans will be rooting for all next Summer."[1] In fact, New York fans would have to root for two summers before their first intercity World Series became tangible, but it was worth the wait. Billed as a battle between Giant manager John McGraw's old-school "scientific" approach to the game and the new, brash brand of long ball introduced by Yankee slugger Babe Ruth, the 1921 World Series would indeed be played exclusively at the Polo Grounds, home to both teams since 1913, and it would be the last of the best-of-nine World Series. With no scheduled days off, the clubs alternated home-team honors daily. The Giants hoped to end their streak of losing four consecutive World Series since their 1905 title, while the upstart Yankees, winners of their first American League championship, looked to end two decades of consistent failure with the ultimate victory. By the time the Series concluded, new records were established for ticket sales (269,976) and receipts ($900,233.00),[2] and *New York Times* scribe Irvin S. Cobb was moved to declare that the eight games were played so well and with such splendid sportsmanship that "it should be written that 1921 has wiped the shield of our hemispheric pastime clean of the befouling smear which [the Black Sox Scandal of] 1919 put upon it."[3]

However, the excitement that surrounded the first seven games of the 1921 World Series waned considerably by the early afternoon of October 13, when the two clubs

Fans watch the action from the outfield. Though far away, the stands afforded a view to many historic events, including the 1921 World Series (collection of Tom Edwards).

arrived for Game Eight. One win away from taking the title and wearing sweaters and mackinaw coats, the Giants gathered around the visitors' dugout while the Yankees took batting practice. A cold, steady wind cut through the small huddles of early-arriving fans. The Polo Grounds would remain sparsely occupied throughout the afternoon. Just 25,000 witnessed the first pitch of the final game of the Series, the upper deck nearly empty. The cold winds and dark sky were not the only reasons for the small turnout; a Giant victory seemed a foregone conclusion to many. The Yankees had won the first two games of the series, but the Giants evened the ledger with victories in Games Three and Four. The American Leaguers then won Game Five before dropping Games Six and Seven to find themselves on the brink of losing the championship. Most of the games had been competitive and well played, but the Yanks lacked pitching depth and Babe Ruth had been reduced from superstar to spectator by a nagging injury that worsened and now threatened his career.

The 1921 season had been dominated by Ruth. He mashed 59 home runs, and a nation of baseball fans obsessively followed his exploits in newspapers and filled ballparks to see his swing firsthand. With Ruth in their lineup, the Yankees had outdrawn the Giants, their landlords, at the Polo Grounds for the first time in 1920. In 1921, at the age of 26, in just his eighth season in the big leagues (his third as a non-pitcher), the Babe broke the career home run record of 138 and singlehandedly surpassed the season home run totals of nine teams. When the second-place New Yorkers hosted first-place Cleveland for four games over the penultimate weekend of the 1921 season, Ruth led the way, going eight for 11 with three doubles and two home runs to flip the standings, despite incurring a nasty gash on his left elbow in the third game and reinjuring it the following day.[4] The Yankees increased their lead during the final week of the season to win the pennant, but their star limped to the postseason on a tender left knee, his wounded elbow worsening with each passing day.

Ruth started each of the first three games of the Series, notwithstanding his inflamed elbow and gimpy knee. Following Game Three, the infected elbow swelled to twice its normal size and a three-inch incision was made to drain pus from the wound.[5] Ruth was ordered to sit out Game Four, but he did not. His arm heavily bandaged, The Bambino was praised in the press for playing through the pain. Although he slugged his only home run of the series, he struggled in the field and the Yankees lost, 4–2. Ruth again spurned doctor's orders and started Game Five. The game's most crucial events unfolded in the top of the fourth when he led off the inning with a surprise bunt single. Bob Meusel then doubled past his brother, Giant left fielder Irish Meusel, scoring Ruth from first. His sprint around the bases gave the Yankees the lead, but it exacted a toll from the weakened star. According to Lyle Spatz and Steve Steinberg in *1921: The Yankees, The Giants, and the Battle for Baseball Supremacy in New York*, "[Ruth] staggered into the dugout, collapsed, and passed out. Dr. George Stewart revived him with spirits of ammonia." Remarkably, the wounded Babe remained in the game (striking out in his next three at bats), and the Yankees won. Afterward, Ruth's attending physicians released a statement: "The glands have taken up the poison, as is usual, but the swelling has reached such proportions that if the arm is used it will force the poison into the system, when the poisoning would become general. When blood poisoning becomes general throughout the system, the seat of the trouble must be removed, and that means amputation. Ruth will not play again in the series."[6]

With their top hitter relegated to the press box for Games Six and Seven, the Yankees soon found themselves one game from elimination. They had been outslugged in Game Six, and then the Giants' Phil Douglas outpitched Carl Mays in Game Seven. Waite Hoyt would get the ball for the Yankees in Game Eight. Having already won twice in the series, allowing no earned runs in 18 pitched, Hoyt gave the Yankees a chance to even the series, but then what? Sid Mercer, writing for the Olean (New York) *Times Herald*, opined: "The Yankees need two games, the Giants one. For the one game[,] McGraw has his choice of two good pitchers [Art Nehf and Jesse Barnes]; for the two games[,] the Yanks have one pitcher [Hoyt]. McGraw is sitting in the golden seat at last after four failures in ten years."[7] To make matters worse for the Yanks, their starting third baseman, Mike McNally, arrived for Game Eight with his arm in a sling, having injured his shoulder in Game Seven.

Hoyt induced a 5–3 groundout to start Game Eight and then issued a pair of walks sandwiched around a foul fly out to first base. Next, the game turned on an ordinary play gone wrong. Roger Peckinpaugh, the Yankees' shortstop and captain since 1914, misplayed a routine ground ball off the bat of High Pockets Kelly. As the ball rolled into left field, Dave Bancroft scored the final and deciding run of the 1921 World Series. Nehf and Hoyt settled into a pitchers' duel the rest of the way, and the defenses tightened. When Hoyt left the mound after retiring the Giants in the top of the ninth, his streak of innings pitched without allowing an earned run reached 27.

With Nehf on the mound to begin the bottom of ninth, Babe Ruth strode to the plate (again against doctor's orders) to pinch-hit for Wally Pipp. He fouled off the first offering and took the second and third for a strike and a ball. Ruth swung hard at the fourth pitch of the inning but grounded out to Kelly at first. Aaron Ward followed with a walk and Yankee fans hopes flickered with Home Run Baker coming to bat. Baker, in

It was not until after the 1922 season that the grandstands were extended into the far reaches of the outfield (collection of Tom Edwards).

the 12th year of his 13-year career, hit a Nehf pitch hard to the hole between first and second. The Associated Press game account reported that

the rap looked like a sure hit[,] and with Ward legging it for third[,] it promised to put the Yankees in a favorable position if it got by.

But it did not pass. Throwing himself at the skimming sphere, [second baseman Johnny] Rawlings ... reached out and clung to it with his left hand. Rolling over and transferring the ball to his right hand, Rawlings made the throw to [first baseman George] Kelly at first while still on the ground, getting Baker by several feet.

It was then Kelly's turn, and with a lightning-like and accurate throw[,] he shot the ball across the diamond into the hands of [t]hird [b]aseman Frank Frisch. A cloud of dust flew up over third as Ward slid into the bag. From the midst of it, Umpire [Ernie] Quigley's form emerged, his right arm flung forth, motioning the runner out. The double play had been completed, the third Yankee of the inning had been retired, the game was over, and the Giants had won it and the world championship.[8]

NOTES

1. William Juliano, "No, No, Frazee: A Look Back at the Reaction Following Babe Ruth's Sale to the Yankees," http://www.captainsblog.info /2012/01/06 (accessed on June 12, 2017).
2. Lyle Spatz and Steve Steinberg, *1921: The Yankees, the Giants, and the Battle for Baseball Supremacy in New York* (Lincoln: University of Nebraska Press, 2010).
3. Irvin S. Cobb, "Fans, Not Players, Quitters, Says Cobb," *New York Times*, October 14, 1921.
4. "Ruth 5 Times 'Out' on Counts by Physicians," *San Francisco Chronicle*, October 13, 1921.
5. *Ibid.*
6. *New York Evening Telegram*, October 11, 1921. In Spatz and Steinberg, 361.
7. Sid Mercer, "Pitching Miracle Only Can Save Yanks Victory," *Olean Times Herald*, October 13, 1921.
8. "Giants Win World Title; Yankees Die Fighting Hard, 1 to 0," *Oneonta Daily Star*, October 14, 1921.

American League 9, National League 7: July 10, 1934
BY STEW THORNLEY

The 1934 All-Star Game is remembered for the performance of New York Giant southpaw Carl Hubbell, who struck out five players in a row who are now in the Hall of Fame. Less remembered is the outstanding outing of Cleveland's Mel Harder, who entered a mess in the fifth inning and went the rest of the way, allowing the American League to hold on for a 9–7 win.

The follow-up to the inaugural All-Star Game, played the year before at Comiskey Park in Chicago, was a hit again as more than 48,000 fans came to the Polo Grounds in New York to see a wild affair.

The National League built a 4–0 lead after three innings. The runs came on a leadoff home run by Frank Frisch and a three-run homer by Joe Medwick, both off American League starter Lefty Gomez. However, the main story occurring in the early innings was not how the Nationals got their runs but how the Americans stayed scoreless during this time.

Hubbell, pitching in the home park of his New York Giants, was following up on a year in which he had led the senior circuit with 23 wins, a 1.66 earned run average, and ten shutouts. At the time of the 1934 All-Star Game, he had 12 wins, on his way to 21 for the year (the second of five consecutive seasons in which he topped 20 wins) and another league-leading ERA. In the All-Star Game, however, Hubbell had a shaky start. He gave up a leadoff single to Charlie Gehringer (who made it to second when Wally Berger fumbled the ball) and walked Heinie Manush. The American League had two on with no outs and an incredible heart of the order coming up. No problem for Hubbell, who relied on his screwball to strike out Babe Ruth, Lou Gehrig, and, after a double steal, Jimmy Foxx.

Hubbell did not let up in the second, fanning Al Simmons and Joe Cronin. Bill Dickey singled to break the strike-out streak, but Hubbell finished the inning by striking out Gomez. Years later, the legend became one of Hubbell striking out six Hall of Famers (although, of course, Gomez made the Hall for his pitching, not hitting, ability). At the time, there was no Hall of Fame, but the feat was still noted. *The Sporting News* wrote, "Carl's fanning Ruth, Gehrig, Foxx, Simmons, and Cronin in succession amounted to one of the greatest pitching achievements of modern times."

Hubbell pitched a scoreless third, as well, but NL manager Bill Terry did not have anyone of his caliber to follow. Terry tried Lon Warneke of the Cubs in the fourth, but the Arkansas Hummingbird was not up to Hubbell's performance. Warneke retired Foxx, the first batter he faced, but then gave up a double to Simmons. Cronin followed with a run-scoring single and, one out later, came home on a pinch-hit triple by Earl Averill to cut the Nationals' lead in half.

The Polo Grounds hosted the second All-Star Game, which is remembered for Carl Hubbell's performance, striking out five straight players who are now in the Hall of Fame (collection of Stew Thornley).

Trouble continued in the fifth, and Warneke gave way to Van Lingle Mungo after walking Ruth and Gehrig, the first two batters in the inning. Foxx greeted Mungo with a single on the first pitch, scoring Ruth and sending Gehrig to third. Simmons beat out an infield hit as Gehrig scored to tie the score, 4–4. After Cronin popped out trying to bunt, Dickey walked to load the bases. Averill, who had remained in the game after batting for Gomez the previous inning, produced another extra-base hit, doubling to right to score two runs and put the Americans ahead. Red Ruffing, who had pitched a scoreless fourth, drove home two more with a single, giving the junior circuit a six-run inning and an 8–4 lead in the game.

Back on the mound in the bottom of the fifth, Ruffing was roughed up. A leadoff walk to Pepper Martin followed by singles to Frisch, Pie Traynor, and Chuck Klein finished Ruffing. Harder came into a situation with two runs already in, two on, and no out. The Cleveland right-hander allowed another of Ruffing's runners to score (on a steal of home by Traynor as part of a double steal) but got out of the inning while preserving his team's lead, which had been cut to 8–7.

The American League completed the scoring in the sixth with another run on doubles by Simmons and Cronin off Dizzy Dean. The slugfest concluded with a 9–7 win for the Americans, their second straight win in what was becoming a regular summertime event. *The Sporting News* wrote, "As a result of the widespread interest the game generated throughout the county and the fact that it is a charitable enterprise, devoid of any mark of commercialism, baseball leaders see in it a fine thing for the propagation of the sport nationally and at the December meetings the club owners are expected to go on record to make it a yearly fixture."

The All-Star Game did become a yearly fixture although over the years it could no longer be said that the game was "devoid of any mark of commercialism." Nevertheless, the excitement of seeing the game's greatest names assembled on one diamond each summer has continued. The 1934 All-Star Game met expectations in terms of interest and entertainment of the game itself. Even though his outstanding outing did not result in his team's winning the game, Carl Hubbell stamped his name on this one with a performance that lives on in the lore as one of the most memorable All-Star Games ever.

All-Star Notes

Although the 1934 All-Star Game is remembered for Carl Hubbell's string of strikeouts, walks were nearly as plentiful in the game. The teams combined for 12 bases on balls, nine given up by the National League (including two by Hubbell). Robert D. Maley, the self-proclaimed sole member of the "Bureau of Unvital Statistics," tracked the pitches in the game with a breakdown on what happened with every pitch from each pitcher. National League hurlers threw 182 pitches, 102 of which were strikes (including balls put into play). Starter Carl Hubbell threw 32 strikes and 21 balls. Warneke threw more balls than strikes (21 to 20). Van Lingle Mungo and Fred Frankhouse were even in balls and strikes (13 each for Mungo and 6 each for Frankhouse). The American League issued only three walks and, as would be expected, had a better overall strike-to-ball breakdown: 96 strikes and 48 balls. Starter Lefty Gomez delivered 28 strikes and 12 balls.

Billy Herman of the National League entered the game twice. Herman hit for Hubbell in the third inning. Later in the game, National League manager Bill Terry needed someone to take over for Frisch. According to *The Sporting News,* Frisch was troubled by charley horses, and the play-by-play account in Retrosheet notes that Frisch sprained his foot while scoring a run in the fifth. Frisch played another inning in the field. In the seventh, Terry requested that Herman be allowed to re-enter the game to relieve Frisch at second base. American League manager Joe Cronin gave his permission, and Herman went back into the game.

One other All-Star Game was played at the Polo Grounds, in 1942 and was the first All-Star Game to be played at night. According to David Vincent, Lyle Spatz, and David W. Smith in *The Midsummer Classic: The Complete History of Baseball's All-Star Game,* the game was originally scheduled for Ebbets Field in Brooklyn. However, the game was moved to the Polo Grounds, which had greater capacity, to allow for a bigger crowd since the gate proceeds were going to charities related to the war effort. A crowd of 34,178 attended and saw the American League win 3–1. The Americans did all their scoring in the first, on a leadoff home run by Lou Boudreau and a two-run homer by Rudy York. The game began at 7:21 p.m. (nearly an hour later than scheduled because of rain) and ended at 9:28, two minutes before a blackout test scheduled for New York City.

Boston Braves 9, New York Giants 0 (forfeit): September 26, 1942 BY JAMES FORR

Warren Spahn's record in 1942: No wins, no losses, one complete game.

That very peculiar statistical line was the product of one very peculiar Saturday afternoon at the Polo Grounds.

Paid attendance for the Boston-New York doubleheader on September 26, 1942, was a paltry 2,916. After all, the games meant nothing. The Giants were a decent team, but they had been mathematically eliminated from the pennant race weeks earlier. And the Braves were the Braves—dreadful, as usual.

However, the paid attendance did not include the nearly 10,000 youngsters who got into the game for free in exchange for their contributions to a scrap metal drive. All over the country at that time, kids were collecting empty tin cans and old pots and pans, which found new life as raw material for the ships, tanks, and planes the United States needed for its march to victory in World War II.

While outside the massive mound of metal grew higher and wider by the minute, inside the Giants took the opener of the twin bill, 6–4, behind a complete game from Carl Hubbell and Mel Ott's 30th home run. The second game began with rookie Warren Spahn on the mound for Boston. Had the 21-year-old Spahn broken in during the era of the internet and 24/7 sports media, his arrival would have been proclaimed by a choir of angels. At Class B Evansville in 1941, he had gone 19–6 with seven shutouts and a microscopic 1.83 earned run average. He made the big-league team out of spring training in 1942, appeared in relief in two games, and then was optioned to Class A Hartford, where again he was nearly unhittable: a 17–12 record with a 1.96 ERA.

Boston manager Casey Stengel declared that his young lefty could become one of the best pitchers in baseball if he stayed healthy.[1] Stengel was right, of course, but on this day Spahn was just a no-name kid struggling with his command in only his second major league start. "I didn't have anything resembling self-confidence," he said later as he looked back at his first few games with the Braves. "I was as tight as a drum and worrying about every pitch."[2]

New York jumped on Spahn early. They capitalized on a pair of walks to score twice in the first inning. Johnny Mize accounted for the first run with a sacrifice fly, and then Babe Young followed with an RBI single. The Braves got one back in the third. Spahn, an outstanding hitter, led off with a single. He raced to third on a Skippy Roberge double, and then trotted home on a groundout by the primeval Paul Waner.

Spahn gave it right back in the fourth, though, as the Giants pecked out a run on an infield hit, a walk, and Dick Bartell's run-scoring single, which made it 3–1. New York stretched out its lead again in the seventh on Babe Barna's two-run triple. Meanwhile Spahn's mound opponent, 24-year-old Bob Carpenter, who was seeking his 12th win of the season, kept the Braves shackled, surrendering just six hits and two runs through eight innings.

By the middle of the eighth it had been a long afternoon and the kids at the Polo Grounds did what kids do when they get tired and bored—they went nuts. Out of nowhere, they began streaming onto the field, first in a trickle, then in a tidal wave. Besieged umpires Ziggy Sears and Tommy Dunn slogged through what the *New York Times* called "the hopeless, tangled, confused mass" toward the Giants dugout, where they called upstairs and ordered that an announcement be made to clear the field.[3] Amid the clamor, though, no one could hear the public address system—not that it would have mattered. City police, security guards, even members of the grounds crew tried to restore order but they found it impossible "to make even a faint impression against the mass swirling on the field."[4]

The umpires had no choice but to forfeit the game to the Braves, 9–0. Giant president Horace Stoneham could not argue with the decision. "It was an unfortunate ending but there was no alternative under the circumstances." Stoneham was disappointed but undeterred. "We will continue to admit youngsters bearing war scrap, but we will try to marshal them in restricted sections tomorrow for our final doubleheader."[5] Stoneham's Plan B was not necessary, however, as rain washed away those last two games.

By rule, all the individual statistics counted and Spahn was credited with a complete game, but neither pitcher received a decision.[6] It was the last baseball fans would see of Spahn for three years. That fall he enlisted in the Army, where he received a Bronze Star and a Purple Heart for his service in Europe.[7]

Although the day turned out to be a split decision for the Giants, at least it was a winning afternoon for Uncle Sam. By the end of the day, the towering junk heap contained 56 tons of scrap metal, including the hollowed out shell of a broken-down car.

NOTES

1. Gregory H. Wolf, ed., *That's Joy in Braveland: The 1957 Milwaukee Braves* (Phoenix: The Society for American Baseball Research, 2014), 190.

2. Todd Anton and Bill Nowlin, eds., *When Baseball Went to War* (Chicago: Triumph Books, 2008), 151.

3. James P. Dawson, "Youthful War-Scrap Crowd Ruins Giants' Triumph at Polo Grounds," *New York Times*, September 27, 1942.

4. *Ibid.*

5. *Ibid.*

6. http://mlb.mlb.com/mlb/official_info/official_rules/official_scorer_10.jsp.

7. Anton and Nowlin, 149–150.

Brooklyn Dodgers 5, New York Yankees 1, New York Giants 0: June 26, 1944

BY MIKE HUBER AND RACHEL HAMELERS

Twenty days after the D–Day invasion of Normandy, a special baseball game took place in New York City. The world was focused on the Pacific and European battlefronts, but on the American home front, the War Loans Sports Committee was developing a series of events to sell War Bonds. One of these events was baseball's ultimate subway series, also known as the Tri-Cornered Game.

The *New York Times* exulted over the unusual game, writing:

> Baseball is more than a hundred years old. Generally speaking, youth is rash and often radical. The ancients are the ultra-conservatives. But, despite its respectable old age, the diamond sport is going completely haywire tonight....
>
> This is a three-ply offering involving Giants, Yankees, and Dodgers in a fantastic fray that is certain of only one result. It will attract a gathering of more than 50,000 and will bring in a sale of approximately $6,000,000 in war bonds.[1]

In this fantastic fray, the three New York City teams played in the same game at the Polo Grounds to a crowd of 50,000 fans. One baseball game with three different teams all fielding, hitting, scoring (at least in the case of the Dodgers and the Yankees), and trying to win the title of New York's best. On the day of the game, the teams had similar positions in the standings (all winning records). The Dodgers and Giants were tied for third place in the National League. (After the Tri-Cornered Game, however, the Dodgers went on a skid, losing 16 consecutive games.) The Yankees were tied with the Boston Red Sox for third place in the American League.

The program from the Tri-Cornered Game at the Polo Grounds in 1944 (collection of Stew Thornley).

Holy Cow!

The attendance plan for the Tri-Cornered Game called for each fan to buy a War Bond as a ticket. There were to be 40,000 unreserved tickets at a cost of $25 each (the bond maturity value), 5,809 reserved seats in the lower stands, each costing a $100 bond, and 3,796 box seats for $1,000 bonds each. That in itself added up to 49,605 fans who pledged $4,416,925. To put this amount in perspective, a $25 War Bond in 1944 actually cost each fan $18.75 (the matured bond could be cashed in for $25); $25 would be worth about $334 in 2014, if multiplied by the annual percentage increases in the Consumer Price Index. The $4,416,925 amount pledged by fans in 1944 would be over $59 million in 2014. In addition to the amount raised by fans, New York Mayor Fiorello La Guardia announced that the city would purchase $50 million in War Bonds. And the Bond Clothing Stores chain purchased a $1 million bond in exchange for an autographed scorecard of the game.

Do the Math

On June 25, the day before the game, the *New York Times* wrote, "As major league baseball starts the tenth week of its campaign, Greater New York's three local clubs will pause in their serious pursuit of pennants for the more serious pursuit of war bond dollars."[2] Another story told fans, "The jig-saw puzzle of working out this procedure baffled the best minds of the game until they called upon a mathematics professor at Columbia University, Paul A. Smith. Without scratching his head more than a few hundred times, the professor came up with the following layout, which calls for eighteen half-innings to be played, thus"[3]:

Inning	*1*	*2*	*3*	*4*	*5*	*6*	*7*	*8*	*9*
Field	D Y	D G	Y G	Y D	G D	G Y	D Y	D G	Y G
Bat	Y D	G D	G Y	D Y	D G	Y G	Y D	G D	G Y
Rest	G G	Y Y	D D	G G	Y Y	D D	G G	Y Y	D D

D = Dodgers, Y = Yankees, G = Giants.
In each box, the first letter was for the top half of the inning; the second letter for the bottom of the inning.

This round-robin format had each team come to bat six times, with it batting three times against each of the other two teams' defenses. In case anyone was confused with this scheme, *New York Times* writer Arthur Daley suggested that "a sufficient number of traffic policemen be installed at strategic points in order to avoid snarls of various descriptions."[4]

Pregame Festivities

An hour or so before the game, 500 wounded servicemen were scheduled to arrive to watch the game. A fungo-hitting contest was held, and an 18-year-old pitcher for Brooklyn named Cal McLish won the event with a 416-foot, five-inch shot. It was McLish's rookie season, and he spent 1945 in military service, away from baseball. To his family, he was known as Calvin Coolidge Julius Caesar Tuskahoma McLish.[5] In a throwing-for-accuracy competition for catchers, the Dodgers' Bobby Bragan came closest to throwing the ball from home plate into a barrel at second base, besting five other backstops. There were three heats in a sprint contest. Snuffy Stirnweiss, who would go on to lead the American League in stolen bases in 1944, beat the Giants' Johnny Rucker, posting a time of 7.8 seconds. Snuffy also had the only stolen base in the game (see the box score below). In the other two heats, Dodger sprinters Eddie Miksis and Luis Olmo bested the Giants' Buddy Kerr and the Yanks' Johnny Lindell, respectively.

Before the game, during infield practice, the famous clown prince of baseball, Al Schacht, entertained the crowd. Milton Berle "boisterously ushered in"[6] musical numbers furnished by the Manhattan Beach–like United States Coast Guard band. Former New York City Mayor James J. Walker introduced a contingent of diamond stars from the New York teams, including Zack Wheat, Nap Rucker, Otto Miller (all from the Dodgers), Wally Schang, Bill Dickey (still active but away in the Navy), and Herb Pennock (from the Yankees), and Roger Bresnahan, George "Hooks" Wiltse, and Moose McCormick (from the Giants). Babe Ruth had been scheduled to appear, but he did not show.

The Game

The Dodgers and Yankees squeezed into the visitors' dugout, while the Giants played from the home quarters. The three managers were Joe McCarthy (Yankees), Mel Ott (Giants), and Leo Durocher (Dodgers). Like all the major league teams, the trio of New York clubs had lost players to the war, resulting in 16-year-olds playing alongside 41-year-old veterans. Mel Ott started the game for the Giants as their right fielder and was credited with a putout. Brooklyn pitcher Ralph Branca was the third pitcher for the Dodgers. Seventy years after the game, he recalled, "We got a great crowd. For the players in the game, what was happening was very strange: three teams playing in one nine-inning game. But you couldn't beat the cause."[7] The *New York Daily News* commented that the game was "the wackiest diamond battle ever conceived," and that spectators were "amused and confused."[8]

As for the game, Brooklyn bested its two rivals. In six turns at the plate, the "Flock,"[9] as the *New York Times* referred to the team, tallied five runs. The Yankees managed a single run, and the Giants got only two hits and were shut out. Wrote the *Times*, "Opposed by the Yankees in the first inning, the Dodgers immediately got off on the right foot by clipping Al Lyons for a run on a trio of singles by Goody Rosen, Augie Galan[,] and Dixie Walker."[10] Walker pulled a leg muscle, and future Hall of Famer Paul Waner replaced him in right field. In the second inning, the Dodgers batted again, this time against the Giants' Johnny Allen. Mickey Owen worked a walk and Eddie Stanky hit a double, driving in Owen. Frenchy Bordagaray singled to drive in Stanky, and the Dodgers had two more runs.

In the eighth inning, batting against Frank Seward and the Giants, Brooklyn's Luis Olmo singled, Jack Bolling tripled, and Eddie Stanky drove Bolling home with a fly ball. "Maybe the craziest thing about the game was we [the Dodgers] left before it was over," recalled Branca.[11] "We won and we weren't there to see it finish." Why? The Dodgers had to catch a train to make it to Chicago for a June 28 doubleheader. Hal Gregg, Les Webber, and Ralph Branca combined for the Dodgers' pitching duties. Buddy Kerr made two errors for the Giants against the Yankees in the ninth inning, which allowed the American Leaguers to score their sole run.

Presumably, only a cause as big as a World War II War Bond benefit could have brought together all the New York major league teams on one field for one unforgettable and probably unrepeatable game.

NOTES

1. Arthur Daley, "Sports of the Times," *New York Times*, June 26, 1944.
2. "3 Baseball Clubs Set for Contest," *New York Times*, June 25, 1944.
3. *Ibid.*

4. Daley.
5. Roger Rubin, "Subway Serious," *New York Daily News*, May 11, 2014.
6. John Drebinger, "50,000 Fans See Dodgers Triumph," *New York Times*, June 27, 1944.
7. Rubin.
8. *Ibid.*
9. Drebinger.
10. *Ibid.*
11. Rubin.

New York Giants 5, Brooklyn Dodgers 4: October 3, 1951 BY SCOTT FERKOVICH

On August 11, 1951, the second-place New York Giants trailed their rivals, the Brooklyn Dodgers, by 13 games. From that point until the end of the season, the Giants won 39 of their final 47 games, an incredible .830 clip. The 154-game season ended with both clubs tied for the top spot in the National League, necessitating a three-game playoff series. After splitting the first two contests, the foes faced off at the Polo Grounds on October 3 for the deciding game.

Despite the high stakes, it was a relatively disappointing crowd that made its way to the ballpark that afternoon. Perhaps it was the threat of rain in the forecast, or maybe the 10–0 drubbing that the Dodgers had inflicted on the Giants the previous day. But whatever the excuse, only 34,320 fans were in attendance. However, in the ensuing decades, tens of thousands more would claim that they were there. What the no-shows missed was one of the most legendary games in baseball history.

The Giants were managed by Leo Durocher, who chose Sal "the Barber" Maglie as his starting pitcher. Maglie had gotten his nickname either because he usually looked like he had not shaved or because the fearless pitcher liked to welcome batters to the plate with a little chin music. He had won 23 games so far that season, including five against Brooklyn. His mound opponent for Charlie Dressen's Dodgers was hard-throwing Don Newcombe, who had won 20.

The Dodgers drew first blood, when Pee Wee Reese scored on a one-out single by Jackie Robinson in the opening frame. Maglie pitched his way out of further damage, however.

In the bottom of the second, the Giants' Whitey Lockman singled with one out, bringing up Bobby Thomson, New York's 27-year-old third baseman, who had been sizzling down the stretch. Earlier, on his way to the ballpark, Thomson had said to himself that it would be great if he could somehow produce three hits that day. He got off to a good start in this at bat, lining one down the left field line. Thinking double all the way, he rounded first with his head down, racing for second. The Dodgers' left fielder, Andy Pafko, had a rifle for an arm, and Lockman, not wanting to get thrown out at third, held at second. Pafko threw the ball to shortstop Reese. Thomson was suddenly caught in no-man's land between first and second, and he was out on Reese's relay to first baseman Gil Hodges. It was a costly baserunning gaffe by Thomson. Instead of runners on first and second with one out, the Giants now had a runner on second with two down. The next batter, Willie Mays, flied out to end the inning. For the moment, Thomson wore the goat horns. In the darkening gloom, the Polo Grounds lights were turned on.

In the fifth, Thomson, still wielding a hot bat, doubled to left. His mates, however, were unable to drive him in, and the score stood 1–0 in favor of the Dodgers. It remained that way until the seventh, when Thomson's deep fly to center scored Monte Irvin from third.

In the eighth, the wheels fell off for the Giants and the exhausted Maglie, as the Dodgers scored three runs to take a commanding 4–1 lead before the Barber was replaced by Larry Jansen. Newcombe, meanwhile, was seemingly growing stronger.

Then came the bottom of the ninth. Many of the Polo Grounds crowd had already begun making their way to the exit ramps. But Alvin Dark singled to open the inning. The next batter, Don Mueller, noticed that Dodger first baseman Gil Hodges was playing close to the bag, as Dark edged his way off first. It was an odd strategy on Hodges' part; there was not much chance of Dark attempting to steal. The Giants, after all, needed base runners. Mueller hit a slow grounder to Hodges' right, just out of his reach. Had the first baseman been playing wider of the bag, he may have easily gobbled it up and started a double play. It went as a single to right field, however, with Dark taking third.

Monte Irvin, the leading RBI man on the Giants and their best clutch hitter, fouled out to Hodges for the first out. At that point, an announcement was made in the press box that World Series credentials for Brooklyn's Ebbets Field could be picked up later that evening at the Biltmore Hotel.

Lockman, the next hitter, doubled to left, scoring Dark and sending Mueller to third. Mueller slid awkwardly into the bag, injuring his ankle. Thus, in the middle of the mounting excitement, the game was halted for several moments as Mueller was carted off the field, pinch runner Clint Hartung taking his place. "The corniest possible sort of Hollywood schmaltz," wrote Red Smith, "stretcher bearers plodding away with an injured Mueller between them, symbolic of the Giants themselves."[1]

Next up, Bobby Thomson. To face him, Dressen brought in Ralph Branca. The Brooklyn righty had been the starter in Game One, giving up a homer to Thomson but pitching well in a 3–1 loss.

Gordon McClendon was calling the game on radio for the Liberty Broadcasting System. "Boy, I'm telling you!" he declared. "What they're going to say about this one I don't know!"[2] Branca somehow sneaked a fastball down the middle for strike one. "A ball I should have swung at," Thomson, a fastball hitter, admitted later.[3]

At 3:58 p.m., Branca's second pitch, another fastball, came in high and tight. Thomson swung, his uppercut driving the ball deep toward the corner in left. Pafko, dashing toward the high wall, ran out of room. The ball landed in the first row, just above the 315 feet sign for a three-run home run. Game over. The Polo Grounds shook as the euphoric crowd erupted. Joe King wrote in *The Sporting News*, "[Thomson's homer] touched off scenes in this place which never before had been witnessed in connection with the winning of a pennant."[4]

By any measure, and for pure excitement, Thomson's home run, referred to down the years as "the shot heard 'round the world," belongs on the short list of the most legendary in baseball history. Some consider it the most famous blast ever. Much of the mystique surrounding the home run lies in the iconic, delirious radio call by Giants broadcaster Russ Hodges ("The Giants win the pennant! The Giants win the pennant! The Giants win the pennant! The Giants win the pennant!")[5] Dodger broadcaster Red Barber's call summed it up: "It is … a home run! And the New York Giants win the National League pennant and the Polo Grounds goes wild!"[6] Gordon McClendon described the home run this way: "Going, going gone! The Giants win the pennant!" Then, after a brief pause, "I don't know what to say! I just don't know what to say! It's

GIANTS CAPTURE PENNANT, BEATING DODGERS 5-4 IN 9TH ON THOMSON'S 3-RUN HOMER

Bobby Thomson's blast in the 1951 playoffs may be the most famous home run of all time (collection of Stew Thornley).

the greatest victory in all of baseball history!"[7] Ernie Harwell, calling the game on the Giants' television network, simply said "It's gone!"[8] Felo Ramirez, describing the game in Spanish for Latin-American listeners, cried "Los Gigantes son los campeones!"[9]

As Thomson raced around the bases to be greeted at home by a throng of ecstatic teammates, the stunned Dodgers began the long walk off the field. All except Jackie Robinson, who can be seen in a well-known photograph taken from center field looking in toward second base. The photo shows the scrum of players at home plate, with Thomson somewhere in the middle. Branca, head hanging, is walking dejectedly away from the mound. Robinson, standing all alone just beyond second base, his back to the camera, is staring, hands on hips, toward home, in order to make sure that Thomson actually touched the plate. It is one of the classic photos of sport, a poignant juxtaposition of dejection and giddy victory. Bobby Thomson had certainly gotten his three hits.

Probably no one in the old ballpark was more delighted at Thomson's home run than the on-deck hitter rookie Willie Mays, who later admitted he was terrified at the prospect of having to bat in such a pressure-packed situation.

Branca, of course, took the loss, while Jansen, who pitched one inning, got the win, his 23rd of the season.

Attending the game that day was the motley quartet of comic actor Jackie Gleason, New York restaurateur Toots Shor, FBI chief J. Edgar Hoover, and crooner Frank Sinatra (who had been given four tickets by Durocher). The group had been drinking all day, and just before Thomson hit his home run, Gleason unceremoniously threw up in the lap of Sinatra, a Giant fan. Said Sinatra later, "The fans are going wild and Thomson comes to bat. Then Gleason throws up all over me! Here's one of the all-time games and I don't even get to see Bobby hit that homer! Only Gleason, a Brooklyn fan, would get sick at a time like that!"[10]

Not only did the game feature perhaps the most famous home run ever hit, the most famous radio call in sports broadcasting history, and one of the most iconic sports photos, but it resulted in one of the most wonderful ledes ever in a newspaper article. The day after the game, Red Smith, writing in the *New York Herald-Tribune,* opened his story "Miracle of Coogan's Bluff" with the famous lines "Now it is done. Now the story ends. And there is no way to tell it. The art of fiction is dead. Reality has strangled invention. Only the utterly impossible, the inexpressibly fantastic, can ever be plausible again."[11]

Notes

1. Red Smith, "Miracle of Coogan's Bluff," *New York Herald-Tribune,* October 4, 1951.
2. http://www.joshuaprager.com/books/echoing-green/audio-book.
3. Ray Robinson, *The Home Run Heard 'Round the World* (Mineola, New York: Dover Publications, Inc., 2011), 226.
4. Joe King, "Giants' Playoff Win Sets New High in Drama," *The Sporting News,* October 10, 1951, 7.
5. Joshua Prager, *The Echoing Green* (New York: Pantheon, 2006), 220, 221.
6. *Ibid.*
7. *Ibid.*
8. "Longtime Tigers Broadcaster Harwell dies at 92," http://www.cbssports.com/mlb/story/13346545/longtime-tigers-broadcaster (accessed on February 15, 2014).
9. Prager, 220, 221.
10. Robinson, 241.
11. Smith.

New York Giants 5, Cleveland Indians 2 (10 Innings): September 29, 1954 by Gregory Wolf

"We were beaten by the longest out and the shortest home run of the year," said an incredulous Al Lopez, skipper of the Cleveland Indians, who had just lost to the New York Giants in Game One of the 1954 World Series, featuring two of the most iconic plays in baseball history.[1] Following Willie Mays' over-the-shoulder, run-saving catch in deep center field to preserve a tie game in the eighth inning, Dusty Rhodes belted a walk-off, pinch-hit three-run homer into the short right field porch in the 10th inning to give the Giants a dramatic 5–2 victory in the Polo Grounds. "It was just another game for us," said Giant pitcher Johnny Antonelli. "We won the pennant with finishes like this all season long."[2]

According to the Associated Press, the Giants (who were 97–57 during the regular season) were 8–5 underdogs against the Indians, winners of a then-record 111 games.[3] But a closer look at the squads reveals two very similar teams. The Indians' pitching staff was their shining diamond. Two 23-game winners, Bob Lemon and Early Wynn, helped Cleveland lead the American League with a stellar 2.78 earned run average. New York's pitching staff, though less glamorous than Cleveland's, paced the National League in ERA (3.09) but, unlike its opponent, relied heavily on its relief corps, the best in baseball. Both squads were average hitting teams that led their respective league in round-trippers.

On a warm autumn afternoon, Wednesday, September 29, 1954, the venerable Polo Grounds was packed with 52,751 spectators. Entertainer Perry Como, supported by Artie

White's orchestra, sang the national anthem. Jimmy Barbieri, the 12-year-old captain of Schnectedy's Little League world championship baseball team, threw out the ceremonial first pitch.[4]

Cleveland wasted no time getting to New York's 37-year-old unflappable curveballer, Sal Maglie (14–6 during the regular season), who drilled leadoff hitter Al Smith on his fourth pitch. Bobby Avila, who had led the AL with a career-high .341 batting average, lined a single in front of charging right fielder Don Mueller who fumbled it, allowing Smith to scamper to third. After Larry Doby and Al Rosen popped up, Vic Wertz smashed a long fly ball over Mueller's head. It "caromed off the wall," wrote John Drebinger of the *New York Times*, "and bounded gaily past the Giants bullpen," before Willie Mays gathered it.[5] Wertz slid easily into third as Smith and Avila scored, giving the Tribe a 2–0 lead. Giant manager Leo Durocher, expecting the worst, had swingman Don Liddle warm up in the bullpen. But the "Barber," so named for his command of the inside of the plate, shrugged off the two runs and settled down.

New York faced Cleveland's 33-year-old ace, right-hander Bob Lemon, who had recorded a major league leading 148 victories in the previous seven seasons. He squelched a Giant threat in the first with runners on first and third and cruised into the bottom of the third inning in a scoreless game. Described by Irving Vaughan of the *Chicago Tribune* as "only steady at times," Lemon struggled with control throughout the game. The Giants' Whitey Lockman and Al Dark led off the inning with consecutive singles. Mueller, who enjoyed a career year, batting .342 and leading the NL with 212 safeties, grounded into a force out as Lockman scored. After a walk to Mays, Hank Thompson blasted a single to right, driving in Mueller to tie the game. While Cleveland's Art Houtteman warmed up in the bullpen, Lemon set down Monte Irvin and Davey Williams to extinguish another rally. Lemon, who had been Cleveland's Opening Day center fielder in 1946 before being converted into a pitcher, gathered his composure and allowed only four base runners (three hits) from the fourth through ninth innings.

New York dodged a bullet in the sixth inning when Wertz led off with a single to right field. Mueller attempted to throw him out at first, but the ball shot over Lockman's head. Wertz should have made it to third, thought skipper Lopez, but the slow-footed slugger's protective shin guard "broke loose and stopped him" at second base.[6]

Two innings later, the left-hand hitting Wertz faced Don Liddle, who had just replaced Maglie, with two on and no outs. He belted the southpaw's fourth pitch deep into center field. Mays, just 23-years old, took sight of the ball and raced with his back facing the diamond toward the wall in front of the bleachers, just a shade right of center field. Mays "travel[ed] on the wings of wind," wrote Drebinger, "to make one of his most amazing catchers." Mays, the NL Most Valuable Player in his first full season, spending most of the previous two in the armed forces, whirled around and heaved the ball to the infield as Doby tagged and raced to third. "Durocher was standing in front of me in the dugout," former Giant batboy Bobby Weinstein told the author. "He turned around and said 'Oh no.' And then he saw Mays run the ball down."[7] After the game, Mays took his fielding exploit in stride, "I had it all the way," he said. "There was nothing too hard about it."[8]

The forgotten star of what Gayle Talbot of the Associated Press called a "real hard rock of a baseball game" was New York reliever Marv Grissom, who snuffed out Cleveland's rallies in the eighth, ninth, and tenth innings. Relieving Liddle after Mays' "preposterous catch" of Wertz's flyball, Grissom walked pinch hitter Dale Mitchell to load the bases.[9] After pinch hitter Dave Pope whiffed, catcher Jim Hegan smashed a deep fly

Willie Mays tracked down Vic Wertz's long drive in the first game of the 1954 World Series (collection of Stew Thornley).

ball to left field. "It looked like a homer," said Al Lopez, "but the wind, blowing from left to right, pulled the ball in."[10] With two outs in the ninth, left fielder Irvin dropped Avila's pop-up for a two-base error, putting a man in scoring position for slugger Doby, who had topped the junior circuit in homers (32) and runs batted in (126). Grissom issued an intentional pass to face Rosen, the 1953 MVP, who flied out to end the threat.

In the "throat-clutching" final inning, Wertz led off the tenth with his fourth hit, a double to the gap in left-center. Pinch runner Rudy Regalado moved to third on Sam Dente's sacrifice bunt. With nerves of steel, Old Tomato Face Grissom intentionally walked Pope, then fanned Bill Glynn and induced Lemon, arguably the best-hitting pitcher in baseball, to line out to first to end the inning with the go-ahead run 90 feet from home.[11] The Indians tossed away multiple scoring chances and left seven runners on base in the last three innings.

The bottom of the 10th provided, in the words of John Drebinger, a "breath-taking finish to as nerve-tingling a struggle as any world series had ever seen."[12] After striking out Mueller, Lemon issued a walk to Mays, who moved into scoring position by stealing second. Lemon then issued an intentional pass to Thompson to play for an inning-ending twin killing. The next batter, Dusty Rhodes, pinch-hitting for Irvin, swung at Lemon's first pitch and belted a pop fly down the right field foul line. "We all thought the ball was going to twist foul," said Lopez after the game.[13] Instead, the ball traveled 270 feet and barely cleared the right field stands, bouncing off a fan, and rolling back onto the field. Rhodes' three-run, walk-off homer gave the Giants a stunning 5–2 victory.

Hailed as a "Chinese homer" (a cheap home run) in the insensitive parlance of the time, Rhodes' round-tripper was just the fourth pinch-hit homer in World Series history and the first to end a game. A poor fielder, Rhodes enjoyed a career-year in 1954, batting .341 with 15 homers and 50 RBIs in just 164 at bats. He also hit two of the Giants' record ten pinch-hit home runs that season.

"It was difficult to find the No. 1 hero in the Giants' clubhouse," said sportswriter Roscoe McGowen of the *New York Times*.[14] From team electrifier Mays and the clutch-hitting Rhodes to Grissom's relentless, pressure-packed pitching, the Giants made a heroic statement in their Game One victory.[15]

NOTES

1. Ed Corrigan, "Giants Jubilant After 10th Inning Series Win; Longest Out, Shortest HR Blamed by Lopez," *Newport* (Rhode Island) *Daily News*, September 30, 1954.

2. *Ibid.*

3. Jack Hand, Associated Press, "Rhodes Pinch Hit Homer, Mays' Magnificent Catch Trip Tribe," *Sarasota Herald-Tribune*, September 29, 1954.

4. Barbieri is among the few players who played in the Little League World Series and the big leagues. In 1966, he saw action in 39 games with the Los Angeles Dodgers.

5. John Drebinger, "Giants Win in 10th From Indians, 5–2, On Rhodes' Homer," *New York Times*, September 30, 1954.

6. Hand.

7. Author's telephone interview with Bobby Weinstein on May 28, 2014.

8. Corrigan.

9. Dan Daniel, "Mays' Catch gets Nod," *Newport* (Rhode Island) *Daily News*, September 30, 1954.

10. Louis Effrat, "Cleveland Contends Wind Contributed to Downfall on Two Important Points," *New York Times*, September 30, 1954.

11. Hand.

12. Drebinger.

13. Effrat.

14. Roscoe McGowen, "Heroics of Mays, Rhodes, Grissom Regarded as Routine by Happy Giants," *New York Times*, September 30, 1954.

15. Gayle Tabot, "Giants Win Series Opener, 502, On Rhodes' Pinch Homer, *Newport* (Rhode Island) *Daily News*, September 30, 1954.

New York Mets 8, Philadelphia Phillies 6: April 28, 1962 BY ALAN COHEN

The end of a terrible era, the absence of National League baseball in New York, was at hand. After four intolerably long seasons, young and old alike, who Dick Young of the *New York Daily News* tabbed the "New Breed," could see their National League heroes in the flesh.

The New York Mets had arrived, and, unfortunately for them and their fans, were off to a very bad beginning. They had lost their first nine games and their sole win had occurred on the road in Pittsburgh. The home folks had yet to see a win.

Saturday, April 28, 1962, was a beautiful day for baseball, and going into the season, it was expected that the visiting Philadelphia Phillies, who had finished dead last the prior season, could be easy prey for the New Yorkers.

It was fairly simple to get a ticket for a Mets game at the Polo Grounds in 1962. The home team drew only 922,000 in their first season, and many of those came to see the Dodgers and Giants. On April 28, 1962, it was especially easy for the ladies who got in for free on "Ladies Day." The attendance was announced at 16,987, 10,978 who paid their way in and most of whom had arrived at the ball yard in Harlem via subway.

The Phillies batted first, of course, and one thing that was obvious was that their uniform numbers took into consideration that some of the spectators may be visually challenged. Large maroon figures emerged from the gray road uniforms of the visitors.

In that very first inning, the fans got to see four of the Philadelphia players cross home plate as the visitors raced to an early lead. It was ugly for the Mets as starter Jay Hook, who had secured the New Yorkers' first-ever win earlier that week, yielded a walk to Tony Taylor and a single to Johnny Callison before Tony Gonzalez pulled a homer down the right field line to put the Phils up 3–0, three batters into the game. Don Demeter, made the score 4–0 with the Phillies' second homer of the inning, a blast that landed atop the left field roof.

When Clayton Dalrymple followed Demeter's homer with a single, manager Casey Stengel signaled for Bob Miller to come in from the bullpen. This was Robert L. Miller, who was at one time known as Robert Gemeinweiser. Mr. Miller, one might say, was well travelled. In his 17-year career, he made 12 stops, and played for ten different teams. He wore 16 different uniform numbers and Mets aficionados remember him as one of two Bob Millers to play for the 1962 squad.

Miller calmed things down and Stengel's men tried to climb back into the game. Charlie Neal sliced a ball down the right field line that carried over the wall for a home run off Jim Owens leading off the second inning to put New York on the scoreboard. But the Phillies reclaimed the four-run advantage when Dalrymple homered off Miller in the fourth inning. After Miller was removed from the game for a pinch hitter in the bottom of the fifth, Dave Hillman entered the game for the Mets and was greeted by Demeter's second homer of the game. The score was 6–1, and it appeared as if the New Yorkers would go down to defeat for the 13th time in their brief 14-game history. Phillie manager Gene Mauch made a defensive replacement, removing Wes Covington and inserting Billy Klaus.

As chronicled by Dick Young, "So it was 6–1 and you'd think the fans would go home, or boo, or throw things. Not The New Breed."[1]

And then, as if by the sheer force of a young boy's wishes, the Mets awoke. After a walk to Gus Bell, the fans erupted and cheered the team on. Frank Thomas launched his fifth homer of the season to the seats in left field to pull the New Yorkers within three runs of the lead. Thomas would go on to hit 32 homers in the season, establishing a single-season Met record that would last until 1975. Charlie Neal followed with his second homer of the game, this one landing atop the roof in left, knocking sore-armed Jim Owens out of the game. Jack Hamilton entered the game and Gilbert Raymond Hodges of Brooklyn greeted him with the third consecutive Met homer and the Amazin's were within a run of the lead. The blast was estimated at 450 feet and landed in the upper deck in left field. To one observer, it was a blast reminiscent of the days of glory.[2] The Polo Grounds jutted out severely from about 250 feet down the line to well over 400 feet in left-center field. Hodges himself "never thought it would go in [to the seats]. Not that far out there. I was just praying for it to hit the wall so I could get on, the way I have been going."[3]

Hodges was in the twilight of his career, and the homer, his second of the season, gave him a career total of 363. He finished the season and his career with 370, one better than Ralph Kiner, who was in the first of his more than 50 years as an announcer with the team. At the time, it gave Hodges more home runs than any other right-handed hitter in National League history. The record was short-lived, however, as Willie Mays, who had slugged his first Polo Grounds round-tripper on May 28, 1951, socked the 371st of his 660 National League homers on April 19, 1963.

The Mets would not have another base hit in the sixth inning, but they would take the lead. With one out, Frank Sullivan, who had relieved Hamilton, walked catcher Chris Cannizzaro (or Canzinari as he was called by Stengel), and John DeMerit was sent into the game to run for Cannizzaro. Next up was pinch hitter Sammy Taylor, who was also walked and then replaced by a pinch runner, Rod (or "Runner Rod" as announcer Bob Murphy loved to call him) Kanehl. A grounder to the first baseman by Rich Ashburn advanced the runners to second and third. That brought up Ed Bouchee, pinch-hitting for Elio Chacon against new Phillie pitcher Chris Short. By this point, even the most ardent of grandstand scorekeepers was on the verge of throwing in his pencil. Short, on his first toss of the game, uncorked a wild pitch. DeMerit scored easily from third, and Kanehl scampered home from second base with the lead run. Kanehl, when interviewed after the game, indicated that coach Solly Hemus had given him the green light rounding third. Hemus was of another opinion. The throw from catcher Dalrymple to pitcher Short seemed to have Kanehl nailed. However, "the pitcher was a little lax,"[4] and Kanehl's hook slide eluded the tag and the Mets had the lead.

Roger Craig took the mound for the home team in the seventh inning and pitched the final three innings, allowing only one hit, to get his first victory in a Met uniform. New York gave him an insurance run in the eighth inning as Jim Hickman homered off Ed Keegan for the Mets' fifth round-tripper of the game. Hickman had replaced Rich Ashburn in center field in the top of the inning, and it was his first major league homer.

Harold Rosenthal, in the next day's *Herald Tribune*, summed things up. "They racked up a six-run inning, batted around, and ran the bases like dervishes, while, in the dugout, Casey Stengel did everything but blow goofus powder into the eyes of the opposition.... He selected pinch runners like a French chef selecting pullets for a state feed and he came up with a dish just as tasty."[5]

It can truly be said that the win was a team effort. At one point or another, 19 Met players were in the contest.

After the win, Casey Stengel jogged all the way to the clubhouse in deepest center field.[6] There, he was greeted and congratulated by M. Donald Grant, the Mets' president. "This is the greatest thrill of all. Those fans make all the others in the world look sick."[7]

NOTES

1. Dick Young, "Mets Explode! Bomb Phils with 5 HRs in 8–6 Thriller," *New York Sunday News*, April 29, 1962.
2. Harold Rosenthal, *New York Herald Tribune*, April 29, 1962.
3. Young.
4. Young.
5. Rosenthal.
6. Jimmie McDowell, "Mets Score Over Phillies by 8–6, Six Markers in Sixth Bring Joy to Casey," *(Trenton, New Jersey) Sunday Times-Advertiser*, April 29, 1962.
7. Young.

National League Latino Players 5, American League Latino Players 2: October 12, 1963
BY RORY COSTELLO *AND* ROBERT DOMINGUEZ

The last baseball game ever played at the Polo Grounds was the one and only Latin American major league players' game. The charity benefit match was not close—the National League defeated the American League, 5–2, and the AL scored only in the ninth inning. Nor did it have any official status. Nonetheless, it gained lasting significance.

Four Hall of Famers took part: NL player-manager Roberto Clemente, Juan Marichal, Orlando Cepeda, and Luis Aparicio. And Tony Oliva and Orestes "Minnie" Miñoso of the AL squad have much support for a place in Cooperstown. In later years, this game became known as an "All-Star" contest. At the time, though, it was billed simply as a "players' game." Most of the other *peloteros* there that day had solid big league careers, but there were a few good journeymen, too. As of Opening Day 2014, Latin Americans made up 23 percent of major league players.[1] On October 12, 1963, stretching was required to fill out the rosters.

For all, however, regional and national honor was involved. As Manny Mota said in 2013: "It was a question of prestige and pride, because we were representing our countries. It was a rare event and all the players had a grand passion for this game because they knew what it signified for us and Latino fans. We were all together for the first time, and, as it turned out, the last time."[2]

Marichal and Cepeda also discussed what it meant. Said Marichal, "It was historic. There was a lot of emotion among all the players, and you could tell the fans were excited about it, too." Cepeda added, "It didn't matter that it was for charity and that it wasn't a 'real' all-star game. When you put on your uniform, you played hard and you tried even harder to win. And that's what everybody did in that game."[3]

Marichal underscored Cepeda's point. "There was a lot of competition in those days between the National League and the American League, and each member of the team really wanted to beat those guys. Everybody gave 100 percent."[4]

The event had extra cultural flavor. Bandleaders Tito Puente and Tito Rodríguez and singer La Lupe performed on the field before the game. Ralph Paniagua, a Latino music promoter and founder of LatinoBaseball.com, said, "When you consider the legendary players involved and the legendary musicians who performed, it was just such an amazing and historic day for the Latino culture that we'll probably never see again."[5]

This game had been in the planning stages since at least early August 1963.[6] The organizer was New York radio and television personality Guy LeBow. According to NL team member Joe Christopher, LeBow "was deep in Latin American business and baseball. He was good friends with Vic Power. He got everybody together that day."[7]

New York entrepreneur O. Roy Chalk was also involved. Chalk—who played sandlot ball as a boy with Lou Gehrig—owned Trans Caribbean Airways and New York City's Spanish-language newspaper, *El Diario–La Prensa*.[8] *El Diario* helped conduct the pregame ceremonies, during which Trans Caribbean executives presented awards.[9]

The first players aboard were the managers, Clemente and Héctor López.[10] The Hispanic-American Baseball Federation, which promoted baseball for Spanish-speaking boys in the U.S., got some of the proceeds from the game.[11] It is easy to see why Clemente got involved—he was known for his goodness where youth was concerned. Marichal, Julián Javier, and José "Joe" Azcué were next to join; further announcements followed.[12]

The game took place on Saturday afternoon. It may be no coincidence that it was Columbus Day, which has also been celebrated in various Latin American countries.[13] However, the date and venue may both simply have reflected availability.

Tickets cost $1.75 to $3.50.[14] Thus, the gate receipts were somewhere between $25,000 and $50,000—based on the announced crowd of 14,235. The number in attendance was far less, though, according to Edward Mandt, one of the few Anglo fans in the park.[15]

The players received $175 apiece. "We didn't make a lot of money back then," Marichal said, laughing. "So whatever it was, it helped." Cepeda recalled lining up in the clubhouse after the game to collect. "After me, Roberto Clemente and Vic Power got paid, we got in line again," he said, also laughing. "The guy never realized he ended up paying us twice."[16]

It is likely that the game was carried on WHOM radio, New York's main Spanish-language station of the day. Behind the mike would have been famed broadcaster Buck Canel, the 1985 Ford Frick Award winner, who was WHOM's sports director.

As the table below shows, Cuba had been the prime source of Latino baseball talent in those days, though Fidel Castro turned off the tap after taking power in January 1959. Today's mother lodes—the Dominican Republic and Venezuela—were just emerging.

Participants in the Latino Players' Game—by Nationality[17]

Cuba (16)
Joe Azcué, Ed Bauta, Julio Bécquer, Leo Cárdenas, Mike de la Hoz,* Chico Fernández, Tony González, Román Mejías, Minnie Miñoso, Aurelio Monteagudo,* Tony Oliva, Pedro Ramos, Cookie Rojas,* Diego Seguí, Tony Taylor, Zoilo Versalles

Dominican Republic (4)
Felipe Alou, Julián Javier, Juan Marichal, Manny Mota

Mexico (1)
Rubén Amaro

Panama (1)
Héctor López

Puerto Rico (5)
Orlando Cepeda, Roberto Clemente, Félix Mantilla, Vic Power, Félix Torres*

U.S. Virgin Islands (2)
Joe Christopher,*Al McBean

Venezuela (2)
Luis Aparicio, Vic Davalillo*

United States
Cuno Barragán, Joe Pignatano
* Did not play

It is noteworthy that two men from the U.S. Virgin Islands were on the NL roster. The V.I. culture is not Latino, but the islands' ties to Latin America are tangible. St. Croix and St. Thomas are just east of Puerto Rico, and for many years, they were a small but steady wellspring of baseball talent. Many islanders starred in the Puerto Rican Winter League. What's more, Christopher and McBean both married Puerto Rican women and learned Spanish.[18]

The U.S.-born players also point out the lack of Latino depth back then. During the 1963 season, not one man born in Latin America played catcher in the National League. Cuno Barragán, from Sacramento, California, was the son of Mexican immigrants.[19] He had played in just one game that season for the Chicago Cubs, with one at bat and three innings behind the plate. The NL's only Caribbean backstop that year was Elmo Plaskett, another Virgin Islander, who caught three games for the Pittsburgh Pirates.

Instead of Plaskett, though, Joe Pignatano played for the NL. Pignatano, an Italian American from Brooklyn, stretched the definition of Latino to the utmost. His playing days in the majors had ended in 1962; in 1963, he spent time with the Buffalo Bisons and Rochester Red Wings of the International League. He worked in Brooklyn during his off-seasons, though, so he was available on short notice. He had also played Dominican winter ball, where he was a teammate of Felipe Alou and Manny Mota.

Also notable: Julio Bécquer had just one at bat in the majors in 1963 (he had spent most of his time after 1961 in Mexican ball). Aurelio Monteagudo, a 19-year-old rookie, got into four games with the Kansas City A's.

Along with the musical guests, the pregame ceremonies had other notable features.

- **A Home Run Derby:** The AL won, with two, by López and Power. Alou hit the NL's lone homer.[20]
- **Awards:** Cepeda accepted one on behalf of his father, Perucho Cepeda, who was honored posthumously for his contributions to baseball in Puerto Rico.[21] Also, the younger Cepeda was named the most popular player in the majors, Marichal the top pitcher, and Power the top player.[22]
- **A Latin American Baseball Hall of Fame:** Perucho Cepeda, Adolfo Luque, Hiram Bithorn, and Pancho Coimbre were named.[23] Nothing else is known of this hall, though, implying that it may never have actually been established.[24]

As for the game itself, it had its moments. Mota, who developed into one of the best pinch hitters ever, had a two-run single batting for Marichal in the fourth. AL starter Pedro Ramos, who allowed four runs in five innings despite striking out eight, took the loss. McBean got the win with four shutout innings in relief of Marichal. McBean also provided the most exciting play in the sixth inning, when he was thrown out at the plate trying to stretch a triple into an inside-the-park homer. "There was a Listerine sign in left field [right of the 422-foot marker]," he recalled in 2014, "and that's where I hit the ball. It was a lot of fun."[25]

By one account, the Latino players' game was intended to be an annual affair. It proved impossible to reunite all the principal figures, however, primarily because a suitable date could not be found.[26]

In autumn 1963, though, the handwriting was already on the wall for the Polo Grounds. In early September, United Press International called the game of October 12 "Baseball's Grand Finale" at Coogan's Bluff, repeating that point a month later.[27] Along with the players' grand passion, the game also echoed part of the stadium's past (the New York Cubans)—and, more broadly, heralded baseball's future.

NOTES

1. "2014 Opening Day Rosters Feature 224 Players Born Outside the U.S.," MLB.com press release, April 1, 2014. Based on the pool of 853 players (750 active 25-man roster players and 103 disabled or restricted major league players) on March 30 rosters.

2. Robert Dominguez, "The Forgotten All-Star Game," *New York Daily News*, July 10, 2013.

3. *Ibid.*

4. *Ibid.*

5. *Ibid.*

6. "Benefit Game Slated," *New Castle (PA) News*, August 8, 1963.

7. Telephone interview, Joe Christopher with Rory Costello, November 15, 2014. LeBow died in August 2008, at the age of 92.

8. David Stout, "O. Roy Chalk, 88, Entrepreneur With Diverse Holdings, Is Dead," *New York Times*, December 2, 1995. Chalk and Gehrig (as well as George and Ira Gershwin) lived on the same block in Harlem. "Chalk Talk," *The New Yorker*, April 25, 1959, 36.

9. Edward Mandt, "Latin American All-Stars: Los Niños del Otoño," *Baseball Research Journal* 17 (1988): 23. Marco Emilio Guerrero, "Con los campeones," *(Santo Domingo, Dominican Republic) Listín Diario*, April 25, 2007.

10. "Marichal, Javier on All-Star Club," *Philadelphia Inquirer*, September 8, 1963.

11. "Cronin Loop Bows Again—in Latin Tilt," *The Sporting News*, October 26, 1963, 22.

12. "Cepeda, Alou Sign for PG Game," *Long Island Star-Journal*, September 12, 1963. This announcement also included Tony González and Zoilo Versalles. "Ramos, Tartabull Sign for PG Fray," *Long Island Star-Journal*, September 18, 1963. José Tartabull appears to have withdrawn. "Aparicio Signs for L-A Game," *Long Island Star-Journal*, September 21, 1963. This announcement also included Al McBean and Ed Bauta.

13. In the U.S., Columbus Day has been celebrated on the second Monday in October only since 1970.

14. "Sports," *Cue: The Weekly Magazine of New York Life*, October 12, 1963.

15. Mandt, 23.

16. Dominguez. This suggests that somebody other than Guy LeBow was the paymaster.

17. Guerrero. Confirmation for Clemente and López as managers: "Baseball Pokes Nose into Football Scene," Tonawanda News (North Tonawanda, New York), October 12, 1963.

18. Rory Costello, *Baseball in the Virgin Islands* (New York: Hungry Joe Publishing, 2000), 27.

19. Rick Cabral, "The Long Journey of Facundo Antonio 'Cuno' Barragan," http://www.baseballsacramento.com/Spotlight-CBarragan.html (accessed on June 15, 2017).

20. Mandt, 23.

21. "National Latins Rally to Down Americans, 5–2," *Fresno (California) Bee*, October 13, 1963.

22. "Cronin Loop Bows Again—in Latin Tilt."

23. "National Latins Rally to Down Americans, 5–2."

24. The authors' efforts turned up nothing else, and the hall's existence was also unknown to three experts on Latin American baseball: Jorge Colón (official historian of the Puerto Rican Winter League), Peter C. Bjarkman, and Tito Rondón. The Puerto Rican origin of three of the four players honored—Cepeda, Coimbre, and Bithorn—could have reflected either or both of two things. First, Puerto Ricans were (and are) the largest Latino population in New York City. And second, Trans Caribbean Airways had its hub in San Juan.

25. Telephone interview, Al McBean with Rory Costello, November 1, 2014.

26. Guerrero.

27. "Marichal, Javier on All-Star Club," and "Join Latin Team," *Bridgeport (Connecticut) Post*, October 6, 1963.

The Polo Grounds
View from the Bleachers

ARNOLD HANO

Watching ball games at the Polo Grounds was sometimes a family affair, sometimes a solo project.

We were three generations of Giant fans. We would sit in a row in the lower deck of the ballpark between home and first, my grandfather Ike, my father, my brother Alfie, and me. Three generations stretching back to the game's early roots. Ike had seen Honus Wagner. My father saw Christy Mathewson. My brother and I saw Carl Hubbell and Hack Wilson. Later on, I would take my son Stephen to see his first game in the Polo Grounds. He saw Jackie Robinson and Willie Mays. Four generations of Giant fans. Talk about masochism! When we were together—Ike, Pop, Alfie, and me—I would lean across and say to Ike, "Tell me about Honus Wagner."

My grandfather was a big man. He was a policeman. He had saved kids from drowning in the East River. He talked bad guys out of their guns and then knocked them cold with his heavy fist. He was my hero.

"Honus Wagner had hands as big as pillows," Ike said.

Today, at 91, I look back to that moment. I envision Honus Wagner, scooping up a ground ball in those hands big as pillows and firing to first. That was a hundred years ago. Together, we had seen Honus Wagner, Christy Mathewson, Dizzy Dean, Carl Hubbell, Mel Ott, Hack Wilson, Rogers Hornsby, and Willie Mays. A roll call of Hall of Famers. Home runs shot into the short right field seats. Blazing fastballs poured past the game's greatest hitters. Dazzling plays in the field. Umpires calling them right and wrong. The game, before us, in the Polo Grounds.

Baseball has the ability to hold people together yet allows us to be ourselves. I would ask my father who was better, Bob Meusel or Emil "Irish" Meusel, left fielders for the Yankees and Giants, respectively. My father was grave and thoughtful, a lawyer once whose practice had dried up during the Depression. "Bob has the stronger arm," he replied. "Emil has more power." Pop hated nicknames. Never Irish. Always Emil. "But who's better?" I persisted. He would shrug, shake his head, and say, "You decide."

Eventually I weaned myself away from the family and became a bleacherite. For one thing, the price was right—50 cents for a seat on a wooden plank, later, 55. During the game, I would collect used soda bottles and redeem them for two cents each at the neighborhood candy store. More important, I had all that open space before me, the whole field. The two dugouts. The two foul poles. I felt I was riding the center fielder's back, looking into the infield play.

When the Giants were scheduled to leave New York, *Sports Illustrated* flew me from California back to the Polo Grounds to cover the last game of the 1957 season. I sat in the bleachers and listened to fans chant, "Go, Horace, go. Stay, Willie, stay." I still own the rain check stub for that final game, with the big 77—the last home game of that last season.

I retain my memories. I remember Mel Ott, raising his right leg and then dropping it as he buried a pitch in the right field seats. I remember a catch by Fred Lindstrom, playing center field because his knees did not allow him to bend for ground balls at third base. He could still run. He raced to the fence in right center and leaped high to one hand the ball as he crashed into the wall. Gus Suhr, who had hit that drive, stood and gave a long stare at Lindstrom. The next day's papers said it might have been the finest catch ever at the Polo Grounds. I saw it. I also saw Willie Mays make the catch and throw of a ball hit by Vic Wertz that saved the first game of the 1954 World Series. I sat in the bleachers that day and was within 50 feet of Mays when he ran down the drive. I wrote about it in a book, *A Day in the Bleachers*, still in print a half-century later.

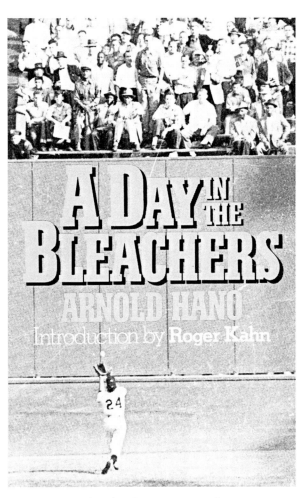

A Day in the Bleachers remains a favorite among baseball fans more than 50 years after Arnold Hano wrote it (collection of Stew Thornley).

Not all my memories are so heroic. One day, Cincinnati outfielder Harry Craft hit a fly ball along the left field line that either wrapped around the pole for a home run or drifted before the pole into the seats for a harmless foul ball. The umpire at home plate called it a home run. The Giants exploded. Catcher Harry Danning began to jump up and down, yelling and pointing. Pitcher Harry Gumbert joined in. So did manager Bill Terry. Eventually each man was ejected. The riotous mood seemed quelled. But not so. Shortstop Billy Jurges decided it was his turn. He faced off with second base umpire George Magerkurth.

The two men went jaw to jaw. A faint spray of saliva came out of the umpire's mouth. Jurges wiped it away. But when the spray continued, Jurges took a step back and released an oyster of his own, right in Magerkurth's face.

The umpire punched Jurges.

Jurges punched him back.

The two men wrestled together and fell to the ground, clawing and punching. Finally players and other umpires cleaved the two men apart. Jurges was, of course, tossed out of the game. I believe he was suspended for ten.

Utility infielder Lou Chiozza replaced him. The very next day, on a pop fly hit into short left field, Chiozza raced back and left fielder Joe Moore raced in. The two men collided. Chiozza was carted off with a broken leg. It must be the first time in baseball history that one man's saliva had broken a teammate's leg.

It was not the only time I saw Jurges in a low moment.

Pitcher Bucky Walters let go a fast ball that struck Jurges on the left temple, fracturing his skull. Players did not wear helmets back then. Jurges lay still and we in the seats fretted: was he dead? Then his body twitched. He recovered, but I do not think he ever played again.

The years have passed. Batting helmets. Batting gloves. Designated hitters. Sixteen teams in a league. Salaries ballooned. So have ticket prices. My father, my grandfather, and my brother are dead.

But my son lives on, a Giant fan. I took him, 11 years old, to that first game he ever saw, in 1955 at the Polo Grounds, a Giant-Dodger game, and we sat in the grandstand. In the first inning, Giant pitcher Jim Hearn gave up a hit and two walks, and the bases were loaded with Gil Hodges up. Hodges lifted a fly ball along the left field line that gently brushed the left field overhang as it descended.

In his very first inning, Stephen had seen a grand slam.

A few innings later, pitcher Jim Hearn hit a home run of his own.

And in the seventh inning, Stephen saw something I had never seen before.

Jackie Robinson came up with the bases loaded again, and again with nobody out. Robinson lifted a pop fly over second baseman Davey Williams' head. The three runners started to run, then paused. Would Williams catch the falling ball? Williams leaped, and the ball ticked off his gloved fingers and popped into the air. The runners raced ahead. But Williams did not give up; his momentum carried him forward and he grasped the ball inches before it hit the grass. One out. He whirled and threw to Alvin Dark, standing at second base with the ball before the runner could scramble back. Two out. Dark tossed the ball to Whitey Lockman, the Giants' first baseman before the retreating runner reached the bag. Three out.

A triple play.

Stephen's first game.

He sat back, elated, exhausted. And later, dejected. The Giants lost that game, 5–3. Welcome to the big leagues, sonny boy.

That's baseball. It exalts you. It breaks your heart. I learned lessons out there in the Polo Grounds. Lessons of the game and of life. Baseball is a game of thrills and spills. So is life. It features courage under fire. So does life. It is drama and melodrama and even comedy. Take umpire George Magerkurth.

One day at Ebbets Field a fan ran out of the stands and tackled Magerkurth. The two men wrestled and flailed away before the startled players and others could pry them apart.

Meanwhile in the stands, a confederate of the assailant was busy picking the pockets of fans standing, leaning forward, their wallets easy prey. It's true, this did not take place in the Polo Grounds but surely the Jurges-Magerkerth scuffle on the Polo Grounds floor became Act One of this two-act farce.

So some of us are richer for the experience. Some of us are poorer. I am who I am because I sat in that great oval arena of baseball and saw the balletic grace of a double play and the clumsy foolery of three men surrounding a fly ball and nobody bothering to catch it. And I saw Willie Mays.

I witnessed victory and defeat, and became part of each.

People today will ask me, where did I grow up? And I answer, only half in jest, I grew up in the Polo Grounds.

The Book and the Batboy

David Butwin

I had a clear vision of the little paperback with the waxy maroon cover. *Bat Boy of the Giants* was full of colorful anecdotes about a New York Giant batboy in the mid–1940s, Garth Garreau, who served such baseball stars as Willard Marshall, Johnny Mize, Sid Gordon, Buddy Kerr, and Bobby Thomson.

In the late 40s, even as I devoured books in the [St. Paul] Mattocks library about sports heroes, I also had a keen interest in woodsmen and pioneers like Jim Bridger, Kit Carson, Wild Bill Hickok (who was plugged by Jack McCall the night he failed to sit with his back to the wall, a mistake I promised I'd never make in a public place), and my main man, Davy Crockett. On a visit to 1735, our family friend Meridel Le Seuer, novelist, prairie progressive, and later a feminist idol, took note of the Crockett biography I was reading and a year or so later came out with a children's book, *Chanticleer of Wilderness Road: A Story of Davy Crockett*. I have an inscribed copy: "From Davy Crockett to Davy Butwin (who introduced us!) and Miriam, Joey and Frances. Davy and the People will make Peace! Love Meridel, Christmas 1951." I treasure that book and others of Meridel's.

On the sports shelves, I passed up the unwieldy tomes of John R. Tunis for books like *Backboard Magic* (whose author, Howard M. Brier, has been called a master of the genre, and from which I vividly recalled the term "crip" for lay-up). These were stories of schoolboy athletes who overcome great odds—shrimpy stature (which particularly spoke to me) or a nasty coach—to make the starting team and win the big game. And there was Johnny Tremain, the boy hero of a classic about an apprentice silversmith in 1770s Boston who overcomes greater odds than a nasty coach when a jet of molten silver disfigures his hand. But the best read of all was the book about a mere batboy.

When I mention the book to [sister] Miriam, she says, "I read it too. I loved that book. I wanted to be a batgirl." Over the years, I thought about the high school boy who lived in a place called Teaneck, New Jersey, and spent a season or two at the Polo Grounds around a team I hadn't learned to hate by 1949, the year the book came out. In the mid–80s I moved out of New York to a Jersey suburb a mile or two from Teaneck, and one day I decided to look for Garth Garreau. The most I could turn up at the Teaneck public library was a page in his high school yearbook, showing a smiling boy with a shining pompadour—"Generous, gregarious and genial Garth…." Then on a pass through the Internet, in a rundown on "Classic Baseball Paperbacks of the 40s and 50s," a thumbnail image of *Bat Boy of the Giants* jumped out from across six decades—same maroon cover, same smiling boy in Giants uniform, three bats crossed on his shoulder.

213

Plumbing the Internet further, I felt a shiver run through me: "Grover, Garreau, and Patterson crash off USS Coral Sea...."

Below a passage headed "The AJ2 Crash of November 8, 1954" was an account posted recently by an ex-Navy flier who had replaced an airman lost in an accident off the aircraft carrier *Coral Sea*: "Our first task was to pick up and pack for shipment home the personal belongings of LT Grover and LTJG Garreau, whose stateroom we were assigned. Their squadron mates apparently had not felt up to the task. At the time I don't think I thought about it too much, but in retrospect it was rather a macabre way to start duty aboard ship with a new squadron."

How many Garth Garreaus could there be? I sent an email to the ex-flier, more or less asking for confirmation and mentioning my regard for the book. Kenneth Jennings (Bertie) Wooster, of Cortland, New York, in the upstate Finger Lakes, wrote back: "Yes, I knew that Garth

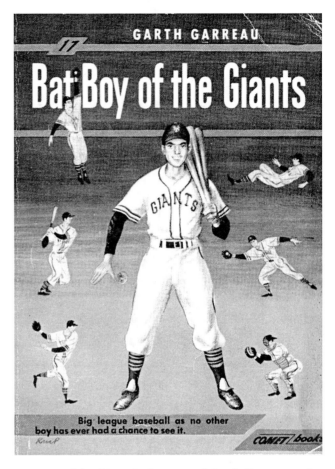

Bat Boy of the Giants is the story of Garth Garreau and his time picking up bats for the Giants in the 1940s (collection of Stew Thornley).

Garreau had been the bat boy for the Giants during the 1947 season and that he had written the book.... Although I stepped into his place, figuratively into his shoes and literally into his bunk, after he was killed, I am not certain whether I had ever met him. It was all so long ago."

Wooster, in his early 80s, a retired college math teacher, said he and Garreau had trained with separate squadrons at the Naval Auxiliary Air Station at Sanford, Florida, as bombardier/navigators with a top-secret nuclear bombing group employing a special plane, the AJ Savage. The plane was designed to deliver the Mark 6 atomic bomb from a carrier deck at a time when Russia was the mortal enemy. He distinctly remembered landing on the *Coral Sea* "two weeks to the day after the crash" as it steamed off Athens.

From another ex-flier whom I tracked down via the Internet, Jack Brennan, came a stunning eyewitness description of the crash. Brennan said the *Coral Sea*, deployed with the Sixth Fleet, was participating in "war games" off the Turkish coast the day of the accident. When Garreau and a mate took off early on November 8, 1954, in the huge long-range bomber, Brennan was manning a tiny rotating cabin called a gun director, from which he could search the skies for enemy targets. His was a cold-eyed account, dramatic in its understatement; I read it as though I were on the deck that November day.

> The pilot brought his engines up to take-off power level; the jet engine was blasting a red-white tail; the signal was made to launch; the huge fuel-laden plane shot forward. But because of the slant of the deck, the right wing was noticeably lower than the left wing. After clearing the carrier, the pilot immediately tried to level the wings; the move went too far. In a split second, the left wing was now lower than the right wing had been a moment before. The desperate pilot made a radical move to right the plane but this time the right wing tip caught the sea. The plane cartwheeled into the sea and there followed an instantaneous, gigantic explosion of aviation fuel. As we passed the tremendous fire-ball fifty yards to starboard, the radiant heat was so intense that I almost panicked as to whether I should get out of the gun director. As the flames moved further aft on our right-hand side, I was looking directly into the Fleet Admiral's eyes. He never moved his eyes to mine; he just kept looking straight ahead with his chin resting on his arms. Only the life-jacketed body of the enlisted crewman was recovered.

Bertie Wooster put me in touch with three or four Navy fliers who might have known Garreau. Bill Edwards, who saw the mishap from the *Coral Sea*'s sister ship *Lake Champlain* as the two were steaming parallel that day, added a touching detail: "Garth really enjoyed his cigar and a good laugh, in that order. I believe all three in the crew smoked cigars and it was said that on low level flights, no one could see thru [*sic*] the cockpit from one side to the other."

Paul Wells, another flyboy, capped his note with a jarring revelation: "Garth and his pilot were very close friends (as was true, I think, of all our crews). In fact, Garth was engaged to his pilot's sister and they were to be married when that deployment was over."

Part of me wanted to hunt down a surviving friend or loved one, but the other part wanted to let go—the reporter who had always hated approaching a grieving source with, "Hi, what can you tell me about your dead son (husband, wife, best friend), and do you have a photo we could run in the paper?" I thought about how that dark day lined up with my own life. On the day of the crash, I was a kid reporter of 14, a few days from covering the Twin City football game for the school newspaper. I punched up the *Times* archive on the computer. And there on November 11, 1954, was a headline: "EX-GIANT BATBOY KILLED."

On page 18 was a three-paragraph story, with the subhead "Parents Get Word of the Death of Garth Garreau in Crash":

> The New York Giants received word yesterday that their former batboy Lieut. (j.g.) Garth Garreau, who wrote a book about his experiences with the baseball club, had died in an airplane crash in the Mediterranean Sea.
>
> Lieutenant Garreau's parents, Mr. and Mrs. Claude Garreau Sr. of Saddle River Township, N.J., were notified by the Navy Department that their son crashed Oct. 8 and his body had not been recovered.
>
> Lieutenant Garreau, who was 23 years old, served as the Giants' batboy in 1945–46–47 and wrote the book[, *Batboy of the Giants*,] in collaboration with Joe King, New York sports writer. He entered the Navy three years ago after his graduation from Michigan State College, where he was a member of the baseball and wrestling teams.

Never mind that the October 8 date was a month off, I was glad to learn that Garth Garreau, who took a ribbing in the book from some of the Giants for his weak arm, had realized his dream of making the college baseball team. On that Armistice Day (as it was called then), the front page of the *Times*, topped by a story about the dedication the day before of the Iwo Jima memorial at Arlington National Cemetery, was etched everywhere with the Cold War, which had brought Garth Garreau to the Med. I tried to place Garth, if not in his ill-fated plane or in a romance with his buddy's sister, then in late autumn 1954. I figured he would have been gloating about his Giants, who had swept the Cleveland Indians in the World Series a month earlier.

Where to turn next? Well, of course. Find the book and read it again.

A week later, I tore open a package and there was the book that had swept me up so long ago, the batboy smiling from the maroon cover. I sat down to read again about Garth Garreau's excellent summer, wincing at his unquenchable optimism, at his treasuring of good luck omens, at his plans for becoming a chemical engineer. Among the Teaneck references was Bischoff's, the soda fountain still there on Cedar Lane where he gathered with his buddies after school. Bobby Thomson, a villain to me and all of Brooklyn for his infamous homer in 1951, was one of Garth's favorite Giants. On opening day 1947, the rookie Thomson kneels beside the nervous batboy in the on-deck circle, telling him, "I need a hit and you'll have to do something about it," then reaches over and crosses one of Garth's fingers over the other for good luck. Thomson smacks a homer and after flying around the bases stops to shake hands with the stunned batboy whose fingers are still crossed, telling Garth, "Nice going, bub."

On a road trip in Pittsburgh, Johnny Mize and the old coach, Hank Gowdy, invite Garth to visit, of all things, an art gallery. Hank Gowdy? That long-retired player's name for some reason graced the smallish MacGregor catcher's glove that I got with Green (or was it Gold Bond?) stamps in 1954 and which Joe used as the starting backstop for the Yankees in the Highland Park Little League. I still haul out the glove for ball tossing in the front yard, childishly proud of the THUMP! I can draw from it on receiving a throw. For 206 pages, I am right beside the batboy as he fetches tobacco plugs and sandwiches before the game, rolls the bat rack onto the field. On that road trip—Pullman berths, first-class hotels, meal allowance for the kid—a Cincinnati player calls out to Garth, "Hey, Teaneck, how did you get so far from home? You're a long way from New Jersey."

"Eric Tipton had started that name when I was a visiting team bat boy."

It was Eric the Red, my first hero [with the St. Paul Saints], a year or two before he came to the Saints. I put the book aside and take a final crack at finding someone, anyone who was close to Garth Garreau. Via Bertie Wooster, I am led to Garth's surviving brother. In his mid–80s, Ed Garreau, who lives north of Atlanta, is warm and availing.

"Yes, Bill Grover and Garth were very good friends," he says, referring to the pilot of the downed plane. Without my prodding, he continues, "It was a freak accident. I think they were performing a refueling exercise, for Franco. It was the largest operational aircraft on any carrier. The order to launch was given, just when the deck was at a slight angle, and you can't have that when a plane is taking off. It was the responsibility of the air officer."

He pauses. I mumble something sympathetic.

"It was terrible," he says finally. "Garth had such promise—he graduated in the top 10 percent of his class at Michigan State. I don't know what his plans were."

Reflecting for a moment, he adds: "He grew up with men [the Giants], so he was a different young man by the time he reached college." I mention the wrestling and baseball teams he'd played for. "Oh yes, he was national junior champion in his weight. He was not big, maybe 5–11, but you couldn't be much taller and still fit in those planes."

I ask Ed about his father, Claude Garreau, who arranged music for the likes of Ray Bloch during the radio days, and who occupies a warm spot in the book.

"I miss him—he was a mensch," Ed says of his dad, using a Yiddish word for a fine and decent person. "He was my best friend. We were a pretty tight family."

Ed Garreau and I keep in touch, comparing acorn drops and monarch sightings in our yards. And the book sits on a shelf near my desk, the batboy ever smiling, three bats on his shoulder.

Dr. Fan

SETH C. "DR. FAN" HAWKINS

Editor's Note: Dr. Hawkins has become one of the most interesting people I've known on a variety of scales, including baseball. He moved to St. Paul, Minnesota, close to me, in the 1990s, inhabiting a Victorian home that doubles as a museum focusing on the Gilded Age of 1865 to 1899. The museum includes a room devoted to James Garfield, the subject of Dr. Hawkins' doctoral dissertation, and to Slovenia, a country he has adopted as his own. Of course, the museum contains a room dedicated to baseball, although the memorabilia it contains, interesting as it is, hardly conveys the impact baseball has had on his life—and his life on baseball.

Dr. Hawkins grew up in New York, taught in Connecticut, and moved to Minnesota after retirement. His resume that earned him the nickname Dr. Fan has an impressive list of achievements in terms of games attended. He has been present for every 3,000th hit going back to 1970 and has attended a regular-season game in every stadium that has hosted one over the last 70 years.

Dr. Hawkins proudly maintains many of his New York traits, particularly an outspoken nature. He has been a source of information—notably first-hand experiences—of attending games at the Polo Grounds, and I have asked him to once again chronicle his encounters and memories.

Here they are.

First Game at the Polo Grounds

It would have been the Saturday, May 7, 1949, as the Giants, behind the pitching of Clint Hartung, beat Stan Musial and the Cardinals, 9–1. The future Dr. Fan and his mother, Florence R. Hawkins, stopped off first at the New York Historical Society at 77th and Central Park West, as the exhibits were worth two added subway fares, and it was on the way (8th Avenue line). Saturday was selected because Mrs. Hawkins had a full-time job, but not because school was still in session: Hawkins began private school in the fall of 1949. ("You can't go to PS40: you'll get knifed.")

First Night Game at Polo Grounds

Mrs. Hawkins did not like the subway after dark. Her sister-in-law, Margaret Remson (Aunt Marge), stepped in and took her nephew to a Tuesday night game in June 1950. Aunt Marge enjoyed the war years and still dressed and was coiffed like Goldie Hawn's pals in *Swing Shift*, and the concept of staying out late on a school or work night did not faze her. Hawkins still remembers the vivid glow that the lights seemed to give to the grass; in an era before color television, it was like the moment in *The Wizard of Oz* when black and white shifts to color.

Last New York Giants Game at the Polo Grounds

We all know far too much about this game. By this date, Mrs. Hawkins had died, and Hawkins was living with Aunt Marge in Flushing so that he could keep his New York City residency to finish at Stuyvesant High School. Wouldn't you? Hawkins sat in the first row above the walkway in the upper deck, just to the third base side of home. In front of the walkway were a few rows of aluminum chairs with black plastic seat cushions. Although not one for civil disobedience, Hawkins was so angry at the Giants for leaving town that he took a seat cushion. He left it with Aunt Marge when he began college in 1958.

Run Fast, and You Too Can Sit Behind Home Plate for $1.30

The Giants, unlike the Dodgers and Yankees, maintained the last three rows of the lower deck, even behind home plate, as general admission. But the main gate that opened earliest was the one nearest the subway, in the far right field corner of the horseshoe. Hawkins was underweight then and could run with the best of them to the long side of the Polo Grounds and sit directly behind the plate for $1.30 (five cents of that was city tax).

Hawkins' First World Series Game and a Mild Scandal Involving the Perfect Attendance Record

Stuyvesant High School, always a very serious place where 70 percent of the teachers had Ph.D.s and where *every* graduate went to college on scholarship, had a few liberal arts teachers who bent a rule when needed. Hawkins was only a freshman in the fall of 1954, but his English teacher, Mr. Brant, was impressed with Hawkins' devotion to major league baseball and arranged somehow, quasi-legally, to get him out of school halfway through the day (Stuyvesant was on early and late double session due to construction renovations of the 1904 building) because Mr. Brant gave Hawkins a ticket for the right field bleachers for Game One of the World Series. In the seventh row, Hawkins got to see "The Catch" by Willie Mays against the Cleveland Indians.

The assumption was that the administration wouldn't have let Mr. Brant take the day off himself. Many theorized that Mr. Brant was also trying to annoy eventual Class of 1958 valedictorian Peter Biskind, whose family had moved to Riverside Drive from Shaker Heights, Ohio, to get Peter a Stuyvesant education, or so the rumor went. Peter's parents must have purchased a large box of Indian hats as he insisted on wearing them to school, and even after the Stuyvesant nerds stole them or ruined them. So Peter was upset that he did not get to see his Indians play. Next year, in creative writing class, Mr. Brant was quite pleased with Hawkins' story about the kidnapping of Herb Score.

Oh yes: the perfect attendance record. Although no one ever really claimed that Hawkins' legally being out a half day ethically compromised his perfect attendance record, it would have served him right, because he always insisted that Henry Eng, who transferred in from junior high (why would anyone willingly spend only three years in Stuyvesant?), should have his alleged perfect attendance record listed with an asterisk, as it was only three years. The classmate in question, amused, began referring to himself as Henry Eng*.

Not Going to the Polo Grounds

The biggest stir that Hawkins created was the day that he did not go to the Polo Grounds. When his mother was in the later stages of her terminal illness, Hawkins stayed with Aunt Marge during the summer of 1956, a period prior to the full-year stay in 1957–1958. Aunt Marge was worried, impatient, fuming between 6:30 and 7:00 p.m. one day when Hawkins came in with his scorebook. Aunt Marge remarked that the Giant game had not gone into extra innings. Hawkins replied that he had not been at that game but at a game in Philadelphia. He had completely forgotten to tell Aunt Marge that, as the son of a railway employee with a free pass, he could take the train to North Philadelphia (with a five-minute walk to Connie Mack Stadium) and sometimes did that. He promised to tell her in advance when he was going to do that!

90 Minutes—What to Do?

Hawkins' mother was a secretary to an insurance broker in Jamaica. After a weekday Polo Grounds day game, he would meet her at the office at the end of her workday (5:30 p.m.). But one day there was a 90-minute game; it was only 3:00 p.m. Having long ago erroneously concluded (but being too timid to actually ask) that Mom's boss would be upset if he sat around the office, he had to improvise something to do for the extra hour. True to his nature as a future graduate of Stuyvesant, he went to the American Museum of Natural History and talked to the Egyptian mummies.

Cheated Out of Game Two

New York City had a peculiar bookending Sunday curfew law that narrowly regulated when a doubleheader could start and how late it could go. There was a Sunday (May 1, 1955, against the Reds) when Game One went into the 16th. Don Mueller was being intentionally walked, but he reached for the intended fourth ball and slapped a single to left.

This was the first year after the size of the catcher's box was reduced, the intent being to make it more difficult for a team to issue an intentional walk. Game Two was postponed because there was not enough time left before the curfew. But, in a way, it was worth it to see Mueller's improvisation.

Do Not Act Like a New Yorker and You Will Get an Autograph

Mayor Robert F. Wagner was autographing scorecards one day before a game, and he had had enough of that and was starting to walk away when Hawkins said, "Please, Mr. Mayor…." Explaining that he was startled that any New Yorker could be so polite, Mayor Wagner turned on a dime and signed Hawkins' scorecard.

Fred Stein

INTERVIEW BY STEVE TREDER

Editor's Note: On October 1, 2014, I entered the University of Minnesota hospital in Minneapolis to have a cancerous tumor removed from the cartilage of my right hip. The surgery was successful in terms of taking out the entire tumor, although it required hip replacement and the cutting out of surrounding muscle and part of the pelvis, leaving me with a challenging recovery for my hip, leg, and foot. The long recuperation period gave me the chance to continue work on this collection on the Polo Grounds, but I didn't realize that it would lead to breaking additional ground on the project.

One of the doctors who looked in on me during my hospital stay was Dan Stein, who specializes in internal medicine. Our conversation quickly turned from my medical condition to baseball. Dr. Stein asked if I was a member of SABR, the Society for American Baseball Research, and I assured him I was. He said his dad had been a SABR member with a strong interest in the Polo Grounds. Even as I began asking his dad's name, I knew the answer: Fred Stein. With his book Under Coogan's Bluff *(among several other books he authored or co-authored), Fred Stein is well known to any aficionado of the Polo Grounds. As with Arnold Hano with* A Day in the Bleachers, *Fred established his expertise of and love for the Polo Grounds through his writing. I called on Fred's research a great deal when I wrote* Land of the Giants: New York's Polo Grounds *in the late 1990s.*

Steve Treder, prominent for his work on The Hardball Times, *got to know Fred and conducted a series of interviews with him, which he generously agreed to allow to be published here, a series of questions and answers that captured a baseball treasure.*

Steve noted that it was many years before that he had purchased Under Coogan's Bluff: A Fan's Recollection of the New York Giants Under Terry and Ott. *"It turned out to be a superb little volume (just 145 pages), self-published, but professional in writing style and thorough, detailed, and historically accurate content," Treder wrote of the book.*

One might assume a self-published book would be, well, you know, "interesting": passionate, but amateurish, meandering, disorganized, in dire need of editing. *Under Coogan's Bluff* was nothing like that; it was crisp, direct, and smart. I distinctly recall the manner in which it captivated my barely-20-year-old imagination: it sat me down in the Polo Grounds grandstand in the late 1930s, and not in any rose-tinted manner. I felt the hardness, the angularity, the peculiar complicated physical and moral reality of everyday New York City in that era, yet the book never presented any of that straight-on; it was subtly implied, a backdrop to the center stage action of Terry, Hubbell and Ott. That, my friends, was really fine baseball writing.

Fred Stein may not be a household name, but to some of us he's a nugget of national treasure.

Treder provided background information on his subject.

Fred Stein was born in New York City on April 21, 1924. He served in the Army from 1943 to 1946, as an infantryman in the European Theatre. In 1949, he earned a bachelor's degree in dairy technology from Penn State and received a masters at Ohio State in dairy and food marketing in 1953. He spent most of his career working for the federal government, in milk marketing from 1952 to 1966, and in water pollution control from 1966 to 1979. He then worked as a pollution consultant from 1980 to 1985. Fred has been a member of the Society for American Baseball Research since 1975. In addition to numerous articles in SABR publications, he's the author of the following books:

> *Under Coogan's Bluff: A Fan's Recollection of the Giants under Terry and Ott* (self-published, 1978)
> *Giants Diary: A Century of Giants Baseball in New York and San Francisco* (co-authored with Nick Peters; North Atlantic Books, 1987)
> *Mel Ott: The Little Giant of Baseball* (McFarland, 1999)
> *And the Skipper Bats Cleanup: A History of the Baseball Player-Manager* (McFarland, 2002)
> *A History of the Baseball Fan* (McFarland, 2005)

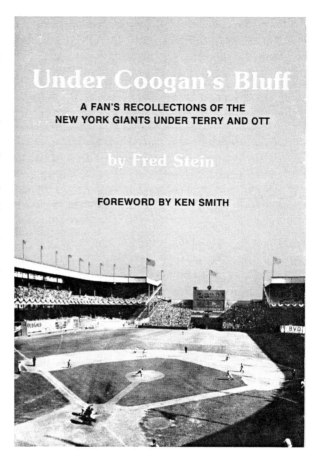

Fred Stein captured his memories and shared them with others in *Under Coogan's Bluff* **(collection of Stew Thornley).**

Here is the interview conducted by Steve Treder with Fred Stein.

Steve Treder: How old were you when you became a baseball fan?

Fred Stein: My first awareness of major league baseball occurred during the 1933 World Series between the New York Giants and the Washington Senators. At that time, all World Series games were broadcast on radio, unlike the Giants' regular-season games, which were not broadcast until 1939 because of an agreement between the three New York teams.

And so I listened to my first major league game on October 7, 1933. Mel Ott's 10th-inning home run won the deciding game for the Giants, and in my nine-year-old mind, he became my special hero.

An uncle took me to my first big league game in the spring of 1934, to celebrate my 10th birthday. We saw the Yankees play the Red Sox, with the main attraction, Babe Ruth, playing in what would be his final season with the Yanks. I remember little about that ballpark visit except the tremendous size of Yankee Stadium. My only recollection of Ruth was his carrying out his well-known superstition of touching second base as he trotted to and from his outfield position.

Treder: Can you recall the first game you watched at the Polo Grounds?

Stein: It was in 1935, I believe in June. My father and I drove to the ballpark and parked on the "Speedway" (now the Harlem River Drive), a parkway overlooking the western side of the stadium. It would be virtually impossible today to park on a street just one block from a major league ballpark, but there were fewer fans and cars 75 years ago.

I became more excited as we neared the stadium and walked down the steep path to the turnstiles. Roger Angell in *The Summer Game* captured a feeling I can relate to in approaching the Polo Grounds. He wrote, "The steepness of the ramp descending [to the ballpark] toward the upper-stand gates, pushed your toes into your shoe tips." We bought grandstand seats for $1.10 apiece, entered the Polo Grounds, and walked to our seats in the upper deck behind third base.

Treder: Was there anything particular about the weather/crowd/stadium/game that especially stood out to you?

Stein: I was struck by the unusual layout of the ballpark, completely unlike the more conventional Yankee Stadium configuration. The Polo Grounds had high fences down each foul line, a mere 257 feet down the right field line and 279 to left. In contrast, center field terminated a distant 483 feet to the base of the clubhouse wall. The center field bleachers, about 460 feet from the plate, were separated by about 25 feet of open space with flights of stairs leading to the separated player clubhouses. Viewing this most unusual stadium was one of my most memorable recollections of the entire day.

I was entranced by the sight of the players. I had read about them in the newspaper, but I'd never seen them in person before. My father and I identified them by their uniform numbers (this was long before names were sewn on the back of the uniforms). I had seen photos of Ott, Carl Hubbell, and Bill Terry, and I had some familiarity with their career achievements.

But the other Giants had been mere names to me. After seeing them on the field, I read all I could about the other regulars: infielders Mark Koenig, Dick Bartell, and Travis Jackson, outfielders Joe Moore and Hank Leiber, catcher Gus Mancuso, and pitchers Hal Schumacher, Freddie Fitzsimmons, Clydell Castleman, and Roy Parmelee. I knew very little about these players that day, but seeing them further stimulated my interest in reading about them in the daily sports sections, *Baseball Magazine*, and later, *The Sporting News*.

I was fascinated by the batting practice and fielding drills preceding the game. I don't remember the drills I'd seen at the Yankee game the year before. But in the Polo Grounds I have a fairly clear memory of Bill Terry's dexterity and grace at first base, and I couldn't take my eyes off the stocky Ott as he finished his practice fly-catching stint with bullet-like throws to home plate and third base. The lineup announcements came out of distant loudspeakers near the center field clubhouse, and the game began.

Treder: Who were the Giants playing? Did they win?

Stein: I believe the Giants defeated the Boston Braves. My only recollection of the game itself is a treasured memory of Ott homering. I was ecstatic, as Mel typically pulled a drive deep into the upper stands in right field.

It was a wonderfully exciting day, with so much to see and absorb. Seeing the Polo Grounds and the Giants was a truly unforgettable experience for a wide-eyed 11-year-old. Best of all, Ott, my favorite, had come through for me as he would do so often in the years to come.

Treder: How did the typical baseball fan in the 1930s follow the teams/games? Was it mostly via the newspaper, or the radio, or were they both about equal?

Stein: Today's fans have so much more to contemplate in following baseball than fans of the past. Baseball buffs in the 1930s followed the game during the season by attending games, listening to radio broadcasts (not available in the New York area in the '30s), and reading daily newspaper sports pages and sport periodicals like the weekly *Sporting News* or the monthly *Baseball Magazine*. During the offseason, fans became preoccupied with player trades and rumors of trades, and there were occasional stories of player signings or holdouts. Then came the welcome days of late February and spring training.

By contrast, today's fans have available daily coverage of baseball happenings throughout the entire year. Each game is covered in detail in multiple editions of a daily newspaper and described and dissected on radio and television, especially on ESPN. Fans can watch each pitch on TV if they are able. Offseason news is largely concerned with financial aspects of the game and player misdeeds or physical rehabilitation.

The immediacy of today's game details compared to delayed news of the 1930s was illustrated by a game in 1935. Giant right-hander Hal Schumacher pitched an apparent no-hitter against the Phillies, and the fans left the Polo Grounds excited by his feat. It was not until the next morning's newspaper arrived that fans learned that what appeared to be a wide throw by Giants shortstop Dick Bartell had been ruled a hit, and that Schumacher had pitched a one-hitter. Today the correct official scorer's ruling is usually available immediately.

Treder: In your observation, were most fans in that era more knowledgeable, or less knowledgeable, about the game and its players than modern fans?

Stein: Baseball fans of today are probably just as passionate about, and supportive of, the game as fans were then. But there are no quantitative research data to indicate, for example, whether a given baseball fan today attends more, or fewer, major league games than a comparable fan of the 1930s. The devoted fans I knew as a youngster at the Polo Grounds attended perhaps an average of about 15 games a season. Some also went to a few minor league games, especially in Newark (the Bears) and for a few years in Jersey City (the Giants).

I now live in Fairfax County, Virginia, and a number of my acquaintances also attend more games in the adjacent Prince William County's minor league ballpark than at the major league Nationals Park in Washington. Interestingly, some fans are turned off by the cost and inconvenience of attending a National game, preferring a more relaxed, easily accessible minor league game. Fan interest in college baseball appears largely limited to the fan's alma mater teams.

Fans are generally more knowledgeable today because of the authoritative radio and television coverage now available, especially insights provided by former major leaguers. The influence of SABR members and their analytical methodology and expanded interest in all phases of the game have been very significant and indicative of the fans' increased knowledge.

Treder: Did fans in those days behave in generally the same manner as modern fans, or are there ways in which there are significant differences?

Stein: It's difficult to detect any significant changes in fan behavior or impact on games since the 1930s. In the earlier period, the ballparks were smaller and most fans sat closer to the players. Pop bottles thrown from the stands were a frequent occurrence in the '30s, but one rarely seen today. This may be an indication of some improvement in fan behavior.

Of course, current fans sitting in seats just off the playing field have affected games importantly—for example, young Yankee fan Jeffrey Maier deflecting a Derek Jeter fly ball into the stands for an important homer in 1996, or Cub fan Steve Bartman interfering with a key catch by left fielder Moises Alou in 2003. These aren't necessarily examples of intentionally bad fan behavior but, regardless, they have affected games significantly.

Treder: Tell us some stories about being a teenaged Giant fan in the Ott era.

Stein: In the spring of 1937, after my 13th birthday, my father decided I was capable of taking the subway by myself to the Polo Grounds and less often to Yankee Stadium. I felt liberated. I went to the Polo Grounds and found myself a congenial niche in the lowest seats just off the field in the right field bleachers, near the Giants' bullpen. There I became friendly with fans of all types and ages. We were a completely disparate group, joined together only by our attachments to baseball and the Giants.

I became a disciple of a most unforgettable fan. He was a rotund, swarthy man named Louie, whose voluminous knowledge of the game and seniority (dating back to the 1920s) as a Polo Grounds bleacher resident greatly impressed us. Louie took his wooden bleacher seat more than two hours before the game and occupied himself watching the players while reading Shakespeare and other classics not normally considered pregame reading fare.

Most impressively, the players recognized his presence during their strolls to and from the Giants' dugout and the deep center field clubhouse. We bleacher fans expected to be ignored when we shouted to our heroes, but the players responded to Louie, smiling at him or exchanging friendly words. As a group, we gloried in the players' recognition of Louie, which we accepted as an indirect recognition of the rest of us in those 55-cent bleacher seats.

Listening to Louie's sophisticated analysis of players on the Giants and visiting teams was alone worth the trip to the game. He knew their strengths and weaknesses and some of their unpublicized off-field activities.

Many years after Louie had departed the Polo Grounds bleachers, *The Sporting News* published this note: "Who says there's no sentiment in baseball? Commissioner Bowie Kuhn received a letter from a tuberculosis hospital in Phoenix. The letter was from a patient who wrote that he was a longtime Giants fan and requesting, in view of the writer's long involvement with the Giants, whether Kuhn could use his influence to convince the New York baseball clubs to subsidize a trip for him to the World Series. The Commissioner wrote back that he would help all he could. The patient's name is Louie Kloppett."

After all those years, I finally learned Louie's last name and whereabouts, although I never learned whether he made it to that World Series.

Though I attended many games at the Polo Grounds in the late '30s and early '40s, one of my favorite recollections of this period came at Yankee Stadium, on July 11, 1939, when a friend and I attended the All-Star Game. I still remember a few things about the game, a 3–1 American League win. I clearly recall Joe DiMaggio's home run a few rows into the left field seats, and Bob Feller coming into the game in relief in the sixth to get an inning-ending double-play ball from Arky Vaughan.

I have a vivid recollection of a night game at the Polo Grounds in May 1941, which dramatically drove home the seriousness of the war in Europe. I was chatting with my bleacher friends in midgame when the public address system came on announcing that the president would be speaking. FDR proclaimed an "unlimited emergency" and the U.S. intention of resisting further Nazi attempts to stop or destroy Allied vessels. I remember that the game was stopped for the fans and players to hear the speech. A number of the players sat listening on the clubhouse stairs, with the game forgotten for nearly an hour.

Treder: Did you watch any ballgames during World War II in which the balata ball was being used? If so, was the game with the balata ball noticeably different from the vantage point of the grandstand?

Stein: I saw a number of games in 1942, that is, until I left home to begin my freshman year at Penn State. I enlisted in the Army in December 1942, and I managed to see the Giants play once in April of '43 before being called into active military service in June. I recall that the infamous balata baseball was used for a brief period after the 1943 season opened. The balata ball was used because of raw material shortages. The new baseball had the resiliency of an overripe grapefruit and the unpredictable airborne gyrations of a flying saucer. In the game I saw, hard-hit ground balls seemed to slow down before reaching an infielder.

Treder: When you were in the service in Europe during the war, were you able to follow baseball back home?

Stein: I was in the service from June 1943 until my Army discharge in March 1946. My only awareness of major league activities came through the *Stars and Stripes* newspaper, which was distributed to the troops. I was astonished to read a report in that newspaper that Tiger left-hander Hal Newhouser was seeking an incredible $35,000 annual salary in 1945. But other than that vague recollection, I don't remember any news of players or teams during the 18 months I was overseas. I was too concerned with other immediate problems, like staying alive, to have baseball news make any impression on me.

My service discharge made it possible for me to attend my last Polo Grounds game on April 16, 1946. Ott's Giants defeated the Phillies, 8–4, and Mel hit his 511th and last career homer in the first inning off Philly left-hander Oscar Judd. Unlike so many of the well-tagged home runs I had seen Ott deliver in earlier years, this was a looping fly that barely reached the right field seats.

The following day, Ott dove for a fly ball (which he didn't catch), injured his knee, and played only sporadically and ineffectively for the rest of his virtual last season as a player. And it typified what became a disastrous, last-place finish for the Giants. I left for Penn State's summer school a few weeks later, and my Polo Grounds years were over.

Treder: Can you remember the first time you saw a baseball game on television?

Stein: Sales of small, 13-inch black-and-white TV sets took off in 1947. I can only recall watching Yankee games on TV that summer, and I don't know if any Giant games were televised.

Treder: Did you see any of the 1947 "Windowbreakers" Giant games?

Stein: Between attending college and other activities, I did not see any games at the Polo Grounds that year. The affectionate "Windowbreakers" nickname was invented by the Giants' traveling secretary, Eddie Brannick. That team hit a then-record 221 home runs, a mark which stood until the Reds tied it in 1956.

Treder: Can you remember the first time you heard about Jackie Robinson and Branch Rickey's plan to racially integrate the Dodgers?

Stein: I never saw Robinson play in person, but I was thrilled at the breaking of the color line. I was pleased to learn that Ott, a proud Southerner, nevertheless instructed his players to treat Robinson "as they would any other rookie."

Treder: It sounds as though your relationship with the Giants, and with baseball generally, was changing quite a bit as you engaged with adulthood.

Stein: In July 1948, Leo Durocher replaced Ott as the Giants' manager. I was saddened at the news but it didn't surprise me. I had begun to feel that the Giants were not destined to win pennants under Ott's leadership, regardless of the reason. Also, by this time, my rooting interests had begun to change. I became unable to subsist psychologically on the fortunes of the Giants alone. So, my baseball interests widened to include all major leaguers, their careers, statistics, playing styles, anecdotes, and so on; in short, most of the wide variety of interests that SABR accommodates today.

Treder: Where were you during the "shot heard 'round the world" game?

Stein: Although my love for the Giants had faded considerably after Ott's dismissal, I was tremendously excited and thrilled after Bobby Thomson's home run. The event revealed an unexpected interest in baseball among many people who normally were oblivious to the game.

When Thomson hit his historic homer, I was working in an office in midtown Manhattan and one of my colleagues was an unfailingly serious, dignified, economics academician who had never shown the slightest interest in baseball. I recall his running up and down the office corridor, opening doors indiscriminately and shouting hysterically, "We won! We won!"

Treder: What was your reaction to the Giants and Dodgers leaving New York City in 1957?

Stein: The immediate impacts of the franchise moves to California were the profound disillusion and feelings of betrayal many fans felt, especially Brooklyn rooters. Since by then I no longer lived and died with the Giants' doings, my decreased feelings for the club cushioned the blow for me. But most significantly, in the ensuing 50 years, many who were then Dodger and Giant fans have largely abandoned their interest in baseball, furious at the realization that professional baseball is not truly a sport, but a business.

Treder: As a kid, you were a huge fan of the Mel Ott-era Giants. Did you ever develop a close rooting interest for another team in the years to follow?

Stein: My rooting interest in the Giants declined after the Ott era ended in 1948, although I had more than a passing interest in Bobby Thomson's miracle homer which won the 1951 pennant. But other interests took over in the ensuing years: graduation from college and graduate school, marriage, children, and government employment in Washington, D.C.

After moving to Washington, I developed a casual interest in the Senators, unexciting clubs with the exception of players like first baseman Mickey Vernon, outfielder Roy Sievers, right-hander Camilo Pascual, and the slugger Harmon Killebrew. But I did enjoy visiting Griffith Stadium, despite mediocre Senator teams, as it gave me opportunities to observe excellent visiting team players.

My enthusiasm for the Senators increased during Gil Hodges' 1964–1967 managerial seasons. And it was fun watching the Senators' improvement under Ted Williams' leadership before Bob Short took the club to Dallas-Fort Worth in 1971. But following that, there was no local major league team in the D.C. area until the Montreal club moved to

Washington in 2005. Before that move, Washington fans had no alternative but to accept the Baltimore Orioles as their "home team."

I continued to follow the game every day, but the focus of my interest had shifted from individual teams to all aspects of the sport and to players whose effectiveness and styles were especially appealing to me. I differ from most baseball lovers in that my rooting interests focus more on players than on teams.

I was an Oriole fan during the Jim Palmer-Eddie Murray-Cal Ripken years largely because I was taken by these players' styles as well as their effectiveness. Similarly, these days I find myself cheering for the Yankees because of my admiration for players like Derek Jeter, Mariano Rivera, Mark Teixeira, and, before the Yanks let him go as a free agent, Hideki Matsui. Among my other favorites were Greg Maddux and currently Albert Pujols and Joe Mauer.

Treder: What have been the baseball books you've most enjoyed reading over the decades?

Stein: I've always been greatly interested in baseball writers and authors. In the years preceding and following World War II, the New York baseball scene included a number of excellent journalists who spent all or part of their careers covering sports, and especially baseball, for New York papers. The most distinctive of the writers included Frank Graham, Dan Daniel, Tom Meany, Red Smith, and Dick Young. During this period, Graham and longtime writer Fred Lieb wrote a number of classic major league team histories, which I read avidly.

Lieb's *Baseball as I Have Known It* is excellent. Graham's *McGraw of the Giants* is superb. Roger Angell has written the most elegant material including my favorite, *The Summer Game*. And the three baseball volumes written by Harold Seymour (as we have recently learned, with considerable help from his wife, Dorothy) are fundamental to historical baseball writing. My favorites among more recent books are Bill James' *The New Bill James Historical Baseball Abstract*, any of Thomas Boswell's efforts, and Paul Dickson's *The Dickson Baseball Dictionary*. Finally, John Thorn's *Total Baseball* is indispensable.

Treder: What was the process through which you conceived of, wrote, and published *Under Coogan's Bluff*?

Stein: With the inspiration of the work of writers such as these, I decided to try my hand at baseball writing. As a youngster in the 1930s through the start of World War II, I had kept a scrapbook on the New York Giants and, with that material in hand, I began to write about the Giants under Bill Terry and Mel Ott. I began my first draft in 1978, 18 months before my government retirement. About halfway through the draft, I became discouraged, reasoning that there would be little interest in the subject, and I stopped writing for a month.

But one night I was watching the Walter Cronkite program and one segment provided me with needed perspective. There was a description of a wealthy Cincinnati Red fan who owned a farm in nearby Kentucky. The Reds had abandoned Crosley Field, their longtime home, and the gentleman farmer was in the process of buying pieces of the old ballpark and reconstructing it on his farm. I told my sons, "If this guy is crazy enough to do that, I'm not crazy in trying to write a little book about my long-gone Giants." And so I returned to my draft, completed it, and self-published it after trying unsuccessfully to find a publisher.

Treder: How did you come to learn about the Society for American Baseball Research? In what ways have you been involved with SABR?

Stein: SABR was largely instrumental in my decision to publish the book. I had joined SABR in 1975 after I was introduced to [SABR founder] Bob Davids at a federal interagency meeting on environmental control. Before I published my book, I was again concerned as to whether there would be enough interest in the book. But several SABR members were enthusiastic about the book and this gave me sufficient confidence to self-publish it, after I was unable to interest a publisher in taking it on. *Under Coogan's Bluff* was a pleasure to write. It became a modest marketing success, but a useful reference for other writers.

Treder: How did you come to collaborate with Nick Peters on *Giants Diary?*

Stein: In the mid–1980s, I began a manuscript on the New York Giants, from their inception in 1882 until the franchise moved to San Francisco after the 1957 season. North Atlantic books was willing to publish the book, and they arranged to have the ensuing seasons covered by Bay Area writer Nick Peters. Nick escorted me on one of the most pleasant experiences of that project. We spent an entire game in the Candlestick Park press box and then sat in on a high-spirited postgame interview with Giants manager Frank Robinson. This was a full-scale baseball writing experience for this novice writer.

Treder: Describe the three books you've written for McFarland.

Stein: The first of those, *Mel Ott: The Little Giant of Baseball*, covers the career of my most favorite player in 75 years of following the game, a player I saw many times and loved for his skill on the field and his high personal qualities. And so I was very pleased to read your insightful article about Ott in *The Hardball Times* in 2007. I was especially interested in the point that Ott's impressive National League home run totals for his time would have been much higher if he had spent his career hitting against the significantly more lively American League baseball used in the 1930s.

My next book, *And the Skipper Bats Cleanup*, was about the outdated player-manager role. It's unthinkable today to imagine, for example, Derek Jeter managing the Yankees in the World Series while serving as their regular shortstop. And yet, in a simpler baseball world in 1933, Joe Cronin accomplished that feat with the Senators. The last player-manager who was a semi-regular player was the Reds' Pete Rose in 1986. Since the post–World War II rise in major league players' salaries and team values, it has made no sense to burden a player with the joint responsibility of managing and playing simultaneously. This book discusses the problems player-managers faced in running a team on the field while coping with the usual physical and mental difficulties players face.

My most recent book, *A History of the Baseball Fan*, recounts the evolution of the fan from the mid–1800s to the present day. The book reviews the involvement of the fan with baseball in several ways. It examines ways in which fans and baseball management have changed over time. It looks at the media and how it has evolved as it reports and analyzes baseball games, players, and impacts American society. It also traces the impact of gambling and attendance levels. And it describes the most famous and infamous fans. Finally, it tells how fans have influenced baseball management decisions and game results.

My interest in baseball writing has added immeasurably to my enjoyment of the game. I highly recommend it to any readers with a similar interest in writing about the game.

Treder and Stein finally met at the SABR convention in Washington, D.C., in the summer of 2009. A year later Treder wrote: "It's with a leaden heart that I must report that Fred Stein passed away last week, at the age of 86, following back surgery. The last email he sent me, just over three weeks ago, concluded with, 'I still am enthusiastic about further contributions. I'll keep in touch to discuss ideas for future articles.' That was the essence of Fred, as I knew him: never dithering, never complaining, always looking ahead. He was a gem."

Home Address
Polo Grounds

Jerry Schwab

My dad, my grandfather, and my great-grandfather were groundskeepers. My grandfather and his dad had been the groundskeepers at different ballparks in Cincinnati. My dad [Matty] had been the superintendent for Ebbets Field [in Brooklyn]. He was responsible for the entire stadium, not just the playing area. But all he was interested in was the field.

When he got an offer from the Giants to be the groundskeeper, and nothing more, at the Polo Grounds, he took it in 1940. The Giants had just raised the field and improved the drainage, and this was a challenging field to maintain. My dad didn't mind. He wanted the field more than he wanted to worry about the stands. He was a groundskeeper, and that was his forte.

My mom [Rose], dad, and I moved from Brooklyn to the Bronx, near Yankee Stadium. We lived in the Concourse Plaza Hotel. Living out of a hotel wasn't that good. My dad thought about moving back to Brooklyn, but he didn't like the idea of that long of a trip back and forth to the Polo Grounds.

My dad found some space under the left field stands where a small apartment could be constructed, and he sold [Giant owner] Horace Stoneham a bill of goods that he could do a better job if he lived right there in the park, so they built an apartment for us. We had been in the hotel about one year and moved into the Polo Grounds when I was around five [in 1947].

It was small, but it was still better than the hotel. We had a kitchen, bathroom, living room, and a bedroom that I got to use. There were windows but not much to see. We could look out of the apartment into a concourse that was between the apartment and the outside of the ballpark on the north. That was a repair area for the subways and cars for the elevated lines. Later it was a high-rise housing development.

We had a few ways in. There was a roll-up door on the left field fence, in foul territory. And we could go out another roll-up door on the outside stadium wall. However, normally when we left we took our car. We could drive under the stands, around the back of home plate, and would go through almost the entire stadium, coping out through a door under the grandstand in right-center field onto Eighth Avenue.

It worked out well for my dad. At night, he often got up every few hours to move these big sprinklers around the field. My dad worked on the field all the time. No automatic sprinklers—it was all done with hoses. I helped him sometimes. I remember situations at three in the morning with me, Mom, and Dad, and a couple of the night watchmen trying to put the covers down because a big storm had come in and there was a game the next day.

I hung around with some of the other kids. Dale Jansen was the son of Larry Jansen, the pitcher. There was Roger and Ed Logan, who were the sons of the clubhouse manager, Eddie Logan. And Chris Durocher, Leo's son. Some of us had uniforms and were able to work out on the field with the players during batting practice. I was left-handed, so I played first base, and my big hero was Johnny Mize, who played first for the Giants. I even had his number, 15, on my back. I was broken-hearted when he was traded to the Yankees.

During a game, Dale Jansen and I spent most of the time in the clubhouse, looking out the windows. We couldn't be right up against the windows, though, because then we could be in the batter's line of sight and be distracting. There was a line in the clubhouse, and you had to stay behind that line so you wouldn't get too close to the window.

Years ago when a relief pitcher was called to replace a starter, it was usually because the starter wasn't doing well. After handing the ball to the new pitcher, the starter would turn and make the long walk across center field to the clubhouse. Dale and I knew he was going to be in a foul mood, and we knew to get out of the clubhouse. We would fly out the back door and into the bleachers until it was calm again.

When very young, I used to watch my dad turn the sprinklers off and on. I decided to try this myself, and I did ... during a game! I suddenly felt my dad lift me up by the scruff of my shirt and turn them off. Boy, did I get in trouble for that one!

When I got older, I helped my dad a lot. There were many wheelbarrow loads of dirt and sand. Matty Schwab took pride in his pitcher's mound as well as the rest of the field. When it rained, it was a rush to get the tarp out. It was huge, but we got it done with the help of the regular crew.

When the Giants were on the road, the entire ball field became my playground. I've had many birthday parties in that huge field. Roy Rogers and Dale Evans attended one year with their horses. It was great! When things got boring, I climbed every inch of that stadium. I could be blindfolded and still find my way around.

When I was 12, I sold sodas and peanuts at the game. "Hustlers," they called us. The concessions company was the same at the Polo Grounds and at Yankee Stadium, so I did it for the Yankees, too. The Giants and Yankees usually didn't play at home at the same time, so I could do it at both stadiums.

We had a regular home in Florida and would go back there before school started every year. Just Mom and I would go, because my dad had to stay around for the rest of the baseball season and then the football season. He'd join us in December. I missed a few of the big events, like Bobby Thomson's home run, because I was already back in school. My dad got to see it, though, and he was a big fan. He sat with the rest of the grounds crew and saw all the games. Sometimes he'd pop into our apartment between innings, because their spot was right near the entrance to it.

Of course, after the 1957 season, the Giants moved to San Francisco. We went with them and for a while I worked for my dad on the grounds crew. My son became bat boy for the Giants. That made him the fifth generation of our family to work on a big league field. Eventually, we moved to Fort Lauderdale in Florida.

I grew up in baseball. It was just part of my life. I didn't really think anything about it because it was all I remember. It was a great experience, and I didn't realize how fortunate I was at the time.

I had a wonderful childhood in the Polo Grounds. The memories I shall cherish forever. I remember playing catch with my dad on those warm summer afternoons in the Polo Grounds. We had the entire field to ourselves—a dream come true for many a young or old Giants fan. It was a good life, living under the stands. The finding of little treasures and money in the stands after a game, how cool was that? I disliked having to go to Florida for school every year. I had to leave the Polo Grounds.

As recently as 2013, I still run into people who remember my dad and the fact that we lived under the stands at the Polo Grounds. My friends never tire of me telling stories about this time in my life.

It was a great life!

Saving the Polo Grounds

Tom Edwards

In the 1980s, I saw an ad in a memorabilia publication for a row of three seats from the Polo Grounds. The owner lived about two hours from where my wife and I lived at the time, so we drove up to check them out. After a very brief negotiation, it was a done deal.

Given their age, I opted to refurbish my newly purchased seats. I disassembled them and had the wrought iron sections sandblasted and powder coated. I sanded the wood and had paint mixed to match the iron. I decided to bring the Polo Grounds seats back to the colors the Giants had during their last season in New York.

When the Polo Grounds opened in the Coogan's Bluff section of upper Manhattan

Tom Edwards has restored seats from the Polo Grounds and other New York stadiums (collection of Tom Edwards).

on June 28, 1911, the seats had wrought iron that was orange, and the wood was gray. The seat numbers were black. It was the first concrete and steel ballpark in New York. Before the Mets brought it back to life in 1962 for their inaugural season, the seats were painted green. The one concession I made to having them restored for their 101st birthday was to outline both NY logos in black.

My final visit to the Polo Grounds was September 2, 1963, for a Met doubleheader with the Reds. Before the first game, I went to the left field seats and sat close to where Bobby Thomson's home run landed. Between games, I walked around to see as much as I could, knowing it would be my last time at a place that had been a big part of baseball history.

At the end of the second game, I headed to the exit near center field, took one more look at the park, bent down, and pulled up some grass. I put it in my 1963 final revised Met yearbook; it's still there.

The Polo Grounds
Was My Playground

Ed Logan

The Polo Grounds. To this day I still have trouble with that name. The structure was actually a stadium for baseball and football and had nothing to do with polo. It should have been called Giants Field because it is where the New York baseball and football Giants played professional ball. On the other hand, it's where I grew up, and it is an indelible part of my history. Ironically, even after almost 60 years in San Francisco, the Giants to this day have not had their own ball park named after them.

My father, Eddie Logan, was the clubhouse manager at the Polo Grounds from the early 1930s to the day the New York Giants baseball team played its last game on September 29, 1957, before moving to San Francisco. By that time, I was 16 years old and I was the last New York Giant bat boy. It was a fitting end to my childhood in that glorious stadium.

My family story actually goes back further than that. My grandfather, Fred W. Logan, was the clubhouse manager for the New York Yankees from the very beginning of that team until he died in 1946. From the Polo Grounds entrance you could see Yankee Stadium across the Harlem River. I hated that view because the Yankees were always the enemy, as were the Brooklyn Dodgers in their Ebbets Field. Fred Logan's Yankee baseball cap is in the archives at the Baseball Hall of Fame in Cooperstown.

I was a war baby, born on April 20, 1941, the year of Pearl Harbor. By the age of five, I had my first tiny baseball uniform. In the family photo album is a picture of me in that uniform standing next to my grandmother, "Nana" Logan, in our old neighborhood in the Highbridge section of the Bronx. Did you know that the famous Giants colors of orange and black were once red and blue? They changed in the mid-'40s. I recall being taken to a Giants game one summer about 1946 or so with family members, probably my dad's sisters Flo and Ann and my mom, Evelyn. We were sitting in the lower stands behind the Giants' dugout. One of them put me over the low fence at the bottom of the stands and told me to "run to daddy," who was in the clubhouse about 450 feet away in center field. Well I did that and stopped the game. My family must have thought that was great fun.

During the years 1950–1956, before I became the New York Giants' last bat boy in 1957, I spent all my summers in the Polo Grounds, many times even when the team was on the road. I actually had a playmate there. His name was Jerry Schwab, who was the son of the Giants' head groundskeeper, Matty Schwab. Matty and Rose Schwab lived in a small apartment under the left field stands during the season. Otherwise, they lived in Florida. In the summers, Jerry would live in the Polo Grounds, too. He and I had full access to the entire ballpark when the team was on the road, and we used to ride our bikes up and down all the ramps to and from the upper decks. Matty once organized an ad hoc little league game for us that took place right on the field. He was able to get two local teams together for that game. My team was the Junior Giants and I played catcher. I got hit in the head with a pitch when I came to bat, and to this day I remember that clunk sound. There was no such thing as batting helmets in those days. I have been scared of fastballs ever since. Matty was a golfer and he used to hit his golf balls from home plate to center field on those away days.

When the Giants were home, my dad would always let me hang around the clubhouse, and eventually I was given a uniform and allowed to shag fly balls in the outfield during batting practice. I got pretty good at it, but I was never allowed in the batting cage. I had my favorite players on the Giants, those who treated me well and called me "Little Logan," but my top favorite at the time was pitcher Jim Hearn. As a result, he allowed me to use his number (21) on my uniform. Of course, the fans then thought I was Jim Hearn's kid. Fans for some reason also thought I was Johnny Logan's kid, although he played for the Braves.

I had another playmate on the field, too: Dale Jansen, the son of Giants pitcher Larry Jansen. He was my age and also had a uniform. Then there was little Chris Durocher, son of the Giants' manager Leo Durocher. He had a uniform with his dad's number 2 on it. It was my task to watch him on the field during practice because he was only five and I was older. In 2013, Chris and I had a reunion when he came to Phoenix to give a talk to a local sports group. We had not seen each other since his dad left the Giants.

My dad took me on several road trips with the Giants in those early 1950s, especially to Brooklyn, Philadelphia, and Boston. One trip stands out in my mind because we rode the train to Chicago, Cincinnati, St. Louis, and Pittsburgh. When I became bat boy in 1957, I was allowed one official road trip to those cities and to Milwaukee, which was in the league by then. That time we flew.

When Bobby Thomson hit that "shot heard 'round the world" to beat the Dodgers in September 1951, I was not at the Polo Grounds, but I was not far away. I was ten years old. It was after school and I was painting my old bike just outside our Bronx apartment building and listening to the game on a portable radio. As soon as I could after the home run, I rode my bike down to the Polo Grounds and tried to get into the clubhouse to see my dad. Because of the crowds, I never got to the door. My dad wound up working until the wee hours of the morning, getting the Giants equipment ready to move to Yankee Stadium for the first game of the 1951 World Series. I did get to go to one of the games at Yankee Stadium with my dad, and there is a press photo of him and me in the Giants' dugout greeting Alvin Dark, who had just hit a home run. Alvin just passed away as I am writing this in November 2014. My dad often told the story of Bobby Thomson rushing up to him in the Giants' clubhouse after his home run with a baseball he said some guy had insisted was the magic one Bobby had hit. Bobby wanted to give the guy two tickets to the World Series game the next day. Dad famously said, "Okay, Bobby, but you're too late. Just put that ball on this chair with all these other balls!"

I was also not at the Polo Grounds on that 1954 World Series day when Willie Mays made that famous catch against Vic Wertz of the Cleveland Indians. However, I had the satisfaction of knowing that dad had originally assigned Willie his number 24 and that I had been given one or more of his old gloves. Eventually, I became his bat boy and often played catch with Willie in the outfield before games, not to mention kneeling with him in the on-deck circle and then watching him hit a homerun with a bat I had just brought him.

My dad also managed the Polo Grounds visiting clubhouse, run by his assistant, George Natriano, whom I called Uncle George. That's what we did with close family friends in those days. When I became bat boy for the 1957 season, I was able to get Uncle George to hire my best buddy from the neighborhood, Billy Sheridan, to be the visiting team's bat boy. Billy was a good ballplayer, better than me. We were both 16. He wound up with the better deal that year because he got to wear all the uniforms of the visiting teams and was given autographed baseballs and equipment from them. In particular, the Milwaukee Braves were hot that season, and Billy hobnobbed with Eddie Mathews and the like.

Speaking of great ballplayers, the Pittsburgh Pirates that season had Roberto Clemente. My farewell to the Polo Grounds included him. The last game that the New York Giants baseball team played at the Polo Grounds in 1957 was against Pittsburgh. The Giant trainer, Frank "Doc" Bowman, was my guardian angel in the dugout, assigned by my dad to make sure I did things right as bat boy. Before the last out in the last of the ninth inning (the Giants lost the game), Doc told me to stick close to him. He said to hold on to my baseball cap and make a run across the field to the clubhouse in center field because the crowd was going to go crazy and the first thing they would do was steal our caps. Both the Pirates and the Giants made this run and it is memorialized in several press photos. In one photo, Robert Clemente (number 21) can be seen reaching the steps up to the visiting clubhouse. In another photo, Bobby Thomson and Willie Mays are dashing to the Giants' staircase. In 2013, I was at the Baseball Hall of Fame in Cooperstown, New York, and was given copies of these photos from their archives.

As it turns out, I was on the field for the final New York Giant game with someone I didn't meet for another 50 years. Moe Resner was a young man who came to the game with a color movie camera and got onto the field for the ceremonies before the game and stayed on the field during the game. He got some great footage, including me in action on my last day as the Giants' bat boy. Eventually the New York Giants Preservation Society learned he had it and urged him to do something with it. Moe transferred the film to a DVD, and it is available for sale.

Moe said he was the last person out of the Polo Grounds that day. We got the chance to know one another when he began selling his DVDs of the final game.

Actually, there was one more ironic farewell to the Polo Grounds for me. In June 1962, the now San Francisco Giants came back to the Polo Grounds to play the New York Mets. I was waiting to enter the U.S. Air Force later that summer, and I attended a game because my dad was there, this time in the visiting clubhouse. After all those years as manager of the home team clubhouse, he said it felt weird to be on the other side. We had our picture taken at the base of the visiting steps. I was never to see the Polo Grounds again.

The Fans Remember

My first game at the Polo Grounds was in the spring of 1955. I had never been to a baseball game. Complete with glove and my NY Giants hat with my two uncles, I was astonished at the green grass and how gorgeous it was. I vividly remember Mays getting a Texas League hit but turning it into a triple! I became an instant fan and still am.

—**Steve Rothschild**
Surprise, Arizona

When I hear Sinatra's "There Used to Be a Ballpark," it reminds me that once upon a time we enjoyed three ball clubs in the Big Apple. And they played in a trio of contrasting ballparks: a bandbox, a bathtub, and a cavernous arena. It all ended after 1957 when the Dodgers and Giants left us for California.

I didn't attend either of their finales, though I could have with little effort. The Dodgers closed shop at cozy Ebbets Field on the 24th of September; five days later, the Giants played their last game at the odd-shaped Polo Grounds. The Pittsburgh Pirates were the opponents in both games.

I was born in the post–Depression '30s and was baseball-smitten during the early 1940s when the St. Louis Cardinals held sway and ruled the decade. I was a kid from the Bronx and could walk to the Polo Grounds and Yankee Stadium, where I'd often sit through Sunday doubleheaders with my dad and older brother. I'd get there early to save them seats in the upper deck, usually between third and home, and watch batting practice and every ground ball of infield drills.

I always felt comfortable and at home in the Polo Grounds, so green and odd-shaped and ancient, but at too-large Yankee Stadium, so foreboding and aloof, I felt like a visitor.

The Giants were run by Mel Ott, who also played right field. Player-managers were not uncommon in those days. I watched him lift his right leg and power many of his 511 home runs into the convenient right field seats, merely 257 feet away. Then he'd take the field and nervously paw at the grass between pitches, inning after inning, game after game, season after season. The great Ott left his mark on the field as well as in the record book.

I was there when the Giants beat the Dodgers, 26–8, in one of the games of a Sunday doubleheader. It was the mid-'40s, wartime baseball, and the Giants had Phil Weintraub, a first baseman who knocked in 11 runs in the 26-run game; the shortstop was Buddy

Kerr, who lived near me until he died a few years ago; I recall that Nap Reyes played third, and tiny George Hausmann was at second. I think Johnny Rucker, from Georgia, was in center field with the unpredictable Danny Gardella in left. Ott, of course, was a fixture in right field. That was his office.

Perhaps Bill Voiselle, a large right-hander from a place called Ninety-Six, South Carolina. It might have been the incomparable Carl Hubbell, whom they called the "Meal Ticket," still throwing screwballs at the tail end of a Hall of Fame career. Certainly the closer was the aptly named Ace Adams.

The Giants' catcher was the lead-footed Ernie "Schnozz" Lombardi, also destined for Cooperstown. Mindful of his awesome power as well as his incredible lack of speed, infielders defended Lombardi on the outfield grass. He held his bat with interlocking fingers, as golfers do.

I remember the wartime Dodgers such as Howie "Stretch" Schultz and Goody Rosen and Eddie Basinski, who played the violin. And they had a 16-year-old kid at shortstop, Tommy Brown, who hit 72 home runs—in batting practice. He kept count.

My favorite time was when the Cardinals came to town and commuted to the Polo Grounds and Ebbets Field from the New Yorker Hotel in midtown. I stalked the lobby and could spot them all: Whitey Kurowski, Marty Marion, Country Slaughter, Harry Brecheen. They wore jackets and ties in those days and many puffed on cigars. I vowed that someday I'd smoke cigars, as well.

At the ballpark they wore their visiting grays with the two redbirds on their chests. I knew them by their gait and their shape: long, gangly Marion, number 4, nervously picking up pebbles at shortstop; Kurowski, with the short right arm, number 1, spitting into his glove at third; the magnificent Mr. Musial, number 6, curled into that signature batting stance. Stan the Man: never booed, home or away. Dubbed "Baseball's Perfect Knight."

I missed the Bobby Thomson game on October 3, 1951, and I was serving in Korea when Willie Mays made The Catch in '54. Later, the fledgling Mets borrowed the Polo Grounds for a couple of years before they moved into Shea in 1964, and I visited the old ball field on occasion.

Finally, when the wrecking ball was summoned to make room for housing, I returned to the partly razed skeleton and hauled away a pair of grandstand seats for $10. They sit like a monument in my basement, seats 3 and 4, green and paint-chipped, facing our washer and dryer. Usually my wife puts our folded laundry on them.

"... and there used to be a ballpark, right here."

—**Bob Mayer**
Westwood, New Jersey

Growing up just north of New York City in Tarrytown, along the Hudson in Westchester County, I was able to see baseball both at the Polo Grounds and Yankee Stadium. I got to Ebbets Field for pro football, a 1948 All-American Football Conference game between Brooklyn and Los Angeles. Not the usual scenario for most people.

My first major league game was at the Polo Grounds in June 1949 when my Cub Scout Pack, dressed in our appropriate uniforms, saw the New York Giants host the Boston Braves. I recall two things about the game, which was a Giant victory. Johnny

Antonelli, who would later become a member of the Giants, relieved for Boston and Johnny Mize hit a tremendous drive (most likely off of Antonelli) to that very spacious center field where Pete Reiser, the former "wall bouncer" with the Dodgers, hauled it in for a very long out just in front of that distinctive bleacher area on the top of which was a Chesterfield cigarette sign if I'm remembering correctly. All of this would have been viewed from roughly the left-center field bleachers.

Pro football also has a place in my memory book as I saw Stout Steve Owen lead his Giants to a very competitive 27–16 loss to the eventual NFL champion Detroit Lions in December 1953. What stands out was the Lions conceding a safety, thus accounting for the "16" in the final score. That game would mark Owen's last with New York as he was fired soon thereafter as the Giants finished at 3–9. While viewing Stout Steve's last game, I also saw the Giants play their last game there two years later as Cleveland's Lou "The Toe" Groza had a late field-goal attempt blocked, keeping the final at 35–35. The next year they were off to Yankee Stadium.

—Roger Godin
St. Paul, Minnesota

I went to the Polo Grounds between the years 1947 to 1957. I grew up in Jersey City and would take the Hudson Tubes and the D train. I would go with family and friends, sitting close to the foul pole in the lower right field stands. Such tickets were priced at $1.25.

I would enjoy watching batting practice since we would get to the ballpark early. Given our seats, we always had a good chance to get a ball. I was lucky once, getting a batting-practice home run hit by Gus Bell. Since we would usually go on Sundays, we would sometimes be fortunate to see a doubleheader. The one I remember the most was on June 15, 1952. The Giants had an 11–0 lead in the first game with [Sal] Maglie pitching and lost, 14–12. I was 11 years old and couldn't believe what I saw. It had to be one of the most heartbreaking losses I suffered through as a Giant fan. I remember seeking some understanding from my father as to what we experienced. Of course, he was at a loss to put it into any perspective. Fortunately, Dave Koslo came back with a shutout in the second game so that the subway ride home was not as depressing as it could have been. The Cardinals were led by Musial and also had Slaughter and Schoendienst.

Of course, it was a sheer delight to watch Willie Mays play center field. What was especially interesting were the continuing debates among the fans of the merits of Mays, Mantle, and the Duke [Snider]. Such debates had Dodger fans, whether white or black, extolling the greatness of Snider. Of course, we Giant fans believed Willie was the greatest ever. Yankee fans were small in number at the Polo Grounds. I certainly believe that observing those fans while a boy had a significant influence on me. The debates were good natured, lively, and added a lot to the experience.

A major highlight was to exit the stadium via the field walking under the clubhouses in center field. To this day, I can still visualize that experience and also looking back towards home plate seeing the Polo Grounds sitting below Coogan's Bluff.

—John J. Burbridge, Jr.
Mebane, North Carolina

I attended my first major league game at the Polo Grounds on August 8, 1963, Cardinals vs. Mets, the last New York playing appearance for Stan Musial. It made me a Cardinal fan for life. It's because of Stan Musial that I developed a lifelong passion for baseball.

My paternal grandfather had immigrated to the United States from Poland before World War I and settled in Bayonne, New Jersey. He was a proud Polish American. During the 1940s, when Musial won three National League batting titles and led the Cardinals to four pennants and three World Series championships, my grandfather became a Stan Musial fan.

Stan Musial's father had immigrated to America from Poland. Stan Musial always was true to his Polish heritage. Poles like my grandfather saw in the talented and humble baseball star a solid symbol of Polish contributions to the American culture.

My father was a Brooklyn Dodger fan, but he, too, rooted for Musial. The Dodger fans at Ebbets Field in Brooklyn respected Musial so much that they gave him the nickname "The Man."

My grandfather and father wanted me to see Musial play in person, so they purchased three tickets for the Cardinals' last scheduled 1963 appearance in New York. On August 8, a Thursday afternoon, we were among the 8,309 who went to the Polo Grounds to watch the Cardinals play the Mets.

Musial was 42 and speculation was that he would retire after the season. Regardless, he would be playing in the Polo Grounds for the final time because the Mets were moving to brand-new Shea Stadium in 1964. The setting was poignant because, prior to the Mets, the Polo Grounds had been the home field of the Giants before their move to San Francisco.

"There's something sentimental about this old place," Musial said in an Associated Press story published before the game. "For one thing, I've always been a Giants fan. When I was a kid, Carl Hubbell and Mel Ott were my heroes. I've enjoyed playing here because of the short fences and the nice crowds. Now, this is goodbye. It's a bit sad."

During our drive into Manhattan from New Jersey, my grandfather and father told me stories about Musial. Then, in a pregame ceremony, the Mets honored him. The crowd gave him an ovation. To a seven-year-old, all this adulation for Stan Musial convinced me then and there that he must be the greatest baseball player. And, because he played for the Cardinals, a seven-year-old's logic said, they must be the greatest baseball team.

Before a pitch was thrown, I was devoted to Stan Musial and the Cardinals.

When the starting lineups were announced, my grandfather and father were disappointed that Musial was being given the day off against Met left-hander Al Jackson.

Still, being at a big league ballgame was thrilling for me. I can recall vividly how the Polo Grounds looked that day from our second-deck seats on the first base line, and how Jackson and Cardinal left-hander Ray Sadecki were receiving praise from fans around us for their pitching, and that my grandfather and father kept commenting how they hoped Musial would be put into the game.

In the ninth inning, with the Mets ahead, 3–2, Jackson walked Julian Javier. With two out, our wishes came true. Musial was sent to pinch hit for reliever Bobby Shantz.

I recall focusing on the figure at the plate. I still can see Musial in his famous batting crouch, the number 6 looking huge on the back of his jersey.

Jackson walked Musial on four pitches. My grandfather and father were hoping he would get a hit for my sake. But I was satisfied just to see the plate appearance. Gary Kolb was put in to pinch run for Musial. Curt Flood then grounded out, ending the game.

In January 2012, I had the privilege to interview Jackson. He is a delightful man. We were nearing the end of the interview in a room at the Mets' training facility in Port St. Lucie, Florida. I was intending to ask Jackson if, by chance, he had any recollection of facing Musial in that August 1963 game at the Polo Grounds.

Instead, Jackson stunned me by bringing it up without me mentioning it.

I was asking Jackson for his impressions of players in Cardinal history. I asked about Flood. Here is the transcript of what Jackson said:

> Great defensive player. He was a great hitter, too. Here was a man who got 200 hits every year. But asking about Flood reminds me of when I was still pitching for the Mets and we were playing the Cardinals in the Polo Grounds. I had a one-run lead in the ninth inning. There were two outs (and a runner on first base) and here comes Stan Musial to pinch-hit.
>
> I always said, "My momma didn't raise no fool." Flood was due up after Musial. And as good a hitter as Flood was, I thought about how years back, [pitcher] Harvey Haddix had told me how dangerous this man Musial was in the clutch. And so I said to myself, "I got a one-run lead in the ninth inning. This man is not going to beat me." I threw four pitches outside and he went on to first base. I got the next man, Flood, to ground out. Game over.

—**Mark Tomasik**
Palm City, Florida

In the summer of 1962, my father took me to see Willie Mays and the San Francisco Giants invade the Polo Grounds for a Wednesday night game against the fledgling New York Mets. My dad, a Scottish immigrant, had absolutely no interest in baseball, but he knew that his 13-year-old son devoured it.

I was a bit of a baseball oddity growing up in New York because I didn't care for any of the local teams—the Yankees, Giants or Dodgers. Beginning in the late 1950s, my heroes played for the Phillies—Richie Ashburn and Bobby Wine, the latter hailing from my hometown of Northport on Long Island's north shore.

As a kid growing up, I knew very little about the illustrious history of the Polo Grounds, but I distinctly remember my fifth or sixth birthday when I received a Giants replica uniform. I proudly wore those cream-colored flannels on that hot and humid day in late July. Sweat lashed down my crimson face much to the consternation of my mother, also a Scottish immigrant, who shared my father's lack of understanding when it came to the importance of baseball to her young son. In this manner, I was initiated into Giant fandom. There is no denying that, as I grew older, I rooted for National League clubs.

When we arrived at the Polo Grounds in the early evening of August 22, I was awestruck by the sheer size of the stadium's exterior walls. But something appeared inexplicably wrong. Scaffolding hung from the facade and it left me with the impression that the building's structure was either being renovated or demolished. I was unsure.

In one of the ticket booths there sat a rather large man who clutched a fistful of game tickets like a deck of cards, and a stubby cigar hung from the corner of his mouth. There were long lines of fans standing in front of the other booths, which added to the overall noise, confusion, and excitement of the scene. And I was a part of the action and about to attend my first major league baseball game.

The ticket salesman conveyed bad news—he didn't have two seats together! My dad pointed in the opposite direction of the booth and shouted for me to "look at that," but I was too smart to totally fall for such a ruse, one whose ploy I had witnessed firsthand in countless episodes of The Three Stooges on television. My head snapped around just in time to catch my dad slipping the man a little incentive—a $10 bill. Miraculously, the fellow discovered a pair of seats together in the third base grandstand.

I don't have an impression of our emergence from the tunnel, but I do recall the wonderful contrast of the green grass that carpeted the field with the brown infield dirt and snow-white bases. I also remember the famous irregularity of the indented wall in deepest center field. My most vivid sensation, however, was the smell of cigar smoke— both stale and fresh—that permeated the air. And my rubber-soled tennis shoes stuck to the cement floor with every step I took, a by-product of spilled beer and soda. The stadium was vibrant with anticipation.

We found our seats on the second level just beyond third base, so we had a panoramic view of the entire ballyard. The players below were warming up or standing in small groups engaged in idle conversation. We shared our row of seats with a rather large family of Puerto Rican descent. It seemed to me that their family practically stretched from aisle to aisle. By the third inning, my dad had struck up a conversation with their patri- arch, and both men retired to the Ballantine beer stand on the concourse only a few rows behind us. Left alone, I talked baseball with one of the young boys sitting beside me. Later in life, I concluded that, from our tiny vantage point, the crowd was a living testa- ment to the multicultural appeal of baseball. After all, our row was a distinct blend of Old World Scottish and New World Hispanic immigrants.

As I already stated, I knew very little about the rich heritage of the Polo Grounds or famous Giant players from bygone eras. Who was John McGraw or where was Coogan's Bluff or what was Bobby Thomson's "shot heard 'round the world"? I was even oblivious to some of the legendary characters who were standing on the field that night: Casey Stengel and Rogers Hornsby, aging veterans like Harvey Kuenn and Don Larsen, who hailed from the last decade, and Mays, Cepeda, McCovey, and the Alou brothers, who represented the modern age. Yet, all I cared about was the Mets' aging centerfielder. Ash- burn had two hits that night, scored the game's first run in the first inning and reached base three times. I still recall the name for the Mets' catcher: Clarence "Choo Choo" Coleman. Who could ever forget a nickname like that?

The Mets, whose team colors embody the departed Giants and Dodgers, went on to win the game, 5–4, one of only 40 victories in that inaugural season of futility. Iron- ically, Roger Craig earned his third save in a campaign when he lost 24 mound starts. As the 33,500 fans filed out of the stadium after the final out had been recorded, I chanced a look back at its curved facade now bathed in artificial street and stadium lights. The shadowy scaffolds seemed to cling to the Polo Grounds in a tight death grip. There was something surreal about this image, but, at the time, my 13-year-old mind could not figure it out. Months later, I eventually realized that the Polo Grounds was dying.

The next day, I clipped the game summary and box score from *Newsday* and placed the article in my sock drawer. Over the next few months, the newsprint gradually yellowed, and one day it mysteriously disappeared. By the time the Polo Grounds turnstiles closed for the final time following the 1963 season, my family had relocated to a Seattle suburb, very far from major league action. But my first (and only) trip to watch a major league game with my father was in the historic Polo Grounds. It is a night I will never forget.

—**John A. Simpson**
Kelso, Washington

I am a charter member of the New Breed. By that I mean that I am old enough to remember the Brooklyn Dodgers and the New York Giants, that I agonized through those four seasons when New York had no National League baseball, and that I greeted the arrival of the New York Mets, even before they had played an exhibition game, with unabated enthusiasm. The chant of the New Breed, "Let's Go Mets," proclaimed grimly, regardless of the score or the inning, was proof that our love would abide forever.

I got to the Polo Grounds the first time on Friday night, August 24, 1962. It was Gil Hodges Night, a celebration of the Mets' most popular player. I was 14. I went to the game with my grandfather, bought a Mets yearbook, which I still have, and got Gil to autograph it before the game. Hodges did not play, but the Mets beat the Dodgers that night, 6–3. What a game it was. Jay Hook bested Don Drysdale. Three Mets—Rod Kanehl, Choo Choo Coleman, and Marv Throneberry—hit home runs, and the Mets scored three runs in the bottom of the eighth to break a 3–3 tie. But it was the top of the ninth that was truly special. Throneberry was playing first base, and every member of the New Breed knew that Marvelous Marv could turn from hero to goat in a flash. Yet on this night the good guys prevailed. Maury Wills opened the ninth by grounding to Throneberry, who tossed the ball to Hook for the first out. Jim Gilliam did exactly the same thing. Then, Willie Davis hit a screaming line drive down the first base line. Throneberry, a lefty, dove, reached across his body, and snared the ball for the final out. It was my first Met game and the team's first triumph at home over the club they had replaced in our hearts.

—Steve Gietschier
Florissant, Missouri

I have vivid recollections of the Polo Grounds because of two overlapping reasons involving the personal and the poetic.

In June of 1951, I had a tryout with the New York Giants at the Polo Grounds just days after I had hit a game-winning two-run double for my Connecticut high school in its first baseball triumph ever over its arch rival—the reason, I guess, for the invitation "to show my wares." A left-handed-hitting catcher, I pulled a ball into the right field stands—"the short porch"—for which the Giants' home field was famous, but, unfortunately, it hooked foul. There was talk of a contract subsequently, but since I had already accepted a scholarship to play ball at Michigan State, I was not much interested, and the talk led nowhere.

Years later, I had the pleasure of often teaching Rolfe Humphries' well-done poem "Polo Grounds" and, in 1969, of treating it in my Duke doctoral dissertation on literature and sports.

I think it's fair to say that the Polo Grounds has treated me well both academically and athletically. As a distinctive stadium, I've enjoyed distinctive ties with it as a field of play and as a fine poet's perception of it in a work of art—memory makers, both.

—Bob Reising
Conway, Arkansas

My oldest memory of the Polo Grounds is April 28, 1946. My uncle, Joe Verboys, took me to see the Giants sweep the Dodgers, 7–3 and 10–4. Leo Durocher and Mel Ott were the managers. And I have been a loyal Giant fan ever since.

I moved to Cocoa Beach, Florida, in 1958 and I am now retired, but I bought a dish in 1999 and watch most games including late-night West Coast games on DirecTV.

I have attended Giant games in 12 major league ballparks.

—John Chioma
Cocoa Beach, Florida

When you grow up without a father, and there is no adult in your life who can appreciate your youthful obsession with baseball, you surely will miss out on certain special, intrinsically American childhood experiences. You will not partake in the sacred father-son "Let's have a catch" ritual, which explains why tears well up whenever I see *Field of Dreams.* And you will not attend a real live baseball game until you are old enough to travel to one on your own.

This explains why I missed out on seeing a ballgame at Ebbets Field. (I grew up in a Brooklyn housing project; to this day, my favorite baseball cap is a powder blue number with a "42" on the front and the name "Jackie" stitched on the side. But alas, I never did see the great Jackie Robinson play in person.) This also explains why I did not attend a baseball game until I was 14 years old. (Happy to say, I've more than made up for this omission in the intervening decades.)

I first visited a big league ballyard in 1963. It was the second and final season in which the Polo Grounds was the home turf of the newly minted New York Mets, and it was the first and only time I ever passed an afternoon at Coogan's Bluff.

The date was May 5. It was a Sunday doubleheader, with the Mets going up against the former New York Giants. The memory of that day, which has floated through my mind ever since, was that Carlton Willey was on the mound for the Mets in one of the games; I would swear that the third Giant batter in Game 1 fouled out to the immortal Choo Choo Coleman; and the cleanup hitter, Willie Mays, was rousingly cheered by 50,000-plus fans. Willie, of course, accomplished what all great showmen do at certain moments in time. He belted a home run.

A bit of research serves to refresh my memory even further. San Francisco won that first game, 6–3. It was the sixth straight victory for the NL champs, leaving the hapless Mets with an 8–15 season record. Met starter Galen Cisco walked the first two batters before hitter #3 made out #1. Then, according to Leonard Koppett, writing in the *New York Times,* Cisco "was tagged for a tremendous home run by Mays, a drive clear over the left field roof at a point some 360 feet along the ground from home plate." The Mets came back to win the second game, 4–2, with Willey tossing a seven-hitter. The paid attendance was 53,880. "Judging by its sound," reported Koppett, "it was the largest pro–Met crowd ever assembled."

For me, it is ironic that, as a dyed-in-the-wool Brooklynite, my first big league game was at the Polo Grounds, rather than Ebbets Field. But still, that one experience is emblazoned in my mind. Plus, given Willie Mays' stature and legend, it seems appropriate that he was the one who belted my first-ever big league dinger.

—Rob Edelman
Amsterdam, New York

From the time I first knew about baseball, I have loved the Polo Grounds. I was born in Flushing, Queens, in 1947, but in 1952 my father's job moved my family to the Washington, D.C., suburb of Fairfax, Virginia, where I spent the rest of my youth.

Fortunately, my older brother, Paul, was already a Giant fan, and I grew up under his baseball tutelage. At the age of six or seven, I read and reread a great comic book history of the Giants, focused particularly on the 1951 pennant race with the Dodgers.

Our father was a stamp collector, not a baseball fan, and occasionally took Paul and me to Senator games. At least it was baseball, and throughout the games, we closely followed the Giants on the scoreboard.

For years after our leaving, we would return for a couple of weeks every summer to stay with our extended family on Long Island, and we would be able to watch Giant and Dodger games on television with our cousins, also Giant fans.

I was entranced by the Polo Grounds, and anytime we were in the New York City area and saw a baseball field, I would ask my parents if that could be the Polo Grounds. No such luck, as I never got to see the Polo Grounds by the time the Giants vacated in 1957.

Because my family had fortuitously purchased a TV in early 1954, and because I was in a split shift second grade with morning classes, I was able to watch all the weekday games in the 1954 World Series. Willie's catch and the vast centerfield—and the softball-size left and right field foul lines—were forever imprinted in my mind.

By a stroke of luck, in August 1957, my grandfather and father took Paul and me to a Giant-Dodger game in Ebbets Field, six weeks before it, too, was vacated. It was the first time in our lives we saw the Giants live, and they won, beating the "Hated Brooks," 5–0.

The creation of the Mets in 1962 gave new life to the Polo Grounds, even if for only two years. Then in high school in Virginia, I was able to attend one Giant-Met game in '62 and a doubleheader in '63 and loved them. I was fascinated by everything about the games and the park.

My home has lithographs and other depictions of the Polo Grounds. I love to bore young or non–New York fans with the history and dimensions of the park. It never gets old.

—**Ron Haas**
DeWitt, Michigan

One August morning in 1951, while I was hanging around the concrete playground of a community center on Manhattan's East 73rd Street, a staff member asked whether I wanted to go to a ball game for free. What a no-brainer—I was bored because my buddies were all elsewhere, and I had never seen a ballgame in person. Since things were so slow, the staffer could only round up one more kid, someone who I had never seen before.

There were a couple of small catches to this terrific offer: the game was at the Polo Grounds—not ideal for a rabid Dodger fan—and the opponents were the Pirates, the National League's perennial doormat in that era. But still, it was a big league game, and it was free. The three of us paid our dime fare (four years earlier, it would have been only half as much), hopped on the Lexington Avenue subway, and took it uptown to the

167th Street station in the Bronx. On the way, we caught a brief glimpse of palatial Yankee Stadium as the train climbed out of its tunnel to become an "el." At 167th Street, we switched trains to "the shuttle," a short el train that crossed the Harlem River to connect the main line with the ballpark. (Three years later that three-stop line would be torn down.)

After arriving, we took our seats in the left field upper deck near the foul line, pretty much above the spot where, five weeks later, Bobby Thomson would hit his legendary home run on a dreary overcast day. Our game, however, was played in full sunlight that did full justice to the park's colors, mainly greens and tans. For a kid whose previous exposure to Polo Grounds imagery was in the form of coarse-screen monochromatic newspaper photos and grainy black-and-white small-screen television, the rich tones and sharpness of these colors were revelations. Similarly, I was awed by just how immense the stands and field were in the flesh, an impression reinforced by the plentiful distance markers on the outfield walls: 315, 360, 414, 447, 455, 475, 450, 443, 404, 336, and 294, running from left to right. For some reason, the Giants had neglected to include the famed 279 and 258 markers at the foul lines, the shortest in the majors for nearly half a century.

The cavernous size of the park meant that the official "crowd" of 7,678 left quite a few seats empty—about 45,000 of them. I doubt that anyone was within 50 feet of us; it felt like we almost had the upper deck to ourselves. This may have been due to experienced fans preferring to sit in the shade, which abounded in both decks of the right field stands and the lower left deck. I've never seen it mentioned, but the famous deep upper-deck overhang was a very effective and welcome sunshade for the southwest-facing lower tier.

My meager funds would not cover a food or drink purchase, but I did spring for a pencil and scorecard published by the famous Harry M. Stevens. It explained how to score a game, and I duly did so. For years, I treasured that folded piece of cardstock, going over it with a Yankee-fan friend (my 73rd Street pals were very ecumenical, rooting for at least five different teams in those days) until it was soiled and dog-eared. Eventually, my mother did what so many moms are genetically wired to do with their sons' irreplaceable treasures—she threw it out without asking.

Even without the prompting of that scorecard, I remember the Giants won a low-scoring game and that Ralph Kiner didn't hit the homer or two that I had hoped he would. The closest he came was a high fly to fairly deep left-center that would most likely have been a four-bagger in Ebbets Field but which didn't have a snowball's chance as Willie Mays floated back and to his right to haul it in without breaking a sweat.

Thanks to Baseball-Reference.com and Retrosheet, I am able to reconstruct salient details of the game more than 63 years later. The date was August 29, 1951, and the Giants won, 3–1, in a speedy 2:02 thanks largely to a homer by Alvin Dark and two triples by Monte Irvin. The winning pitcher was Jim Hearn (13–7, en route to a career-best 17–9 season), and the loser was Murry Dickson (17–12, who finished with a career-high 20 wins). Although the Giants' lineup was easily recognizable to me as a faithful box score reading New Yorker, the Pirates' starting nine bore such unfamiliar names as Pete Castiglione, Clyde McCullough, George Strickland, and Dick Cole, as well as much better-known ones such as Frank Thomas, Gus Bell, and, of course, Kiner, who was well on his way to setting a seemingly unbreakable record by leading the league in home runs in each of his first seven seasons.

One aspect of that game didn't emerge until several weeks later. Had the Giants magically lost that game (perhaps Al Dark's two-run homer was the result of a telescopically stolen sign?), there would have been no end-of-season playoff necessary, and my beloved Dodgers would have won the 1951 NL pennant.

—John Pastier
San Jose, California

A plaque to mark the site of the Polo Grounds was unveiled in the early 1970s (collection of Stew Thornley).

The Players Remember

Bob Oldis was a catcher for three teams in the majors between 1955 and 1963 before becoming a coach and a scout. For his entire career, he was a part of two World Series champion teams, as a player with Pittsburgh in 1960 and as a scout with Florida in 2003.

It is a long walk after a game to the clubhouse after a loss.

But the field was such a treat, like it was laid out and anything could happen—short home runs down the line or a drive to center that should be an easy home run. Then a guy by the name of Willie Mays would suck it up for an easy out.

Bob Miller was the Robert G. Miller of the Bob Miller tandem with the Robert L. Miller. Bob G., a southpaw, unlike right-hander Bob L., signed out of high school with Detroit and made his debut three weeks before his 18th birthday. He came to the Mets in a May 1962 trade with Cincinnati and won his final two big league games at the Polo Grounds.

The Polo Grounds was definitely a hitter's park. It was extremely short down both the left field foul line as well as the right field foul line.

In addition, there was about a 12-foot-to-15-foot overhang in both left and right field, which made the foul lines even closer. Many home runs were just pop fly hits that landed in the overhang.

Stan Williams was effective as a starter for the Los Angeles Dodgers, New York Yankees, and Cleveland Indians and was even better out of the bullpen for the Minnesota Twins in 1970. Playing for the Dodgers, Williams pitched his first game at the Polo Grounds on July 14, 1962 (the game he writes about). Although the Mets might have avoided a loss (at least for the time being) had the game been rained out before the fifth inning was completed, it would have meant issuing rain checks to the more than 37,000 fans, many drawn by Old-Timers Day, which included Ralph Branca pitching to Bobby Thomson nearly 11 years after giving up Thomson's pennant-winning home run. Of the Met outfielders during the two years they played at the Polo Grounds, Jimmy Piersall had nine kids, Frank Thomas eight, Gus Bell eight, and Richie Ashburn five.

The year 1962—the first year of the "Mighty Mets." Playing for the L.A. Dodgers, I pitched one of the doubleheader games. It was a holiday and the stands were packed. At the end of the fourth inning, we had a 19–3 lead. It started to rain and by the fifth it rained so hard you could barely see home plate. Casey Stengel (the Mets' manager) ran his hitters to home plate with orders to hit the first pitch. They didn't want a rain out and needed to get the gate in.

I saw what was happening and grooved half-speed fast balls right down the middle. Our center fielder, (3-Dog) Willie Davis, caught about 1,300 feet of fly balls to deep center field. We got the inning in, it stopped raining, and the game went the full nine innings. Not only did I want the win, but I had a three-run home run at stake, as well. The Mets went on to lose 120 games that year.

One interesting point you may not be aware of: The Mets' three starting outfielders had over 30 children between them. Jim Piersall was one. I don't recall the other two.

Willard Hunter played for the Dodgers and Mets in 1962. He pitched a two-hitter for the Mets on June 20 in a rain-shortened, six-inning second game of a doubleheader—unfortunately, both hits he allowed were homers by Hank Aaron, and he lost to the Braves, 3–2.

They say it's all in the mind. You try to get the batters to hit up the middle. Right and left field were only around 200 feet down the line. The tiers jut out far, which made it seem closer.

Sorry that's all I have. Maybe other ballplayers had a better idea.

Ray Daviault made his major league debut in the Mets' first home game, which was played on April 13, 1962. His one win in the majors came that July 7 against St. Louis when Marv Throneberry hit a two-run homer in the last of the ninth inning for a 5–4 New York victory.

The Polo Grounds was for me a dream come true. It was the first place that I played in the major leagues.

When the crowd sang the national anthem. it was quite an honor for me to be on the same line with Gil Hodges, Roger Craig, Richie Ashburn, and all the well-known players and coaches.

Casey Stengel would say that to win in the Polo Grounds you have to make them hit to center field, which was easy to say but not easy to do. I remember one day when Lou Brock hit one to center field for a home run, and the next day Hank Aaron hit one, too. After that Casey stopped talking about center field!

Rogers Hornsby showed me the places where Babe Ruth hit his home runs. Great baseball players played here before I did.

My father was proud of me. He watched me playing on the television. My only regret is that he was never able to come to the Polo Grounds in person to see me pitch a game.

The first game that I won was at the Polo Grounds against St. Louis, a memory that I will never forget.

Ernie Broglio pitched for the St. Louis Cardinals and Chicago Cubs between 1959 and 1966. His first appearance in relief was July 7, 1962, and he gave up a two-run homer to Marv Throneberry in the last of the ninth to provide a victory for the Mets and Ray Daviault. He did better his next time at the Polo Grounds, going the distance in a 7–4 win on August 18 despite giving up another home run to Throneberry.

A ballpark with a lot of history. Mostly of the Giants and later the Mets.

What comes to mind is the distance to center field. It's at least a $10 ride in a cab from home plate to the center field bleachers.

For a pitcher, tough to pitch with the short left and right field fences.

Moe Morhardt played for the Chicago Cubs in 1961 and 1962 and was a pinch-hitter in one game at the Polo Grounds, on May 16, 1962. A multisport athlete at the University of Connecticut, Morhardt twice helped the Huskies reach the College World Series. He later coached baseball in high school and college in Connecticut and is a member of the Manchester (Connecticut) Sports Hall of Fame.

Your research certainly has some depth when you contact a guy who played only one series there.

Like most people, my experience goes to October 3, 1951, as I sat in front of the little black TV witnessing the "shot heard 'round the world" (first sporting event televised coast to coast), when Bobby Thomson lifted Ralph Branca's second fastball into history.

Fans and players remember the Polo Grounds fondly (collection of Tom Edwards).

(I was in eighth grade at the time and, like so many others, skipped school to see the game even though I was a Yankee fan.)

Being there years later (1962) with the Cubs inside that ancient clubhouse, a two-level dungeon out in the "horseshoe" behind the center field wall, you could still sense the excitement of '51 clinging to the inner walls.

The Mets were the temporary tenant at the time, and, of course, Casey Stengel was the manager, and he had played with the Giants himself, hitting that World Series inside-the-park home run. I recall taking throws during b. p. [batting practice], and as I caught a throw, he was passing behind me. As I turned to make a throw our eyes met, and he gave me that famous wink of his. I was momentarily stuck being a rookie on the opposition, but it has stayed with me as a warm, fraternal baseball moment.

Johnny Edwards went to high school in Columbus, Ohio, stayed in that city as he played for the Ohio State University, and, after a little more than two seasons in the minors, returned to the state to play for the Cincinnati Reds. He also played for St. Louis and Houston and spent his entire major league career, 1961–1974, in the National League. Regarded as a top catcher, Edwards received two Gold Gloves and was on the All-Star team three times. In 2008, he was named to the Ohio State Varsity "O" Alumni Association Hall of Fame.

#1. How far to center field, short down the right field line.

#2. The fans were fanatic. Many would stand during the whole ball game.

#3. The clubhouse was located in right field. You had to walk up steps next to fans to get there. They would throw things at you, spit on you, and [they] left a bad impression.

#4. We lost a doubleheader to the Mets in 1962. Our manager (Fred Hutchinson) was so mad he sent us back to [the] hotel without showering and gave us five minutes to dress. When we came to the ballpark the next day, he had destroyed all of the clubhouse furniture.

Sammy Ellis pitched for the Cincinnati Reds, California Angels, and Chicago White Sox between 1962 and 1969. In his only appearance at the Polo Grounds, September 16, 1962, he hit Gene Woodling—not Throneberry—with a pitch. Woodling had to be replaced by a pinch-runner and never played again.

Sammy Ellis died May 13, 2016.

September 1962, called up for September. In relief, hit Marv Throneberry in the knee with a curve.

He never played again.

Bobby Shantz, pitching for St. Louis, gave up the home run (a grand slam with all the runs unearned) to Rod Kanehl on July 6, 1962. With the Philadelphia Athletics in 1952, Shantz had a record of 24–7 with a 2.48 ERA and was named the American League Most Valuable Player. A southpaw, Shantz received nine Gold Gloves even though he was primarily a relief pitcher in most of those seasons.

I really cannot remember very much about the Polo Grounds. Seemed like a real big park with a short left field fence down the line. I do remember a guy named Rod Kanehl hitting a home run off me down the line. I thought it was a pop fly!

Jeoff Long flied out in his only at bat at the Polo Grounds on August 7, 1963. Signed by St. Louis as a pitcher out of high school in Erlanger, Kentucky, Long switched to playing first base and the outfield. He spent parts of two seasons in the majors, 1963 and 1964, with the Cardinals and Chicago White Sox.

I had only one at bat in a pinch-hit role against the Mets, in 1963, the year I was called up to the Cardinals. The pitcher I faced was Tracy Stallard (who became one of my best friends when our careers were over). I flied out to left field. I don't think Tracy and I ever discussed that meeting.

I have been able to say I batted against a very famous pitcher. Tracy gave up number 61 to Roger [Maris], as you know.

I always noted when I was in the old ballparks who had played there through baseball history. I would imagine who had been in the locker rooms, etc. There sure were a lot of players to think of. The old parks were really something. All of them I can recall Waite Hoyt talking about over the radio as a child listening to the Reds' games.

Lastly, I can say I played or was in all of them in that era, except Ebbets Field.

Ken MacKenzie pitched for the New York Mets in 1962 and 1963. He had gone to Yale and later coached there after his playing days. Met manager Casey Stengel reportedly said, "His signing with us makes him the lowest paid member of the class of Yale '56."

Two things: First, the entrance that we used was out on the center field side of the Polo Grounds. There were stairs up to the offices and clubhouses for the players.

We arrived in New York from spring games—the last in Baltimore. Went to the ballpark and got ready for our first road trip—to St. Louis. It was raining. As we were getting on the bus, Lou Niss (traveling secretary) called Joe Christopher aside. They wanted to see him upstairs. As we left, there was Joe, standing in the rain, a small suitcase beside him and a paper bag in one hand. Lunch? To this day I don't think Joe had a place to spend the night or knew where he would be tomorrow. It could have been any one of us.

Second, the locker room was pretty shabby. Casey's office up on the right as you walked in, then down about eight steps to the players' room, then through an open door to the trainer's room (two tables), then through another open doorway to the showers. Lockers were closely spaced—and small. Rod Kanehl was to my left and then, sort of first on the right as you came down the steps, was Roger Craig. When you are that close, you get to know your teammates pretty well.

Third (I lied), our second son, Geoffrey, was born in June of '63. We were living in an apartment in the East Village, which meant on Mondays and Thursdays the alternate-side parking changed, so you had to do the switch. Once Geoffrey was born, my wife couldn't handle the parking with two kids in tow, so I got permission, along with Roger Craig, to park in the Polo Grounds, under the left field stands. It was like a deserted, run-down barn under there. Steel girders, earthen floor, no lights. Like an abandoned building.

Well, it sort of was. But even the paint job outside couldn't disguise the fact that this was supposed to be a VERY temporary (one year) rental for a VERY transient team.

Frank Torre had his best years with Milwaukee during the Braves' pennant-winning seasons in 1957 and 1958. Part of a notable baseball family, his dad, Joe Sr., was a scout, and his younger brother, Joe Jr., went on to a Hall of Fame career as a player and manager. As a member of the Philadelphia Phillies, Torre played against the Mets in 1962 and 1963. He later became vice president of the Baseball Assistance Team (BAT), which helps former players with hardships.
Frank Torre died September 13, 2014.

Watching Willie Mays cover center field like no one else.
One of my favorite parks to hit in. I refer to the short left and right field lines.

Russ Kemmerer spent his first seven seasons in the majors pitching in the American League and finished in the National League with the Houston Colt .45s. His last win in the major leagues came in the second half of a doubleheader on September 20, 1962, at the Polo Grounds as he pitched the final four innings in a 5–4 12-inning victory after Houston had tied the contest with a run in the top of the ninth. Kemmerer had also finished the first game in relief, though the W went to starter Jim Golden. The home run contest prior to the Red Sox-Giant game was June 28, 1954, at the Polo Grounds. Kemmerer remembers well, as the New York Times reported that Williams "put on an amazing exhibition," going "five-for-five, every one a tremendous clout."
Russ Kemmerer died December 8, 2014.

I don't have a lot of memories about the Polo Grounds since I played in the American League most of my career. But one of the memories I do have is winning two games in one day against the Mets. It was a doubleheader and I came into both games in relief.

The only other time I was there was an exhibition game when I was with the Red Sox. The teams had a home run hitting contest prior to the game. Each team had three hitters. I believe the Giants had Willie Mays, Monte Irvin, and I think Dusty Rhodes. The Sox players were Dick Gernert, Jackie Jensen, and Ted Williams. If my memory is correct, Dusty hit two into the seats, Monte and Willie hit three for the Giants. Gernert hit two and Jensen hit two. Ted Williams stepped into the batter's box and launched five pitches into the seats. The last one hit the top of the roof.

Billy Pierce played in the Esquire game at the Polo Grounds on August 7, 1944. Known as "Mr. Zero," Pierce, then 17, started for the East team, struck out six batters in six innings, and was the winning pitcher. The following year he signed with his hometown team, the Detroit Tigers, and pitched in the majors for 18 seasons, being credited with 211 victories and having his number 19 retired by the White Sox.
Billy Pierce died July 31, 2015.

Most exciting time I spent there was in 1944 at the Esquire All-American Boys game.

My manager was Connie Mack. West manager was Mel Ott. Coach was Carl Hubbell. Quite a thrill.

Ken McMullen had a 16-year career as a third baseman in the majors, starting with the Los Angeles Dodgers in 1962.

How deep center field was. Locker rooms in dead center and overhang in outfield.

Ron Brand caught in the National League between 1963 and 1969. In his first year, with the Pittsburgh Pirates, he played in three games at the Polo Grounds. Brand later was a player-manager and a manager in the minor leagues.

I remember pulling up under the elevated subway track as a 23-year-old rookie with the Pittsburgh Pirates in 1963. I looked across the tracks and there stood Yankee Stadium. I had not known they were so close together.

The clubhouse was up some stairs in an opening in the center field fence. I'm sure it was the only one of its kind in major league baseball.

The Polo Grounds was the home field for the New York Mets, which were only two years into their existence.

As I walked onto the field, I recalled practicing there for the "Hearst All-Star Classic" in 1957 as a 17-year-old high-school player. At that time, the Giants were still there, and we saw a game between them and the Brooklyn Dodgers.

I recall visualizing Willie Mays making his great catch and throw on Vic Wertz's drive in the 1954 World Series.

I was fortunate to play in a few games as a Pirate rookie in that park. I remember thinking of all the greats who had played on that field, sat in the bullpen against the left field wall, and dressed and showered in the rickety old locker room. I remember how short the fences were down the lines and how far it was to center field.

One member of the Mets that year was Duke Snider, the great former Dodger. I felt such a thrill to be catching right next to him.

I will always be grateful to have played on that famous field, and I can still feel the thrill of being there.

Ty Cline played at the Polo Grounds with the Milwaukee Braves in 1963. An All-American at Clemson University, where he pitched, patrolled the outfield, and helped the Tigers make it to the College World Series, Cline performed in the majors from 1960 to 1971.

The view from the clubhouse in center was great. A long walk down to the field and thinking about Mays' great catch.

Joe Hicks played for the Chicago White Sox, Washington Senators, and New York Mets from 1959 to 1963.

I first learned about the Polo Grounds as an eight-year-old listening to games on my family's battery-operated radio in the early 1940s. In rural Virginia when the sun set,

I could pick up a radio station in New York that broadcast the Brooklyn Dodger games with announcers Red Barber, through the 1953 season, then, beginning in 1950, Vin Scully, and later, beginning in 1956, Jerry Doggett.

Of course, when the Dodgers played the Giants on the road, games were played at the Polo Grounds. I could visualize it being a hitter-friendly ballpark for players like Mel Ott, Johnny Mize, Ernie Lombardi, and, of course, Bobby Thomson, who hit the shot in 1951 that won the pennant.

It never occurred to me back in those days that I would, 20 years later, be playing in that historic ballpark and not only playing, but experiencing the most exciting moment of my professional baseball career. The date was July 17, 1963. The defending National League champion San Francisco Giants came to New York to play the Mets. Gaylord Perry started for the Giants, and we roughed him up for six runs early on and the game was tied 7–7 going into the extra innings.

Galen Cisco was pitching perfect relief ball for us. In the bottom of the 11th, our leadoff hitter, Joe Christopher, singled to left field off Don Larsen, the only pitcher in history to pitch a perfect game in the World Series. I came to bat knowing that our manager, Casey Stengel, would want me to sacrifice the runner into scoring position. I laid down a real good bunt, but it rolled foul down the third base line. Walking back to the plate from first base, I look over at third base coach Solly Hemus, and Casey had taken off the bunt sign. I'm guessing that Casey, being Larsen's manager in 1956 when Larsen pitched his perfect game, thought he would throw me a high fastball, which is hard to bunt. Casey was right! Here comes the high fastball, and I pull it down the right field line into the upper deck for a game-winning home run. This, of course, was the highlight of my professional baseball career.

Don Schwall won 15 games his rookie season for the Boston Red Sox in 1961 but never reached double figures in victories again. He made the American League All-Star team in 1961, even though he started the season in the minor leagues, and was named Rookie of the Year. Schwall pitched a four-hit shutout for the Pirates in his first game at the Polo Grounds on May 31, 1963.

I remember pitching a game against the Mets, for whom Duke Snider was finishing his career. He hit a shot off me to dead center, which struck the wall 475 feet away on one bounce. However, his advancing age caught up to him, and he stopped at second base. It had to be the longest double ever hit!

Bill Virdon had a long career as a player and manager and was the National League Rookie of the Year for St. Louis in 1957 as well as the starting center fielder for the 1960 World Series champion Pittsburgh Pirates.

Willie Mays' over-the-shoulder catch in deep center and many others.
The long walk from the clubhouse to home plate.
The long open area from regular center field to the stairs up to the clubhouse.

After serving in the Marines and fighting in the Pacific during World War II and then attending Western Michigan College, Wayne Terwilliger started in professional baseball in 1948 and was still in the game more than 60 years later, managing Fort Worth in an independent league until 2005 and then coaching for the team. His major league playing career spanned 1949 to 1960.

Polo Grounds—one of my favorite ballparks even though I didn't stay that long with the Giants. Of course, playing alongside some of those Giant players was exciting—Willie Mays, Al Dark, Whitey Lockman and being on the postgame show with Laraine Day was another highlight—got $50 for that!!

Hit my first home run in the Polo Grounds—off Dave Koslo (in the upper deck in left field) with the Cubs in 1949.

Watched Bobby Thomson's famous "game ender" in '51 with the Dodgers. Spent a lot of my time walking the street in the city—visiting Stillman's boxing place and then back on the subway to the Polo Grounds.

Al Moran was a shortstop for the Mets in 1963 and 1964.

I can remember how deep center field was. We would walk from the clubhouse in center field to the dugouts—was a long way to take batting and infield practice. Left field and right field were short. The infield was all right. It was an old park compared to the park where we would play in.

I have fond memories. Hit a home run off Warren Spahn to right field. Hank Aaron retrieved the ball and gave it to me. I had him sign it after the game.

I can remember Casey Stengel's favorite sleeping spot in the corner of the dugout, all the fans screaming, the old dugout board all broke. It needed painting. You could hear the team outside third base all night long.

It was a memory for me. I played in the last game held at the Polo Grounds.

I still have fond memories.

Ron Taylor pitched for the Mets from 1967 to 1971, winning nine games for the championship team in 1969, but he played at the Polo Grounds as a member of the St. Louis Cardinals. After his playing career, he went to medical school and became the team physician for the Toronto Blue Jays. In 1985, Taylor was voted into the Canadian Baseball Hall of Fame.

Deep center field.
Very short foul poles.
April 1962 [the first month of the Mets' inaugural season].

George Altman played for the Kansas City Monarchs in the Negro American League in 1955 and, after military service, for the Cubs, Cardinals, and Mets in the National League between 1959 and 1967. He then played for Lotte in the Pacific League and Hanshin in the Central League in Japan. His two home runs off Wilmer "Vinegar Bend" Mizell came when he was playing for the Cubs against the Mets at the Polo Grounds May 15, 1962.

Lou Brock hitting the ball into the center field bleachers. Was it 450 or 470 feet?

Hitting two home runs off of tough left-hander Vinegar Bend Mizell.

Casey Stengel explaining a Mets loss by saying, "We may have won except I have [a] player that wants to be a sailor." Of course, no one understood what he meant.

Explanation: We have runners on first and second late in a close ballgame. This dictates that batter Frank Thomas, a right-handed hitter, hit the ball to the right side to move the runners along. Instead, he hit a sharp grounder to third for a double play to kill the rally. There was a sign down the left field line saying, "Hit this sign and win a boat." So Casey was implying that Frank was trying to win a boat rather than playing team ball and moving the runners along.

Roger Craig was the first pitcher for the New York Mets, getting the start in the 1962 opener. He lost 24 games that year and 22 the next (including 18 in a row) and epitomized the early Mets as well as anyone, including Marv Throneberry. Aside from his two years with New York, Craig had a winning record in a major league career that went from 1955 to 1966. He later was a pitching coach for the Detroit Tigers when they won the 1984 World Series and then managed San Francisco to a division title in 1987 and a pennant in 1989.

As you know, the Polo Grounds was a unique ballpark. You could hit a 424-foot drive to center field and it would be an out. You could hit a ball down the right field line 250 feet and it would be a home run. The most unusual thing was both bullpens were in the playing field—left-center and right-center. The clubhouse was in dead center field about 470 feet away. It was a long walk when you got knocked out of the game.

Jim Campbell was a catcher for Houston in 1962 and 1963. Jim Wynn's first home run, which Campbell corralled, was July 14, 1963. The next day, Campbell hit his home run off Craig.

What I remember most about the Polo Grounds was how huge it was. The clubhouse in center field was a mile from the dugouts.

I hit a home run off Roger Craig down the left field line that went about 190 feet. If it had gone another foot, it would have been a foul ball. Later in the game, I hit a ball about 450 feet to center that was just a fly out.

Because the bullpens were so far out, they were in the field of play. I was warming up a pitcher when Jimmy Wynn slugged his first major league home run. It hit into the bleachers right above me and bounced to me. I caught the ball and gave it to him after the game.

Don Demeter was primarily an outfielder for several teams and once went nearly three seasons in the outfield without an error. A native of Oklahoma City, he later became a pastor, president of the minor-league Oklahoma City 89ers, and was elected to the Oklahoma Sports Hall of Fame. Demeter was playing left field for the Phillies when Piersall hit his 100th home run.

In 1962, I played third base for the Phillies. I was able to see into the Mets' dugout. Casey Stengel was managing. Usually the Mets had to change pitchers almost every inning. It was an expansion team with very little pitching.

I recall Gil Hodges pinching Casey to awaken him from a sound nap so the pitchers could make a change.

Also, I saw Jimmy Piersall running backwards after hitting his 100th home run.

Doug Clemens was an outfielder in the National League from 1960 to 1969. As a member of the Cardinals he played one game at the Polo Grounds on April 18, 1962, starting in right field and getting a single in three times up.

The biggest memory, which I saw on TV, was the Mays catch of Vic Wertz's drive to center during the '54 World Series.

I was with the Cardinals and Johnny Keane, the manager, told Ray Sadecki to intentionally walk a Met to put a runner on first as second and third were occupied—to create a force out or double play. Score tied, bottom of the ninth. Sadecki throws a ball in the dirt, and catcher Carl Sawatski misses it. Run scores—game over!

Cuno Barragan caught for the Chicago Cubs from 1961 to 1963.

A day game at the Polo Grounds, in early 1962, after warming up the starting pitcher, I went in to change my sweatshirt in the dressing room. The dressing rooms, for both teams, were in center field. While dressing, I was watching out the window for the game to start. Lou Brock, left-hand hitting center fielder for the Cubs, hit a home-run shot that struck the top of the screen in center field and bounced into the stands. It must have been in 50 feet. The only other left-handed hitter to ever hit a ball in that area was Babe Ruth. Word has it, the only right-handed hitter to hit one in that area was Joe Adcock, who played for the Braves.

On a personal note, it's hard to believe how Wes Westrum, catcher for the New York Giants 1947–1957, caught so many games in the Polo Grounds. It was very hard to see from behind home plate because of the Rheingold Beer sign shining, day and night, in center field. It was a real distraction to a catcher.

It was great to play in that era of baseball. Thank you for asking.

Known as "Possum," Larry Burright was a middle infielder for the Dodgers and Mets from 1962 to 1964.

I liked the playing field infield area. Short porch in right, though. Long way to center. If you hit one out in center, it was a long one. Left was pretty far. It was a long walk from the dugout to clubhouse in center.

Overall, I enjoyed playing there. I can still picture looking out from the dugout to center. And playing for Casey.

Ted Savage played for Philadelphia and Pittsburgh during the Polo Grounds years of 1962 and 1963 and later played for a number of teams between 1965 and 1971.

He attended Lincoln University in Jefferson City, Missouri, and after his playing career was over, he received a doctorate in urban studies from St. Louis University. In 2006, he was inducted into the Lincoln University Alumni Hall of Fame.

I made a leaping catch against the right field wall, and it was then I felt like I belonged in the big show. Just knowing and remembering all the greats who performed there only made me feel special. The stories that were told by older players who played many games there would pump me up to do good or the best I could. Can't remember much more. Sorry, I am an old man now. Just glad I can remember anything (smile).

Dick Ellsworth won 22 games for the Chicago Cubs in 1962. His son Steve later pitched for the Boston Red Sox.

A tough park for pitchers, with the very short fence down the lines.

You wanted to pitch complete games because if you were relieved, it was a long walk in front of the fans all the way to the clubhouse behind dead center field!

Frank Funk signed with the New York Giants in 1954. He worked his way through the minors, with three different organizations, before reaching the majors with the Cleveland Indians in September 1960. After two more seasons with Cleveland, he was traded to Milwaukee. His first game with the Braves, April 19, 1963, was the only game he ever pitched in the majors at the Polo Grounds. Funk pitched five more seasons in the minors before becoming a manager in the minors and a coach in the majors.

I signed to play with the Giants out of high school, when they were still in the Polo Grounds. I was a kid from Bethesda, Maryland, who hadn't even slept over at somebody else's house.

They gave me a bus ticket to go up to New York to the Henry Hudson Hotel, and they told me the next day, which was a Sunday, to go out of the hotel, go left, and go down into the subway and get the D express train to 151st Street. Okay, that should be easy.

I got on the subway, and that thing started flying by those stops so fast I couldn't even read them out the window. Oh, my God, I thought that I was going to end up someplace in Tokyo. But it came to a spark-flying screeching halt at 151st, and I jumped off that thing as quick as I could. And then all I did was go up the steps, and there I was at the Polo Grounds.

It was a great experience. The first person, one of the players in the clubhouse, who treated me really, really well was Johnny Antonelli. He just came over and shook my hand and welcomed me and all that kind of stuff. And he was very, very nice.

One of the things I remember on that Sunday, after the pitchers were finished, the Giants would usually run them in the outfield, and Frank Shellenback was the pitching coach then. He's running the pitchers, and Sal Maglie was there, and he [Shellenback] said, "Well, are you going to run?" He [Maglie] replied, "Naw, I'm going to go in and read the paper. You can run those young guys."

During batting practice, they had me come in and do some pitching. Frank Shellenback finally said to Bobby Thomson, who hit that shot heard 'round the world, the year before I think it was, to take some cuts—they had me pitch to Bobby Thomson. I got two strikes on him, and I threw that little kind-of slider, a slurve, and I threw pretty hard, so he wasn't going to stand around there and let some high-school kid drill him in the ribs, so he backed off and it was a strike. They called him out.

Now everybody was ragging on him. "Yeah, you the guy who hit that home run?" And he said, "Throw me that pitch again, kid." I threw one I thought was even better, and he hit it in the top deck, the upper deck in the Polo Grounds.

That's pretty much what I remember when I first signed to go there. I couldn't get over the vendors. I kept hearing the vendors saying, "Get yer beer heer," and I had never heard people talk like that before, and I thought that was kind of interesting.

With the Braves when we went in there to play, the one thing that I do remember was I was called up to warm up in the bullpen, and, of course, where the bullpen was, two or three decks up were fans. And Bob Uecker was catching. It didn't take me very many pitches, and I was starting to heat it up pretty good, and here are these people throwing their lunches down at him, and wads of paper, and halves of sandwich, and the ball's flying right at him, and they had these older fellows up in the stands, and they were walking around, were supposed to be the security.

So Uecker hollers up there, "Hey, what are you doing up there? Let's go!" And the guy starts blowing his whistle, and Uecker hollered up there, "The hell with that whistle. Get your guy out!"

That just cracked me up.

That's what I remember about the Polo Grounds. I had never been in a ballpark that big in my life when I first signed. I walked in there and saw those three decks high, and I thought, "Whoa!" It was mind-boggling to me. You'd feel like the tops of those stands were going to come in on you.

Even when we went in there to play when I was with the Braves, the Polo Grounds had some kind of a charisma about it almost like Yankee Stadium—so many great players that played there and done great things. Willie Mays making that catch over his shoulder was in the Polo Grounds.

It gave you a feeling that there were a lot of great players looking down on you when you were in there.

It was something. I had never even been in a clubhouse or anything before joining the Giants. I was just walking around with my mouth hanging open it was so neat.

I'll never forget it.

Eddie Kasko, playing for the St. Louis Cardinals, hit his first major league home run off Jim Constable of the Giants in the first game of a doubleheader on Tuesday, August 20, 1957. The brawl he talks of was noted in the next day's *New York Times*: "In a wild post-game melee on the field some heavy-fisted fan knocked another fan and a Polo Grounds usher unconscious. Several minutes elapsed before park and city police were able to restore order." Kasko, the starting shortstop for the National League champion Cincinnati Reds and an All-Star in 1961, was originally signed by the St. Louis Browns in 1949 and finished his playing career with the Boston Red Sox in 1966 but stayed with the organization as a manager in the minors and majors and then in the Boston front office into the 1990s.

I remember it was my first year in the big leagues. Being born and raised up there— I was born and raised just outside of New York, in New Jersey—it was a great memory for me coming back. I always had a lot of friends and relatives and everything coming up there.

I guess the one, biggest memory I have about the Polo Grounds was that I hit my first home run there in the first game of a doubleheader. I don't remember the pitcher—I think it was a red-headed guy. I had a lot of friends up there—high school friends and family and that sort of thing.

The clubhouses were in dead center field, and they also had the gate out there. The fans would come out on the field and go out that gate and catch the subways out there. So a lot of people would walk out with the players.

A lot of my friends came down from their seats, and they were trying to sit in the aisle so they could come over the fence and walk out with me to the clubhouse, and they would go out through the center field gate.

When they came down, the usher said, "No, you can't come down here." And they said, "All we want to do is walk out to the clubhouse. We know the guy." Of course, they're saying this with a New Jersey accent. And the usher said, "Well, you can't come down here now. You can't come down until the game is over."

And the next thing, one says, "Hey, don't push. You don't want us here—don't push." And then one thing led to another, and the last out was made, and I'm walking out to the clubhouse, and I hear all the commotion out there. I turn around, and I see the biggest brawl going on I've ever seen in a ballpark.

All I'm thinking is, "Geez, I hope that's not the guys." And it was.

Of course, the writers came in after the game, and all they wanted to talk about was the brawl because a lot of them, in those days, didn't have the computers where they send their stories in. They had to wait there and do their stories after the game and then send them in that way. So they were watching the brawl. They said it was the best one they had seen at the Polo Grounds in quite a while.

They arrested three of my buddies and took them down to, I think, the 151st Street precinct and were booking them down there. Another friend of mine that I grew up with, a brother [of one of the men arrested] came down to spring them. The police sergeant said, "You want one or you want all three?" And he said, "Three of them."

Well, my friend didn't have enough money to get them out. They spent the night in jail. They got out the next day and got fined. I think they just got fined. I don't think they had anything else going on with them.

So that was one of my memories of the Polo Grounds.

Bobby Locke played for five teams between 1959 and 1968. As a member of the Philadelphia Phillies, he pitched his only game as a major leaguer at the Polo Grounds, getting the win with 4⅔ innings of scoreless relief in the second game of a doubleheader on April 29, 1962. As he points out, he also pitched in the Hearst Classic on August 20, 1952. Locke struck out six batters in the game but was the losing pitcher for the U.S. All-Stars, as the New York All-Stars won in 11 innings.

1952—I pitched in the U.S.A. All-Star Game at the Polo Grounds. Very short fence in left field.

Al Worthington broke into the majors with a shutout in his first game, July 6, 1953, at the Polo Grounds. He gave up only two hits, both doubles, in the fifth and the ninth against the Phillies. Worthington later became a reliable relief pitcher and finished his career in the majors in Minnesota with the Twins, from 1964 to 1969. In the 1970s and 1980s, he was the baseball coach at Liberty Baptist College (now Liberty University) in Lynchburg, Virginia, and then became the school's athletic director and the pitching coach under Bobby Richardson.

The first time I saw the Polo Grounds was in June of 1953. The Giants had called me up from their AAA team, the Minneapolis Millers. I stood in the outfield and looked at the most beautiful baseball stadium I had ever seen. This was a double-decked stadium, and I had never played in one.

We did not have a double-decked stadium in Alabama. The stadium seemed to be enormous. The gaps were so green and beautiful. The stadium was beautiful, and I thought, "You are going to pitch here." I was excited.

The first game I pitched there was against the Philadelphia Phillies. I shut them out, 6–0. The stadium looked like a horseshoe. Right field and left field were short. If a hitter could pull the ball, a home run was not too far away.

Because my fastball was a natural slider, which caused batters to hit a number of ground balls off me, I liked small baseball fields. In the Polo Grounds, even though the distance was short down the right field and left field lines, you had to hit a line drive home run. Otherwise, the ball would strike the facing of the stadium above the first deck. A pop fly would go into the upper deck.

I was there when Willie Mays caught Vic Wertz's drive to center field. I would say this was one of the all-time catches. Mays caught the ball over his shoulder while he was running for the ball. After Mays caught the ball, I thought, "So what? That was Willie Mays out there." A great, great catch.

Center field was enormous. You had to really hit the ball for a home run into center field. In fact, I never saw a ball hit into center field for a home run. To hit a home run in the Polo Grounds, you had to pull the ball.

In the 1954 World Series against Cleveland, Dusty Rhodes pinch-hit two or three home runs down the right field line to win and help us win the first two games.

The clubhouse was spacious. There was plenty of room for everyone. Both clubhouses were in direct center field. You walked from the clubhouse down the ten or so steps right on the field.

The green grass at the Polo Grounds was the only green grass my two children saw in 1953. We lived in an apartment, and everything was cement.

When Leo [Durocher] took me out of a game, which was often, the walk to the clubhouse was a long trek.

The stadium held about 50,000 people. The Dodger-Giant rivalry was probably the biggest rivalry in the U.S. Being from Alabama, I thought the Alabama-Auburn teams were the biggest until I experienced the Dodger-Giant rivalry. Nothing could compare with this. The stadium was full of people screaming during batting practice. What a series.

Hoyt Wilhelm had the greatest control of himself of any pitcher I ever saw. To go into a Dodger game as a Giant reliever and hold a lead was incredible. If the stadium had a roof, the noise from the crowd would have removed it.

The Polo Grounds was fantastic, remarkable, and beautiful. The Polo Grounds held a remarkable place in my heart like no other stadium has had on me. The Polo Grounds held an attachment for me that I will never forget. It really felt like it was a part of you. It was really a part of me.

Bobby Gene Smith was an original Met, playing eight games for them before being traded to the Chicago Cubs, who traded him to the St. Louis Cardinals, the team for whom he had first played in 1957. He became Bobby Gene with the Cardinals, who also had Bob G. Smith and Hal Smith in addition to Bob "Riverboat" Smith in spring training.

Bobby Gene Smith died November 24, 2015.

Having to wear football shoes in the outfield during the opening series with the Mets in 1962. Snowing and very cold.

Ellis Burton hit his Polo Grounds home run June 26, 1963, off Al Jackson of the Mets.

Ellis Burton died October 1, 2013.

I hit one over the left field stands.

Jim Schaffer caught in the majors from 1961 to 1967 and then spent ten seasons as a coach with the Texas Rangers and Kansas City Royals. He homered at the Polo Grounds off Tracy Stallard in the second game of a doubleheader on August 11, 1963. The game Schaeffer refers to was June 26, 1963, when Tim Harkness hit a grand slam with two out in the last of the 14th to give the Mets an 8–6 win over Chicago.

The Polo Grounds was a unique place to play because of the dimensions. There, stands hung over the playing field. I remember a grand slam home run hit against the Cubs that nicked the overhang of the stands, and the ball was caught by our left fielder. It happened right in front of me because the bullpen was in the playing field.

Another game that was in extra innings and very long, Casey Stengel was sleeping in the corner of the dugout toward home plate. His first baseman hit a home run to win the game and he got up, waving his index finger over his head and headed for the club-house in center field.

Too many 250- to 260-[foot] home runs.

Dick Schofield was a switch-hitting shortstop who played in the majors from 1953 to 1971, including being a member of the 1960 World Series champion Pittsburgh Pirates and the 1968 pennant-winning St. Louis Cardinals. His home run off Hearn at the Polo Grounds was August 26, 1953. Schofield's son, Dick, and grandson, Jayson Werth, followed him to the major leagues.

Played there in 1953 with St. Louis when I was 18 years old and remember almost all the names of the Giant players because they could hit and they had good pitchers.

Hit a home run off Jim Hearn when I was 18, so I remember that.

1962 Mets—played there when I was with Pirates. The Mets had many guys from many teams in the expansion. They had some really good players, but not much pitching.

Rick Herrscher hit his home run in the first game of a doubleheader off Jim O'Toole, capping a four-run third inning to give the Mets a 4–0 lead on their way to a 5–2 win.

August 5, 1962:

The day Marilyn Monroe died.

The day Rick Herrscher got his first base hit in the major leagues!

It was a home run with two men on to help defeat the Cincinnati Reds with their volatile manager, Freddie Hutchinson.

Jim O'Toole pitched for the Cincinnati Reds from 1958 to 1966 and finished his major league career with the Chicago White Sox the following year. He won 19 games for the Reds in 1961 and pitched in the World Series against the Yankees. The doubleheader sweep by the Mets occurred on August 4, 1962, the day before O'Toole gave up Rick Herrscher's first major league home run.

Jim O'Toole died December 26, 2015.

Hutch [Fred Hutchinson], the manager of the Reds in 1962—after losing both ends of doubleheader, he gave us 30 minutes to get out of clubhouse.

Bad experience going up stairs to the clubhouse. Fans threw things at you.

Ted Wills played for Cincinnati in 1962 and pitched two games in the Polo Grounds.

All bad! The fans were terrible! They would throw bottles or whatever at the other team. Also, in '62, the home team had a bad habit of throwing at your better hitters. In return, we had to do the same per our manager, [Fred] Hutchinson.

Denny Lemaster pitched in the National League from 1962 to 1972. Although he described the Polo Grounds as a nightmare, Lemaster did well in the three games he pitched there in 1963. He started and was the winning pitcher in one of the games and relieved in two others. In all, he gave up only one run in 9⅔ innings.

It was a big nightmare.

Pete Richert pitched for the Los Angeles Dodgers from 1962 to 1964 and later became a relief ace with Baltimore and pitched in three World Series for the Orioles.

A band box.

Jacke Davis tripled off Jackson in the first game of a doubleheader April 29, 1962, the only game he played at the Polo Grounds. He later coached baseball at Carthage High School in Texas and Panola College in Carthage.

The oddest-looking baseball field I was ever on.

My first hit in the big leagues was in the Polo Grounds off Al Jackson, a triple. It was exciting, too, because Casey Stengel was the Mets manager.

Bob Anderson pitched for the Chicago Cubs from 1957 to 1962 and the Detroit Tigers in 1963. He gave up his home run to Sauer on August 22, 1957, and hit his triple off Craig in the first game of a doubleheader on June 15, 1962. Anderson was the winning pitching in that game and two days later relieved in the game in which Brock homered into the center field seats.

Bob Anderson died March 12, 2015.

1. Awesome size of outfield.

2. Hank Sauer's home run against me in '57. Hank was my favorite player when I was young and he was with the Cubs. I lost my admiration for him after he hit the homer.

3. My own triple to the left field bullpen off Roger Craig. Any other park—it was gone!!

4. Lou Brock's homer over the center field fence. What a drive!!

Jerry Kindall played for a College World Series championship team—Minnesota in 1956—and later coached Arizona to three titles. As a major leaguer, he was a member of the Chicago Cubs, Cleveland Indians, and Minnesota Twins between 1956 and 1965. Kindall did better than he remembered at the Polo Grounds. He had a pinch-hit single in his first game there, May 5, 1957, and two hits and two walks in the next game. Overall, he played seven games in the Polo Grounds and had five hits in 20 at bats. His tag out of Willie Mays on the steal attempt was July 15, 1957. Kindall finished his career as a senior advisor for USA Baseball.

Jerry Kindall died December 24, 2017.

I joined the Cubs on July 1, 1956.

Players at that time were on their own to get to the park. After taking the wrong train from Grand Central Station to Ebbets Field, I wisely joined three Cub teammates in a cab for the first game versus the Giants at the Polo Grounds.

I couldn't wait to see the oddest configuration of any ballparks ever. The long walk from the clubhouse to our dugout remains imbedded in my mind to this day: avoiding the batting practice balls from the Giant hitters and intently looking for a glimpse of Mays, Monte Irvin, Alvin Dark, Al Worthington, et al.

Remember, I grew up in St. Paul and had cheered for a good many of the Dodgers (St. Paul Saints [were the farm team]) and Giants (Minneapolis Millers) as they played in the American Association. I was disappointed none of the guys greeted me!

The Giants played a lot of day games, so the afternoon shadows were tough at the plate. I remember playing third base several times in the Polo Grounds and tagging out Willie Mays on an attempted steal.

The crowds were slim in those years, but I could imagine Bobby Thomson's home run in 1951 and Mays' great catch in 1954 at the clubhouse steps.

I estimate I had 10–15 at bats those two years but do not recall any hits. (I do remember taking a called third strike and the long walk from home plate to the third base dugout.) And I recall with great pride having dinner with Cub third base coach Pepper Martin after day games in the venerable and venerated Polo Grounds.

What a blessing to have played in such an historic and iconic baseball field!

Frank Linzy pitched in one game in the Polo Grounds in 1963. His first full season was 1965 when he finished third for Rookie of the Year in the National League as he pitched 81⅔ innings with a 1.43 ERA for the Giants. A hard-throwing right-hander, Linzy was the fireman for the Giants for the rest of the 1960s.

I was there for only one series and it was a weird-shaped park—240 down the lines and 457 to center field. The clubhouse was in center field and the owners didn't care about the players in those days.

Jack Fisher pitched a six-hitter for the Giants and beat the Mets, 5–3, despite the two home runs by Snider on May 3, 1963, in his first game at the Polo Grounds. He pitched in relief in one other game there.

I started only one game there—in 1963.

I was with the Giants and won the game and Duke Snider hit two home runs off me down the right field line. I'll bet the total distance of both were not over 500 feet!

Also, during batting practice, both Willie McCovey and Orlando Cepeda hit balls into the center field bleachers.

Earl Averill was on the bench for the Phillies when Piersall hit his 100th career home run in the first game of a doubleheader at the Polo Grounds on June 23, 1963. Averill himself played only one game at the Polo Grounds, striking out while pinch hitting for Art Mahaffey on May 7, 1963. The son of Hall of Famer Earl Averill, Averill played seven seasons in the majors.

Earl Averill died May 13, 2015.

As a Phillie, I played in the game in which Jim Piersall hit a home run and ran around the bases facing backwards.

Carl Erskine pitched for the Brooklyn/Los Angeles Dodgers from 1948 to 1959. Known as "Oisk" in Brooklyn, he was a key part of the "Boys of Summer" and a regular in the rotation for the pennant-winning teams between 1952 and 1956. His two-hitter at the Polo Grounds was August 11, 1953, and the brawl he mentions was a few weeks later, on September 6. Regarding sign stealing, Erskine is referring to the revelation that the Giants in 1951 had worked out a system of stealing the signs from opposing teams' catchers and relaying them through signals to their batters.

I used to think the Polo Grounds was in the Bronx—a fan straightened me out. I pitched there several times—once a two-hitter. Hank Thompson, left-handed-hitting third baseman, got both hits, two bloop singles back of second.

I was present when [Carl] Furillo, enraged because Ruben Gomez hit him with a pitch, thought [Giant manager] Leo Durocher had ordered it. Furillo attacked Leo and had him on the ground in a choke hold, when either Jim Hearn or Monte Irvin kicked Furillo's wrist and broke it. Furillo was hitting .344. He finished the season leading the league in batting average but missed the 1953 World Series.

Of course, we suspected the Giants were stealing signs from the clubhouse window, but we never protested.

And, finally, I was throwing with [Ralph] Branca in the bullpen during the third playoff game in 1951 when Dressen called the pen and asked coach Clyde Sukeforth, "Are they ready?"

"Yes," said Sukey, "but Erskine is bouncing his overhand curve."

"Let me have Branca," said Dressen.

When I'm asked what my best pitch was during my career I say, "The curve ball I bounced in the bullpen at the Polo Grounds just before the shot heard 'round the world."

Jay Hook was the first winning pitcher for the Mets, pitching a five-hitter as New York, after having lost its first nine games, beat Pittsburgh, 9–1, on April 23, 1962. Hook pitched three years for the Mets after five seasons with Cincinnati.

The shape of the Polo Grounds was good and bad. Very short down the lines but very expansive in left- and right-center.

The clubhouse was upstairs in center field. When a pitcher was taken out of a game, it was a long, lonely walk to the clubhouse.

The New York fans were terrific toward the Mets in the first couple of years. Casey Stengel did a great job of selling the club to sportswriters and fans.

Jim Marshall started at first base in the Mets' first game at the Polo Grounds and doubled off Tom Sturdivant in the fifth inning. His batting average was .344 when the Mets traded him to Pittsburgh for Vinegar Bend Mizell in May 1962. Marshall finished his major league career with the Pirates that year and played for Chunichi in the Japan Central League the next three seasons. He later managed the Chicago Cubs and Oakland Athletics.

Being an original Met: Great.

Opening day lineup at the Polo Grounds. Booed because Gil Hodges couldn't play. Mayor Wagner also booed.

First extra-base hit in the Polo Grounds that opening day!! A double down the line.

Background for hitting was outstanding. Hit over .300 for Mets before trade.

Fans were great—with a losing team. I always love and miss the Polo Grounds. Don't let people forget the Polo Grounds. Wrigley Field in Chicago—same good feeling!

❖ ❖ ❖

Jim Dickson watched Jim Wynn hit his first career home run July 14, 1963, and the next day played in his only game at the Polo Grounds, pitching the last of the eighth.

I was there with the Colt .45s and remember the shape of the field. Clubhouse behind the outfield.

Game situation is what sticks in my mind. Unless I'm totally senile, Jimmy Wynn had two home runs there—a line shot in left-center is the one sticking in my mind.

Got to see a lot of places where history was made in baseball and am forever thankful for that.

Ernie Bowman, a middle infielder for the Giants from 1961 to 1963, had his big day against the Mets on August 23, 1962.

I remember a game: I started that day and we had Hall of Famers playing, including Marichal pitching. I hit a home run in the fifth inning to tie the score, 1–1. When I came back [to the dugout], Mays, McCovey, Cepeda all said, "That's where Bobby Thomson hit his."

We went on to the 10th inning, and I singled home a run. It was against Al Jackson. He pitched the whole game. The headlines—I've got all of the papers—said "Bowman Beats Mets."

So the next day we go to Philadelphia, and I go to the park, look at the lineup card, and guess what. I wasn't on it. Man, I was mad. The guys said, "But you got all the RBIs."

I got to play in the World Series in Yankee Stadium with the Giants. I got to play in both of the parks. But I didn't get to play in Ebbets Field because the Dodgers had already moved west.

The Polo Grounds. Unreal. I'm still fascinated by it. I really am. Think about Mays and everything. Willie instructed me on how to grab my hat and glove and run like crazy to center field to get in the dressing room after the game.

It was just amazing. The people were fantastic, and I'm just a poor country boy out of Tennessee from a poor neighborhood in an all-black section. I was a different breed, I guess. I was never prejudiced or anything like that. I got along so well.

I grew up in Johnson City and still live there. That was the neighborhood I grew up in, and there was no trouble for me. I was the state 100-yard dash champion, broad jump champion, high jump champion, and all this stuff, and even with all the blacks there, I was still right along with them.

The fans [at the Polo Grounds], boy, you'd do good, and it didn't matter who you were for or anything, you got a cheer from somebody in the Polo Grounds.

Paul Brown pitched for the Philadelphia Phillies from 1961 to 1963 and again in 1968. His brother Jackie also pitched in the major leagues, and his son, Daren, pitched in the Toronto Blue Jays organization and managed the Seattle Mariners in 2010.

It was kind of run down when we played there in the '60s. But what I remember most are the short distances down the foul lines (being a pitcher, that's not good) and seeing the part of the field where Willie Mays made "the catch."

Originally signed by the New York Yankees, Cal Neeman caught in the major leagues from 1957 to 1963.
Cal Neeman died October 1, 2015.

It was a privilege to play there.

One game I never forgot was that we lost when Whitey Lockman hit a ninth-inning home run to tie the game and a game-winning home run to beat us in extra innings.

Don Larsen was 3–21 with a 4.37 ERA for Baltimore in 1954. He had more success with his next team, the New York Yankees, and had one of his better outings in the fifth game of the 1956 World Series.

I never played that much in the Polo Grounds; 1962 with the San Francisco Giants was the first time, and to my surprise, Casey Stengel was the Mets' manager, and he had all the players nobody else wanted.

The park was huge and odd-shaped.

Roger Craig had a year as bad as I had with the 1954 Orioles. I remember Mays' great catch in the Series, and here he is with the Giants. Good feeling.

Bob Friend got married September 30, 1957, the day after tossing a six-hitter for the Pirates in the final game for the New York Giants. Friend pitched for Pittsburgh from 1951 to 1965, winning 22 games with them in 1958, and he finished his career the following year in New York, with the Yankees and the Mets. His memory of his prowess over the early Mets is accurate as he won 12 straight games against them between April 15, 1962, and June 24, 1962. Bob Friend died February 3, 2019.

I pitched the last game at the Polo Grounds against the Giants before they left. It was quite a day, and I got married the next day—such a memorable situation.

I still have the picture of Giants left fielder Dusty Rhodes. He made the final out, grounded out, and I have the picture of it that we both signed. I remember him well—he always pulled the ball down the right field line.

It was a tough place to pitch. During those years, we had a bad ball club, and they had those strong teams in the first half of the '50s. They had [Larry] Jansen and all those outstanding pitchers, and they threw those sliders that made you hit the ball to center field, and it was about 470 feet to center.

We were a young ball club, and the Giants, with Leo Durocher managing, it was a tough deal for us, there was no question about it.

The Giant pitchers learned how to pitch in there. It was Sal Maglie and [Jim] Hearn and people like that. They made you hit the ball to center field, and Mays made all those great catches in center field. They had terrific outfielders—Monte Irvin and Bobby Thomson and those guys. They knew how to play it, and Don Mueller and Whitey Lockman. I remember all those guys who played there—Alvin Dark, Wes Westrum.

Later, I had good luck against the Mets. They were a young team, though they had some veterans like Richie Ashburn and Duke Snider. I think I won 12 straight against the Mets in those years.

I pitched in all the great ballparks, and they were great parks. I had good luck in New York, against both the strong Dodger teams in the early '50s and the Giants.

I had an appreciation of those ballparks: Ebbets Field, the Polo Grounds, Yankee Stadium. It was a wonderful experience and I have many fond memories of it.

The '50s and '60s, no question about it, were the golden years. It was a great era, and I was fortunate enough to play during that time.

Mike McCormick was signed as a bonus player by the New York Giants in 1956 and pitched 16 seasons in the majors, most of them with the Giants. In 1967, he won 22 games for San Francisco and received the Cy Young Award.

I joined the New York Giants at the tender age of 17. As you can imagine, I was enamored by just being there. I remember the first day as the players broke me in by nailing my baseball shoes to the wooden floor in front of my locker. The culprit was Don Mueller. The time I spent was depressing for New York fans as knowledge of leaving for San Francisco was staring them in the face. My year and a half was exciting for me, but the fans had given up as attendance was very low, 600,000, which made for many small crowds. Having gone back to the Polo Grounds with the introduction of the Mets in 1962 was exciting as those Giant fans again had National League baseball.

Playing for the Los Angeles Dodgers, Maury Wills hit his home runs from both sides of the plate in the first game of a doubleheader on May 30, 1962. He also stole his 24th base in the game, en route to a record (since broken) of 104 stolen bases that year, when he was named the National League Most Valuable Player. Wills managed the Seattle Mariners in 1980 and 1981 and was the third black manager (after Frank Robinson and Larry Doby) in the major leagues.

In 1962, I hit two home runs in a single game in the Polo Grounds vs. the Mets—one right-handed and one from the left side. The right side was into the stands in left field. The left side was an inside-the-park home run to center (over 500 feet away). The center fielder was playing me close. I hit it over his head. By the time the ball was returned to the infield, I was sitting on the bench, catching my breath. I was elated to hear that only a few players had hit two homers in a game—one from each side of the plate. Then I was told that Mickey Mantle had done it eight times (to "burst my bubble").

Dallas Green gave up Piersall's 100th home run on June 23, 1963. Signed by Philadelphia out of the University of Delaware, Green pitched eight years in the majors with the Phillies, Senators, and Mets. He moved into the front office and was also a manager for eight seasons, leading Philadelphia to a World Series title in 1980.

Dallas Green died March 22, 2017.

Pitching for Philadelphia vs. the Mets. Jim Piersall hit his 100th home run that barely got over the right field wall and ran the bases backwards.

John DeMerit's home run at the Polo Grounds was off Dick Ellsworth of the Cubs May 16, 1962. DeMerit played baseball and basketball for the Wisconsin Badgers and signed a bonus contract with the Milwaukee Braves in 1957. Selected by the Mets in the expansion draft, he was a pinch runner in the Mets' first game at the Polo Grounds.

1962

1. Hit a home run in to the upper deck in left field against the Cubs.

2. During batting practice one day, Casey came out to center field and tried to show me where a rock in the playing field should be. He claimed that this rock helped him determine where he should position himself when he played there.

3. Rheingold Beer was a big sponsor of the Mets with a huge sign above the center field scoreboard that bothered the hitters' view. The team had a large supply of 24-can cases stored next to the clubhouse and had a hard time giving it away to the ballplayers.

4. [Coach] Cookie Lavagetto got impatient with a crowded shower room one day and resorted to taking a splash bath with the used water in the whirlpool tank. He dried off quickly, dressed, and left in a hurry.

5. Casey giving pregame talks in the clubhouse, and then Solly Hemus and the coaches trying to explain what he said.

Charlie James was an outfielder for the St. Louis Cardinals and Cincinnati Reds from 1960 to 1965 and was with the Cardinals during the two years the Polo Grounds was used.

I always hit well in this ballpark. It was a very historic, beautiful place to play. Willie Mays made some great catches there.

Dave Roberts came up with Houston in 1962, played a full season for the Colts in 1964, and then played one more season in the majors, with Pittsburgh in 1966. His home run in his first game in the Polo Grounds, on September 18, 1962, came off Larry Foss.

As a young boy, all I knew of the Polo Grounds was that Mel Ott made it his own "playground" with the ease of hitting home runs.

My first game in that historic park was in September of '62. I was a late call up by the Colt .45s after batting .322 in the American Association. I called my mentor who lives in New York and invited him to the game.

I think I singled in the second, then I think it was the fifth. A pitcher I had seen in the minors tried to fastball me inside. I swung and the ball went out of sight over the roof in right field. Wow!

Even my teammates thought it was a big deal. After the game, my mentor, Jackie Bruthwaite, was there to meet me. We went to dinner. This was a bigger thrill than my first big league hit.

About the Contributors

David **Butwin** grew up in St. Paul, Minnesota, and rooted for the St. Paul Saints, a farm team of the Brooklyn Dodgers, and against the Minneapolis Millers, a farm team of the New York Giants. By extension, he rooted for the Dodgers and against the Giants. He now lives in Leonia, New Jersey, and Owls Head, Maine.

Alan **Cohen** is a retired insurance underwriter who has been a member of the Society for American Baseball Research (SABR) since 2011. He has written 50 biographies for the SABR BioProject and done 42 game summaries for the SABR Baseball Games Project. He is the datacaster for the Hartford Yard Goats of the Class AA Eastern League. A native of Long Island, he now lives in West Hartford, Connecticut, with his wife, Frances.

Rory **Costello** grew up as a Mets fan in Connecticut but did not have the opportunity to see a game at the Polo Grounds. He now lives in Brooklyn with his wife, Noriko, and son, Kai.

Robert **Dominguez** is a veteran editor and reporter for the *New York Daily News* and managing editor of *Viva*, the *News'* monthly Latino lifestyle magazine. The coauthor of *Bronx Bummers*, he is also a playwright, theater director, and the creator of a photographic novel series.

Tom **Edwards** was born in Brooklyn in 1949 to parents who were Dodger fans. A freelance writer, photographer, and comedian, he has written for a number of nationally distributed publications, done photo shoots with Minnesota Twin and Minnesota Viking players, and performed stand-up comedy of his material during open mic nights at comedy clubs.

Scott **Ferkovich** writes about all things baseball for websites such as TheNationalPastimeMuseum.com, HardballTimes.com, and DetroitAthletic.com. Also, he has appeared in the *Detroit Free Press* and *USA Today* and was the editor of *Detroit the Unconquerable* and *Tigers by the Tale*.

T.S. **Flynn** is an educator and writer in Minneapolis who has published short fiction, essays, reviews, and articles. His blog, *It's a Long Season*, has earned wide acclaim, and he is working on his first book-length project, an excavation of the 65-year baseball career of Tom Sheehan.

James **Forr**, along with coauthor David Proctor, is a recipient of the McFarland-SABR Baseball Research Award for his biography of *Pie Traynor*. He lives in Scottsdale, Arizona.

Rachel **Hamelers** is the math and science librarian at Muhlenberg College in Allentown, Pennsylvania. She spent many hours of her childhood at Houston Astro games and still mourns the state of the Astrodome. She lives outside of Philadelphia with her husband, Mike, and daughter, Lainie.

Arnold **Hano** grew up in New York and became a Giants fan at an early age. He was at the Polo Grounds for the first game of the 1954 World Series and chronicled the hours he spent at the ballpark that day in a book, *A Day in the Bleachers*, which is often cited as the first baseball book of its kind that was written for adults. He later moved to California, where he taught writing and continued as a freelance writer.

Seth C. "Dr. Fan" **Hawkins** has been proclaimed Dr. Fan for his feats as a baseball spectator. Born in 1943, he has missed visiting only one major league baseball stadium used in his lifetime—League Park in Cleveland. He has been to a regular-season major league game in every ballpark occupied by major league franchises since 1952, including stadiums where just a few games were played, and been present for every 3,000th hit going back to Hank Aaron's milestone in 1970.

Richard **Hershberger**, a paralegal in Maryland, has published numerous articles on early baseball in SABR publications and in *Base Ball: A Journal of the Early Game*.

Mike **Huber**, a Baltimore Oriole fan since 1968 and a SABR member since 1996, is the dean of academic life at Muhlenberg College in Allentown, Pennsylvania. He enjoys modeling, simulating, and predicting rare events in baseball and has been publishing his sabermetrics research in books and journals for close to 20 years.

Norm **King** is a retired project manager with the Canadian government. A member of SABR, he has contributed biographies and game summaries to books about the 1957 Milwaukee Braves, the 1934 St. Louis Cardinals, and the 1965 Minnesota Twins. Norm, who died July 31, 2018, lived in Ottawa, Ontario, with his beautiful wife and best friend, Lucile.

Bill **Lamb** spent more than 30 years as a state/county prosecutor in New Jersey. Now retired, he lives with his family in Meredith, New Hampshire.

Ed **Logan** is a career investigator, senior executive manager, government regulator, and retired Lt. Colonel from the U.S. Air Force who lives in Litchfield Park, Arizona. Since leaving government service in 2003, he has been active with assignments with his own firm, Logan Management Consulting.

John **Pastier** has been an architect, city planner, design critic, and university teacher. The lead author of *Historic Ballparks* and *Ballparks Yesterday and Today*, he is a coeditor of and contributor to *Tiger Stadium: Essays and Memories of Detroit's Historic Ballpark, 1912–2009*, was a consultant on Camden Yards, Safeco Field, Petco Park, and two minor league ballparks, and was an expert witness for the city of Chicago, supporting historic landmark status for Wrigley Field.

Joel **Rippel** is the author or coauthor of seven books on Minnesota sports history and has contributed to several SABR publications, including *The National Pastime* and *The Emerald Guide to Baseball*.

Jerry **Schwab** is part of a multigenerational family of groundskeepers. During the time his dad, Matty, was the groundskeeper at the Polo Grounds, Jerry lived in an apartment under the left field bleachers for part of the year. The Schwabs moved with the Giants to San Francisco and Jerry worked for his dad on the grounds crew at Candlestick Park.

Ron **Selter** is a retired economist formerly with the Air Force Space Program and the author of the award-winning book *Ballparks of the Deadball Era*. A SABR member since 1989, he has made presentations at both SABR regional meetings and national conventions.

Stew **Thornley** has written a number of books about baseball history, including *Land of the Giants: New York's Polo Grounds*. An official scorer for Minnesota Twins home games, he is a member of the Major League Baseball Official Scoring Advisory Committee.

Steve **Treder** contributed a weekly column to HardballTimes.com from its founding in 2004 through 2011 and has been a coauthor of many of *The Hardball Times Baseball Annual* and *The Hardball Times Season Preview* books. A frequent presenter at baseball forums, he is senior vice president at Western Management Group, a compensation consulting firm headquartered in Los Gatos, California.

Dan **VanDeMortel** became a Giants fan in upstate New York and moved to San Francisco to follow the team more closely. As a research paralegal, he has written extensively on Northern Ireland political and legal affairs, and his Giants-related writing has appeared in San Francisco's *Nob Hill Gazette* and SABR's *The National Pastime*.

Gregory **Wolf**, a lifelong Pirates fan, was born in Pittsburgh, but now resides in the Windy City area with his wife, Margaret, and daughter, Gabriela. A professor of German and holder of the Dennis and Jean Bauman Endowed Chair of the Humanities at North Central College in Naperville, Illinois, he was the editor of *Thar's Joy in Braveland: The 1957 Milwaukee Braves*, as well as of books on the 1929 Chicago Cubs and the 1965 Minnesota Twins.

Bibliography

Enders, Eric. *Ballparks Then & Now*. San Diego: Thunder Bay Press, 2002.

Graham, Frank. *The New York Giants: An Informal History*. New York: G. P. Putnam's Sons, 1952.

Hodges, Russ, and Al Hirshberg. *My Giants*. New York: Doubleday, 1963.

Hynd, Noel. *The Giants of the Polo Grounds: The Glorious Times of Baseball's New York Giants*. New York: Doubleday, 1988.

Lowry, Philip J. *Green Cathedrals: The Ultimate Celebration of Major League and Negro League Ballparks*. New York: Walker, 2006.

Mele, Andrew Paul. *The Boys of Brooklyn: The Parade Grounds, Brooklyn's Field of Dreams*. Bloomington: AuthorHouse, 2008.

Murphy, Cait. *Crazy '08: How a Cast of Cranks, Rogues, Boneheads, and Magnates Created the Greatest Year in Baseball History*. New York: HarperCollins, 2007.

Palacios, Oscar A. *The Ballpark Sourcebook: Diamond Diagrams*. 2nd ed. Skokie, IL: STATS, Inc., 1998.

Reidenbaugh, Lowell. *Take Me Out to the Ball Park*. St. Louis: The Sporting News Publishing Co., 1983.

Ritter, Lawrence S. *Lost Ballparks: A Celebration of Baseball's Legendary Fields*. New York: Penguin, 1992.

Sandalow, Marc, and Jim Sutton. *Ballparks: A Panoramic History*. Edison, NJ: Chartwell Books, Inc., 2004.

Smith, Curt. *Storied Stadiums: Baseball's History Through Its Ballparks*. New York: Carroll & Graf, 2001.

Thornley, Stew. *Land of the Giants: New York's Polo Grounds*. Philadelphia: Temple University Press, 2000.

Vincent, David, Lyle Spatz, and David W. Smith. *The Midsummer Classic: The Complete History of Baseball's All-Star Game*. Lincoln: University of Nebraska Press, 2001.

Index